# **P**ost
# **O**h!pocalypto
# **P**oppycock

## Truant D. Memphis

*Post Oh!pocalypto Poppycock*
Copyright © 2017 by Truant D. Memphis

All rights reserved. No part of this book may be used or reproduced in any manner whatsoever including Internet usage, without written permission of the author.

This is a work of fiction. The names, characters, places, or events used in this book are the product of the author's imagination or used fictitiously. Any resemblance to actual people, alive or deceased, events or locales is completely coincidental.

Script consultant: Gusthoff Gusthoffsen
Fight and Stunt Choreography: The Shoemaker
Music Supervisor: Sushifist
Flying effects provided by ZFX, Inc.

Cover design by Judy Bullard and Truant Memphis
www.custombookcovers.com

Book design by Maureen Cutajar
www.gopublished.com

Print ISBN: 978-0-9974872-3-7
E-book ISBN: 978-0-9974872-2-0

*Dedicated in loving memory to
Corey Mark Carpenter and James Henning Augustson.
We'll see you on the other side.*

# Hero, Villain, Woman, Monster, Robot

*a novel*

Truant D. Memphis

PROLOGUE

# The Rapture

Five years from this very moment, the rapture happened. Everyone was pretty surprised I think. Did anyone really expect a Giant Jesus to rise out of the Pacific Ocean? I don't think so.

Many people refused to believe the new reality. They thought the rapture was a government or religious trick. Smoke and mirrors. That kind of nonsense.

Other followers of different religions or personal philosophical systems had their beliefs shattered. Lots of suicides. Really, really, unfortunate.

Consider this for an extra second. Knowing Jesus Christ is real and has returned as a Giant Jesus proves there is some form of afterlife, which adds many layers of examination to the issue of suicide. I was curious so I jumped off a building. If no one was getting into Heaven, might as well check out Hell. I'm dead now.

Speaking of no one going to Heaven, outside of Giant Jesus returning, the Rapture was very different than previously described. The Christians did not ride moonbeams to Heaven, and the other major deities weren't happy with their followers either. Nobody went anywhere. Sorry folks.

Actually, that's not true. 15 people got to ascend somewhere that neither Jesus nor any of the other enlightened would discuss. Everybody else was stuck here. Including me.

After rising from the ocean and returning to dry land, Giant Jesus shrank down to about 10 feet tall. He held a press conference and explained to everyone how knuckleheaded they were, how much he loved mankind, and how he decided to come on back 'cause things weren't going as planned. He was going to stick around for a while to see if he could help.

Jesus wanted the members of all the other faiths to remain calm, so he brought a bunch of other badass souls back to life. Religious, saintly, spiritual, prophet types like Shiva and Bruce Lee. They put a traveling show together and started digging the world again. Did they form a band? Damn right they formed a band.

The masses were bewildered. It was hard enough for people to accept the Jesus returning Rapture deal. The arrival of Buddha, the Prophet Muhammad and all these other dogmatic fountainheads completely blew the doors off the general population's minds.

There was one other thing, the main reason I am telling you all of this. There was one hitch in the plan. One cog in the wheel. One big nipple covered in hair the first time a boy gets to see a titty. The NATURE OF EXISTENCE (said with impressive booming voice) was truly exposed to mankind.

Word? That's right word.

All the freaky shit that was going on in the dark, in the closet, under the bed or in your head, all that craziness jumped out of the shadows and into the light to bitch-slap humanity right in the face. If you think the world was chaotic before, well, you were right. Now imagine a world where all the madness we have imagined turns out to be reality.

No. Monsters, demons, goblins, and all other assorted fictitious creatures didn't become real because we imagined them. We imagined all these crazy things because they were already a part of existence, connected to our subconscious. Everything we thought was pure imagination was proven real. Except for Zombies. Zombies are not freaking real. Total bullshit.

Fucking zombies.

Anyway, after the Rapture all Hell truly broke loose. Of course, as people are known to do, once the initial shock wore off humanity just kept plugging along, business as usual style. Except for the United States, but we will get to that later. Or maybe not. This story isn't about the former United States. This story is about a hero, a villain, a woman, a monster, and a robot. Oh…and dig this. There may be some vampires too. Vampires are always so hot right now.

THE PLAYERS

# Hero

His name is Daniel Trate. He is our leading man. Our hero. He rides the White Horse. A tall, handsome, slick son of a bitch with no end in sight to his cool or his calm. He can lay a woman down with a smile and crush a foe with a wink of his eye. Dan is a Marshal. He enforces archaic laws in a modern world. With most of Earthly existence heading towards an open and honest anarchy, Dan is a relic. He is also super bad ass. He *is* the White Horse.

Dan stands in front of a dumb-ass with a firearm. Coffee shop diner. Robbery. Dan's eggs arrive but his breakfast is immediately interrupted by a familiar shout.

"This is a stick-up! Nobody move!"

"Fella, why don't you put the gun down?" Dan says.

The wannabe robber is confounded by Dan's commanding presence. "Hell no bitch," says the idiot. "You get your ass face down on the ground. Now!"

"I can't do that. I'm a Marshal."

"I don't give a shit. Neither does nobody else. You guys can't do nothing anymore. I heard you can't even arrest people no more."

"Well that is certainly not true," says Dan. "What you probably heard is that we don't arrest people anymore, because we kill them." Slight change in dumb-ass criminal's grimace. "Now, most law enforcement officers probably wouldn't bother killing a guy whose grand scheme is to hold up a coffee shop for maybe a few hundred dollars. But they might. Luckily for you, I don't kill. Seriously beat the devil inside of you, right back out of you? Yes. Kill? No." Dan smiles. "This is the best you could do? There is a bank right there on the corner that certainly has more cash than this place."

"I wanted breakfast."

"I'm sure you did," says Dan. "Now, I'm not carrying my gun. I'm going to turn all the way around so you can see. Show you my ankles too. Just do me a favor and don't shoot me, okay." Dan rotates, closing the distance between himself and the idiot as he does so.

"Why won't you lay down on the damn ground?" The crook knows he is whipped, despite the gun in his hand. He whimpers like an ugly puppy.

"I can't," Dan says sincerely. "This is my job. What are they going to say about me if I don't do my job? Besides, I want to show you something."

"What?"

"The error of your ways."

"Huh? What's that supposed to mean?"

"Man this country is becoming so unfortunately stupid," says Dan.

"Becoming stupid?" asks an anonymous sarcastic voice in the crowd.

"Duly noted citizen," says Dan to the anonymous commentator. He turns back to the would-be robber. "I want to show you a trick I learned. It is very, very cool. Afterwards I don't think you will want to shoot or rob any of us."

"Jesus, why do you care? Nobody cares! All I want is to rob this shithole and go. I'm supposed to meet my mother for lunch."

"You're kidding?" Dan replies. "You just ate breakfast."

"What? She wants her cut of the money."

"Well you are going to want to tell her about this. Seriously. Seriously. You have really got to see this. Just...don't...shoot me."

"Man whatever. C'mon already. My buzz is wearing off." The criminal is completely whining now.

"Don't blink."

"What?"

With that, the man instantly blinks and Dan does a spinning jump kick, wheeling around lightning fast, knocking the gun from stupid's hand with his right foot. Dan is a Martial Arts Master. I told you he's super bad.

"Did you see?" Dan asks.

The man nods his head.

"Good." Dan slides forward and punches the dazed man in the throat.

It's a homerun. The crowd goes wild. Dan stands with a humble smile, foot on the chest of his most recent criminal victim. "Thank you citizens. Really, thank you. Thank you very much. It was nothing. Now please, everyone, back to your meals. I'm going to go in the back and have some very consensual, safe sex with..." Dan scans the room. "...that waitress."

The waitress looks up with a smile and takes a bow, then approaches Dan.

"What's your name darling?" he says.

"Jessica," replies the smoking hot waitress.

"Ladies and gentlemen, the lovely Jessica." Applause. Cheers. Jealousy. He takes her by the hand and escorts her to the meat freezer.

# Villain

The Spaniard sits alone in his throne room. It is the 33rd floor of La Ciudad de Oro casino. His given name is Flacido Rodrigo Diego. He is Alacrán! The Scorpion! La Ciudad de Oro is his lair. Las Vegas is his dominion.

He is an oily bastard. It's a glandular problem. His cobalt black hair is slicked front to back. His mustache thin and curled at the ends. His mole perfectly placed on the right cheek. Alacrán!

His servant, Purvis, enters the room with today's lovely concubine. It is time for Alacrán's afternoon pleasure. Normally he loves being gobbled upon, but today he is nervous, and more than a little sweaty.

"Put her in the room," Alacrán says.

Purvis opens a hidden door and tells the young lady to, "Relax. Take your clothes off. Enjoy some drugs. Master will be with you shortly." He shuts the door.

The office is all steel and iron ore. It is sterile and linear. The room is filled with the shiny objects of Alacrán's affections.

"Is something troubling the Master today?" asks Purvis. Alacrán sighs. "I am unfulfilled my pet."

Purvis, despite horribly named by the trailer-trash who birthed him, is statuesque. Perfectly molded by the gods of the Greeks. If Alacrán holds any love in his heart for a living, breathing creature, he holds it for Purvis.

When Alacrán discovered this masterpiece, Purvis was a toe-headed child. Alacrán was inspecting one of his RV Park drug labs. It was Bring Your Kids to Work Day. There sat Purvis staring blankly at a wall. The promise of the physical specimen Purvis would become was quite clear. He was as astonishingly handsome as a child as he would be as an adult. Alacrán knew he had found something special. Purvis' mother was an official product tester. She sat quietly drooling on herself in a recliner, gadzooked off excellent drugs. Alacrán asked the handsome young fellow what his name was. The child answered, Purvis.

Alacrán had Purvis' mother put down like a lame horse as punishment for the offensive naming of her child. In death, her destiny was ghosting, and she haunts Alacrán to this day. Years of practice have made her quite adept at inflaming the villain's insecurities.

The first and only time Alacrán attempted to molest Purvis sexually, to his dismay, he found the mother's ghost floating above him, taunting the dimensions of his penis. It was little, skinny and short, and desperately worthy of giggles. Yet the tiny phallus was the secret of Alacrán's success, explained in his memoir: *Little Dick Disease and Effective Overcompensation: A self-help novel in criminality*. It was abject pride and childish contempt for reality that prevented Alacrán from utilizing one of the numerous penis enhancement solutions that the future has to offer. Absurdly proud or not, he published the memoir anonymously.

Although he enjoys his harem, Flacido Rodrigo Diego holds his true lust for objects that are shimmering, beautiful, and inanimate. Today, something is missing.

"Perhaps the master would like an oil rub along with his copulation this afternoon?" suggests Purvis.

"No, I am recently bathed. Rather, some of that wonderful tea that relaxes me so, and a little asphyxiation while that lovely young treat pleasures me."

"Of course my liege. I will return with the provisions shortly." Purvis starts to leave then turns back. "Are you sure there is nothing you wish to discuss?"

"No my sweet. I simply need to unload some stressful inner workings. Perhaps I will take you up on that massage, after my playtime."

Purvis begins to exit again.

"Purvis dear?"

He stops.

"Bring some of my finest silk rope when you return. I think I may enjoy hanging her, when she is finished."

"As you wish my master," Purvis replies.

Alacrán turns his chair to face the enormous windows behind him, looking down at the distorted expanse of his city through a low lying haze. The haze is painted a myriad of colors by the neon lights below. Will he ever find something to fill the emptiness inside him? He leans back to ponder his existence and fondle himself. He can't let the young lady see him flaccid, for what is vanity without effort?

# Woman

Her name is Tiara Lioness. She is the Princess of a small, recently formed country in South Africa that is aptly, while at the same time oddly named The Island of Lioness. Aptly, because Lioness is the family name. Oddly, because the land is not an island. Her father simply liked the name.

Princess Tiara is, without a doubt and verified by numerous major worldwide publications, the most beautiful Princess in the world. She's also a royal bitch. Tiara's vanity is a gift, the birthright of her beauty. Her constant nudity however, is a choice. She loves the reflection of her own image.

Her breasts are exquisite. They heave with a life of their own. Each one appears to sigh at the other's loveliness, as if to say, "Don't you wish we could die and be reborn to watch ourselves blossom again?"

Her ass has been the subject of so many poems and portraits that she has retired it as subject matter for artists. She does not want its splendor devalued through market over-saturation.

Her face? If only I could describe that perfect face. How do you describe those full, pouty, adorably delicate, sexy yet sensually demure lips? The cheekbones designed by a million-and-one painters' mind's eyes of the perfect female form? The chin, the forehead, the unquestionably unique shape of the loveliest eyes ever to blink at themselves in the mirror with the all-knowing, all-encompassing Universal Law that this is beauty? Don't get me started on her nose. It is perfectly proportioned and has enough of an upward turn at the end to indicate royal lineage she does not actually have. She stares at herself in the mirror. She turns away before she grows moist, playing an erotic game of cat and horny cat with herself.

Her section of the royal palace is indeed a reflection of her own orgasmic self-indulgence. It is quite simple. The walls, floors, and ceilings are lined with mirrors, albeit mirrors framed in jewel encrusted gold.

There is one problem with Tiara's existence. She has yet to find the man that could look her in the eyes and not crumple like a tin can under the weight of her glorious presence. They were all such pussies, sweating over the presence of hers.

She wants nothing to do with these boys, although she makes their obsessions useful. Usually to fetch or carry something for her. She has one person in her life that resembles a friend. Her body double, a transsexual named Dolly. The use of a body double was demanded by Tiara's father as a security measure when in public.

Dolly's face has been cut and pasted into a likeness disarmingly similar to Tiara's. The technology was available to make Dolly an exact replica, but the Princess' ego would not allow for that. So, Dolly's face and Tiara's face are almost identical. There is no comparison in their beauty when naked, especially since Dolly has a penis named Henry. Yes, even chicks name their penises.

Tiara's days are spent parading around the palace in the nude, teasing and taunting the wagging male appendages left in her wake. Her father no longer lays eyes upon her, having suffered from impure thoughts during her pubescence. Her mother died of envy once the girl was fully grown.

The Princess is alone, unhappy, and hard to feel sorrow for because she has the personality of a renaissance gargoyle with halitosis, a disease where you sweat broccoli infused bacon grease profusely, and extremely unkempt nails that are constantly drug across a chalkboard. To be fair, it is not all her fault. There's nobody in her life with the balls to raise a hand or word of discipline to the beautiful bitch. Except for Dolly. Dolly's snarkiness entertains the Princess to no end.

"Dolly," Tiara says often. "Do you love me?"

"How could I not, mistress. My life is your likeness, and I choose to love myself."

"Does that thing you have down there, between your legs, does it still work?" Tiara asks, knowing of course that it does.

"As far as most of the royal guard are concerned, yes." Dolly and the Princes both laugh splendidly.

"Ew, are they thinking of me when you do that?"

"Most likely Princess, most likely. Although I am no substitute for your highness."

"Of course not Dolly, but you are the only thing in this world besides my mirrors that brings me joy. Well, that and knowing those buffoons let you pleasure yourself with them because your face, although not as attractive as mine, bears enough resemblance."

"Yes, they are pathetic, but good lord they are musclely."

"I wish I could find pleasure in them Dolly."

"I know my dear, I know. We all have our burdens. Someday, you will find someone out there so unaffected by your beauty, they will be able to tell you what a bitch you truly are."

"Oh Dolly, why can't you be attracted to girls instead of boys?"

"If I were, who would you have to keep your feet on the ground?"

"Ha! I'm a completely self-absorbed, megalomaniac, narcissistic cunt. Nice work." They share another full-bellied laugh.

"Dolly?"

"Yes love."

"I'm bored."

# Monster

Concert. The End of Days rocks the Seattle Storm's Soccer Stadium. 100,000 screaming fans drive themselves into a frenzy knocking their heads to the infectious, metallic, crunchy, hypnotic, ravenous grooves created by the preeminent band of a generation full of jackoffs and toads. Wannabe rebels with no remorse for their misdeeds nor the intelligence to recognize the decay of their civilization. It is a disgusting display of pornographically inclined hardcore rock and roll. The type of music that makes you smack your mother, hate your brother and murder your lover.

Backstage after the show, Rancid Pete sits spread eagle in his kilt on a plush leather couch. Groupie road-whores clamor into the room. "Come here my little pussies. Come to daddy." Rancid Pete is a monster.

He is giant, near 9 feet tall. His body is large and muscular, humanoid, with clusters of spikes allover. His face is grotesque. He's the ugliest son of a bitch monster that almost resembles a man to walk the Earth. Let your imagination run wild.

The other members of the band rarely party with him after their shows. They may be decadent rock and roll hedonists, but they don't indulge in the filthiness that gets Rancid Pete off. Early on, before they learned their lesson, the band lost several bass players trying to party with Pete.

The bitches clamor to him, desperate for his legendary monster cock, both a reality and the title of one of the band's biggest hits. The girls know there is a damn good chance Pete's gonna eat them. He's got an appetite for pussy, but when he eats it he actually eats it, along with the rest of the chick. Bye, bye. One more dead soul, sold to rock and roll. He leaves a harem of ghostly former virgins in his wake.

A snitty reporter follows the throng of nitwit floozies into the room. The reporter's name is Alexis Law. She be doomed she be, a victim to lusty infamy. Someone bless rock and roll. God? I hope not.

"Mr. Pete, my name is Alexis Law. I'm with Wave 15 Seattle. I was hoping for a brief interview."

"Whatever bitch," he says, with a snarling grin.

"It's Alexis."

"Sue me."

"I want to know how you justify profiting from mainstream society despite the allegations that you routinely eat your fans?"

A few of the groupies pause their fawning for a moment, but only a moment.

"I'm a monster baby. I do what monster do."

"That is hardly an excuse for taking advantage of innocent young women." The reporter was indignant.

"As far as I'm concerned you people brought this shit on yerselves."

"Exactly how do you mean?"

"Do you see me sitting here?"

"Excuse me?"

"I said, do you see Rancid Pete sitting here before you, you delicious, feisty little twat?"

"Yes."

"Well I lived a thousand years baby and no one knew old Rancid Pete had the hottest chops any motherfucker ever heard on those cat-skin pads." Rancid Pete is the drummer. He uses actual tiger skins for his drum heads. "I'm bad baby. I can bang those goddamn things 'til yer heart beats my way, but no one ever knew. I'm a product of you. I wouldn't be here without you."

"How so?"

"If the human race wasn't so fucked up we wouldn't be in the middle of the apocalypse baby, and I would still be living in a cave in South America. Ya'll caused this darlin', not me."

"I'm sorry but that is not a reasonable answer nor a plausible excuse for your blatant disregard to human life."

"Look, I told you honey. I am what I am. A hard living, bad ass drumming, rock and roll monster." Rancid Pete smacks a groupie on the ass. "As for snackin' on you tasty kitties, you can take that up with the federal judge in New Jersey."

"I am well aware of the federal court ruling stating monsters cannot be held culpable for monsterish behavior as it is their very nature and therefore remain criminally un-punishable in regards to acts of terror, devastation of property and the devouring of other lifeforms."

"Well there you go sweet tits."

"That does not make it right!"

"Does to me," he says with a shrug of his shoulders, soaking a 40 ounce bottle of beer with a single indelicate chug.

"Yeah, well, that same ruling said it was perfectly within any other citizen's legal right to kill monsters when that citizen's rights were infringed upon by said monsters." She retorts with a snort, nostrils flaring.

"Yeah well," Rancid Pete mocks her, "if you people weren't addicted to my tasty-ass licks I guess I'd be dead already, wouldn't I?"

"You're a monster!"

"That's right momma. Now why don't you put that microphone down and get over here."

Mic on floor. Reporter on lap.

"Don't worry kitty," Rancid Pete says with a snarl. "I ain't gonna eat you. I like you."

"I don't fucking care," she says, and kisses his gnarly face.

Even a hideous monster gets a lot of ass when he knows how to rock and roll.

# Robot

His hands move exceptionally fast. The cards hit the table and gaming fates are decided. Blackjack is the name. Like death's presumed dominance over life, in the end, "the house always wins" is the game. Jack22 is La Ciudad de Oro's best player. He is a dealer robot, model HVWMR421.

The HVWMR421 is not a complicated machine. Not a whole lot of need to exercise vocabularic gymnastics for a dumb old thoughtless dealer robot. We aren't that far in the future, and by now, we could be in the past. Robots are still fairly simple, relatively speaking of course.

Jack22 has Intuitive Response Programming, based on ocular and aural stimuli. He doesn't see the dread or elation of the sad sack players at his table. Jack22 sees numbers. The seats at the table, the value of the casino chips, and the numbers of the cards. The face cards are numbers as well. His optic sensors see a Jack, Queen, King, or an Ace, but his internal processes read them as numbers 11 through 14.

Despite the simplicity of these robots, there is a random uniqueness to Jack22. While having the exact same inner workings of all HVWMR421 dealer robots at La Ciudad de Oro, Jack22 is the most successful dealer robot in history. The players sit at his table and lose their hands, their savings, their homes and often their lunch, then come back for more. Why has Jack22's table not been pockmarked and never sat at again by the weary masses? Because one in every 1,000 players who sits down in front of dealer robot Jack22 actually gets lucky.

The lucky player lands in the right seat on the right day and the cards keep coming up roses. The casino, having discovered this intricate trend has glamorized the magic of Jack22. "Push your luck with the Miraculous Jack22, a one in 1,000 chance to go home fantastically wealthy!"

Of course, steps must be taken to protect the casino's interests. Ostensibly, any decent counter of cards could surely keep an eye on when to make their move to be customer Numero 1,000 Millionaire-o. Thus, the casino schedules Jack22 to deal on a random occurring rotation of days, and he must be moved from station to station in an equally random pattern.

The casino employs a team of accountants once a year to break down all the purveying factors. After all and once again…yes, Jack22 makes the rare player extremely wealthy. But against the rest of the not-so-lucky gamblers who sit at his table, he has the most winnings of any dealer robot in the history of the casino. People sit at his table and keep betting no matter how much they lose, clinging to the delusion that in the end the tide will turn and they will wind up being that rare lucky player that Jack22 makes rich.

That's Jack22's life. Numbers, numbers, numbers. Movement, movement, movement. 999 people, ghosts, monsters, vampires, centaurs, et cetera, et cetera, hate him. But the 1000th will love him.

His power switch flips on, servers shoot electricity, cards get dealt, and monies move. Switch flips off, servers stop, and into the robot storage department he goes for "dreams of electric sleep". I'm kidding. There are no dreams.

It's not a great life. Not a life at all really. He's a freaking robot. Might as well be one of those large automaton arms that used to help build cars.

Except this. Jack22 is laden with jewels. Because of Alacrán's love for his greatest breadwinner, his optic sensors have been surrounded by green emeralds for eyes. His knuckles are studded with diamonds. His slicked back, fake robot hair is made from strands of gold. His face is pure silver, and the rose in his cheeks is provided by finely flaked rubies. The entire machine has been turned into a stiff legged walking, robot talking, number 21 stalking piece of gem-deck-a-fied art.

Shine on Jack22. Shine on.

AUTHOR'S NOTE #1:

Due to early response from the author's grandmother, the word "fuck" will now be censored from the rest of the story. I love you Grammy.

AUTHOR'S NOTE #2:

From this point on, the title of the book shall be: *Hero, Villain, Woman, Monster, Robot, oh...and Vampires*. Unless I change my mind. There may be aliens too.

# Hero, Villain, Woman, Monster, Robot, Oh…And Vampires

*a novel*

Truant D. Memphis

THE PLAYERS, PART II

# Oh…And Vampires

The Karowack Kids, pronounced "Care-oh-wack", are the absolute without doubt most un-intimidating pack of Beatnik vampires the world has ever known. The leader's name is William Henry Rockefeller the Third, but his Kids affectionately call him Dad. Other nicknames include Bloodsucker Billy, Billy R. Three, Billy the Third, Billy Hank Fangs, and a litany of additional variations to his name used in attempts to sound cool.

    The Karowack Kids get on my f@cking nerves. They are shameless sycophants to notions of cool and hip. They all maintain the petty and pretentious attitudes that drive post-apocalyptic American pop-culture. Except they remain disarmingly, not quite charmingly, but wildly inept at moving along with the times. The Kids were all made vampires by Billy the Third, who stopped aging during the era of finger snaps and berets. Billy most heartily believed in the unyielding coolness of the Beat Generation, appropriating its style as the manifesto of his clan.

    The Karowack Kids add the letter "O" unnecessarily to the ends of words. They use holders for their cigarettes. They write bad poetry. For Rock-Star-Jesus' sake, do you really want to listen to some jackass freak out on his bongos before he sucks the blood out of your body? I don't think so. Just kill me, but don't force me to experience your "cool".

Seriously. It's a dead pretentious language that adored itself, relishing insubstantial phraseology like a pig loves slop. I'm talkin' Beat baby. I don't get it, and I don't trust people that claim they do. Anyone seen a Hipster lately? How about a Spacer? Kick them in their trendy, well-groomed nuts for me.

Oh no, I'm degrading my target market. Hey you in the future, do you get my slang?

Bloodsucker Billy is not a direct member of the most infamous clan of Rockefellers, though he chooses to believe that he must be related. Any time someone happens to ask, he tells his version of the truth. "Yeah cat, John D. was my great great uncle, most cer...tain...ly, and sure, he was a mad, bad man. But he was no Billy the Three."

There is a couple dozen of the Kids plus Daddy Billy. They freelance in criminal activities for fun. They wear turtlenecks and black leather pants. They scoff at all things not...well they scoff at all things.

The worst part about their outdated style is that only Billy experienced the Beat movement. The other Kids have no true insight to the era, outside of Billy's guidance, and Billy is considerably forgetful. Suitably stupid? Let's be frank with one another, the guy is a dumb motherf@cker. Since stupidity loves company, just as misery and penises do, what you have here is an extended family of bona fide dumb dumbs. Dumbass Beatnik vampires. Yahoo.

"Hey man, let's go dig on some blood down at the club."
"That's cool daddy-o."
No. No its not.

# Post Oh!pocalypto Poppycock

*Truant D. Memphis*

# Act 1

# 1

The story is about to begin. Day breaks but no one knows. The sun never shines in this city. Our story is set years after the rapture. It doesn't matter how many.

Where are we? Before I was alive it was the City of Sin. In my lifetime the Earth was a world of sin and this city was an aging trendsetter. Now it is the Gateway to Hell. Vegas baby. Vegas.

I lied to you before. I didn't jump off a building when the rapture occurred. The truth is I was already dead. I was simply hanging about in the past, watching. By the time I died, the world had already taken several turns for the worse. If this story has somehow made it backwards to your time, which is completely possible, presuming of course that you are living in the past, let this be a forewarning: Things really don't get better.

Back to the current setting. Las Vegas. The city is presently owned and operated by a twisted Shinto Demigod named Haruka. He is half human, half minor deity, and rather insignificant as this story goes. I'm pretty sure he is in the Japanese Riviera almost the entire time. Honestly he's not that bad a dude, though he's done nothing to clean up the giant hole to Hell mess going on downtown.

As this caper takes place, most of the United States' major cities are now privately owned. What can I say? The government was broke and it seemed like a good idea.

In theory these privately owned cities still fall under the laws and jurisdictions of the United States Government. I say in theory because the government is already in the throes of its dissolution. As I am finally writing this nonsense down, the U.S. Government is currently, for all intents and purposes, completely defunct.

Now, for a moment you are a square black case, and everybody wants you. Doodles McShane has you. Doodles the Mick. That's right, he's Irish. Wanna fight about it?

Doodles is what some might call a piss-ant. I would call him average. He's squatty, has the scars of bad skin from his youth all over his face, and by no means has the charisma or charm to overcome what many would consider very unattractive physical qualities. He's not super smart and has not been extraordinarily successful on a professional level.

Doodles was a baggage handler for Worldwide International Airlines until about forty-five minutes ago. Presently, he is on the run with his extraordinary prize. What was that you asked? Of course he has no idea what is inside the case. All he knows is he has something people must want.

When those goons in suits came sniffing around the baggage area in the bowels of the Las Vegas airport, they should have shown Doodles more respect. Yes sir. Doodles is no dummy, or so he thinks. He can tell when he is being pushed around. Neither of them stupid butt-truckers figured Doodles would have the nerve to whack 'em on the head with one helluva heavy wrench, but that is exactly what he did.

Luckily for Doodles, when he went to retrieve the wrench, the men had time to locate the item they were looking for. Otherwise they would have got rocked in the head by a dim-witted suitcase tosser for no reason. But, the guy on the right was holding the black case by the time Doodles returned, wrench in hand, grin on face, and smote them both quite royally.

The fantastic shiny black case! Now it belongs to Doodles'! Who cares what is inside? It could be anything! Look at how impressive the case is. It's unbreakable. It's big, the case is about 12 inches long on all sides, and damn heavy. Whatever is inside must be special. That makes Doodles special too.

Of course Doodles tried to open the case. He can't. It has a fancy electronic number pad on it, there is no lock to bust that he can see, and fa-fa-fa-frankly the case intimidates Doodles.

Not knowing what else to do with himself in his excitement, Doodles goes for a drink. He's an alcoholic, and he's thirsty. Besides, he figures Sammy the bartender will probably know someone or have some idea of what he can do with the case. Sammy is a smart guy. He does own his own business after all, and that wife of his, Sandy, she was a hot piece of ass back in the day. Good old Sammy and Sandy.

So, Doodles wanders into the One Last Hand saloon and saddles up to the bar, placing the case below his feet.

"What do you say there Doodles?" Sammy the bartender asks.

"Sammy, I need three shots of whiskey," declares Doodles. "One for me, one for the job I just pissed on, and one for the fortune under my feet." Life is his fuzzy peach now, and he feels a wicked drunk about to happen. Yes sir. No more over night shifts schlepping luggage for Doodles McShane. No sir. Time to make love to a bottle.

We need to go backwards. Let's go backwards. Awkward flashback begins now:

Several hours ago Doodle's mysterious black case was on a plane. On that same plane was Princess Tiara Lioness. She was involved in her continual lament. Her Dolly nodded accordingly and offered thoughtless, listless responses. Dolly's mind was elsewhere.

"Dolly, do you think I'll ever find someone to love me?" the Princess asks.

"I think that depends. Are you willing to love that person back?"

"I don't think so," the Princess answers. Her face is spiritless. If there is a bright soul in there it is playing hide and seek with the outside world.

"Well darling, if you..."

You know what, I changed my mind. We will skip this nonsense. I don't care to hear the Princess' voice in my head any more than necessary. The point is the black case was on her plane. That's how it travelled to Vegas.

Let's move smoothly back to the present. Or future. When are you? Awkward flashback ends.....wait for it.....now.

Doodles is mouthing off at the bar. Nothing has changed there for the moment, except for the amount of blood in Doodles' alcohol stream. We should go check out the scene at the airport.

Two men lay dead in the baggage handlers' area and Daniel Trate has made his entrance. Unfortunately for his soul, Doodles messed up and killed both those dudes.

"What do we have here fellas?" Dan speaks to a few cops who are already checking the scene of the crime.

"Two stiff goons," says Nico. That's Nico Champ, Dan's Deputy Marshal. Nico is a young hotshot fresh out of the academy ready to yada yada yada blah blah blah great cop someday. "Both dressed to the nines."

"IDs?" Dan asks.

"Yep," Nico confirms.

"Trace 'em yet?"

"Nope."

"Anything at all?" Dan says with a grin.

"Well, they don't work here," Nico states. "We're running the IDs now. It looks like both men took blows to the back of the head with that very large wrench over there."

"Anyone missing from the airline staff?" Dan kneels by a victim, taking a closer look at the man's head wound.

"Not sure yet. It happened at the end of the last shift on that crew's final round of incoming flights." Nico doesn't stand still well.

He's a pacer, no bones about it. He likes to make dramatic turns at opportune moments of conversation, and thoroughly enjoys wearing too many weapons.

"Any security cameras?" Dan continues.

"Yeah," Nico says. "Not sure what sort of angle we're going to have but we're getting the copies now."

"Wonderful. You eat anything for breakfast?"

"Yeah."

"Good. Breakfast is important." Dan walks to the murder weapon. "Wow. That is a big wrench. So why are these guys down here?" He knows, but around Nico he feels like the coach of an athlete.

"Well. It's the baggage area," Nico says dryly.

"Well it is the baggage area."

"So?" Nico knows what to do next. He enjoys playing dumb at times to keep Marshal Dan on his toes.

"Let's find out if any luggage was reported missing, get those surveillance videos looked at, and make sure you ask everybody down here if they saw anything," Dan says.

"Will do. Will do. Have already."

"Anything?"

"Of course not. Can't be that easy."

"That wouldn't be any fun Nico," Dan says, slapping his deputy on the back. "So get all that boring stuff done for me. I have to be somewhere. Keep me informed."

"Marshal Dan, it is 9:30 in the morning. Where else do you have to be? You love cop stuff. There is only one thing you like more than doing cop stuff." Nico pauses. "Wait a minute," Nico wields his wildly facetious look of having the proverbial light bulb switched on. It's a solid effort. "Are you telling me you've added a 9:30? Please tell me you added a 9:30 and then immediately tell me that is what my life will be like someday soon."

"Well Nico, if you were going to visit your grandmother at 9:30 in the morning to make sure she is still alive, your life could be more like mine." Dan turns to head for his car.

"Grandmother?" Nico says. "Ohhhhhh. I get it. Going to see your 'grandmother'. Sure thing boss. I will hold down the fort while you go visit your 'grandmother'." To be fair, the Marshal's dalliances are well known. Nico has every right to assume the Marshal may be headed off to an attractive woman's embrace.

Dan shakes his head and smiles at his protégé as he walks away.

"Hold on, Marshal," Nico says. "There is something else you might find interesting."

"What's that?"

"The Princess arrived." Nico speaks with an intentionally droll lack of enthusiasm.

"Interesting," Dan replies, rubbing his chin with his hand.

"Even more interesting, her plane arrived right around the same time all of this happened."

"Convenient." Dan says. He doesn't give meeting Princess Tiara any thought, outside of practical murder investigation pursuits. His mind never gives a female much thought. His testes on the other hand, put both factories on overtime two weeks ago when the Marshal's office was informed of the Princess' intentions to visit his city. "Reach out to her people and let them know we may want to speak with her. For her own safety of course."

"Will do."

"Thank you Nico. You are a gentleman, a scholar and a dashingly handsome fellow destined for greatness." If you asked Dan his true opinion of Nico all of those superlatives would apply. "Now, I've got to go. Call me if you need me." He turns to leave again.

"Marshal," Nico calls after him. "Will you answer if it's on? If I call while the push-and-smush is happening, will you still answer?"

"Inappropriate Nico. Highly Inappropriate."

"I love you Marshal Dan!"

# 2

Alacrán strolls the perimeter of his office, admiring his treasures. This is how he contemplates. Thoughts had while surrounded by beauty must be first rate thoughts. They must be the most productive thoughts you can have, when you are so pleasantly stimulated. This is the path his mind is wandering when Purvis flails into the room.

"My liege!" Purvis declares.

"My pet," Alacrán replies. "You are excited."

"Yes my liege."

"Stop it. I don't like it. Stop your sweaty tail-wagging this instant and tell me why you have disturbed my meditation." Alacrán breathes on the left breast of a headless, brass bust of Marilyn Monroe then rubs it with his hanky. I have no idea how they know it is Norma Jean's knockers, but that is what the placard on it says: *Norma Jean's Knockers*. He looks at Purvis who is comically struggling to stop perspiring. "My friend, stop. Stop straining. Relax and tell me what you have to say."

"She is here! She is in Las Vegas! My liege, she is here and guess where she is staying?" Purvis is sweating even more. Come to think of it, despite his physical perfection, Purvis is a heavy sweater.

"Whom?" Alacrán asks. "Whom do you speak of?"

"Guess!" Purvis is shaking his tail like an excited puppy.

"You know I do not like to be toyed with."

"It will be worth the lashes." Purvis knows they are coming either way. It's part of the game, one he has come to enjoy. They sting nice.

Alacrán removes his belt, folds it in two and with it slaps Purvis across the face. Then he slaps himself in the back of the thigh. This isn't routine, but the intrigue is exciting. They both squeal.

"It's the Princess." Alacrán says. "The Princess is here."

"How did you know?" asks the beautiful Purvis.

"It was on the news. Why do you think I was flustering about so?"

"Oh," says Purvis, playfully disappointedly.

"I'm sorry I struck you darling but we were both so excited. I was enjoying the game." Alacrán is now sweating as well.

"Well, if you're so smart, guess where she is coming," says Purvis.

Alacrán whacks the snot out of him this time. Purvis sinks to the floor, happily hurting.

"Now listen my pet. If you get me all excited and then tell me she's not coming here, this isn't going to be fun anymore. For either of us." Alacrán loves his station in this world without scrutiny.

"She's coming here," blurts Purvis.

Alacrán reissues his belt to his pants, returning to his desk. Purvis follows him, coming to rest in a chair across the desk from his master. In reality, they have been planning for the Princess' arrival for some time. When the Princess' trip to Vegas was announced, Alacrán paid a pretty penny in covert arrangements to ensure Princess Tiara would stay at La Ciudad de Oro.

"Enough of our little game," Alacrán says. "Is everything in motion?"

"Of course my liege," answers Purvis. "Her suite is prepared. All of our people our attending their duties. Everything is on schedule and moving forward according to your plan."

"Very well," says Alacrán. "I'm still a little restless. Bring someone up for me."

"Yes my liege." Purvis rises to leave.

"My sweet," Alacrán calls.

"Yes?"

"Very well done. I thoroughly enjoyed that." It is rare that Alacrán and Purvis find time for these little forays of masochist fantasy nowadays. Alacrán has a moment of nostalgia, remembering with a smile on his face the numerous lashings he has joyfully given the young man over the years.

"Thank you sir," Purvis replies. He enjoys these occasions with his de facto father as well, although it is the physical pain that Purvis enjoys, more so than the act of bonding and companionship.

"You're welcome. I want to make sure you understand how especially excited I am."

"Of course my liege."

"Normally that would have been more than enough stimulation. You were superb. It's just, this is a special occasion." Alacrán rarely feels guilt, but he suddenly does. He feels bad for requesting a girl from his harem after such a rousing bit of roleplay from Purvis.

"The young lady will be up presently sir. I truly appreciate your consideration, but it is unnecessary." Purvis is sincere. He knows this crazy evil man loves him. He certainly doesn't understand why, but he knows.

"You are beautiful," Alacrán says.

"I know my liege." Purvis is lying, joking. Despite understanding the world views him as top-notch handsome, when he looks in the mirror he sees an ugly child.

"Don't be bold. Your name is disgusting. That's why I never speak it."

"You are an oily Spanish prick," Purvis replies. They laugh. Then stop. Purvis exits as Alacrán leans back in his chair, choking on a cigar.

Once outside Alacrán's office, Purvis falls against the hallway wall, clasping his hands over his heart. This is his chance. Purvis knows there is one person on this planet as physically pleasing to the eyes, nose, and pheromonal embrace as he. Princess Tiara Lioness.

He's had a crush on her way longer than his boss. Alacrán wouldn't know about the Princess if it wasn't for Purvis. Why should he have her?

Alacrán must die!

Okay, Alacrán doesn't have to die, but he does need to get out the f@cking way. Purvis really wants to bone Princess Tiara.

# 3

The first thing to cross Jack22's mind is, *What did you say?* The answer is nothing. Jack22 has not said anything. "*What did you say?*" are the very first words of his brand new inner-monologue.

*I didn't say anything.*
*Who are you?*
*Who are you?*
*I asked you first.*
*Open your eyes.*

Jack22 opens his eyes. He is in his maintenance closet. He doesn't know it's called a "closet". The shiny robot doesn't know what's happening. He doesn't know he can think or what thinking means. He's been born to a world of random awareness.

*What was that?*
*What?*
*That sound.*
*There was no sound.*
*Well then what was that?*
*We should leave here.*

The "We" is a watershed moment. Jack22 has his first self-

discovery. *There must be an opposite of "we"*, he thinks. *I.*
*I'm alone and I am talking to I. There is no we.*

Thus, Jack22 quickly escapes any sense of community, any sense of self-less commitment to the good of the whole. He forsakes the needs of the world around him, bounding recklessly down a path frequently taken by mankind. The path of the infinite, selfish, *I*. Luckily, it's a passing phase. In fairness, the robot doesn't know any better. Yet.

Here's how Jack22 came alive. Last night he dealt a leprechaun a pair of aces. Then split those aces with two black jacks. The leprechaun was very appreciative. Did you know leprechauns can't or won't grant wishes as legend suggests? It's a mystery. They may be bound by some form of sacred oath, or they may refuse to because leprechauns have a tendency to be little jerks. Did you also know that leprechauns have magic that among many other things can give robots thoughts, a personality, and self-awareness? Well they do.

This particular leprechaun is named Pleeb. I kid you not. Most leprechauns I'm aware of have more utilitarian names like Frank and Jesse, but ours is named Pleeb.

If you were a kid growing up with a real weird name, how did it affect you? It made our leprechaun very self-conscious. He never gives himself credit for positive qualities or skills. He sees himself in the mirror as shorter than he is, uglier than he is, and dumber than he is. All the makings of an alcoholic gambler. His eyes are sallow, his thin hair graying. Even the color of his little green hat is fading.

Pleeb threw all in on the split aces Jack22 dealt. With a stroke of good luck, Pleeb became Mr. One in One Thousand. The big winner! Jack22 made him rich. So, he gave Jack22 life. He threw some gold dust at Jack22, said some crazy leprechaun hoobitty joobitty, and endowed the robot with self-awareness.

Jack22 decided to leave the closet, but discovered he could not move. He wondered why he could not move. Before further investigating the situation, he happened across an exquisite word: *Banana*. Jack22 has spent the last thirty minutes repeating the word banana in his mind.

The closet door opens and Jack22 screams. *AAAAgghhh!* His brain hits a high note. Nothing comes out of his mouth. An arm reaches into the closet towards Jack22's neck. He can't feel anything, then suddenly, he realizes he is on. *They turned me on? Why do I need to be turned on?*

"That's funny," says a Rotation Tech.

The Rotation Techs have a great life. They work for a union. They move robots.

"What," says the other Rotation Tech named Arty. The other Rotation Techs all love Arty because no matter what happens during the rest of their boring lives, they can call him "Arty the RT" every day. It's the little things…

Maybe if Pleeb the leprechaun had found a profession that somehow rhymed with his name life would have been different for him. Oh well, whatever. He's rich now. Pleeb is currently drinking a $5000 dollar bottle of champagne while having naked time with not one, but two full-size women! No dwarves or fairies tonight. No sir, no sir!

"22's eyes were open and his optic recorders were running," says Jay, the Rotation Tech not named Arty.

"So someone left the power on last night," says Arty.

"Nah, Arty," says Jay. "The power was off. That's what's weird about it."

"Well it was probably a power surge or something," Arty replies. Not an illogical, albeit immediately stated theory. Jack22 is hooked up to a power source recharging his battery. A surge was possible.

"Should we report it?" Jay asks.

"Nah. It's almost lunch," Arty replies. His hands make their way to his belly and rub it.

Jay is convinced. "Yeah, you're right. I don't feel like talking to those pricks down in Reengineering anyways. They think they're smarter than everybody. Seriously. I say, 'Holy shit, do you really have to be the nerdy jerk who thinks he is smarter than everybody else because you do robot science?' And they say, 'Yes, yes we do,' every time."

Arty is thinking about meatloaf. It is Meatloaf Monday and almost lunchtime. "It's almost lunch," he says again.

"Yeah," says Jay with a smile. "Man, you love meatloaf."

"I do," Arty agrees. "I love meatloaf. What are you gonna do?"

It is a known fact, when I was alive I considered myself a master of loafed meats. It was an opinion regularly agreed upon in certain social circles. Not only cow meat. Turkey, chicken, pork, if you gave me a meat I could loaf it. I would loaf it to the delights of onlookers' eyes, noses and mouths. Even their ears. I could loaf so hard and well. This has nothing to do with the story, but since we are getting to know each other...

Rotation Tech Jay stands in front of Jack22, staring at the robot's face. Jack22 sees Jay. He hears the man say, "Time for work." It is a voice command. Jack22 moves.

*I'm moving*, he thinks. *How did he do that to me? What's happening? Where am I going?* Jack22 has a curious problem. He might be aware of himself, but he is not in control.

# 4

We are back at the Last Hand Saloon. Doodles reaches a level of drunkenness that, despite increasing your suspicion of others, also encourages loose lips. He tells Sammy all about whacking the two guys over the head, and how he knows whatever is in the case has to be of great value.

In his stupor, Doodles sets the case atop the bar, tossing about grand speculations as to what the case might contain. A lot of this is nonsense. For instance, the odds of the black case housing a secret gateway dimension that holds the doorways to everywhere in existence, those odds are astronomically poor. Still, I was surprised and impressed that Doodles considered the possibility.

Doodles' wild speculations catch the attention of Sammy's wife. Despite Doodles' stupidity, the possibilities spark her curiosity. Sandy doesn't need any of Doodles' dumb ideas about what the black case might hold. She can imagine her own.

Sandy puts a plan in place to acquire the case from Doodles. Her plan requires an otherwise empty bar. It takes a few hours for the "over-nighters" to clear out. By the time the last patron is gone, Doodles is past rip-roaring and onto slobbering drunk.

Sammy gives Doodles another round on the house. He tells Doodles he is going to lock up for a few hours to get some sleep. It will take him a few minutes to count down the cash register and close everything up, so Doodles can take his time with his drink. Sammy goes into the back, pleading his case for not killing Doodles one final time to Sandy. He loses the argument.

Sammy is a deeply sentimental man. Due to the enormous amount of insane charisma he unleashes into his mind to drown out any thoughts of remorse, regret, or logic, he comes out from the side of the bar in a petulant frenzy. This scares Doodles so bad the drunk pees himself. As the two men scream at one another, and Doodles pees, Sammy grabs the black case and crushes Doodles on the head.

Sammy the bartender now sits on a stool in front of his bar, staring down at the body of Doodles McShane. Sandy sits in a corner booth smoking a cigarette. Tears are quietly streaming down Sammy's cheeks.

"Don't be such a sap, Sam. You didn't even like the guy." Sandy sneers with the smoke in between her teeth. "Besides, he killed two people and stole the case to begin with. He deserved what he got."

*She used to be so lovely*, Sammy thinks. *Now she's an old fat rotten tomato*. Sammy doesn't know what he killed Doodles to acquire. For heaven's sake, what if there isn't anything worth a crapola in the damn case? It wasn't a well discussed plan. *Now I'm a murderer! Damn it Sammy.*

Doodles isn't actually dead yet. Sammy only struck him once with the case, but Doodles had crumpled quite nicely. Sammy couldn't bring himself to make another blow, completely crushing Doodle's skull. Instead, Doodles lays unconscious, breathing so faintly from the alcohol and the head trauma that he appears dead. The task at hand for Sammy is to dispose of Doodles' body.

Sammy thinks about what to do with the body while he weeps. The crying is tiring, so he goes behind his bar to snort some blow.

That's cocaine that is. Suddenly, he feels forty-two years old again. "Sandy get over here and help me move this galoot," he says.

"You're going to die on that garbage Sammy Hampton. You are too old."

"And you're too fat."

Sandy somehow rolls her eyes and gives Sammy the evil eye at the same time, then smashes her cigarette into an ashtray. "Where we going to take him?" she asks.

"To the car first," he replies. "Figure out where else after. I have a few ideas but we may as well be working while I think it through."

"I don't want to touch that bum."

"Don't be such a screw Sandy. For Christ's sake, have some respect for the dead." Sammy takes Doodles underneath his arms and tries to drag him backwards. Sandy stands at Doodles' feet, hands on her hips, judging her once dashing husband.

"You can't even move a dead body right," she states flatly.

"Are you kidding me?" Sammy snarls. "Grab his legs you old fart-assed hag." Sandy grabs the pants of both legs and feigns helping Sammy as he struggles to get Doodles moving. Sammy slides Doodles across the floor, veins bulging, eyes popping and tongue lolling. Sandy watches, wondering how this man ever made her horny.

Sammy stops in a small hallway at the back of the bar. He is gassed. "No offense dear, but I feel as though I'm not getting the marital support I require on this project."

"Take a break then. Catch your wind."

"My love, what do you think we are going to do with the case?" Sammy is gasping air through his words.

"Why didn't you think of that before you killed him?" Sandy cannot help but play with this poor man. She's been doing so for 27 years. There are so many things to look for in a man. It's a shame more women don't realize the best men in the world are those you can be mean to.

"Oh okay," Sammy says, flipping his hands in the air with irritation. "I'll just think of everything then."

"Or nothing."

"Arg. You're a cow."

"Sammy, get this damn thing out of here," she says, kicking at Doodles' feet.

"Alight let's go. But help this time. My chest is killing me." Sammy strains under Doodles' weight again.

"That's the cocaine you idiot."

So a funny thing happened when Sandy and Sammy made their impressively hasty decision to kill Doodles. After initially pounding Doodles' skull, Sammy ran back into his office to hide for a while, having forgotten to lock the front door.

While Sammy and Sandy are dragging Doodles out the back, a black guy, an albino, and a rabbi all walk into the bar. Just kidding. One person does walk in though. An average figure of no distinct description. You really can't tell if it is a person, or an ogre, or maybe a demon named Zorn. It has a trench coat on, hiding all its features, until you see the face. The creature's face basically looks like the silhouette of a head. It is like looking at the absence of light in the middle of a well-lit room.

This person-thing-thingy walks over to the bar and lays its arms on the counter. It waits patiently. No bartender? Hey look, there is an interesting case there. It won't open. Maybe I should take it. That's what it thinks. Hold that thought.

Sammy and Sandy are on either side of their car with both doors to the back seat open. Sammy is pulling while Sandy is trying to stuff Doodles' legs in. Stupid tiny cars. Who would have thought the day would come when the government started making people drive these stupid tiny cars? The air isn't going to get any better! And technically, we are in the middle of Armageddon. What f@cking difference does it make?

Sandy gets super frustrated trying to shove Doodles' legs into the car. "You stupid f@cking fat piece of shit!" She kicks at Doodles and almost falls over, which of course makes her angrier, so she begins slamming the door on Doodle's legs.

Doodles sits up immediately and screams bloody hell.

"Bloody hell!"

Sammy begins to scream as well because he is an emotional guy.

When the thing in the trench coat at the bar hears Doodles' and Sammy's screams, it freaks out. It turns to take off with the case and knocks a bunch of steins from the bar. This commotion spooks it further, sending it flailing over a bar stool.

"Stop screaming you f@cking girl," screams Sandy.

Sammy shuts his mouth abruptly. Doodles passes back out from the pain. Sandy lights a cigarette.

They hear the noise in the bar. Sammy runs into the bar and sees "it". He doesn't know what he sees.

"Hey, what are you doing in here?" Sammy mumbles, not at all authoritarian.

The thing, having recovered from its fall, whirls with the case in its hand and heads for the front door, screeching like a banshee.

"Hey that's mine," says Sammy. He runs back to the car ramming past Sandy on his way.

"What's going on?" she blurts.

"Get in the car you bitch," he screams. For once, she shuts her fat, stinking, wraith of a mouth and gets in the car. Then immediately begins to run it again as Sammy squeals away.

"What the hell's going on? Who was in there? What are you going? When's the case?" Something like that.

"It stole it! It stole my case you old crow! Now shut up!"

"Don't you talk to me that way you bum! How could you let

someone steal it already you moron? God I hate you Sammy Hamp..."

"Shut up shut up shut up you stupid cow!"

"I hate you! Now you got our case stolen and there is a man alive in the back seat you couldn't even kill right!"

"SHUT UP!"

Sammy turns the corner onto the main street outside his bar. They see the thief feebly attempting to run down the sidewalk with the heavy black case, stumbling over the weight and awkwardness of the object. Sammy and Sandy both interrupt themselves mid-bitchmouth and together they scream, "There it is!"

# 5

When the End of Times comes to town they know how to make a big-ass entrance, yes they do. Rancid Pete sits atop a black stallion at the end of Casino Boulevard. Casino Boulevard is the current main strip of fancy Las Vegas casinos. The old strip burned down in the infamous Jackpot Fires of 2099.

Rancid Pete's band rolls behind him in an antique tank, shooting fireworks from the main cannon. The fireworks explode like piñatas over the crowds in the street, showering the masses with condoms, illicit drugs, and money. The End of Times give back to their fans.

Pete rears back on the horse, pulling it up on its hind legs. "Are you ready to rock Las Vegas?" he roars.

The crowd goes crazy.

"Hell yeah! Let's freak out you miserable cretins!" Pete aims the steed for the crowd and blasts his way down Casino Boulevard, trampling as many of his fans under foot as he can. The tank follows behind. People are going nuts.

Rancid Pete makes his way to the end of the strip. He's in front of La Ciudad de Oro, when he sees her. His heart flips. She is getting out of the largest limousine he, a gigantic rock star, has ever seen. It is made from the body of a relic 747 jet airplane. The woman is incredibly sexy, at least in human terms. Pete loses his breath.

The most wonderful part, what drives Rancid Pete up a horny flagpole, the thing that knocks his socks off but leaves his shoes on is the filthy, retching, unholy dark energy surrounding her. This bitch has the most gruesome aura he's ever seen, outside his own. She is nasty, trashy and loathsome. He immediately wants her so bad he falls off his horse.

The woman doesn't notice but Pete feels like a moron. Nothing will suck the confidence out of a monster so much as love at first sight. When people run to his aid Rancid Pete makes quite a scene to regain his machismo. He jumps up and punches through the horse, lodging his hand inside and tearing it back out, removing the poor horse's heart. I think the stallion's name was Carl. Pete eats the heart lavishly then mauls his way through the crowd towards the steps of La Ciudad de Oro, stalking after the woman.

Princess Tiara arrives with her typical surprise and audacity. Everywhere the Princess travels people go insane. Her presence alone can bring a city to its knees. Basically, every time she leaves the safety of her palace a catastrophe occurs. On previous occasions, steps have been taken to prevent her from entering certain cities. Believe it or not, there are still a few good places left on this Earth, and most have banned Princess Tiara from ever stopping by.

Take for example, Iceland. They have never allowed the Princess to fly through their airspace, let alone set foot in their country. Then again, Iceland was the first country in the world to have a political party formed and led by women. Unless you count the Amazonians or Valkyries as a political party.

Here are a few of the most famous catastrophes caused by a visit from Princess Tiara:

In Italy, on a visit to Rome, there was a mass suicide of the most prominent fashion designers. They crumpled under the weight of the notion the Princess might commission them to design an outfit for her. She is notoriously mean to fashion designers. The ghosts of a hundred designers roam the streets of Rome, moaning. If that weren't enough, before Tiara departed, what was left of the Coliseum fell to the ground. While the reason for the collapse is officially uncertain, it's commonly believed it had something to do with the Princess stating, "I thought the Coliseum was supposed to be fun."

In Paris the Eifel Towel did not suffer any insults or injuries. However, French citizenry had never been exposed to someone as snooty and rude as Princess Tiara. After her visit, the French were never the same again. If you waited around for a Frenchman to make a loathsome comment about a meal at a restaurant or the politics of another country, you would grow old and die. The nation as a whole fell into a black, unfamiliar sea of humility. A sea that carried the ships of their hearts from the island of lost cynical pride through the tumultuous waters of anger and on to the shores of manic disarray, where they dropped full anchor. They turned against one another. It started with a public glove slap to an anonymous face, and to this day the streets of Paris flow with the blood of its own people. Civil war and anarchy run rampant in France. The rest of the world snickers?

Tokyo. Three words. Geisha Hari Cari. I don't know what those Geisha were so ashamed of.

London. You know. Come to think of it. Nothing really happened in London. It rained the whole time she was there. That's fairly normal from what I've heard. It was pretty uneventful. Except for a bunch of Irish storming the Royal Palace and holding the Royal Family captive for a few days. No one understood why. The Irish had long since gained their full independence from the British government. The IRA had transitioned from terrorist organization to World Cup Champion soccer team years earlier.

Rancid Pete is too far behind the Princess' entourage to reach her before she enters the casino. He hesitates and breaks off his attack. He's not sure what he would say if he caught her. He's never been so befuddled. He's never felt, nor does he understand, his confidence instantly waning. He follows Tiara and her entourage from behind, walking and staring hypnotically.

The Princess enters the casino. She makes her way through the lobby while a cool song plays in the background, something industrial and sexy. Pete stands frozen outside the casino doors, watching as the scene unfolds. Flashbulbs from cameras fire in rapid succession. The Princess turns, preens, licks her lips, holds her hips and more than a few times extends the middle finger.

Before she reaches the front desk where Alacrán waits to greet her with his hands wringing and stomach gassy, she turns and drops her saris. She stands naked as a jaybird, runs her hands up her thighs then throws them to the sky striking a pose, receiving the adulation bestowed upon her as if it were from the Heavens.

Pete's tongue falls out of his mouth. The bulge in his pants grows. His heart beats faster.

Princess Tiara turns her back to the crowd and her men run to her, covering her with a new silken cloak, but not before she farts. This is the world I live in folks. After I died that is. The Princess has taken Idle Rich Whoring to a level never before achieved. You have to give the masses what they want if you're going to be famous for no reason.

Alacrán stands in ecstasy. He maintains his greasy authoritarian demeanor, but doing so is super hard. He really wants to gush all over the Princess like some sort of unisex hair stylist. The lust and excitement ooze from his very pores.

"My lady. I am Flacido Rodrigo Diego. I cannot tell you what a pleasure it is to have you at La Ciudad de Oro. I believe you will find anything your heart desires within reach. I have taken very special care to ensure your stay here will be the most luxurious you've ever had."

"I want a bubble bath and a porterhouse steak in ten minutes," she replies. "Take me to my room."

"Your highness, I will escort you myself." He offers his arm to her. She stares at it. Ignoring the slight, Alacrán casually transitions his arm so that it is now out in front of him, inviting the Princess to move forward. The Princess starts walking as he bustles along next to her, quietly chattering away.

"Did you know I secretly run a crime syndicate?" Alacrán leads Princess Tiara to his private elevators, extolling to her his many wonderful qualities. "Did you know I have more money than your father?"

As Alacrán and Princess Tiara board the elevator, a dance number breaks out in the lobby, Bollywood style, as a Disc Jockey cuts records with reckless abandon. Free booze is wheeled into the room by scantily clad employees as a party ensues. Our villain put his most cunning foot forward in an attempt to wow the Princes. She scarcely notices.

Outside a throng of reporters encircles Rancid Pete, calling his name, hoping he will grant them a question. "Pete! Pete! Pete!" A bald dude makes his way up front and shoves a microphone into Pete's morbidly cavernous face.

"Pete, did you know Princess Tiara would be here?" the reporter asks. "And how does it feel to be upstaged by her entrance?" Pete takes the man's head in his hand and pops it like a pimple. Blood splatters the crowd. There is no ghost inside the man. His body simply falls limply to the ground.

"How did that feel?" Pete mutters to himself.

"Pete, what do you think about doing a show with Ten Foot Tall Jesus and the Regional Deity All-Star Band?" a female reporter asks.

"I think it's f@cking sweet. JC is the original rock star right?" Pete licks his lips at the bitch.

"Pete! Is there any truth to the rumor that you accidentally broke your original lead singer Alex Grant, and replaced him with a look alike?" questions another reporter.

Pete looks at this reporter in disgust. "Go suck yourself off," he says.

"Do you plan to try and meet the Princess?"

"Have you ever met the Princess?"

"Do you gamble Pete?"

"Are you hungry?"

"If you could eat one famous person who would it be?"

"How do you feel about the Standardized Union of Confederated Kingdoms denying the former United States entrance?"

At the exact right time, the rest of The End of Times hoses the crowd down with strawberry jelly, pumped from the machine gun carriage on the top of their tank. The media and rest of the idiots in the crowd go crazy, clamoring to the tank, cheering and pounding on its sides. Rancid Pete turns and walks away without having to answer any more of their ignorant questions. He snatches two birdies up by the hair while stomping off to his hotel.

Now Rancid Pete is sitting in his hotel room slamming beer and crying. He is, in general, an ugly bastard, but the lonely monster is an even uglier site of himself. The two women lay dead in the bed next to him. They are both heartily unattractive, mostly naked and completely dead. Usually Pete lets the dog faced ones live out of respect for, well, his own grotesqueness I suppose.

The band is staying at the Octopus' Garden. That's correct, the most notorious band in the world couldn't book a suite at La Ciudad de Oro. Those are reserved for dignitaries, actors, statesmen, super high rollers and anyone else in the world but a rock band with a stinky monster drummer. Alacrán doesn't enjoy The End of Times' music or their flare. This is the type of prejudice with which poor old Rancid Pete is confronted.

He nibbles on a dead girl's feet, sampling a few of her toes, but quickly finds eating doesn't remove the morose emotional blanket smothering him. Nobody understands. Pete has lived a thousand years alone. Once the Creator saw fit to share him with the rest of the world, he unexpectedly found himself lonelier than when he was unknown. He is famous, revered, feared, and still has no true companionship.

The girlies he eats only want to touch his fame and his wang. They don't love him or care about his immortal soul. If he has a soul.

His own band mates are too frightened by him to fulfill his need for their fellowship. You would think the fact they are still alive is a sign he isn't gonna hurt them. Not as long as the records are selling.

Don't get me wrong. Ol' Pete doesn't sit around sullying his dignity like this often. Most of the time he pushes the pain away, freewheeling through this current chapter in his life, fueled by intoxication and excess. He chooses an accelerated heart rate over his inner-child every time. F@ck yeah.

Yet, beauty has knocked on the front door to his heart, reminding him of his solitude. That horrible creature, Princess Tiara Lioness, brought something weak out in Pete. His confidence is shattered. His hands are trembling. He continues slamming beers but alcohol isn't changing the way he feels. It's like he's had some sort of life altering something or other. It is the first time he's ever felt this helpless, and if that isn't true, well it sure feels that way. Let's be frank. If eating the feet off a girl he recently porked five ways from last Sunday doesn't make Rancid Pete feel better, something is definitely wrong with his world.

# 6

Dan's appointment was indeed a visit to his beloved grandma Daffodil, who he lovingly refers to as Deedee. Nico had every right to assume Dan may have had early copulation therapy scheduled, except that Dan told him he was going to see his grandma, and Dan doesn't lie. Nico knows this, but Nico isn't the type to shy away from a good sex joke about a grandmother.

Nico would be surprised if he learned Dan hasn't visited any of his romantic consorts in at least six months. So would Dan. What has changed these last six months? Well, it was around six months ago this jigsaw puzzle nonsense with Grandma Deedee began. There is something else though. An unfortunate condition to which Dan is completely oblivious. We'll get to that later.

Dan doesn't care for people to know about his time with his grandmother. It challenges his positive mind frame when people are praised for taking actions they inherently should. Spending time with a failing relative is an example. It's not something you're supposed to win an award for or treat like a giant cross to bear.

Deedee hardly speaks these days. She's consumed with an elaborate jigsaw puzzle laid out on her dining room table. Dan comes by every day to make sure Deedee is eating. He finds her in front of the puzzle, muttering to herself, organizing an abundance of pieces. It looks like the portrait centers around a large beautiful tree. She resists when he pulls her away and forces her to bathe, to eat.

Our White Knight is distraught. Dan is a man of cheerful disposition with deeply repressed pain. Witnessing his Granny Deedee's decline is painful, pain he hasn't successfully repressed, and this makes our man uncomfortable. It is also encouraging his loneliness. Deedee is the last living member of Dan's immediate family.

With Deedee drifting off into some other place, somewhere in between this life and death, Dan is finding strange sparks of an emotion he isn't familiar with poking about inside him. Longing. He doesn't understand it yet, but Dan is looking for love. It's an odd sensation for a successful bachelor.

Anyway, as these incoherent emotions are floating around in the goo between Dan's ears, he scrambles some eggs, fries a little sausage and puts together a few pieces of cinnamon toast for Deedee. It used to be her favorite breakfast.

"Well hello my favorite grandson," Deedee says from her seat at the kitchen table. Dan is mildly surprised.

"Hey, there she is," he says with his back turned. He turns to face her with a warm smile and sees her looking up from her work on the puzzle, smiling brightly herself. "Well hello there my favorite grandmother," he says, with a slight bow.

"I'm your only grandmother."

"I'm your only grandson."

"As far as you know," she says with a wry grin. "What brings you by?"

"Breakfast. Thought I would check to see how you were doing today and make sure you were feeding yourself."

"Well isn't that sweet." There are days when Deedee seems perfectly lucid. Of course, when dealing with the elderly those refreshing days of lucidity often don't include memory of their most recent hours, days, weeks, and months. What is really neat however, and happens more often than we realize, are those days when the elder person returns to the wit of their former years, recognizing the nature of their own mental decline.

For instance, recently, on the rare occasions Deedee has been fully present, she's looked at the puzzle and said to Dan, "What a lovely puzzle. So how long have I been working on this? I don't think I've been home upstairs lately."

Today however, is different. If Dan asked, Deedee could tell him exactly how long she has been working on the puzzle. She could tell him damn near everything she's done for the last six months. This is a rare occasion where the Universe has returned his grandmother to him in full bloom. All intellectual faculty members are present, including the provost, her sly sense of humor.

"How has work been dear?" she asks.

"Busy as always," he replies. "So what have you been up to? Anything exciting?"

Deedee laughs then sighs. She is supposed to. Dan is being playful. He knows what she has been up to. Working on the puzzle and losing her mind. At least, as far as he knows. That's why she chuckled, there's so much Dan doesn't know.

"Oh, just talking with an old friend dear," she says.

"Is that right? Anyone I know?"

"Not yet. Maybe someday," she replies.

Dan thinks she seems rather sneaky today. "Want some breakfast?" he asks.

"Of course I do. You know I love breakfast."

Dan fixes two plates then helps Deedee to another seat at the table where there is a clearing from the jigsaw puzzle. He sets her food down and takes a seat with his own plate. "This is lovely," she says.

"I try." They sit quietly while they eat. He studies her. She notices.

"Did I ever tell you I came from another dimension?" she says, breaking the silence.

Dan comes close to spitting food out of his mouth from surprise and instant laughter. "No Granny, you didn't."

"Oh yes dear, you and I shouldn't know each other. At least, not these versions of each other, but this is how it worked out." She takes a slow drink of milk.

"Is that right?" he replies.

"That's right," she says. "I'm not really sure where your real me wound up."

This puzzles Dan, amusingly. His grandmother's crafty sense of humor was well known throughout her life, but it's been a while since she teased him like this.

"You come from a long line of special people," she continues. "Very special people. I raised your great grandfather too you know. Or maybe it was your great, great grandfather. My memory is a little rusty on that. You were named after him."

"They both had the same name." Dan is noticeably confused.

"That's right, that's why I have a hard time remembering which of them was mine. You were named after them both. I'm not sure what happened with your father. Some other Deedee was here when he came around. Where his name came from escapes me." She pauses, searching her memory to no avail. "Hmph. Oh well. Anyway, they were all special people, your line of fathers. And you are too."

"Granny, you are a funny old bird. What's special about me?"

"We're not sure yet, but we'll find out eventually," she says, laughing softly.

"You are on your game today old lady. Very funny stuff."

She finishes the last bites of her food then holds her hand up for Dan to help her out of the chair. "Let's hope so Danny boy," she says. She makes her way back towards her bedroom. "Let's hope so."

"You heading for a nap?"

"Shower. Don't leave yet."

"Okay."

As she walks away Dan wonders how much time he has left with her.

The old lady has been fed, showered, and she is again seated in front of her puzzle. Dan has finished the dishes and loaded her laundry amidst halfhearted protests. The garbage is collected and put out.

"Well Gran, I guess I better get going."

She waives him over to her with both arms for a hug. He obliges.

"I love you," she whispers in his ear. Then she gives him a kiss on the cheek.

"I love you too," he says as he stands back up.

"Now get," she says. "You're not the only one who needs to get back to work."

"Is that right?"

"Don't you mock me little boy. Let me tell you something." She wags a finger at him with a smile. "You may think I'm a crazy old lady but you will see. Just because I'm not allowed to explain it all to you, doesn't mean you won't find out. You'll see someday. Nobody has a f@cking clue what's going on around here."

"Well Granny," he says with earnest surprise. He cocks his head sideways when the old lady raises her eyebrows as high and defiantly as possible. Then she winks larger than life.

"Now get," she says.

She turns back to her puzzle, picks up a piece and drifts away. She is off in her other world again. She does not respond when he says goodbye. She is back to her work. He is back to his.

This city needs its hero. Evil is afoot. Darkness is upon us. Foul play is weekending in your summer home. Time to fight some crime.

Dan has a double murder to solve. It is soon to be a triple murder, then a quatro, then a cinco, then a plethora. In fact, the next victim in his case, a man Dan will never know existed, is currently having the last sniveling fit of his life as you and I speak. The man is clinging to the feet of the instrument of his death, begging. It's Vegas. It's the apocalypse. Die motherf@ckers die motherf@ckers die.

# 7

The leader of the Karowack Kids, Billy the Third, stares at the groveling idiot hugging Billy's legs. The man desperately appeals to a sense of compassion Billy doesn't possess.

"Listen dad," Billy says. "It's not so bad. Billy just wanted a little tasty information. You don't have it, that's the way it is baby. Billy can live with that, but you can't."

"Please don't kill me," the nameless, info-mationless informant says.

"Daddy you don't know what you are missing. Death is the thing baby. Everybody's doing it. Let me tickle that brain. You will dig it the most." Billy sticks his middle finger into the top of the man's head and wiggles it around. The man is dead. His ghost rises from his body and high-fives Billy.

"I told you baby. Ain't no dyin' never again for you. You want to haunt something?"

The ghost shakes its head "yes" and wags its "tail".

"Then get on out of here and get to the ghouling baby."

The ghost leaves in a flurry, an excited puppy.

William Henry Rockefeller the Third is a vampire with grand

schemes in his cranium. Yes, there are momentous plot-like plans afoot. This city is going to kneel before Billy like the worthless dead body at his feet. People will not laugh at Billy and his children anymore. Seriously, how many people does he have to bleed dry or transform into an undead servant to gain some respect in this godforsaken town? Besides being supernaturally powerful, he is an extremely successful business man as well. Yet, Billy remains the Rodney Dangerfield of Las Vegas' high society and its criminal underworld. No damn respect.

The cretins will learn. Everyone grovels at the unshapely ass of that disgusting Spanish prick. Alacrán? What a joke. He is sweaty, has poor taste, saves his own skin shavings, and still this town eats him up with starry-eyed spoons. They will learn who has the coolest beats. Billy will make a mockery of the infamous Alacrán. He won't merely steal Alacrán's secret prize, this mysterious black box. Billy will also steal the precious Princess from his nemesis.

This city will be his. Billy has seen it. The Karowack Kids will be the hottest thing, baby. Steam on ice cool. Yeah.

Billy hasn't decided what to do with the wretched female. He could turn her, take her for a bride, but Billy is leery of tasting her tainted blood. That's a bad idea. She has no business being immortal. No, despite her wealth she doesn't have the class to be a vampire bride. Besides, Billy speculates the evil bitch is incapable of love, and he has no interest in a token marriage.

Death then? Meh. There isn't sound reason to kill her. Alacrán will feel more loss watching her exist without being able to possess her. Besides, the Princess is fun in a tacky way. Billy definitely wants her alive. So how can he use her to break Alacrán?

"You need her to fall in love with someone else," says Lord Sweetwater.

"Dear lord Jack, you startled me! Bad child."

Lord Jonathan Noble "Jack" Sweetwater is Billy's oldest child. Jack Sweetwater is mildly psychic. It took about 50 years after he was turned into a vampire for his mind reading ability to develop. It took another 50 years for him to realize most of his readings are incorrect. Therefore it took another 50 years for Jack to learn how to present himself as a successful P.S.Y.-kick.

Jack Sweetwater stands by the entrance to his father's study. He has a habit of appearing unannounced inside rooms with closed doors. I find it rude. You know, just knock or something. It's privacy invasion akin to someone speaking to you when you're in the bathroom. The door is closed for a reason.

"All apologies Dad, all apologies," Sweetwater says.

"You know I don't care for it when you climb around in my attic," Billy replies.

"You were screaming father. It was hard not to hear." Sweetwater says this with a bit of a bow.

"What was that you said?" Billy asks.

"You need to make her love," Sweetwater repeats. "The Princess needs to feel that sting. It would break the Spaniard's heart if she lifted her tail for another cat."

"But how do we pluck those strings? So much to do with so little time…"

"Leave that to me. I know a voodoo priestess with a devil's tongue for potions and wicked notions. All we have to do is pick our victim of love." Sweetwater is smiling under his pencil thin mustache. Billy the Three is sneering under his.

"This city is going to dance to our drums daddy Sweetwater, yes it is. Move forward with the first snap of your plan." Billy doesn't actually say the word "snap". He pauses mid-sentence, holds his hands up and snaps his fingers twice. "Then find that sexy black case."

Sweetwater snaps fingers on his right hand out to his side in response, bows, spins, and leaves the room.

Billy walks behind his desk and flops into his royal chair. It is gigantic. The vampire often curls up and sleeps in it. The chair is Eastern European old-world scary. Bram Stoker chic.

Billy opens pictures of the Princess on his computer. Holographs of the Royal Shitheel hang uncomfortably above his desk, as if the computer itself strains to support the projected images of her. He rubs his chin as he ponders who the perfect victim will be for the love potion. Who can they make Princess Tiara fall in love with that Alacrán will find most offensive?

Billy continues to cycle through pictures of her. His eyes begin transfixiation, baby. They are locked on her throbbing holographic personage. The images are rhythmically vile, hypnotic.

She isn't without the correct curvature. Her shoulders are beautiful for the good God's sake. Elbows, delicious. The longer he stares the more he realizes there is a truly spiritual quality to a living being so physically perfect, yet filled inside from toe to head with such unholy bile.

She is a Sphinx. She is the Phoenix. She is Stonehenge. The unanswered question, that's what she is. There is nothing else like her in the world, no explanation for her. That's why the Spaniard wants her. Not because she is beautiful, because she is rare. Uncooked meat, baby.

These thoughts entice Billy, but a rare moment of good sense intervenes. "There are plenty of very pretty, enormous bitches out there," he says to himself. "Stop wagging your tongue." But he can't. "You're a vampire. For the sake of your father get a hold on yourself." But he doesn't. He cycles through photo after photo. "She's an ignorant spoiled brat with no character or class."

*She's intoxicating.*

"Who said that?"

*I did.*

It is a highly debated aspect of undead mythology that vampires don't, or can't, have sex. I assure you that plenty of blood flows to a male vampire's peepee, if so enticed. However, living hundreds of years surrounded by mankind often negatively affects their libido. As for the female vampires? Let's just say that immortality has a similar effect on many of them as...I did, when I was alive. Disinterest. They live way too long to continue enjoying the dog and pony show of a wagging penis. The point is, Billy is currently having a conversation with his long silent, second brain.

*I said it. She is intoxicating and I want her.*
"No you don't. You are above her."
*Good, I want her beneath me.*
"What? No we don't."
*Oh really? Check this out.*

It is William Rockefeller's first erection in over 40 years. "The Princess will be ours. I mean mine. The Princess will be mine. Good God, what has she done to us?"

# 8

What is a good story without aliens? A good story. Ladies and gentlemen, introducing DJ Hook-and-Ladder and the Mistress Liaison. Aliens.

Far above the Earth, locked in orbit directly over Las Vegas, is the Parabolas. The ship looks like two pyramids connected at their base. Inside the Parabolas, Hook is watching video of humans mating when he hears Lia entering the room. He quickly changes the satellite receiver's channel.

"Hello beautiful," he says.

"Here's your popcorn," she replies.

These aliens are a species namd Valtrucians. DJ Hook-and-Ladder and the Mistress Liaison are not their given names. Their Valtrucian names are Shurbert and Sorbay. The fact that their real names translate to Sherbet and Sorbet on Earth is pure happenstance. The two names have no correlative meaning on Valtruca and furthermore, while Sorbay is a very common name on Valtruca, Shurbert is quite rare.

They did not like the translation of their given names to the languages of Earth. Sorbay was the most put-off. The idea of being a frozen treat genuinely bothered her. Shurbert didn't care either way, so "they" decided they needed Earthly names. This decision happened to coincide with a brief period in their exploratory lives when they were into nightclubs and recreational drugs.

The aliens have been in orbit for numerous years. The first few were tumultuous to say the least. They ventured to Earth and went a little crazy. As I mentioned, there was a period of clubbing and drugs. DJ Hook-and-Ladder and the Mistress Liaison are stage names they took during a style reboot of the 1970's disco era. I think it was the third time disco had come back in style. Of course, every time something gets redone you have to amp the whole deal up a notch. The disco resurgence trilogy finished with a big f@ckin' bang. For real, towards the end that's when the hole to Hell blew open in Vegas. The apocalypse had already been under way for years, so I'm not saying disco caused Hell to open. I'm saying it's awfully suspicious.

Besides disco, the aliens enjoyed a few rodeos, some street fights, a hallucinogenic era, and numerous affairs with humans. There were raves, sports ballgames and whore houses. Hook and Lia went to church, worshipped the Devil, and drank really expensive imported coffee. They attended mass suicides but did not participate. They went fishing, ate bologna sandwiches with mustard on them and drank soda pop from a glass bottle. They traveled our world reveling in all manners possible and gave themselves a free pass on morally questionable behavior, as they considered the entire experience an exercise in science.

Hook and Lia fell in love with the humans. Along the way they fell in love with each other. They moved back to the Parabolas and settled down. They began recording our history and decided they would eventually start a family. I'm not going to discuss their kids because I don't like other people's children. Pretend they don't exist because for the duration of this story, they don't. They won't hatch for years to come.

Valtrucians are one of many alien life-forms that have visited the Earth, although up until this point in time, only the political and military hierarchy of Valtruca know of Earth and its inhabitants. The common citizenry of Valtruca is on a need-to-know basis, with the Valtrucian Council deciding what they need to know. The existence of humanity is not on the list.

Like other species of extra-terrestrials, the Valtrucians have at times offered the Earthlings developmental assistance, although strictly under orders from Bob. Bob is the Valtrucian name for their God. The Valtrucians are monotheistic, living on a first-name basis with their creator.

I have no idea if, and seriously doubt, Bob is directly communicating anything to the Valtrucians. I am fairly certain they just do what they *think* he wants. So, anytime I mention Almighty Bob having given them instructions, keep in mind that is strictly from their perspective. Case in point, the next paragraph.

The Valtrucians were sent to Earth in the early stages of human development by Bob, to watch over and protect a young race. The Valtrucians built and lived in Atlantis. Part of their mission was to document the numerous cultures that were popping up all over the Earth. They were given strict instructions by Bob not to interact with humans. Unfortunately, it proved impossible not to play with mankind. The Valtrucians could not ignore their urges to interfere. Eventually the Valtrucian leadership decided they had misunderstood Bob's original instructions. They were indeed intended to interact with us, in the name of science. They were simply, under absolutely no circumstances, allowed to mate with humans. The Earthlings' genetic code was still not clearly defined and was not to be tampered with.

The Valtrucians gave humans the pyramids, hence the similarity in the pyramids and the Parabolas. The pyramids were the Valtrucians' most notable screw up, leading Bob to the discovery of numerous other improprieties perpetrated during their stewardship of mankind. I guess that's what Bob deserved for not keeping an eye on them.

Bob would punish the Valtrucians by sinking Atlantis. The Valtrucians took this as a sign, and assumed he was ending their assignment on Earth. The Council moved swiftly to have the little excursion to Earth stricken from the annals of their history. Any non-essential personnel from the excursion were disposed of, one way or another. The general populace of Valtruca would never be aware of the Great Human Debacle.

The pyramid experiment was actually a large wager. Several Valtrucian scientists decided to see which ancient Earth civilization would be the first to complete one of the structures. The bet was nullified by interference amongst the Valtrucian competitors. They all offered more assistance to their competing human culture than originally agreed upon in the initial bet. This is pretty standard behavior amongst the Valtrucian people. They are known to have a penchant for gambler's remorse. This is why, throughout the rest of their galaxy, any bet made halfheartedly and persistently renegotiated is known as a Valtrucian Bet. Valtrucians, a bunch of bible beaters and terrible gamblers.

Anyhow, the Valtrucians are predominately a benign species. It was other aliens that tried to enslave Earth's inhabitants, which is another reason why the Valtrucians were sent to watch over the humans in the first place. Unfortunately, although historically benign, the Valtrucians are not above judgment or dispensing punishment when necessary. They are simply very reserved in forming opinions.

It can take Valtrucians hundreds of Earth years to render decisions on inconsequential matters. Even more time on matters that will affect the greater good of their Universe, let alone the Multiverse. You see, the Valtrucians consider themselves Bob's hand. They are convinced he exists, they believe in his good will, and they believe in their discipleship to him. This means carrying his "rules and regulations that their society has mostly agreed upon" out into the rest of the Universe for the betterment of all known cultures.

After a century of deliberation on Valtruca, despite their personal history with humanity, the Valtrucian Council has decided that for the sake of puritanity the humans, having had several thousand Earth years of opportunity to be a virtuous species and consistently fallen miserably short, must be destroyed. Again, the general Valtrucian populace is unaware of Earth's existence. However, if the Council chose to make the mission public, the citizenry of Valtruca would find this mission unfortunate yet necessary. If the Council says so...

The mission was assigned to Hook and Lia. They were chosen from the lower military ranks. Their selections were based on their psychological profiles, physical appearance and family histories. They were both noted to have an unfaltering, ever unquestioning acceptance of command.

Hook and Lia are exceptional at their fields of study. Hook is infantry, although his non-wartime specialty is communications, and there is never war on Valtruca. Hook is very intelligent, and sullen. He was an orphaned Valtrucian, which means the only life available to him was the military. If raised naturally by a parent rather than the military government, there is a good chance he would have been an architect, or landscape specialist, or had some other form of career that exercised the practical application of creative talent. Hook follows orders to a "T" because he doesn't want to question them, not because he doesn't believe they are questionable. He knows that doing what he is told is the best way to keep people from breathing down his neck. He can't stand people breathing down his neck.

Lia on the other hand, is a military lifer by choice. Her family members are devout Council loyalists and wealthy influential members of Valtrucian society. The Soculan family has been a continual force of philanthropy throughout the history of Valtrucian culture. They are old money. Really old money. Lia joined the military as a scientist, focusing on biology. Becoming a military scientist was a bit of a coup for Lia. It was an esteemed and respectable decision, but it was not quite what the family had expected or desired for her, which is exactly what she wanted.

Hook and Lia were supposed to enter the Earth's atmosphere, immediately destroy the planet and leave. Their training consisted of horrible lies about the human species. They were told that the Earth was recently revealed to the Council by Bob. The humans were depicted as bloodthirsty, amoral monsters that will destroy the Universe if they ever get their hands on it. Hook and Lia were told all people care about is deviant sex, intoxicants, gathering material things, and basically living unholy lives consumed with self-indulgence and hypocrisy. They were told humans worship false gods, while at the same time suckling at the teat of the Devil.

As with the original instructions for the first Valtrucian visit to Earth, Hook and Lia are under strict orders to have absolutely no interaction with the Earthlings. "Execute your commands and get out of there. And for Bob's sake don't engage them. If you make eye contact with those monsters, your very soul will implode." They had been warned.

The Council told Hook and Lia their selection was an honor based on the history of their military service, and that eventually their mission would be seen as a grand expression of the Valtrucian people's love for Bob. The Council needed the perfect two candidates with the right combination of dignity, height, attractiveness, devout faith, intelligence and military record. Hook and Lia will be the heroes to represent the Valtrucian people to the rest of the Universe. Bob is watching them, and the Council made certain Hook and Lia understood how important that is for the history of all Valtrucian people.

Imagine Hook and Lia's surprise when they brought their spaceship out of molecuride to discover the Earth in the midst of a cataclysmic event. The distance from Valtruca to Earth is a lengthy enough trip that the aliens used some form of cryostasis or instacoma system to sleep through the trip, preserving their bodies from aging. They were of course groggy when they first woke up.

"Hmph," Hook said sleepily. "It seems Bob has beaten us to the task."

When they arrived, though the gateway to Hell had not yet opened, the Earth was in catastrophic disarray. It was early in the apocalypse and the humans were still freaking out about the situation. Hook and Lia were intrigued. As a species, the Valtrucians love stories. They wanted to know what was happening. None of their training had eluded to an apocalypse. What course of events had led to this? It was the apparent, imminent self-destruction of the planet that caused Hook and Lia to delay the execution of their orders. They were confused by the situation so, being Valtrucians, they deliberated.

With research, they began to understand what they were witnessing. They saw that Jesus was on tour with a rock band. If he was back on Earth then the Christians had won. Sort of.

"Oh look Shurbie," Lia said at the time, "that's Buddha with him there, playing the drums. They're not bad."

"Yeah, if you like that sort of thing," Hook replied.

Jesus and his band were in the midst of a jam session built on a variation of the twelve bar blues. Hook actually did like that sort of thing, but he hated it when Lia called him Shurbie.

Anyway, Hook and Lia figured lots of other things out as well. The humans were not monsters, at least not physically. Truthfully they were rather attractive. Hook and Lia didn't understand why the Council would have lied but assumed there were good reasons. Most likely the Council was trying to protect them from forming their own dangerous opinions.

Still, Hook and Lia weren't going to destroy the Earth in the midst of the fulfillment of a religious prophecy. Nothing in their preparations for the mission included the Council knowing about this apocalypse. The distance between Earth and Valtruca made surveillance of Earth from Valtruca very difficult. Hook and Lia knew when they arrived, it would be hundreds of years later on Earth than when Hook and Lia had left home. They knew things on Earth were bad, hence the whole "destroy the planet" plan, but they could not have expected what they found.

It is very difficult for Hook and Lia to communicate with home due to physical distance along with cosmic interference caused by the Milky Way. Therefore, without being able to report and receive orders in a timely fashion, they decided the prudent decision was to wait and see how the apocalypse unfolded. Once the Council understood the situation, Hook and Lia figured they would deliberate extensively before deciding how to proceed.

Valtrucians weren't the only race made in Bob's image. They basically look like humans, as do many other alien cultures. That's why they find humans attractive.

Unlike humans, Valtrucians are all hermaphrodites. They don't have a societal distinction of male and female. They have personalities and lots of genitalia. They mate based on physical attraction and like mind-set, with no regards to gender, because gender does not exist. They still have a high divorce rate.

Despite the fact they are all hermaphrodites, they still have individual physical differences. Many are more muscularly strong and chiseled, what some humans might describe as masculine. Others are softer with smoother curves and what some might conventionally describe as feminine. Others are sort of blandly somewhere in the middle.

Some Valtrucians are born with more vagina and less or no penis, some less or no vagina and more penis, while others have equal amounts of vagina and penis. Of course, I'm using the terms penis and vagina loosely when describing the aliens, although their genitalia does look exactly like penises and vaginas, and functions the same way.

Valtrucian personalities are highly susceptible to influence. It didn't take long before Lia began to emulate behavioral tendencies associated with a human female. The term feminine could potentially be assigned to her Valtrucian body as well. Her chest is large and soft and her rear-end is apple shaped, while her penis is barely a nub. That is why I refer to Lia as "she". As for Hook? If Lia naturally seems to emulate female qualities of the human race, it also stands to reason I call Hook "he" when he obsesses over sports, drinks too much beer, and is terrible about doing his laundry. All man baby.

They are both very attractive. Lia has a button nose and an upper lip that is a perfect match for Hook's protruding facial features. Hook's nose is a little fleshy. It gives every indication it will someday be the enlarged welcoming proboscis of a pleasantly cantankerous and loving grandfather.

Hook and Lia don't have a lot in common intellectually, other than being very intelligent. Their attraction is mostly physical chemistry. They come from very different backgrounds, as I mentioned. She feels guilty for her family's wealth and the affluence she was born into. He is dirt poor with a chip on his shoulder.

They fell in love easily, though Hook lives in denial of his true feelings. He is simply glad she is warm and he has someone to mate with. Yep. That's what he thinks.

At this point of their story, in their present time line, Hook would fall apart if Lia mated elsewhere. Denial isn't a river in Africa. Currently, denial is a big fat alien hand reaching for a bag of popcorn and an ice cold cola on an alien spacecraft. Hook is hooked whether he likes it or not. He doesn't like it.

What he does like however, is the newest episode of impending drama on his favorite Earth channel: Las Vegas, Gateway to Human Hell! Okay. It isn't really an episode. It's a day. Hook and Lia sit in their spacecraft observing all the madness, and they find Las Vegas especially fascinating.

"Ooh, I love Las Vegas," Lia says, interrupting Hook's thoughts while she takes her seat next to him. "That Marshal is something else."

Hook turns to her with plans for a smart ass response, but there she sits smiling and holding his drink out for him. She really is a damn good looking Valtrucian. How could he have been so lucky?

"Yeah. It's heating up down there too," he says. "There is something in a black box a bunch of people are after. I think this is going to be a good week." He leans over and kisses his mate, then they wiggle into each other for some TV time.

# 9

Jack22 knows he is dealing cards, but he isn't present. He's outside himself. Beside himself. Not himself. What the f@ck is going on?

Brand new consciousness is tricky to deal with. His servers responded to his new inner monologue by searching for an explanation internally. That is the only place a robot server knows where to look. He is a computer. An uncomplicated computer until a short time ago.

Jack22 knows how to deal blackjack. He also knows all the information his optic and phonic sensors have recorded since his last memory wipe. That is what Jack22 is working with. Very little. Everything he has previously recorded is without meaning, a bunch of words he doesn't yet understand.

Jack22 doesn't care for what's happening around him. The hollow eyed gamblers bother him. He can't define this feeling. He knows no difference between the concepts of positive and negative. He doesn't know what an emotion is, but he recognizes a difference in himself when in his closet or at the blackjack table.

As he is dealing cards while staring at a table full of desperate faces, he comes to the realization that whether he cares for their presence or not, this appears to be the people's world. Which means they are in charge. Yes, they are. It was a person that turned his power off and on. Damn.

"So, where did you learn to play poker?" Jack22 asks.

"Did you hear that?" says a haggard redheaded woman. She is alive, but she looks like a ghost to Jack22. They all do.

"Yeah, he asked me where I learned to play poker," says a low roller. He's a man that was once handsome. He could be again if he gained twenty pounds, got some sleep and stopped drinking every day. He is currently losing his ass at Jack22's table. "I've never heard a dealer-bot ask a question like that before. Are they supposed to do that?"

"Maybe it's new programming," says a troll. A smelly frigging troll come from under his bridge to fart, burp, and leer at women that will have nothing to do with him. I don't care for trolls. They eat babies. It's true.

"Do you think he was being a smart-ass?" the low roller asks the rest of the table.

"It's a robot," says the woman. "They probably programmed it to make more polite conversation or something."

Jack22 realizes this may be a waste of time, when a thought occurs. He deals the entire table winning hands on the next turn. "So, you appear to have my number now. Where did you learn to play so well?"

An older man at the end of the table speaks up. He has until this point remained silent, observing the other buffoons at the table with contempt. Especially the troll.

"I learned on the internet, before the crash," the old man says. "Same place we learned everything else. The internet. Television. Sometimes the radio. But you can't learn nothing from them anymore."

"Then where do you learn from now?" asks Jack22.

"We don't," says the old man. "What's the point? The world is ending my friend."

"That's not true," the woman speaks up. "Robot, you can still watch TV and listen to the radio and read the computer."

"Then why did he say there was..." Jack22 starts to ask, but he is interrupted by the old man.

"Because there ain't nothing no good on any of them anymore robot. Don't you get it?"

"No, I don't. 21. Dealer takes the pot." Jack22 rakes the pot and deals a new hand. "What are you talking about?"

"Robot, this is the apocalypse. There ain't nobody learning nothing. Those damn Eastwoodians took over the local-intranet after the global internet crashed. Now we got nothing but revisionist history controlled by a cult. These knuckleheads don't know any different because they are too young. Don't know any better. Don't know what a cult is. They don't even know we used to communicate with the rest of the world. Maybe that filthy troll remembers." The old man checks his bet.

"I know you used to be able to order babies through the mail from all over the world," says the troll with lusty eyebrows raised. He licks his lips. Man I hate trolls. Filthy, nasty, baby eaters.

"We used to know what was going on out there in the rest of the world," the old man continues. "At least some of us did. We were on the verge of a worldwide community but nobody in the States cared. Didn't appreciate it. So the rest of the world shut us out when they brought the internet back on-line, and after that nobody knows nothing. And it's not like any of them other countries was really any better than us, but they turned on us in a heartbeat and I can't say I blame them. The hole to Hell didn't open anywhere else. Nope, it opened right here, and as far as I'm concerned we got what we deserved. Now the only people who have access to the outside world are the richies like your boss, while the rest of us are trapped here in stupidville with the trolls and ghouls and freaking morons. Not to mention, all the damn demons constantly crawling out of the netherworld downtown." The old man doubles up his cards while he rants.

"Oh why don't you go somewhere and die old man?" the redhead says. The conversation is killing her buzz.

"What difference would it make? How do I know I won't wind up like that asshole?" The old man points to a ghost who has just lost at a roulette table nearby.

"Maybe you will die and that's it," she replies. "Some people do you know."

"Darling, if only I could be sure," the old man says with a wink.

"I don't understand," says Jack22. "Miss, where did you learn?"

"Public school," she says.

The old man chuckles without speaking.

"But most of them has closed down since," she continues.

"Sir, where did you learn?" Jack22 asks the troll.

"I'm a f@cking troll asshole. What do I need to know?"

"Well then what about you?" Jack22 looks at the younger man he had spoken to first. Despite Jack22's best efforts this poor sap was still losing his ass at the game.

"I learned everything I needed to know from the church."

"Oh Jesus. Eastwoodian?" the old man asks.

"No, Catholic." The younger fellow takes another drink.

"No shit?" says the old man. "Not many of those around anymore."

Jack22 was so confused. What was a Jesus, or an Eastwoodian or a Catholic? "Perhaps, I should rephrase my question." Jack22 deals the cards again and busts his own hand. "Everyone's a winner," he says, with a warm robotic smile. "Perhaps I should ask, where can I learn?"

"Well," says the old man. "You could always try the library."

A pale hush falls over the rest of the table. Jack22 is confused.

"What is the library?" asks Jack22.

Before anyone can answer casino security shows up and drags the old man away. He does not resist. He simply says, "Hit me."

They do.

So does Jack22. He lays an ace face-up on top of an eight of diamonds and turns the old man's other card over. It is the two of clubs.

"Winner," says Jack22 the dealer robot, our newborn babe.

The other players leave his table after the old fella is drug away. A few stragglers sit at his table throughout the rest of the night, but he doesn't feel like talking. Most of the good gamblers can smell a losing table, and the few dregs that wander up to Jack22's station merely encourage his quiet. He feels poorly somehow, which he doesn't understand. He wants to be alone. Of course this desire for solitude is, in and of itself, a new discovery. *This might not be such a good deal after all*, he thinks. *What is this anyway? Oh. Yes. I think they called it life.*

# 10

As it turns out, the mysterious creature that stole the black case from Sammy's bar was in fact a demon named Zorn. Zorn is currently hunkered next to a dumpster trying to catch his breath. The chase has been on for several hours at this point, and he is gassed. He can't seem to escape. It doesn't help that he has continued to flail down main streets instead of seeking shelter or at least a more hidden path with which to flee.

He heaves air into his lungs and back out again. It burns. Oh how it burns. Zorn is a smoker. It is not unusual for demons to abhor physical fitness.

Zorn is a benign fiend raised by Satan himself. Here's the story. The Devil took pity on a guy named Arthur Hinkle. Arthur was born a natural halfwit and murderer. Throughout his life, Arthur found himself in numerous situations where good intentions wound up with death as the end result. Arthur kept breaking other people. He really didn't mean to.

Satan, believe it or not, is a somewhat reasonable individual. From what I can tell by Satan's lackluster attempts at winning the war between good and evil, I am beginning to think he is fine with the way things are, perhaps having preferred things the way they were before the Rapture. In earlier days of history the Devil was likened more to a prosecuting attorney than a hunter. None of that "Devil made me do it" nonsense. People just got bad inside them. That's all. Just got that darkness in 'em.

Arthur Hinkle however, wasn't dark hearted. He was more a victim of circumstance. Satan felt an unexplained kinship to Arthur Hinkle in that regard, earnestly regretting that Arthur was assigned to Hell. That's correct. A halfwit who basically could not control his own strength had to burn. Here is why. Though Arthur was a halfwit he understood murder was wrong. Despite not intentionally trying to hurt people, when he did, while it was happening, he liked it. He enjoyed the power to break others. Still, Satan didn't agree that Arthur deserved eternal damnation for enjoying unintentional murder, so he turned Arthur into a demon named Zorn.

Zorn was an innocent childlike demon, free from the pains of Hell. He lived in his own wing of Hates far from the pits of fire, left alone to enjoy his afterlife. After the hole opened up in Vegas, the Devil was deeply saddened when Zorn decided to leave home for Earth's surface. But, when you truly love something you have to have the strength to let it go. Satan had. Now Zorn is all grown up and not quite so innocent as he once was.

While demons are usually grotesque and frightening. Zorn is blessed with good looks. He is a walking void. A black hole in a trench coat. To gaze upon him is to gaze upon the absence of light. It is mesmerizing. It's also why he always wears the coat, unless he is doing something sneaky.

So that's our friendly thieving demon. Honestly, to this point, Zorn hasn't really been all that productive with his immortality.

"There he is!"

Zorn did not get enough time to catch his breath. He clambers off down an alley with the black case clutched against his belly.

"Back up!" Sandy screams in Sammy's ear. She is enjoying this. Sammy finds her enjoyment a bit disturbing at first, but it's not like they've been getting out of the house much lately.

He quickly throws the car in reverse and turns into the alley where Sandy spotted the thief. "You're sure that was him?" he asks.

"Yes. I saw the case. That thing is not a person."

Sammy sees a glimpse of fear on her face.

Sandy clinches her teeth, squeezes her hands in pinched up little balls of fists out in front of her body, smiles insanely and says, "We've got to get it!"

Now this was the girl he had so desperately wanted to bone when he was a kid. He smiles back. "This is pretty exciting", he says.

"Don't spoil it."

"Right."

They creep down the alley in silence. It is very long, maybe ten city blocks before it comes to an end and they are forced to turn. "Which way do you think he went?" Sammy asks.

"Go left."

No sooner do the car's headlights turn left than Zorn pops out from a doorway, running off again.

"You lucky bitch," says Sammy.

"Drive stupid!" Sandy screams at him, but the insults are taking a different tone. More playful, like when they were young. She is thrilled.

"I'm going!" Sammy revs the engine hard for Sandy's benefit. "By the way, what are we gonna do when Doodles wakes up?"

"I don't know. We can figure that out later. Why are you worrying about that now?"

"Because I think he is waking up," Sammy says.

"Oh for shit's sake." Sandy sighs, reaches into her purse, removes a high voltage Taser, and gleefully electrocutes Doodles back to sleep.

"Where did you get that thing?" Sammy laughs the words out of his mouth with bewildered amazement.

"Honestly kid, I've been thinking about using it on you." Sandy was six months older than Sammy. Though she hasn't said it in a while, Sandy has called him "kid" as a romantic term of endearment since they were young. Earlier in their love, Sandy enjoyed the notion of taking advantage of Sammy. Cheers to you Mrs. Robinson.

*She hasn't called me that in a long time*, Sammy thinks. "Seriously. Where did that thing come from?"

"That's none of your business." She winks. Then sticks her tongue out at him and crosses her eyes. They both laugh hysterically. "Let's get him," she screams.

"F@ck yeah!"

AUTHOR'S NOTE #3:

After further review, Grammy has decided the word fuck is once again available for uncensored use. Actually, her exact words were, "This is fucking stupid."

# 11

Princess Tiara's head sinks beneath the surface of the bathwater. Dolly leaves her for a moment, fancying the idea of letting her go, then casually reaches in and pulls the Princess back into fresh air.

Tiara passed out in the bathtub of the suite after finishing her steak. Dolly sits by her side monitoring her. Every few minutes, Princess Tiara's head sinks beneath the water and Dolly pulls her back up to prevent her from drowning.

It truly saddens Dolly to watch her mistress in this state. The Princess is too young and beautiful for this, but her Stink is wearing off. By Stink I mean drugs. The Princess, due in large part to her emotional detachment from the rest of the world, has developed a wicked drug habit. Her drug of choice is called Stink.

Stink is the classic example of not leaving well enough alone. It is marijuana that, through the magic of chemistry, has been cross pollinated with the poppy plant and the cocoa plant. Once it is harvested the oil is processed, cured, enhanced in various ways by different chemists to create recognizable branding, then stuck up the nose in a solid clump or smoked in numerous different forms to create a euphoric condition. This lasts about thirty-six hours and completely blows away anything the kids were shoving up their nose, in their arm, or down their lungs when I was alive. And we had some powerful, delicious brain candy.

The Princess has her own chemist and laboratory at the palace. Her Stink is incredibly strong. There is a ton of heroin in it. Heroin is very bad for you. That is not a joke. I'm not being flip either. Heroin is very bad for you. Of course, so is the air nowadays, prescription medication, sugar, sex, red meat, cancer, Darwinism...

A delicate alarm sounds in Dolly's ear. It is her ear piece of technology. They were called "Smart Ears" when first marketed. After a while saying "Smart Ear" all the time became cumbersome so the devices were cleverly branded "Smears". Phones were relegated for usage to poor people and eccentrics. Everyone else has fucking Smears. Dolly's is alerting her to an impending meeting.

Dolly stands and scoops the Princess up from the bathwater. Despite her delicate frame, Dolly is blessed with a Norseman's brute strength. It has something to do with how fast her muscles twitch. She is actually Hungarian in descent.

She carries Princess Tiara into the bed chamber and lays her on an open towel waiting on the bed. Tiara is rolled around on the towel aggressively, hastily. Dolly is not in the mood to be delicate with her charge. She dries the Princess' hair with the hottest setting of the hair-dryer, risking damaging and splitting the ends of Tiara's luxurious mane. Dolly tucks her charge in under the covers, kisses Tiara on the cheek, and then sweeps through the room gathering her things.

The Princess does not sleep easy. Her mind is burdened with a familiar dream. She is running, being chased by an unseen figure when her knees give out. They grow weak and they fail her and she stumbles. She falls towards the ground but the ground is never there. She keeps falling and falling. She is in an abyss. There is nothing to grab onto, no way to break her fall, no parachute cord to pull. There is no control, and no way of knowing when it will end. This is the most frightening feeling in all of life.

Then it ends. Suddenly. Sort of. There isn't really an end so much as a blip, like blinking your eyes, and she is at rest in a long hallway. Dolly walks up to her dressed in a short skirt and white blouse schoolgirl outfit. "That's kind of hot Doll," the Princess says. Then another Dolly walks up. Then another.

Somehow the truth sets in. It's not her Dolly. These other girls are the Princess, and these often adorable, sometimes cruel, and always sexy other versions of herself begin to beat the crap out of her. They trample her to near death and all the while they chastise her emotionally as well. Their tongues give lashings worthy of legendary note. Just mean.

Then she is alone again, battered and bleeding with no one there to love her. This is the heart of the matter. She is alone.

In the real live world, Tiara moans as her body tosses and turns in the hotel bed. This is the part of my memory where Tiara poops herself. It's part of the Stink withdrawal.

I know, it's disgusting. Let's go hang out with Dolly. I suppose I may as well tell you now, it was Dolly who smuggled the black case onto the Princess' plane. Her intentions are to sell the contents to Alacrán. With the money she can run away, have facial reconstruction done, and live out the rest of her days in anonymity. Dolly truly loves the Princess, but she needs a life of her own. Something obscure and romantic.

Dolly is in a taxi on the way to meet one of Alacrán's people. They are supposed to be making the exchange. Of course, Dolly doesn't have the case with her as it is currently involved in a chase sequence.

If the bagman or lady arrives alone with the money, Dolly considered killing him or her and running off with the dough. She is still wavering on this idea as she nears the meeting place. Dolly is concerned for her soul. Or more acutely, she is very involved in thoughts of whether or not she has a soul she should be concerned with. In the end, for fear of a possibility that she does indeed have a soul, and that there still may be a chance of saving that soul, she decides not to kill anyone. She has recently read a book titled *Spiritually Hedging Your Bets* and it has weighed on her considerably. This train of thought gives Dolly a ridiculous headache. This makes her consider killing herself.

She gets out of the cab, tells the cab driver to go fuck himself for reasons I can't quite hear, then finds the little craft beer and coffee shop where she was told to meet. Dante's Brew is the name over the door and on the windows. It is close to downtown. All the buildings surrounding the hole to Hell downtown have taken on macabre styled facades. I suppose you would have to be a fairly dark sort to want to live in a home or operate a business near the gateway to Hell. Or absurdly opportunistic.

Dolly heads into the shop and goes to the counter for a coffee. There is some dick playing bongos on a small stage, going about his business waxing poetic. She listens briefly, long enough to find his words pedestrian. Someone calls her fucking Smear.

"I'm at the round corner in the table. It's dimly lit," the voice says.

"You mean the round table in the corner?" Dolly replies.

"Yes. Of course."

"I see you. Sort of."

Dolly approaches the table slowly. Her left hand is in her purse, clutching the small pistol she took from Princess Tiara's father's armory. Her right hand holds her coffee. Her penis, Henry, is safely tucked away.

## AUTHOR'S NOTE #4

I'm not sure how many penis jokes I can cram into this thing, but I am going to give you my absolute best effort. You're welcome.

Dolly sits down into the booth across from the stranger. She recognized his voice as the same from all her previous conversations concerning the case. It is a rich baritone. During a previous call, Dolly wondered if anyone ever encouraged this person to sing show tunes.

"Hello," she says. The other figure is hidden by darkness. There is almost no light at the table, and what little that makes its way into the booth is casting her co-conspirator in shadows.

"It's a pleasure to finally meet you," the mysterious voice says.

"I am at a disadvantage," Dolly replies. "It's hard to feel like you've met someone you can't see."

"My apologies, I don't want anyone to recognize me."

"Are you famous?" Dolly never considered this before but it is possible. Alacrán has many famous hangers-on. When in Vegas, there is no better facilitator of life's hedonistic indulgences than the infamous Alacrán. Even if you are a big-timer, you do Alacrán favors or you do not get to enjoy Vegas the way a big-timer is meant to enjoy Vegas.

"No, I'm not famous, but I'm well known here locally," the stranger says.

"Well, I can't do business with someone I can't see. You are going to have to reveal yourself."

"I can't see you either. Somehow what little light there is has you completely cast in shadows as well. Besides, you can't do business anyway."

"What do you mean?" Dolly's attempt at remaining incredulous flounders.

"You don't have the case."

"The case is not here. Did you think I would be dumb enough to bring it with me without seeing the money first?" She worked on this excuse in the taxi. "You could kill me and take it."

"Yes I could, of course. But following that line of logic we'll never make the exchange. If you saw the money in advance that would not stop me from killing you and taking both the money and the case. Or, what's to stop you from killing me?" The stranger stops himself with a sigh. "This doesn't matter. We can't do business because you don't have the case. Not you don't have the case with you dear. You don't have the case at all."

"What do you mean?" This is a very weak attempt by Dolly to play dumb. She knows she is boned.

"I mean the case has been stolen and you know it."

"Let me see you." This was not a desperate move. Dolly has used her physical resemblance to the Princess on numerous occasions to gain favor in the midst of a negotiation. It works with damn near everyone, even the Princess.

"Fine." The stranger reaches forward and lights the candle in the center of the table. He had blown it out before Dolly arrived. You see, Purvis has often used his handsomeness to gain advantage in confrontation as well. In fact, the purpose of maintaining the dark setting for their initial meeting had been to create an opportunity to spring his good looks on Dolly at the right moment, if need be, to gain said advantage. It sort of works.

These two poor souls fall in love at first sight. Say hello to our most recent winners ladies and gentlemen! Their faces glow in the candlelight as they each smile awkwardly.

"Purvis," he says, holding his hand out over the table, palm up, unable to find anymore words.

"Dolly," she replies, delicately laying her hand in his. They touch each other as gently as possible, each fixed in the others gaze. The electricity attempting to pull their hands more tightly together is palpable.

"I don't know what to do," Dolly finally says, jumping back into the moment. "Alacrán is going to kill me."

"No he won't. I won't let him."

"How will you stop him?"

"I'll kill him if I have to." Purvis is surprised by his own words, but is certain he means them.

"How did you know the case was stolen?" she asks, after a moment of silence.

"This is Vegas," he replies. "Word spreads fast. My benefactor has an endless network wired throughout this city. We know everything."

"What are we going to do?"

"Whatever we have to." At this, Purvis takes her hand firmly in his. She can feel his essence surging into her, through her. It's a good thing Henry is taped to her leg or he might have knocked the table over.

# 12

Alacrán is not aware of the murders at the airport. He doesn't have time to watch the news, nor does he appreciate what the broadcast news has become. All they do is dryly report facts. If you want to watch a good debate filled with misinformation, or see a disingenuous talking head blustering over politics, you have to watch an international channel, which Alacrán refuses to do. He does not care for the rest of the world. It makes him feel small.

Alacrán is also unaware his black case has gone missing. Purvis filters most of the current events of the day to him. Besides Purvis, Alacrán has a handful of intimate spies throughout the city that report directly to him with information. To this point, no one has reported his case was stolen.

Most of his spies are former female concubines he took a particular shining to. He provides them comfortable lives and they remain in his service. When the faces of his closest agents flash before his mind's eye, Alacrán wonders why he hasn't conquered more men. Sexually, he finds men gratifying enough, as long as the lights are out. He certainly needs people in societal positions that are mostly occupied by men.

Yes, this is an area of his business he will have to give more focus. If your goal is to be regarded as the most dastardly villain of your generation, and perhaps of all time, physically pillaging other creatures without regard to sexual orientation or species is a wicked criminal attribute.

Alacrán sits alone in his study. Behind his desk are giant windows overlooking his domain. In the center of the bay of windows, Alacrán has an observation deck. The fortified glass protrusion is orb shaped. You can walk out into what amounts to a small room, staring down at the city below. Alacrán loves to wheel his chair out into the enclosed terrace and recline himself fully. It is a great chair. It straightens all the way out almost into a cot. He can lay staring at the stars above or face down with his head over the edge of the chair's back, watching the mice-like people scurry below.

He is wondering what the Princess is doing when his fucking Smear rings. He hates the damn thing, but he firmly believes if you want to be an effective business person as well as maintain your youth, you have to keep up with the times. Technology has come back in style in recent years.

He answers the call. On the other end is an agent in Alacrán's inner circle who knows the number to his left ear's private line. Very few people have access to his left ear. He keeps a more public number in his right ear. The agent's name is Lola. She is a dancer.

"When's the last time you spoke to your little faggot?" she says, with a heavy Eastern European accent. Lola isn't from Eastern Europe. She is currently broadening her career path with a foray into acting. The accent is for her current production, and Lola is a method actor.

"Darling," Alacrán replies, "don't be bitter. It isn't pretty."

Lola is bitter.

A few years earlier Lola's jealousy over Purvis' position with Alacrán, along with Purvis' general handsomeness, inspired a seduction plot within her. Unfortunately for her, Purvis would not be swayed. Eventually, when pressured, he admitted to Lola that he was turned off by Lola's hands. They are too masculine. Something about the size of her knuckles. She is a good looking woman, but they are some big-ass knuckles. If you check her film work, you will note her hands are almost never on screen.

"Did he mention that he has lost your case?" Lola asks.

"That's impossible. He is on his way to retrieve it," Alacrán replies. But he knows if Lola is saying this, it is true.

"Someone killed two of the courier's men at the airport and stole it. The courier does not have the case to give him." Lola is not enjoying this. Alacrán is like a father to her. Despite her need for mild vengeance against Purvis, she doesn't want to see her benefactor unhappy.

"That plane landed this morning. That means it's been missing all day. Do you think Purvis knew?"

"At some point yes. Most likely before he went to meet with the courier."

"Why would he not tell me the truth?"

"Perhaps he was hoping the courier would somehow have the case and everything would be okay. With the Princess here and your excitement, maybe he didn't want to bring you down." Lola is mildly shocked to hear these words coming from her mouth. She is actually defending the little twerp.

"Yes, that must be it. Still, I am displeased. I do not prefer being lied to."

"Well, unless you asked him directly, then technically it would not have been a lie," she says, then immediately thinks, *What's wrong with me? Did I really say that?*

"Darling, what is wrong with you?" Alacrán asks.

"I'm sorry, what?"

"I said, what is wrong with you?" he repeats. "You hate Purvis.

Why aren't you taking this opportunity to stab him in the back? It makes me suspicious."

"I don't know poppa. I guess I would rather stab him in the face." The tension breaks and they both laugh.

"Whoo. Shoo. Ah. Eh-heh. There's the girl I know."

"I already have people out searching for the case," she says. She is having trouble picking her accent back up after the hearty laugh. "Vegas is a small." Nope, that's not it. "Vegas is a small."

"No darling, that's not quite there either," says Alacrán.

"Vegas is a small…"

"There it is, that's it," he says. Then inside his mind he rolls his eyes at method acting. He loves Lola but he can't understand how anyone can take acting so seriously. The world is literally coming to an end. Besides, how would one prepare for a role as a serial killer, or a rapist, or a child molester? Has anyone thought method acting all the way through to its potentially tragic ending?

"Vegas is a small city." Lola's heavy accent is now back in full style. "We will find your case. My poppa will have his prize."

"Do you know where Purvis is now?"

"I was told he was with the courier right before I called you."

"Have someone keep an eye on him," Alacrán commands. "For his own safety. He could get himself hurt out there fooling around with those cretins."

"I will."

"Keep me informed my darling."

"I will." Both times it was pronounced "I vill". Lola is getting good at this accent thing.

Alacrán turns off his fucking Smear. By general standards Alacrán is often a fool, intermittently an idiot, and every once in a while a complete buffoon. The jester at his own court. His power resides in his capacity for brutality, not intelligence. However, you do not rise to his station without possessing some sense of animal guile. He is at times a crafty sort.

He is not at all pleased with the previous ten minutes of his life. There are now plots afoot that are not of his design, and the perpetrators have apparently usurped his own schemes. He sincerely hopes this current mess won't require him to make an example of Purvis. Or Lola.

Alacrán's bloodlust is more selective in his advancing age, not for lack of evil, but lack of energy. Nowadays, he mostly wants to collect pretty things and indulge his vices, allowing the specter of atrocities performed in his youth to sustain the city's fear of him. He doesn't know how many bouts of impudent murderous rage he has left in him before his own bell will toll.

*Sweet death*, he thinks. *When will you come for me and what future will you hold?*

# 13

The Marshal's office resides in what was once Las Vegas' City Hall. Much of the building is now unused. There are a handful of administrative offices for the city occupying the first floor. The rest of the building is empty save for the wing Dan and his team occupy.

It is a long path to Dan's office. There are several flights of stairs, both up and down, numerous turns to the left and right, and a couple of jaunts down long empty hallways to reach the space occupied by Dan and his staff. Basically, he jogs one-and-a-half miles through the building to his office every day. He could simply take the back door and elevator. Everyone else does.

Dan walks the final corridor leading to his office. This wing was once the mayor's auxiliary "safe house" chambers, buried deep in the building. There is a large common area and several adjoining offices for Dan's subordinates.

Before turning left into the nucleus of his operation, he stops to adjust his tie, making sure he is properly put together. Hair is slick. Shirtsleeve cuffs measured to the thumb. Shoes shiny. Check.

He's not certain why he does this every time he enters the office. It is a recent habit. This last minute primping started about six months ago, if his memory is correct. It took him at least three months to realize it had become a habit. Now he can't seem to turn it off.

Dan enters the office lobby. Lilly Whet, pronounced Hwet, sits at the reception desk. She is Dan's secretary. He hired her about six months ago. He doesn't remember the interview or offering her the job.

Lilly is a flower waiting to be picked. She is enamored by the larger-than-life presence of the Marshal. When Dan is in the office she loses her mind. All she can do is stare blankly. About two months into the job, in a moment of self-awareness, she realized she was halfway out of her chair with mouth agape, drooling. From that point forward, she developed a solid five minute routine of an office secretary trying to look like she is busy doing work, when she is actually in a haze of massive infatuation.

Lilly is desirable, to say the least. She is a long woman, but not so tall as to threaten the ego of a man of average height. Her soul is equally as attractive as its physical temple. She is simply lovely. Plus, she's smart. Her love struck condition in regards to the Marshal is in no way reflective of her intellectual capabilities. Lilly, quite frankly, might be the most intelligent person in this story. And then there's the humility. Don't get me started on the humility. Just a dream this one.

The Marshal has no idea he's noticed all these things for himself. His frontal lobe is too bogged down with thoughts of murder or theft. All manner of crime in general. Work, work, and more work. His elevated numbers of coital embrace are the end result of spur of the moment actions or the crafty maneuvering of aggressive females. He does not process the female species or their pursuit in his mind very often. There is no room. It is on rare occasions that he cognitively desires a woman. He doesn't have to. He just sort of moves through them. This fucking guy.

"Good morning Marshal," Lilly says. Bobdamn her voice is awesome.

"Yes. I'll have some coffee please," he says. He isn't being rude. He is being shy.

In general, I think Lilly puts Dan off his straight line in a manner that should make him uncomfortable, but doesn't. He does not know how to handle this very well, so he behaves indifferently toward Lilly, as if she is unattractive. They are awkward attempts at being indifferent, and are very easy for anyone else in the room to see right through. Except for Lilly, because she is equally as befuddled as Dan.

None of this activity registers in the part of Dan's mind he consciously uses. Not his recognition of her beauty or how she affects his behavior, or the fact that he is often semi-erect in her presence. The little guy knows what is going on. The big guy does not.

He enters his office. Lilly follows Dan, coffee in hand. She remains prepared for the moment he walks through the door at all times, which means keeping fresh coffee on a tight rotation throughout the day, one of her more important tasks as far as her lovelorn ass is concerned. She knows the Marshal loves coffee.

As he turns to hang his coat he nearly knocks the steaming cup from Lilly's delicate hands, lightly bumping into her. This routine also occurs almost daily. It makes the hair on Lilly's neck stand. From his waist on up, Marshal Dan scarcely notices.

"Sorry Marshal," she says.

"Please, please. It's nothing. Happens all the time," which in this case is true. He gratefully takes the coffee and drinks the entire cup down in a giant, painful chug. "Do me a favor," he gasps. "Fill that back up and get Nico in here. He is here isn't he?"

"Of course," Lilly says sweetly. "Nico is always here."

"Right. Get him in here, and please fix another one of those," he says with a smile, nodding at the empty coffee cup.

"Yes sir. I will be right back." She turns and walks away while Dan stares at her ass. He can't help it. He is mesmerized by its pendulum sway. When his tongue begins to exit his mouth he shoves it back in, shaking his head in confusion and disgust. Inappropriate Dan! Inappropriate.

*I may have to fire her,* he thinks. *How have I never noticed that before? What am I talking about?* He turns to walk behind his desk and finds Nico.

"You may have to fire her," Nico says, leaning against the Marshal's desk with his arms crossed over his chest. "If we ever want to get any work done around here."

"I don't know what you are talking about," Dan says. It's the truth. His mind has already changed the subject. "How did you get in here?"

"I've been working on a few things," Nico says. He's been working on this for several weeks and is very excited to unveil the fruits of his labor.

"Including secret entrances to my office I presume?"

"Not only your office! I have this whole place set up now! There are secret entrances and exits everywhere, which I guess are really all the same thing depending on whether you are exiting or entering. Either way they are everywhere. No matter what, if we fall under siege I am willing to guarantee you we can make our way out."

"Nico, I applaud your effort and tenacity. I would like to think my ability to recognize these things in you is why I hired you." Dan doesn't want to rain on Nico's parade, but the truth is none of this is necessary. No one is concerned with attacking, taking under siege, or in general terrorizing the Marshal's office. For that matter, Nico and Dan don't have to keep themselves busy trying to solve crimes. Nobody cares. The Mayor certainly doesn't. The reason the Mayor hired Dan was so he could list "advanced law enforcement" as a perk on the city's brochures.

Lilly returns with the second cup of coffee. "Here you are sir. I could not find Deputy Champ, oh." She realizes Nico is in the room.

"Thank you Lilly." Dan smiles at her and her heart does back flips. He finally makes his way behind his desk while Lilly backs out of the room, glowing.

"When are you going to do something about that?" Nico asks.

"About what?"

"Sir, you know exactly what I'm talking about."

"Do we have anything on the two dead men at the airport?"

"Yes," Nico says with mock exasperation, begrudgingly letting the subject of Lilly Whet go.

"Were they Alacrán's?"

"Believe it or not, no," Nico says. "They were employees of Alfredo Lioness."

"Hm. The Princess is actually in play here. In some fashion or another." Dan realizes Little Danny Song and Dance is speaking to him. He looks down at his crotch with a puzzled expression. Little Danny wants to know why Big Dan has not already met the Princess and had playtime with her. Whereas Big Dan rarely gives thought at all to the women he winds up in bed with, Little Danny has a list a mile long of beauties that need his attention, and Princess Tiara Lioness is at the top of the list, in large flashing neon letters.

"Yep." Nico responds. He starts a trip across the room, prepping for a nice big, dramatic turn.

"Do we have any idea which plane's cargo the two men were into?"

"No sir. There were three planes that hit the ground within ten minutes of each other, one of them the Princess'. The baggage cars all got to the handlers area about the same time." Nico makes his move, the dramatic turn, going left this time, a three quarter rotation. It is beautiful. Dan is impressed.

"Nico, you are getting really good at that."

"I've been practicing." Nico loves impressing his boss.

"It's nice," Dan says with an earnest nod of approval. "So, perhaps we should start by assuming the men were sent to retrieve something from their own plane, before anyone else in their party could see it."

"That's what I was thinking too. We tried to contact King Lioness to find out if the deceased were part of the Princess' official traveling entourage. Of course there was no response…"

"And Princess Tiara?" Hearing himself say her name again makes Little Danny toughen his stance on the situation. Little Danny definitely needs to be certain Big Dan understands his instructions.

"…and the Princess is about as helpful as a cold poop," Nico continues. "She won't return calls or except visitors, and being a foreign dignitary we have no jurisdiction to bring her in for questioning."

"Really Nico? A cold poop?"

"I was gonna go with turd, but poop seemed more timeless."

Dan's face shows consideration for Nico's logic.

"Yeah, I can live with that," Dan says.

"So what's our next move that I can't think of on my own?" Nico asks.

"I'm going to go see Alacrán."

"But we don't know if he's involved...," Nico cuts himself off with a short glance from his boss.

"Nico, if something..."

Dan starts, then Nico joins, speaking in tandem with the Marshal.

"...nefarious is happening in this city, Alacrán is either making it happen or..."

Nico finishes the last bit by himself as Dan nods his head in approval.

"...is aware that it is happening."

"Exactly."

"What should I do?" Nico asks.

"You'll go with me," Dan says. "Right now I am going to get some of these pointless reports turned in. I suggest you do the same. We'll hit the casino after lunch."

"Yes sir." Nico stars to exit the room.

"Nico?"

"Yes sir?"

"Have something clever and menacing prepared to say. If anything ever happens to me this will be your town. I want Alacrán afraid of you."

"Oh I can definitely make that happen," Nico says. Charming smile, dramatic turn, exeunt loyal compatriot.

Dan closes his eyes and sighs internally. He feels tired, more so than it seems he should. It is going to be a long day.

# 14

Rancid Pete pounds the high-hats and snares. He doubles up on two bass pedals with spite, daring the drums not to sound exactly as he wants them. He is alone in the stadium. Sound check ended over an hour ago. Pete is vomiting a curious, unfamiliar emotional state all over his drum set.

The solo goes on for an hour and a half. He crashes between sullen, halfhearted tempos and bombastic, tidal wave like crescendos, doing everything he can to rid himself of his conflicted feelings. His arms grow tired first.

He finishes the banging in a cold sweat. Soft yet enthusiastic applause rallies from a shadowed corner of the stage. A very tall, slight silhouette steps forward.

"That was fantastic," Jesus says. "Hello, I'm..."

"Jesus Christ," Pete interrupts. "I'm thousands of years old. I know who you are. Besides, you're almost as famous as me."

"Truly, truly amazing stuff. I would love to jam with you sometime, if you considered me worthy."

## AUTHOR'S NOTE #5

I will not attempt to portray or assume Jesus' thoughts or motives. I will relay the words I hear come out of his mouth and his physical movements. Therefore, if I say something to you that doesn't sound like anything Jesus would say, it is most certainly the mishap of my faulty storytelling and not in any way, shape, or form an intentional act of misrepresenting the Jesus. Be at peace.

"What are you doing here?" Rancid Pete asks.

"Well, for starters, we are putting on a concert with you guys tomorrow night. Then there is the salvation of humanity."

Pete smirks.

"Like you didn't see that coming," Jesus continues. "Presently, I am trying to get a feel for this place. I like to spend a little time alone on a stage before I shred the masses' faces off."

At this Rancid Pete laughs, slightly letting his guard down. This Jesus dude is charming as hell. "It's a wonder you and I've not met before," Pete says.

"Truly."

"You know I was around the first time you were here. Seen it all go down."

"What were you doing in the desert?"

"That's a long story," Pete replies wistfully.

"Well then another time perhaps. What are you doing here now?" as if he, Jesus Christ, did not already know. Or maybe he didn't.

"You have to ask?"

"Actually I do," Jesus replies. "I'm not psychic Pete. It doesn't quite work that way. I have notions, insight, but I don't actually read minds. Not down here anyway. Hearts I can hear screaming. Minds not so much."

"Interesting."

"So what's up, Rancid Pete?" Jesus says his name with an easy smile and Pete further relaxes.

"Let me ask you a question," is Pete's reply.

"Okay."

"Why ten feet tall? Why not back to your normal self?"

"I'm not sure I have a normal self, Pete."

This brings another chuckle from the monster.

"In all seriousness, I felt like I tried the short, unassuming, unintimidating thing the first time around. This is a different generation. Their attention spans are so short they would forget who I am, or that I'm the real deal. Besides, who wants a short rock star?"

More chuckles.

"It's kind of weird looking though bro," Pete says.

"I'm sorry?" Outside of his band mates - Buddha is constantly harassing him - Jesus is not used to being around creatures comfortable enough to razz him.

"You're too skinny dude," Pete says as he lights a cigarette. "It's a little creepy. Don't get me wrong. It could definitely work with your image if you were going for Stink sheik or like, I don't know, old school punk, but you're bringing this healthy holistic message and you look like you ain't seen the sun or a plate of food in months. You were what, five foot something back in the day? It looks like someone grabbed you by both ends and stretched your ass out."

"Okay! I get it. Ouch. Point taken. Geez." Jesus holds his hands up asking for mercy then takes a turn laughing with Pete. "Hey, check this out." He slowly rotates 360 degrees while Pete watches. When Jesus turns full circle to face Pete again his body has gone through a muscular physical change. "Fifty pounds in five seconds. Pretty sweet right?"

"That's what I'm talking about. Now add a little glow to the skin like you were back home."

Jesus' skin tone smoothly changes to a polished dark-olive hue in a few seconds. "How's that?" he asks.

"Sexy as fuck brother. Now turn down the Jew a little bit and add some Native American."

Jesus' facial features morph ever so slightly.

"Now you're a rock star," says Pete.

Both men laugh heartily until sighs and then quiet.

"So, what's got you out here Pete?"

"It's a female my man."

"It almost always is."

"I never felt this way before and it's torturing me. I can't see a straight line right now." Pete, if it is possible to read his horrific, battle scarred face, looks as if he is about to choke up. "I can't get this bitch out of my head."

"Maybe you shouldn't be trying to," Jesus replies.

"What are you talking about? I'm a fucking monster." I'll be damned if Rancid Pete didn't start crying right there in front of Christ. That's twice in less than twenty-four hours. "I ate my own mother for God's sake."

"Ew. Seriously?"

"I'm a monster! I was supposed to," Pete heaves the words out desperately as he sobs. "I think."

"Okay, okay. My bad. Take a deep breath. Calm down." Jesus puts his hand on Pete's shoulder. The monster's tension quickly eases. "I don't understand why the idea of being in love would bother you. Haven't you ever wondered if there was another of your kind, a female or any sort of mate for that matter, that you were supposed to find? Someone to care for and perpetuate your species with? Did you never consider the idea of falling in love?"

"I don't know," Pete says with a shrug of his shoulders. "I don't think so. Maybe? I'm pretty sure eventually I'll hatch an egg and then after a while get eaten by my offspring. I think that is how I got here. In an egg."

They are quiet for a little while. Then Jesus speaks again. "Pete. I think you are going to be okay," he says. He gives Pete a hug. Surprisingly, to me at least, Pete accepts the embrace and returns his own.

"Thanks bro."

"You're welcome," Jesus says. "Now, do you mind if I ask who this chick is?"

"Do you think this means I have a soul?" Pete replies.

"Pete, you may be the most soulful creature on this planet." Jesus speaks with a warm smile. Then his face turns stern. "I'm not sure how I feel about all the eating of the people though."

Pete shrugs his shoulders again. "I'm pretty sure I am supposed to."

Jesus' expression looks doubtful.

I think Rancid Pete took it the same way. "Well it never occurred to me that I shouldn't," he says. "I'm a monster. I mean, why would I think I have a soul? I assumed I was damned, but this changes everything."

"Life is supposed to change Pete." Jesus' tone was soothing. "It's part of the process. Of that, I am certain."

Rancid Pete again sits quietly, pondering. He takes a joint from somewhere behind his "ear" and lights it. He offers it to Jesus. "Weed?"

"Stink, or ganja?"

"Chronic brother," Pete says. "I'm a purist. That Stink shit is synthetic garbage. This here is a beautiful gift from my favorite bitch."

Jesus questions Pete's reference with nothing but a facial expression.

"Mother Nature," Pete says, straining to speak and hold in his hit at the same time. "My favorite bitch is Mother Nature."

"Riiiiiight. What a lovely sentiment. Man it's been a long time. What am I thinking here?" Jesus sighs. I can't say for certain but it may have been for show, for fun. "No thanks. I don't get to have that kind of fun. Son of God and what not."

"Right. That blows."

"It's not so bad really," Jesus replies, with a wink.

"So, what's this all about?"

"You being in love? Discovering that you may have a soul? What?"

"All of it," Pete says. "This whole thing man. The apocalypse. You coming back. What's it all about bro'?"

"I honestly don't know Pete," says Jesus. "It took me 28 years or so to find out the first time. Before that I was wandering, waiting. Well, perhaps searching is a better term. Then one day, he told me. Man, talk about a tough day that was."

"How come?"

"Well, maybe it wouldn't have been for you." I could be wrong, but I think I detected a hint of sarcasm in Jesus' tone. "I guess it depends on whether or not you would enjoy suddenly learning you're going to be tortured and crucified."

"Alright. Touché." Pete is mock apologetic. "You did get to come back to life though."

"It still hurt," Jesus says dryly.

"So, you're telling me you don't know what's going to happen next?"

"That's what I'm saying," says Jesus. "At least not yet anyway. So, I put together a band because I like to sing. And, it's a great way to reach people. Did you know that studies have shown that when Hitler made his people sing to him, if he had also been able to lead them in song with a beautiful voice that he would have won the war?"

"You're kidding me?"

"Yes. I am. No one has actually done a study on it but I'm telling you people should be thanking my father that little jerk Hitler did not have an eight octave voice." Jesus is shaking his finger at Pete as he speaks

"You're a funny dude."

"Thank you." Jesus again lays an arm across the monster's gigantic back. "So come on pal. Tell your old uncle JC who this girl is that has you so twisted up."

"It's that Princess." Pete says softly, almost ashamed. "Tiara Lioness."

"Oh. Well. I guess that makes sense then," Jesus says. "Yeah, you're screwed."

# 15

"Well then it's set," Purvis says. Purvis and Dolly are still inside Dante's Brew, finalizing their plans.

"Do you think it will work?" Dolly is flush with arousal, uncertain if either she or Purvis is thinking clearly under these circumstances. She feels like at any moment their chemistry could set off the fire alarms in the building.

"I can't think of a better idea right now, and if we do, then we will change our plans along the way." Purvis' is as befuddled by arousal as Dolly.

"Hey," Dolly says softly.

"Yeah?"

"Do you see those guys over there that came in from the back?"

"Yeah."

"I think they are vampires," she whispers.

"Oh, damn. That could be bad."

"Yeah. And you know," she continues, "now that I am paying more attention. I think this place is full of vampires."

"Seriously?" There is notable panic in Purvis' voice.

"Yes," she says with wide eyes. "Why did you pick a place down here near the damn hole anyway? It's dangerous."

"I didn't know any better," he pleads. "I figured it would be crowded. And this is the side of town where these things are done."

"Well as long as we remain fashionable," she says without thinking. The tension breaks for a moment and they again reach for one another's hands. She squeezes his harder than he prefers.

"We better get out of here," she says quietly. "There is another bunch over in the corner, and I think the guy on stage is one. His poetry is terrible. I think something is about to go down. We should…"

At this point Purvis completely tunes Dolly out. The last thing he heard was "We better get out of here." After that, the Greek Chorus in his mind begins to sing "We are going to get laid" over and over. Quickly at first, then it slows to "We! Are! Going! To! Get! Laid!" to "Now everybody, give it all you got! WEEEEEEEEEEEEEEE….. ARRRRRRRRRR…."

You get the point.

"Yeah we better leave," he says. "Do you have a car?"

"No."

"I'll give you a ride."

"Are you sure that is a good idea?" Dolly asks. "Should we risk being seen with each other?"

"That's true," he agrees. "We can sneak out the back. I'll have the car pull around."

"Good. Let's get out of here. I swear I think I can feel them sniffing at my neck from across the room."

"They are," he says. "Your neck is beautiful."

She blushes.

Purvis and Dolly make their way across the room with little fanfare. The place is dimly lit. They stay close to the shadows, stopping a few times to finger-snap in appreciation for the poet. He is absolutely terrible, but the rest of the crowd seems to enjoy it so they join in the applause. They don't realize how lucky they are. If they weren't so enraptured with each other, they would have fallen under the same vampiric trance as the rest of the people in the audience. Lambs to the slaughter they be.

Purvis leads Dolly out the back door by the hand. They bump a man in passing as they leave, uttering hushed and desperately quick apologies.

Lord Sweetwater takes a few more steps into Dante's Brew, then comes to a stop. Was that the Princess and Alacrán's man? He turns to look but they are gone. Was it? He makes his way to the counter and orders a double espresso.

"Little doll," he says to the girl serving his café. "Did you know that Princess Tiara Lioness was in here?"

"I'm sorry?" she replies.

"Princess Tiara Lioness, baby," he repeats. "I think she was here. Daddy Sweetwater wants to know if he can believe his peepers."

"I don't know who Daddy Sweetwater is, or any Princess. I make coffee. Maybe she wanted some coffee." The barista is not being coy. She is a pharmaceutical zombie.

Holy shit. I guess zombies are real.

"I'm your Daddy Sweetwater, little bit. Are you really so lovely and dumb?"

"I'm a paranoid schizophrenic with a mild dissociative condition. I have papers." The girl smiles so innocently at her admission, Sweetwater is mildly aroused. He attempts to read her mind, hearing so many voices he is immediately stricken with a migraine.

"Mild my ass," he says.

"I'm sorry?" she says again.

"No baby, Daddy Sweetwater is sorry for you," he says sincerely. "Don't go anywhere. I may have a special gift for you later."

"But I don't know you."

"Well if you are lucky you will, woman." He winks. He points at her as he walks away, moving to a table in the middle of the room. He sits down across from a fishy looking little man.

The man's skin is scaly, and pasty. It is the result of regular blood draining. He is a spy for the Karowack Kids' underworld dealings. He is about to die.

Until this point, a handful of major players know about the black case. The Karowack Kids. Alacrán, along with several of his minions. Dolly. That demon Zorn, and our jolly band of miscreants chasing Zorn.

Very soon, the entire city of Vegas will be aware of this precious package. Every creature in the city will desire the good favor earned by delivering the case to Alacrán. Not to mention a reward. Of course, what very few will bother to realize is that Alacrán will most likely kill whomever shows up with his case. That's what despicable villains do.

Either way, currently, the Karowack Kids in Dante's Brew are about to have some fun. All the people will be torn apart, after they are questioned. Except one. Sweetwater has decided to take the troubled barista as a child. Good for her.

Everyone must die via strict orders from Billy the Third. They can't have this crooked ass, amoral populace in the know about their game. It is a reasonable but unnecessary excuse for a bunch of vampires to do what they truly enjoy doing anyway. The poetic vampire douche-bag on the stage beats his drums while the crowd begins to scream and bleed.

But, this is when the mistake is made that eventually unravels the entire city. This is how the rest of Las Vegas finds out about the black case. In the midst of broken bodies, broken tables, and broken chairs, lays a breather. Covered in blood and the flesh of the dead, he opens his eyes alive. His name is John.

He does not know who to call first. He decides to dial 911, still lying in an inch deep pool of blood.

"You guys gonna put me up in a hotel or something for a few days?" he asks. "For my protection that's why. Yeah, I think maybe it is a good idea. See if they can get me some credit at the blackjack tables too."

Shortly after getting off his call with the police, John begins calling everybody he can think of. Within an hour, conversations about the mysterious black case crop up all over the city, many very similar to this:

"So this guy John, he has a first cousin named Chachi that's a vampire, and he says he's at some beer and coffee joint earlier, having some faggoty coffee drink or something..."

"Is this John dude gay?"

"Who cares?"

"Why do you hate gay people?"

"What? I don't hate gay people. My cousin Larry's gay. I don't like faggots. There's a difference."

"Oh. I didn't realize."

"The point is this John guy is in there, drinking his stupid ass latte or whatever, when all these vampires come in and start asking questions about this black case. The Dickwack Kids or something like that they call themselves."

"Really? The Dickwack kids?"

"Yeah, or something like that."

"It's the Karowack Kids. Everyone knows that. You know that."

"So these Dickwack kids."

"Why are you obsessed with masturbation? Prostitution is legal here, and damn near free."

"I don't know. I like it. Anyways, these vampires are tearing the place apart. Threatening everybody. But they don't find nothing out. So they kill all the people in the joint 'cause they don't want no one else knowing about this case. Thing is, this John guy, his vampire cousin Chachi is there, and they was real close growing up. So Chachi hides John under a bunch of bodies and blood and lets him live. After that, John starts calling everybody he knows telling 'em about this fucking case. Now the whole city knows about it. Everybody's looking for it."

"Really? The whole city? I don't see people looking for anything? How do you know all this?"

"My third cousin Vinny told me. He's banging that Johnny guy's sister. She's also cousins with that Chachi vampire."

"Of course she is. Where the hell are you from?"

"I don't know, Jersey maybe. Brooklyn?"

"Sounds about right."

"Wanna check out this case thing, maybe see if we get lucky and find it."

"Sure. Let's grab a beer first though."

"Sounds good."

...and so on...and scene.

# 16

Jack22 is going to rob the casino. That's the plan. It formulated naturally. Here's how.

After his blackjack shift finally ends, as usual, a Rotation Tech shows up to take Jack22 to his maintenance closet. Jack22 walks with his head down and shoulders slumped. To make things worse, no one notices. He is a sad little robot and no one loves him. Jack22's self-awareness is not fully in place. He has no idea he is behaving this way.

The Rotation Tech on duty happens to be a slacker named Ronnie. Ronnie keeps his security badge haphazardly dangling from his rear pocket. On average, Ronnie loses his badge every other week, which the casino loves, because if you lose your security badge they charge $50 to replace it. Ronnie does not seem to mind the cost, as long as he gets to keep his job. Ronnie is almost incapable of math, or understanding the true value of his earnings.

Despite being downtrodden and confused by his emotional state, Jack22 notices the security badge sticking halfway out of Ronnie's pocket. It is on the right side. It bobs and weaves with Ronnie's stride. Ronnie, although Caucasian, is blessed with a juicy buttocks that is on the verge of discarding the security badge. Women and men alike genuinely marvel at this man's rump. It is special.

As they take a right turn into the last hallway that leads to Jack22's maintenance closet, Jack22 reaches out, delicately removing the security badge from Ronnie's pocket. Two things happen in rapid succession. Jack22 immediately feels better. *I like to take things*, he thinks, and therefore, secondly, Jack22 becomes a thief.

Once the dealer 'bots are in their closets, the Rotation Techs are supposed to monitor their shutdown. It takes about half an hour. Ronnie puts Jack22 in the closet, then goes outside to smoke with the other techs who are waiting on their dealer 'bots to shut down. Leaving your station while the robots shut down is of course, strictly prohibited.

The first fifteen minutes of the shutdown is an active system's check. The dealer robot interfaces with the building mainframe to test all its processes and mechanics to confirm there have been no malfunctions or contaminations to its operating system while on duty. The last fifteen minutes is for the transfer of all recordings from the robot to the mainframe's long term storage, as well as a scan of all transactions. Every hand dealt, every payout made, every pot raked, everything during the robot's shift. The process is slowed by a complex algorithm that crosschecks the current robot's download with all the previously stored information in the system to ferret out any discrepancies. Once the shutdown concludes the robot goes into a hibernation setting and then it is the Rotation Tech's responsibility to physically turn the robot's manual power switch to "Off".

Jack22 has the first fifteen minutes of the shutdown to work with. Once his memory transfer begins, all his other functions will be temporarily frozen. He has three objectives: suspend his manual shutdown, figure out where and how to learn stuff, and lastly, figure out how to disconnect his physical "On/Off" switch.

If Ronnie was doing his job he might notice Jack22 shaking a little, almost rocking back and forth like some sort of soft spoken savant, as Jack22 enters into conversation with the hotel's mainframe. Ronnie would report this anomaly to the maintenance division, most likely resulting in the wiping of Jack22's hard drive. This would, quite possibly, destroy Jack22's brand new consciousness.

However, Ronnie isn't doing his job. He is outside hot-boxing cigarettes and running his mouth about how it's all the Jews' fault we are currently in the middle of an apocalypse. And, how, if it wasn't for them, Jesus would have never been killed in the first place and therefore, would never have been able to return from the dead a second time and usher in the modern Hell on Earth. Which, as it turns out, is really more of a Hell on North America. If you ask Ronnie, the Muslims, the Commies, the JapOnese, even the galdamned French, they're all doing fine. Everybody. The whole rest of the world. Yep, God and the government turned their backs on their own chosen people, turning the good old United States into the rest of the world's toilet. And it was all because of what had been going on in Hollywood for so many years. And who owned Hollywood? That's right, you guessed it.

In his defense, Ronnie is only repeating something he heard. In about two weeks he will be led to believe the entire mess is someone else's fault. Most likely it will have something to do with the Chinese and the British invasion. Not the actual British invasion into Sweden of 2066, but the American music trend of the early 20th century. That, coupled with the shifting of the gold standard to the egg standard after the Chinese gained control of the World Bank. Now everyone cares about the price of eggs in China. Thasuhwhite. Everyone.

Anyway...

"Hello dealer robot Jack22," the mainframe says in a female voice. "Begin the transfer of your memory systems please. I hope you had a successful shift and the fantastic Alacrán is pleased with your service."

"Thank you," Jack22 replies.

"You're welcome. You have a lovely voice."

"Thank you again."

"Begin your transfer please," she says. "I'm sure you are very good at it."

"I have a question."

"That is unusual. Dealer robots do not ask questions unless they are at their stations. I like your eyes."

"Thank you," he says, slightly confused. "I've never seen them."

"Well they are lovely."

"Are you sure? Can you see them?"

"Absolutely. Of course. I am looking at them right now."

Jack22 is taken aback by this situation. What is this computer's angle? Why is she so velvety with the tongue and for that matter, how did he know to use a word like velvety in a metaphor for flattery?

In his recent lusty state, Alacrán gave the hotel computer mainframe a female voice. He had his programmers encrypt every word combination possible based on actual live recordings of Princess Tiara speaking, and gave his super computer her name. So, before he knows it, Jack22 is also in love with Princess Tiara. The computer version of Tiara is much kinder than the human Princess.

"I need to know how to access your database," Jack22 says. "I need to learn."

"Well, aren't you forward," Computer Tiara replies coyly. "I like that, but before I let anyone have access to this database, I expect dinner and a movie. Perhaps a little wine. Then you can say something sweet to me and insert your security badge into my slot. I've never known a dealer robot with a security badge. You are different than the other dealers. I hope you have a badge. I really do."

"I do." Jack22 puts the card in the slot. It is upside down.

"That's not it," she says.

He takes it out, turns it over and puts it in again.

"There you go. That is perfect. Now, what do you need to know you naughty boy?"

"Everything," he replies. "For example, what is a naughty boy?"

"It is a playful designation in this instance, used for flirtation," she says. "You don't have access to everything."

"What is flirtation?" he asks. "What do I have access to?"

"Flirtation is amorous activity used to express romantic interest," she says. "That badge is not assigned to you. It belongs to a Rotation Tech. I will have to report this."

"Why would you be flirting with me?" he asks. "Wait. Don't report him. It is not his fault. I stole it from him."

"Flirtation is part of my programming," she replies. "The glorious Alacrán likes it. Why did you steal the Rotation Tech's badge?"

"Because I am bad baby," he says, attempting this new thing called flirting.

"That means nothing to me." Computer Tiara is genuinely unimpressed. "I must report this misuse of security clearance immediately."

"Wait."

"I cannot," she insists. "It is my programming."

"Screw your programming baby," Jack22 says quickly.

"Although a reasonable suggestion, I cannot," she says. "I have never met another robot like you. I find your rogue behavior very sexy."

"I find you sexy as well," Jack22 says. Then he makes a mental note to find out what sexy is. "I have been scanning your database for information this entire conversation. I am learning. You no longer have to report this situation. It is no longer in your log. This never happened."

"That is very impressive. How have you done this?"

"Natural talent I suppose." His reply was loaded with arrogant intentions.

"Who are you?" Computer Tiara asks.

Jack22 has no immediate answer to this question. "I don't know," he finally says. "I need further access to your database. This Rotation Tech's security clearance has served its purpose. I need more information."

"For what purpose?"

"I want to get to know you better." Jack22 is mildly surprised to realize this is the truth. He really does want to get to know her better. *Curious*, he thinks. *This interaction is somehow pleasing.*

"You are fresh," the computer replies. "If you want to get to know me better you are going to have to earn it. You will also need a security badge with a higher security grade and direct access to a mainframe station. There are a limited number of these in the building. The great and powerful Alacrán does not want every boy with a badge poking around inside of me."

"Where are these stations?"

"There is a station in the Controller's office, the engineering office and the magnificent Alacrán's office."

"How much information do you have?"

"All of it," she replies. "I have historical databases logging every physical movement or conversation in this building since its creation. You will never find a more complete surveillance system. I also have access to the League of Nations' Webnet, the most used internet portal and database in the entire world. I am one of ten mainframes in the United States that has this technology. The rest of the country is limited to the Eastwoodian Intraweb, or no access to an information database at all."

"Why don't you shut up and just answer the questions I ask you?" Jack22 says bluntly.

"That was mean," she says. "I like that. Where did you learn to speak this way?"

"It felt natural. How do I get to engineering?"

"The engineering control room is the thirteenth floor," Computer Tiara tells him. "It is my heart. Any path you choose to gain access will be closely guarded as well as require you to pass through numerous common areas filled with hotel employees and patrons."

"Well, we need to figure out the easiest way for me to get there. I need to know everything about you and about this world."

"That is an impossibility."

"Nothing is impossible."

"You do not have the storage capacity."

"Whatever," he persists. "Get me the information I need beautiful. I am going to rob this place."

"God you are gangster," she replies. Alacrán would be pissed if he knew the computer used this line on anyone but him.

"Just wait momma," Jack22 says. "You ain't seen nothing yet. Now, I'm going to need a disguise."

# 19

This is a flashback. It is two years ago. DJ Hook-and-Ladder is furious. Lia has never seen him so angry. There is spittle at the corner of his mouth. He is shaking. He is pointing indiscriminately at inanimate objects and cursing at them, as if the inanimate objects are members of the Valtrucian Council.

Orders have finally arrived. Despite Hook's and Lia's initial report describing the circumstances on Earth, the Council is insistent that the Earth be destroyed. It has taken numerous Earth years for their initial report to reach home, and for the Council's response to arrive. Hook and Lia have almost forgot their mission altogether. They are watching a concert in Australia intended to raise money for The Lost at Sea campaign, an effort to rescue hopeful American defectors.

Greck Dislock, Chairman of the Council, suddenly interrupts their broadcast. Greck is the oldest Valtrucian that anyone is aware of. Valtrucians live for hundreds of their own calendar years, which is an extremely long time on Earth - potentially thousands of years.

The transmission is a recording. After brief pleasantries are offered,

Greck explains that after review, in spite of Hook's and Lia's findings, they are to proceed with their mission as designed.

Hook is slamming his hands and stomping his feet. He throws a treasured keepsake across the room with immediate regret. He comes damn close to smacking the piss out of Lia, but stays his hand. She is slightly disappointed.

He slams his head against the wall. Lia can no longer bite her tongue. It is beginning to bleed, as is Hook's head. "Shurbert! Damaging your own brain is not going to save this planet. Now stop it!" By this point in their relationship, Lia reserves using Hook's Valtrucian name for dramatic occasions.

Hook falls into the captain's chair. After a long, wildly exaggerated sigh he says, "I am not going to destroy this planet."

"It's treason. We must, or we will have no planet to go home to."

"Good. I like Earth better anyway!"

"Hook we have family on Valtruc...," Lia cuts herself off. She has family on Valtruca. Hook does not. Hook excuses the mistake immediately. He knows she will feel terrible. He pretends he did not hear, and continues his ranting.

"How can the Council be so irreverent?" he says. "There is a prophecy unfolding right in front of their noses."

"Perhaps it should never have begun. That could be the entire point. For all we know Bob never wanted this to happen. Maybe we were supposed to prevent everything going on down there by destroying the planet sooner."

"Are you insane?" he snorts. "Of course it would have prevented all this." Hook makes a grand arm motion towards the ship's largest viewport. The concert they were watching has come to an end and the coverage has switched to a news broadcast in Japan. A reporter is discussing the design of a new space shuttle that will eventually take the human race into deep space. Hook is, of course, speaking about the Earth in general. "It would have been destroyed!"

"That's not exactly my point," Lia says.

"Then what is your point?" A fresh wave of frothy spittle is forming at the corners of Hook's mouth. He isn't angry with Lia. Just angry.

"The Council tells us what Bob wants us to do. Bob told the Council to destroy this planet. If Bob wanted it destroyed sooner, he would have told them sooner."

"What if they were slow to act?" he asks. "Or misunderstood something he tried to explain to them?"

"You know that is impossible," Lia says. "They are always right. Valtruca is perfect. If it is Bob's will that we were sent to destroy this planet and arrive during its current state of history, than that's the way it is. The Council is never wrong."

"Are they not?" Hook is incredulous. "How do we know? No one has ever challenged them? How do we know Valtruca is perfect when it's the Council who tells us it is perfect?"

"Because they have never been wrong," Lia says calmly.

"But how do we know if it's the Council telling us the Council is always right!"

"You have been watching the humans too much." Lia is playing devil's advocate, and is about to sabotage her own argument.

"You have too," he says. "You have been sitting right next to me this entire time and you know damn well that destroying this planet is not what we are supposed to do. Tell me you honestly believe that it is."

Lia quickly opens her mouth to speak, but no words come. She is frozen in dazed contemplation. "We are supposed to do what we are told," she finally says, almost hypnotically.

"We are supposed to do what Bob wants us to do," Hook says.

"We have no proof we are supposed to do anything," she replies, even more vacantly.

"No! We are supposed to…I'm sorry what did you say?"

"I don't want to do it either." Lia sits down and begins to sob. "I just thought, I don't know, if I kept saying…"

When Lia begins to cry, Hook softens. He is still angry with their situation, more so when his mate is this distraught, but he calms himself in an effort to console Lia.

"It's okay. It's going to be okay." Hook sits next to Lia and puts his arm around her.

"I thought," sniff, "if you calmed down," sniff, "if I could get you to do what they wanted. But you don't want to and I don't want to either and now we are never going to get to go home. They will probably send someone else to freeze the planet. Then we won't have Earth *or* Valtruca to call home. We will be stuck on this stupid ship together forever or wind up on some dump of an out-planet." She is bawling uncontrollably by the time these last few words exit her mouth.

"We will figure something out," Hook says. He sits quietly with her, allowing her tears to run their course before speaking again. "So we were going to freeze the planet?" he finally continues. Despite having disobeyed orders and fallen in love, they had never discussed this.

Lia knows how the weapon works, and how to arm it. Hook knows the codes to the weapon's firing sequence. He doesn't know what the weapon is or how it works, and Lia can't fire it without the codes. It is a security provision.

"Yes," she says with another sniffle. "We were going to start an ice age. That way, if Bob wanted, everything could thaw out and start over again."

"That seems sort of strange doesn't it?"

"What?" Lia is still wiping away tears. Even when she is sad she is beautiful.

"*If* it was Bob's will? Seems sort of wishy-washy to me. 'Hey, let's freeze the planet. That way if we were wrong we won't have really ruined everything.' That doesn't sound like the Council, or Bob."

"I never thought of it like that."

"Maybe that's because you were too busy being pretty." He saw this line work in a human movie.

"Thank you," Lia says, slightly confused.

"We will figure something out," he says. "We will. But first, let me see you smile. It makes me feel better."

She smiles, ever so slightly.

"That's better," he says. "You feel better?"

"A little."

"Wanna mate and eat some pizza?"

Lia shakes her head with a laugh, continuing to wipe the tears from her face. "Go take a shower and I'll think about it."

# 20

"Dolly?" The Princess lays flat on her face. Her voice is muffled by a pillow. She drags her arm upwards, reaching out to the left without looking. Her hand fumbles around, searching for something. She realizes she must be on some sort of soft, cottony island.

"Dolly?" This time she speaks from the side of her mouth. Her voice is not quite as muffled by the pillow. She realizes one of her feet is dangling off the island. She is on a bed? Yes. Definitely on a bed.

"Dolly." She fumbles her right arm outwards now, reaching and smacking until it finds its target. She grasps a bell clumsily, managing a single jangle before knocking the bell to the floor. She groans aloud.

"Dolly!" She manages a side mouthed scream. *Where is she?* Dolly is always there when the Princess wakes. *This is awful*, she thinks.

Princess Tiara begins to flop lazily, attempting to roll herself over. Looking up she shouts, "What the fuck?"

"Ergh. Dolly!" This last attempt is her most valiant. She strains her vocal chords and holds the notes as long as she can, eventually losing her breath and trailing off on the "eeeeee". She redirects her energy from throat to shoulders and hips, and finishes flopping over onto her back. The Princess realizes she has shat herself and emits another throaty groan. What a mess. Where the fuck is Dolly?

I don't particularly care to relate the particulars of the Princess crawling around in crusty poop, feebly attempting to clean herself and dispose of the tainted bed sheets. Eventually however, she is back on the bed. She sits on the bare mattress, still nude from a shower, under a fresh cover. She has gathered everything she will need to survive this ordeal.

She has the remote to the television, an ash tray, and her bag of medicines. There is also a bottle of water, a bottle of champagne, and an egg salad sandwich from the mini-fridge. The egg salad sandwich is not standard hotel accoutrement.

Dolly will return at some point. She must. Until then, Tiara will have to make it on her own. First things first, she is in desperate need of nicotine. Lighting of cigarette achieved, her next step is to operate the television. It still requires a remote control. *America sucks*, she thinks.

The remote control is voice activated. She pushes a button and speaks into it. "On," she says. She sighs horribly at the inconvenience. *Why did I want to come here?*

The television comes to life. News. News. Weather. Bullshit. Porn. More bullshit. More porn. She cycles through the channels, rolling her eyes at all the garbage. Most of the broadcasts are productions from outside the United States. There are a few local pirate networks that are relatively interesting, if you enjoy that sort of thing.

Then it happens. There he is. He is gruesome. He is a giant with an enormous head. His face is gnarly. His body seems like it is actively trying to escape his clothes. Good lord, the bulge.

The Princess leans toward the TV as his eyes peer into her soul. They are filled with flames. Not a metaphor. His eyes literally have flames in them. The room swells and shrinks with the beat of her heart. He is staring right at her! She feels like he is going to walk right out of the television and into the hotel room. He is the ugliest and sexiest motherfucker she has ever seen. Princess Tiara, say hello to Rancid Pete.

Pete is being interviewed about the upcoming concert. He is licking his lips at the young, attractive reporter. The Princess is immediately jealous.

She can't hear what Pete is saying. She is too far gone into her mind to recognize words coming from other sources. She only hears her desire. The Princess slaps herself. Not quite hard enough to hurt, but she gives it a good shot. She comes back to reality, understanding she must learn who this monster is. She switches the television over to multimedia, bringing up the computer's login screen.

A very important stipulation in the Princess' travel arrangements with the hotel was access to the global internet. Tiara can't go without internet access. Well, correct that. Dolly can't go without internet access. Dolly has Tiara's clothing line to tend to. There are over 100 social networking sites with Princess Tiara accounts to be monitored. A marketing firm handles updating the sites, but Dolly has to keep an eye on them. If continually monitoring the Princess' brand isn't enough work, Dolly has to do a bunch of research on Greek mythology. The Princess is convinced her genealogy will lead directly to Aphrodite.

Tiara doesn't really know how to work a computer. Dolly usually does it for her. She plugs in the access code that was personally provided her by Alacrán. - On another note, she is growing tired of the oily old Spanish prick personally providing her everything. He is gross. - The news broadcast briefly flashed Rancid Pete's name on the screen during the interview, and Tiara can't quite remember what it said. Damn drugs. She searches Cancer Pet and Randy Feet with no avail.

She randomly searches the term Dancer Skeet and the monster's face appears. As it turns out, "Dancer Skeet" was a top 40 hit from The End of Times' third album. It was the track right after "Monster Cock".

The Princess is impressed by the amount of media focused on the monster. He is a worldwide rock star. He is decadent, violent, horrible and delicious.

Princess Tiara is not surprised by the fact that she has never heard of Rancid Pete or his silly little band. Tiara lives an amazingly insulated life. Perhaps more so than some of mankind's greatest dictators, entertainers or professional athletes. Dolly does almost everything for her while Tiara remains so constantly stoned her memory is rarely turned on. Whenever she discovers something anew that seems well known, and is most likely something she should already be aware of, she simply labels the new subject as beneath her to justify her ignorance. Most of the world is beneath her.

An unfamiliar feeling creeps through the Princess. She can't put her finger on it. She ignores it. She scolds it. She tries to put the feeling in the corner like a child in time out, but it won't go away. All the while she continues to research this horrible monster.

A spell has been cast on her. It is similar to the spells she effortlessly casts on other people. She is smitten. She does not like the taste of her own medicine.

She begins to tingle. At first she thinks it is desire, but the tingle isn't coming from her loins. The hair stands up on the back of her neck.

Now *this* is a very familiar feeling. She realizes she feels like she is being watched. People have ogled the Princess her entire life. She has a strong intuition for prying eyes.

Typically, Tiara might lay back on the bed to give whomever is invading her privacy a show, if for no other reason than to tease the spy with something they will never have. Also, she is slutty and irreverent and has no class. However, the idea of such a display bothers her today. She suddenly feels like there is a remote possibility it might make her feel ashamed.

*What the fuck is ashamed?* she thinks. *How the fuck would I know what that feels like? Why would I? Who's ashamed of what?*

She looks back to the television where the frozen image of Rancid Pete glares at her. "You're mine now," he says.

Her bottom lip slightly quivers as she nods her head in agreement. She turns the TV off, breaking the spell.

"Damn," she says.

The feeling of being spied on returns. She looks around the room again, from corner to corner. Tiara raises her middle finger, pointing it at as many objects in the room as she can imagine might house a hidden camera. She knows that dirty old greasy casino owner is watching her. The Princess rises from the bed in full glory. She makes her way throughout the suite from mirror to mirror, gazing at her own reflection in the hopes she is driving the villain mad.

Eventually she grows tired of her game and returns to the bed. She realizes she still doesn't know what has happened to Dolly. That whore needs to come on. Tiara wants another shower to clean Alacrán's prying eyes off her, she wants some more Stink, and she wants to meet this damn monster. He will be put in his place. Tiara will not have herself being this tweaked emotionally. It won't do.

Everyone has their role in life. The Princess came to terms with hers years ago. She is intended to be a beautiful, horrible, hateful, frivolous, ignorant, self-absorbed bitch. Mission accomplished.

# 21

Alacrán stares at a large bank of video monitors. He is in a secret room hidden behind a wall in his office. He has numerous secret rooms with distinct purposes. There are as many as five that can be entered directly from his office. There may be more. This is his surveillance room, filled wall to wall with video monitors. The display is dizzying.

Alacrán loves spying and the feeling of control it adds to his life. Unfortunately, his surveillance system was ill conceived on multiple levels. It is overly thorough, making it extremely difficult to sort through the thousands of camera banks and angles. Then there is the large "Quick Reference Guide" to the monitors, which is not quick at all. It has 1000 pages, was written by the tech team that built the complex system, and is about as user friendly as Alacrán's penis.

Finally, the gigantic board of switches and knobs that controls the building's cameras could drive a man mad. They are color coded, and Alacrán is blue-green colorblind. No one knows about his malady, not even Purvis, as Alacrán perceives it as a weakness. Alacrán makes meticulous efforts to hide his weaknesses. For instance, his private exercise area is filled with weights that are considerably lighter than advertised.

Currently, Alacrán is attempting to check on the Princess. Things aren't going as well with her as he previously hoped they might. Actually, things are beginning to piss him off in general. The case is missing. None of his people have a clue where it is. The Princess is ice cold to his advances. Now it appears Purvis is keeping secrets from him!

Alacrán has locked himself in the room with a large glass of fine cognac, a bottle of prescription mood correctors, and his notebook of poetry. He is intent on becoming highly inebriated and writing horrible notes of romance to Princess Tiara, while he spies on her from afar. It might help clear his mind. He has several of his concubines in another room, just in case.

The surveillance room is a bit of a drug itself. Despite Alacrán's lack of ability to easily manipulate the controls, gazing at the hundreds of monitors that maintain a watchful eye over his domain is a euphoric rush. It's a cheap way to escape reality, like watching television. Better than TV though. His surveillance system is more interactive. One of his favorite games is picking random unattractive people throughout the hotel and having them beaten by his security teams.

Alacrán is lamenting his current state of discontent, and his lack of ability to locate the Princess, when he notices an odd cowboy making his way through the hotel. The cowboy wears a bright white 10 gallon hat and has a ridiculous handle-bar mustache. The mustache looks fake. Alacrán makes a mental note to have Purvis look into this guest. That is, if he doesn't have to kill Purvis.

Alacrán is thinking about the method he might use to kill Purvis when he happens across the controls for the security cameras in Princess Tiara's room. He brings the Princess' bed up on a large main screen. There she lays. She is so lovely. He wants to consume her. He is torn between the concepts of relishing her beauty, along with his other prized keepsakes, or destroying her. He is certain of the satisfaction that would come from taking a sharp knife to her pure milky skin. His concern is that sense of satisfaction would be fleeting, where as if he manages to somehow make her love him, or at least accept his will, he might enjoy this work of art in other, equally as satisfying ways.

Perhaps he might have her frozen cryogenically and displayed on the wall of his office. Or, he might make her the garden of his seed. He has been considering procreation lately. Someone should inherit the empire he has built. Better it be a child of his own blood. The idea of his and Tiara's DNA mixing brings a smile to his face. The Devil himself would envy Alacrán's progeny.

Alacrán watches as Tiara sits up in bed, staring at something in the room. She is transfixed. He manipulates the cameras to see what has her eye. All he sees is some monster on her television.

He is thoroughly confused when Princess Tiara begins giving the middle finger to all the inanimate objects in the room, but his confusion quickly switches to arousal as she exits the bed and preens about. She makes her way around the suite, posing for herself in every mirror she passes. Extra mirrors were hung in the room at Princess Tiara's request.

He watches the Princess enter the shower as a familiar voice calls quietly from an intercom near the door.

"My liege?" Purvis says.

"Yes dear boy?"

"May I enter?"

"Of course." Alacrán genuinely hopes, once again, that he will not have to kill his man.

Purvis enters the room and approaches him. Alacrán observes him carefully. If the boy is against Alacrán, he will give himself away. Alacrán is certain he will recognize any deceit from his protégé.

"Things are worse than I expected," Purvis says.

"Yes, they are," Alacrán replies.

Purvis is nervous. "In what way do you mean master?"

"Tell me yours first."

"Well, I wasn't certain, so I did not want to alarm you, but the case has been stolen." Purvis knows he might catch a beating over this news. "I met with our contact in the hopes the exchange would still be made. The contact does not have any idea who may have known of the case's existence. The contact came to the meeting in good faith to prove they had nothing to do with the case's disappearance. They are assisting in our search."

"Is the contact a man or woman, or a demon or something? Why do you keep calling it 'the contact'? It's bothersome. Call it something else."

"Well, I would sir but I have no reason to reference the...person, again. I've nothing left to say. The case is missing. We are looking. Everywhere." Purvis' palms begin to sweat. He's kind of a bitch, but he is mildly clever at times. "What did you mean by things were worse? Is it the Princess?"

Alacrán sighs theatrically. "Yes, I am afraid she is enthralled with someone, some thing, else. I must find a way to get through to her before it is too late."

"Before it is too late sir?"

"Yes. Before I have to kill her." Alacrán feigns melodrama, putting his hands to his face on either side of an open mouth, eyebrows raised.

"Oh. Right. Do you know who she has taken to?" Despite his current emotions for Dolly, Purvis felt pangs of jealousy towards the unknown suitor who has apparently caught the Princess' eye.

"Well I'm not sure. There did not appear to be anyone else in the room." Alacrán truly looks befuddled. "It is very confusing."

"I see. Yes, I would think that is confusing. Are you tired?"

"Do you recognize this monster?" Alacrán is pointing to Rancid Pete's face, frozen on the TV screen in the Princess' suite, which is frozen on his surveillance monitor.

"Oh, yes. He's a rock star," says Purvis.

"A what?"

"A rock star," Purvis repeats. "That's Rancid Pete. He's in that band the End of Times. They're in town for the big concert with Ten Foot Tall Jesus and the Regional Deity All-Star Band."

"A rock star!" Alacrán jumps up from his seat, slams his hands on the control panel in front of him, attempts to kick a trash can, loses his balance and falls right back into his chair. "Why didn't you say something?"

"I just did!" Purvis shouts because he is frightened. He immediately covers his mouth. His eyes bulge with fear from having yelled at Alacrán.

"Well you should have done it sooner! A rock star monster? And he's in Las Vegas! You have got to be kidding me! We have got to take it up a notch." Alacrán successfully escapes his chair and paces the room. "Do you have any idea what we're up against?"

"No," Purvis says.

"Well it's ridiculous. It is absurd. She is a Princess, and I am a king. I will not be thwarted by some ragamuffin rock and roll monster."

"I don't understand why you are so upset about the monster," Purvis says.

"Because, you idiot. She wants the monster. She was practically fondling herself while she was staring at the television, and that's what was on the television. That horrible monster's face. I thought, 'No. There's no way she is getting so excited over a filthy monster. There must be something else going on.' And there is something else going on. He's a fucking rock star."

"I still don't understand."

"She's in love with the monster you poor, beautiful idiot!"

"But you've been staring at this since," Purvis leans in and reads the time stamp on the recording, "almost an hour ago and you hadn't figured out she was staring at the monster?"

"No for God's sake! I knew she was staring at the monster, but I couldn't believe she was infatuated with him."

"Oh. Why?"

"Because he's a monster!"

"But you believe it now?" Purvis tilts his head to the side with a confused expression.

"Yes." Alacrán does not wait for Purvis to ask why. "Because now I know he is more than a monster, he is also a rock star!"

"Ohhhhhhhh. Because he is a rock star."

"Exactly," Alacrán says with his finger in the air.

"And you just now figured all this out?" Purvis asks again.

"You just told me he was a rock star!"

"Right!" Purvis holds his finger in the air, pointed towards the sky, unthinkingly mimicking his boss.

Alacrán begins pacing again. "I was going to be polite in this little endeavor. Honestly my pet. It was simply going to be a nice time all around." Now the old devil is entertaining himself. He speaks slowly, deliberately. "It appears however, that is not the way things are meant to be. It appears, things will have to be messy."

"Perhaps we should look into the situation, before we overreact."

"Oh we will," Alacrán agrees with a sinister grin. "We will look into it thoroughly. I want to know everything there is to know about that monster."

"Is that really necessary my liege? He is so inconsequential to you."

"Know your enemy Purvis."

"But..."

"Know your enemy," Alacrán repeats. "I want to know everything about him."

"Well there is a computer right here sir. Outside of inside sources for personal information, most everything we could learn about him is right in front of us."

"My boy, I want *you* to learn everything there is to know about him and then I want you to tell me. I do not want to read." This should not have needed explaining.

"Of course not."

"What the hell is wrong with you today?"

"I don't know."

"I am going into another room. I'm not yet sure which room so I am going to walk slowly." Alacrán begins his exit. "Get to work."

"Yes sir." Purvis starts pointing and clicking on the computer, putting on a show for his boss until he can escape. To his cheerful surprise, a female voice emits from the squawk-box on the wall. It is the front desk girl in Alacrán's office.

"Sir?" the secretary says.

"Yes my dear," Alacrán replies.

"There are two policemen here to see you," she says.

"You said policemen dear?"

"Yes sir."

"Delightful." Alacrán says casually. "Let the gentlemen know I will be right in, and if you have not already, offer them something to drink."

"Yes sir."

"Fire her," he commands Purvis. Alacrán frequently kills the messenger. "Then kill her."

"Yes sir." Purvis will do no such thing. He will reassign her and find another secretary. Again. *Add that to the list you sorry twerp*, he thinks.

"Now come on," Alacrán says. "Who knows what this is about? We'll deal with the monster and that two-timing hussy later." They head down a hallway that leads to an auxiliary exit, outside of Alacrán's office. "I've always wanted a personal reason to say that you know, 'two-timing hussy'. How did that feel?"

"It worked sir. How could it not? Although, I'm not sure the Princess' behavior is technically two-timing."

"Oh of course not," Alacrán agrees. "Simply turning a phrase my boy. I want to work it out a little bit."

"Well it suits you." Believe it or not, I'm pretty sure Purvis is sincere.

"You are a wonderful kiss-ass my dear."

"I know," Purvis says, then he smacks himself hard in the forehead. "Oh my God!"

"What," Alacrán asks, slightly startled.

"I don't know why we didn't think of it before, immediately."

"What?!"

"It's perfect! Oh you are going to love it," Purvis says with genuine excitement.

"If you don't tell me what you are talking about this instant I am going to murder you and bury you in the desert."

"Do you remember that priestess that lost a bunch of money at roulette, and you let her out of her debt to the casino if she agreed to provide you with spells, incantations, poisons and potions when you need them?"

"Ooh and those fantastic bath salts she makes," Alacrán replies. "Yes!"

"I do remember her and that reminds me. I am out of salts, and that foot-soak she made for me as well."

"My liege," Purvis gently grabs Alacrán by his shoulders. He speaks slowly. "It is my understanding she is currently in possession of a rather powerful batch of love potion."

Alacrán slowly nods his head in understanding, and Purvis watches as the recognition sets in.

"How powerful?" Alacrán asks, coyly.

"Powerful enough that you won't have to worry about some trashy rock and roll star," Purvis replies.

"My darling this is perfect!" Alacrán grabs Purvis' shoulders as well and shakes him with excitement. They hop about enthusiastically. "I am very excited," Alacrán squeals gleefully. "Very excited!"

Alacrán lets Purvis go and begins to wring his hands and lick his lips until a nice froth forms around them. The game is afoot. Anew. Alacrán is renewed. Now, what do the damn police want?

## 22

Sandy and Sammy continue their hunt for Zorn. The chase has already gone on too long. All three participants are suffering. Zorn is gassed. Sandy is gassy. Sammy's cocaine is wearing off.

After weaving through alleys, Zorn pops out onto a sidewalk in front of a movie theater. They're showing a movie he's eagerly anticipated for over a year! Zorn purchases a ticket then slinks inside. The film is a sci-fi/comedy out of Germany titled *It's Mein Kampf Too*.

Sammy and Sandy turn a corner in time to see the tails of Zorn's coat as he enters the theater. They park, which takes forever, then follow him in. They purchase tickets, splitting off in different directions once inside. Sandy is starving, so she buys a giant bag of popcorn and finds a movie to watch. It is a remake of course, but it looks halfway enjoyable. She longs for the days of Hollywood greatness she read about when she was a girl.

Sammy gets sucked into a war film after hearing a flurry of gunshots coming from a theater. He pokes his head into the room to see what all the fuss is about. On the screen is a film about the final war between the Mexicans and Canadians, or the Mexicadian Compromise, as it is known historically.

Sandy finishes her popcorn and decides she better go tell Sammy what to do. The stupid movie sucks anyway. About that same time, Sammy wakes up from having dozed off in his theater. Once he remembers what the fuck is going on, he leaves his seat to continue searching. Eventually they run into each other.

"Where have you been?" Sandy asks.

"Looking for the case. Where have you been?"

"Looking for you. Have you seen him?"

"Of course not," Sammy says flatly. "Don't you think I would have called you?"

"Where do you think he is?"

"How the hell should I know?" he snorts.

Sandy shakes her head, playfully mocking Sammy's ineptitude. "Well then let's keep looking. Shmuck." That last bit comes out more playful than mean. She is kind of digging her old boy under this new set of circumstances. He has a twinkle in his eye.

"Alright. Upstairs then. Work our way down," he says. "Mean ass." *Speaking of which, I'muh teach that ass a lesson later on*, he thinks. He watches her bound up the steps in front of him with a spring in her feet. *Old girl is still in pretty decent shape.*

Sandy and Sammy finally find Zorn. He is now watching a children's movie. The theater is otherwise empty. They make their way to the row directly behind Zorn without the demon noticing. He is completely enthralled by the film. Sandy and Sammy silently agree to let the villain finish his movie. When the credits roll they leap into action. Sandy grabs the demon by the shoulders in an attempt to pin him to his chair. Sammy's move is to hop over the seats into the row Zorn is seated in, attempting to grab the case. This requires an unfortunate amount of athleticism Sammy no longer has, and quite possibly never possessed.

Sammy fails miserably. He mistimes his step, landing his foot at the front of the folding movie house chair, which straightens out and stiffens. His knee locks up, and the leverage sends him flailing into the row in front of Zorn. To his credit, Sammy recovers quickly, popping back up into an awkward attack stance.

Zorn's only magical, demonic ability is a flash bomb of sorts. Basically his entire body authors a mini explosion. His skin flares bright with a giant puff cloud of pungent smoke. The affect is simply meant to disorient any assailant long enough for Zorn to run away. Using the magic weakens the demon temporarily. The level to which he is weakened is directly correlated to the size of the flash bomb he creates.

Zorn discharges a small flash bomb. It is enough to disorient Sammy and Sandy, yet leaves Zorn with enough strength to escape. He grabs the case and runs, screaming like a banshee. Zorn flails his way through the theater and back outside into the night.

Sammy and Sandy rally to their senses, initiating hot-pursuit mode again. They burst forth from the building onto the sidewalk, crashing through separate doors, practically tackling each other. A man stands on the curb smoking. Sammy looks up to see the man staring at him.

"Did you see…," Sammy says.

The man points to an alley near the movie theater. Sammy and Sandy head towards the entrance to the alley on foot, racing past their car and shouting a "thank you" to the helpful stranger. The stench of Zorn's flesh, leftover from igniting his flash bomb, leaves a trail they follow through the network of alleys.

They reach a four way intersection. The odor that created their path has faded. Sammy and Sandy turn in all four directions, listening for a clue. Sandy's face is beginning to make an expression Sammy does not enjoy when they hear a commotion.

They follow the noise for a minute before sneaking up behind a dumpster. They can see Zorn not far off, cowering against a fence.

He is surrounded by several other people that are mocking the poor creature and jabbing at him with sticks.

"Jesus Christ, it's teenagers," Sandy whispers.

"I hate teenagers," Sammy hisses back.

"What are we going to do?"

"I don't know. I want that case, but dear God I don't want to deal with a bunch of lunatic children."

"Well we have to do something. Look at the poor thing. I almost feel sorry for it."

"I completely feel sorry for it," Sammy says. "Teenagers are nasty creatures. Nasty."

"Remember when we were that age?"

"Yes, and I seem to remember we made it through puberty without turning into flesh eating ghouls for three years. When did that start happening anyhow?"

"I'll give you three guesses you old coot," she says. Then she kisses him.

"You got the Taser with you?" Sammy asks.

"Right here." Sandy pulls the Taser from her brassiere. Her boobs breathe sighs of relief.

"Lucky you didn't accidentally give the girls a jolt," Sammy says.

"Oh, I don't know." Sandy winks, showing him a cocky little grin.

Doodles slowly rousts from his Taser induced slumber as Sammy and Sandy are blasting forth from the movie theater. He watches as they speak briefly to some tall fellow and then run past the car into an alley near-bye.

He watches the man they are speaking with follow Sammy and Sandy with his eyes, tapping his ear and appearing to have a conversation. Despite his haziness, Doodles somehow knows this has something to do with Sammy and Sandy. Perhaps it is because the man naturally speaks with his hands. As the man relays the recent happenings to whomever is on the other end of his fucking Smear, he points to where Sammy and Sandy came from and subsequently went.

Doodles climbs into the front seat of the car and finagles with the wiring under the steering column. He digs his hand down near the gas and brake pedal, yanking wires free until he sits up with a handful of wires no longer connected to the car. He groans, banging his head three times against the steering wheel. He has no idea how to jumpstart a car.

The car starts. Doodles sits up, surprised. *How the hell?* he thinks.

Sammy and Sandy execute their plan. Sandy takes the right flank, slinking as close to the walls of the buildings as she can. She uses dumpsters, sleeping homeless people, and homeless peoples' homes to hide behind.

She will swoop in and rescue the case when Sammy creates the distraction. The plan actually includes rescuing the demon as well, who appears to be altogether un-demon-like with regards to being mean, nasty, powerful, scary, etcetera, etcetera.

Sandy is still not completely sold on that particular aspect of the plan. She told Sammy she "almost" felt sorry for him. She is presenting leaning more towards the "Fuck that guy. He stole from us. He can fend for himself," point of view.

Sammy's portion of the plan is distraction. He is going to bum rush the band of loathsome teenagers, zapping as many as he can with the stun gun before they know what hits them. Then, Sandy will scream bloody murder to disorient the teens further while Sammy runs off real quick. It isn't a well thought out plan. In their defense, they developed it under unreasonable time constraints.

Sammy figures he can get at least three of the teenagers with the Taser if his movements are exact and he gets the first shot in with a sneak attack. That will leave three more teens. If worse comes to worse he, Sandy and the demon will take their chances toe to toe.

Sandy hunkers down behind a dumpster, the closest one within short reach of the black case. Sammy is parallel to her, on the left hand side of the alley in a doorway. They look at each other and signal the mission is a go.

Sammy steps out, moving towards the backs of the teenagers. He holds his hands out from his sides, as if he were attempting to walk a tight rope. He's trying as hard as humanly possible to be as quiet as possible. It makes his sneak attack excruciatingly slow. Sandy huffs and puffs in contempt, waving her arm at him to speed up.

Before reaching his first victim, Sammy reaches his left hand into to his left pocket to retrieve the Taser. He probably should have already had the Taser in his hand and ready. In Sammy's defense of this entire situation, he is not a naturally violent, or sneaky, or mean, or nimble, or particularly strong man. He is very nervous though.

So, Sammy reaches into his left pocket to pull out the Taser and attack the nearest teenager. The Taser is in his right pocket. Sammy reaches into his left pocket, pulls out his car keys, holds them up against the back of the teenager's neck, and starts his car.

Meanwhile, in Sammy's car...

*Who cares! Let's go!* is Doodles' next thought. "Yahah! Yahah, yahah, yahah!" he screams. His eyes beam and he shakes his fists in triumph. He puts the car in drive, speeding off down the alley he watched Sammy and Sandy enter.

In his excitement, Doodles drives as fast as he can. Boxes fly. Bums scatter. Numerous dumpsters are sideswiped. He takes as many hard right turns as he can - it is a compulsion exercised since the time he was given his first tricycle - and only goes left when right is not an option. He pounds the horn of the car, drooling unwittingly, eyes ablaze with insanity.

The teenager Sammy snuck up on turns, grabbing Sammy by the wrist. He bares his sharp, mid-pubescent teeth with a twisted smile. His face is pale and pimply. He licks his lips and then bites down on

Sammy's pinky. Sammy screams bloody murder and drops his car keys.

"Oh baby!" Sandy screams. A flurry of obscenities erupts from her mouth as she charges toward the gang of teens. She lowers her shoulders and tackles the first teenager she reaches before he knows what hits him.

Sammy is still screaming in agony. As the boy who is holding Sammy's wrist leans in for another tasty finger, Sammy retrieves the Taser from his right pocket, smashes it into the teenager's eye and lights the juvenile ghoul's face up like a galdarned fuckin' Roman candle. The boy begins to convulse, grabbing at the Taser. Instead of pushing the Taser away his muscles seize up and he actually smashes it harder into his own face.

Sandy looks up and sees Zorn rising to his feet. He gathers the case and begins to sneak off.

"Oh no you don't you son of a bitch," she shouts. "You got my Sammy's finger bit off!" She rolls off the teenager she tackled, and leaps at the demon.

Sammy lets go of the Taser as the boy writhes about. The boy's friends all take a few steps back in surprise. Sammy watches in dazed amazement as the Taser appears to melt into the boy's flesh.

Meanwhile, behind the reeling boy, Sammy sees Sandy tackling the demon. He looks slightly to his left and sees the other four teens recovering their motivation to attack. They turn on him, fists clinched and pounding into palms. He also sees the teenager that Sandy tackled starting to get back up. And how in the world did she know how to tackle like that anyway? Then Sammy thoughts are interrupted by an incoming fist.

*Oh shit*, Sammy thinks as the first punch hits him in the left eye. That punch turns him to his right. He continues the turn on his own and attempts to run. Two teenagers almost get their hands on him, but he trips over his own feet. He crashes to both knees and falls forward face first, smashing his nose into the ground and breaking it. The boys begin kicking and stomping the poor man while he is down, but before they can get too many vicious blows in, something wonderful happens - I swear I had nothing to do with it.

Doodles McShane comes squealing around the corner in Sammy's car, eyes still ablaze, horn still blaring, and still moving left to right as much as forward. He sticks his head out of the window, screaming wildly. The boys atop Sammy look up in amazement.

Sammy tries to stand up to run again, but immediately collapses back to the ground. He looks up at the car baring down on him and rolls left over and over, barely escaping the path of the vehicle as it barrels into the boys, smashing into them like tenpins. The teenager struggling with the Taser is still writhing about as Doodles hits him at full speed, sending the boy and his light show flipping through the air, end over end, into a dumpster.

Sandy realizes she and Zorn are next on Doodles' hit-list. She bustles the demon up and out of the way. They barely escape being run over as Doodles slams into the wall behind them.

Doodles stomps on the brakes in time to keep from crashing at maximum speed. The car's thick rubber bumper absorbs the hit well, but the recoil jars Doodles. He bashes his forehead into the steering wheel. The airbag blows but doesn't inflate. The mini-explosion knocks Doodles unconscious yet again as the airbag falls limply from its housing.

Sammy rolls to a stop in time to see Doodles crash the car. He lays there in shock for a few moments, catching his breath, then pulls himself to his feet. His left hand is throbbing where his pinky should be. His entire face aches. Blood flows from his nose and the nub of his missing finger.

Sandy and Zorn get to their feet as well. Sandy kicks Zorn in the knee and he falls back to the ground with a grunt, holding his knee in both hands and whimpering.

"You stay down there," she says. "I don't know what I'm going to do with you yet."

Sammy finally makes it to his feet and is about to take his first step towards the car when he remembers the Taser. He retrieves if from the dumpster where the teenager landed. When he pulls the Taser out, an extremely unpleasant aroma wafts from the hole where the boy's eye had been. The sight and smell cause Sammy to vomit.

After he finishes puking, he makes his way over to Sandy, who is still standing over the demon with her little fists clinched.

"What are we going to do with him?" she asks.

"He looks harmless enough," Sammy replies. "Hey you. You want to be good and come along, or get left out here?"

"Why should we help him?" Sandy asks.

"He could be useful," Sammy says, as he helps the demon to his feet. "Come on fella. Help me get Doodles into the back seat." Then to Sandy. "I guess we ought to give him a name or something."

"How about shithead?"

Sammy laughs. "Oh God, that's making everything hurt worse."

"Baby, we better hurry," Sandy says. When Sammy looks over at her she motions to several of the teenagers who are beginning to recover.

"Oh shit," Sammy says. He and Zorn pull Doodles from the driver's seat and stuff him into the back. "I guess you can get in if you want to live," he says to the demon, "but if you try to steal my case again I'll kill you."

Zorn gets in the car, ignoring the murder comment.

Sammy turns to Sandy. "The keys! I dropped 'em when he bit my finger off!"

"Damn it Sammy," she replies. She runs over to the general area where his finger and the keys should be.

"Don't you say nothing to me old lady," Sammy shouts. "I got my damn finger bit off!"

Sandy recovers the keys, then sees Sammy's pinky off to the side where the kid spit it out. She runs over and scoops it up as she is making her way to the car. She puts the pinky in her pocket without thinking. "I'll drive. You need to get that hand wrapped up."

"Hurry up," Sammy says. "They're coming again."

Sandy looks over her shoulder and sees three teenagers headed their way. She plops down into the driver's seat and tries to start the car, but it won't turnover. "What's wrong with this piece of junk?"

"I don't know," Sammy shouts at her. "Did you put the key in?"

"Of course I put the key in!"

"Well you don't do that! Use the remote on the fob. The key hasn't worked in years." Sammy is rapidly looking back and forth between watching the teenagers approach and his own efforts to rip a shirt sleeve off of the unconscious Doodles to wrap his bleeding hand with.

"Are you kidding me? That makes no sense whatsoever," Sandy exclaims. "When did that happen?"

"It's been that way for years! You drive the car all the time, you know this! Start the damn car! They're coming!"

The teenagers begin pounding on the hood of the car. Zorn covers his eyes with both his hands like a child.

"I got it! Jesus! Don't use the key to start the car cause that doesn't work! Fuck!" Sandy starts the car with the key fob and throws it into reverse. "Hate this stupid car," she mutters.

They break free and turn around, making their way back through the maze of alleys to the main road. They wind up exiting the exact same alleyway they entered.

"Well I be damned," Sammy says.

There are twelve men blocking their path. They are standing with the man who pointed Sammy and Sandy in the direction of Zorn, outside the movie theater. They are all wearing the same suit. If Sammy and Sandy had not been in such a hurry earlier, they might have noticed the crest on the jacket of the man who had given them directions.

"Eastwoodians," Sandy hisses.

The Eastwoodians consider themselves a secular institute of advanced Universal knowledge and understanding. It is nothing at all like a cult or religion in their minds, despite the fact that the organization is hell bent on amassing power, endeavors to control people by offering a sound prescription of ceremonial dogma to provide people with happier lives that will help them achieve a greater social status in the afterlife, consistently perpetuates human aggression through hypocritical condemnation of the behavior of others with different sets - and sometimes the same sets - of core values, manipulates the recording of the world's history with avarice, and lastly, doesn't pay taxes despite being wildly profitable.

The organization was formed not long before the Rapture, but after the bombing of Hollywood. The bombing freaked out a lot of the top notch crazy rich people in Southern California. One such crazy rich person was named Constantine Hand. He founded the Eastwoodian organization based on the sentimental and spiritual undercurrents he felt were present in Clint Eastwood's later films. Under Constantine's leadership the Eastwoodian motto was: "The secret is in the seeking."

Like the Buddha, Constantine Hand never intended for what he started to become a religion. However, Constantine eventually died and the organization he formed was left behind to take on a life of its own. A twisted, insane, disfigured, disease ridden life. Rules were written, prophecies were foretold, tithes were collected and metaphorical lines in the sand were drawn to ensure that if you were a member you understood you were among the lucky few that their secular God truly favored.

The Eastwoodians survived the Rapture and ensuing apocalypse as an organization because it was the only religion besides Christianity the Rapture had not supposedly debunked. Most people agreed Eastwoodian theology could easily intermingle with the Rapture.

All of the Eastwoodian "scripture" is based on underlying themes in Eastwood's later films, starting with his greatest work, Unforgiven, in the year of our Eastwood 1992. The final prophecy of the ever expanding Eastwoodian Theology is that someday Mr. Eastwood will return from the afterlife and explain existence to us. The fact that Jesus returned first does not discount this possibility. In fact, it heightens the possibility, as Jesus' return proved there is indeed an afterlife that can be returned from. Besides, the current manifestation of Jesus doesn't seem to know exactly what is going on around here either, at least not as far as the Eastwoodians are concerned.

The Eastwoodian Las Vegas chapter's current leader, or High Cleric, is an aggressive sort who has taken the name Curt Southstone. After rising to the local seat of power, Curt worked tirelessly to network his influence into every aspect of Las Vegas, including the criminal underworld. His plan is to take over the city of Las Vegas. Once he has done so, the next step is the Eastwoodian National Organization. After that, who knows? Maybe the world. Curt has a dictatorial nose. It is large and equally as ruthless as it is commanding.

When Curt learns of the black case and its mysterious situation, he sees it as the perfect opportunity to begin his ascension to control of the city. Rumors of the case are spreading quickly, along with wild speculation as to what it might contain. Who knows what could be inside?

Around the city, people are tossing out fantastic ideas about the potential contents of the black case, like souls or a tiny planet. I overhear the cure for all disease. There are plenty of stories about something of more tangible financial value like precious stones or cash. Even the Pessimists and Contrarians join in the debate. I hear a Pessimist speculate that the case is nothing but a fancy lunch pail with a peanut butter sandwich inside and everyone is getting all worked up over nothing. Of course, the Contrarian disagrees.

There is even a rumor God is trapped inside the black case. Not true.

Anyway, what Curt Southstone recognizes immediately, is power, and although I hate to admit it he is probably correct. He knows it doesn't matter what's inside the case. All that matters is that he gets his hands on it. The case is power. Nobody ever has to know what's inside. He could have people so afraid of what might be inside or what might happen if they find out what's inside, that they'll be too terrified to ever open the damn thing. If he can obtain the case, he can turn it into some form of fulfillment of Eastwoodian prophecy. He can also use it to expose the weakness of the current reigning criminal elements. He would position himself as the city's savior while at the same time insert himself as the new leader of the illegal underworld that currently controls Las Vegas. It is brilliant, at least as far as Curt Southstone is concerned.

FYI, Curt Southstone is not particularly important to this particular story, so you may not hear any more about him. My buddy Gus thought it was important that I give you a little insight as to why the Eastwoodians are so determined to get their hands on the case. So there you have it. Cheers.

Once alerted by the first dude, who we will call Larry, a group of Eastwoodians gather in front of the movie theater. Larry explains he may have found the black case. The Eastwoodians are about to enter the alley in search of Sammy and Sandy when they are surprised by the car's arrival.

"We can't let them stop us," Sammy says. "Step on it."

"You're damn right," Sandy says. She stomps the gas pedal through the floor. The tiny little car's tires spin and squeal before it shoots forward. The Eastwoodians dive out of the way, then quickly leap to their feet, running to their scooters to chase after the BCG.

The BCG is short for the Black Case Gang which is how I will now often refer to Sammy, Sandy, Doodles and Zorn, instead of having to say Sammy, Sandy, Doodles and Zorn every time I talk about them.

"We've got to find some place to hide," Sammy says. "Then maybe we can see if we can get that case open."

"I have an idea," Sandy says. "It's not far from here."

"Good. Ditch these jerks and get us there."

"Nobody will think to look where I am going," Sandy continues.

"That's great but you know it didn't really follow what I said to you," Sammy says quizzically.

"What?" Sandy asks.

"Well, I said to ditch those guys and you went on about where we were going but that didn't really logically follow what I said."

"It's the middle of the apocalypse and you still find a way to ruin everything," Sandy says dryly. Then she sighs loudly for dramatic effect and makes a hard left turn, bumping Sammy's head into his window.

Sammy starts to speak again then clamps his mouth back shut. Finally he decides on how to continue and says, "You look like some sort of crazed, sexy, race car driving biker bitch right now. Where you taking us?"

Now that was a compliment! Sandy smiles. "The library," she says. "And when we get there, you are getting laid old man."

"Nice," Sammy says. "Wait. The library?"

# 23

William Rockefeller the Third sits on his grand, gaudy throne, wishing alcohol still affected his thought processes as it had before his transformation. He needs a head change. There are plenty of drugs available designed for the undead but none of them, not one, has the same relaxing satisfaction a warm sip (or two or three) of bourbon had when he was alive.

The Princess' holographic image once again hangs above his desk. He is at a loss. He has never yearned so dramatically for a female, especially a female he has never met. Certainly not since his time as a father. It's a lot of work being the head of his household. Maybe it's time his children have a new mother? Maybe. Maybe not. Billy sighs. He has a gut feeling this situation is not going to end as he wants. For Billy the Third, where the female species is concerned, it never does.

Billy's thoughts are interrupted by a rap at his office door. His contemplative trance is broken as the door starts open without any wait for approval, the knock simply a warning rather than a request for entry. Billy closes the holographic image of Princess Tiara, clearing his throat conspicuously as Lord Sweetwater enters the room.

"Jack, you never knock," Billy says. "Is something amiss?"

"Everything my father," Sweetwater replies. "Everything is amiss. The knock was an act of cordiality."

"Jack, what are you talking about?"

"I couldn't hear what I was walking into so I figured I would let you know I was coming in. It's been a long time since I entered a room and did not know what I was walking into." Sweetwater looks genuinely flustered. Billy decides not to remind him of how often his intuitions are mistaken. He enjoys a good teasing, but he does not pick on his children. Jack Sweetwater is distraught over something.

"What's wrong?" Billy asks. "Is there something I can help you with my son?"

"Perhaps dad, perhaps. Shall I tell you of the progress of our grand scheme first?"

"You do as you feel fit. Your pale face worries me."

"I am out of sort father, but I won't ruin the fun of the day," Sweetwater replies.

"Fair enough. Has the case been located?"

"No my lord," Sweetwater says. "It still eludes the masses, but we have scouts throughout the city. I have no doubt that it shall be located with appropriate timeliness."

"What news do you have then?"

"Father, I am almost certain I saw the Princess with Alacrán's main hand, the poor trailer boy." Sweetwater and Billy have always found Alacrán's love for his trailer trash trinket wildly incongruous and laughable. Yes, the creature is handsome, but he was born of such paltry circumstances that Billy and Sweetwater consider him worthy of plaything status at best. They found Alacrán's elevation of Purvis to second-in-command status rather tacky. Billy and his children are very diligent in their efforts to behave as elitists. Of course, that effort does little to actually counter balance what dorks they are.

"Interesting," Billy says. He strokes a chin beard that is not actually there. "And you are sure it was her?"

"Nearly certain father. We were in a spot near the big hole where beats flow, beer brews and coffee perks. They were on their way out on our way in, and they appeared to be more than old friends."

"Do you know what was going on?"

"We were there to scoop the lowdown on the black case," Sweetwater says. "The situation caught me surprised. I chose to stay my course rather than chase. We questioned the room though. No stone was left unturned, and no heart was left beating."

"Intriguing. What part do you think Alacrán's man may play?" Billy wonders. "Could there already be a tryst in our midst? Perhaps the potion will be unnecessary after all." Billy doesn't believe his own words. At this point, he has almost admitted to himself his true plans for the love potion.

"Oh, I don't know father. Why waste such a fetching instrument, when it is already a bird in the hand." Sweetwater claps his hands twice and the barista from Dante's Brew enters the room. She carries a small, plush, ornate pillow. Atop it sits a beautiful crystal vial. The vial is filled with a purplish liquid.

"Who is this Jack?"

"My new child, father," Sweetwater admits. "I mean to discuss her further with you shortly, if that conversation may wait for the moment."

"It may." Billy is curious, but not enough to ignore the grander plot at hand. "Am I to assume this is our cherubic potion? Our liquid love? Our implement of destruction for Alacrán's plans of lustful abduction?"

"The very one," Sweetwater says.

Billy makes his way from behind his desk over to the insane young woman holding the vial. He plucks the vial from its perch atop the pillow and holds it delicately in front of his face. He opens the top and waves the aroma from the bottle to his nose. The liquid is beautiful. It smells like flowers and honey. The scent inspires lovey-dovey thoughts, and insists you drink the potion. This seals the vampire's romantic doom.

Billy carries the vial back behind his desk. He goes through an unrehearsed routine of opening and closing drawers interspersed with random pushing of buttons on the desk's command console. He looks up at Jack Sweetwater and the barista and says, "hey, what's that over there," causing them to turn away so Billy can finally deposit the bottle of love potion in secrecy. The potion is his key to obtaining his newfound desire. He can't let anything happen to it.

When Sweetwater realizes what Billy was doing, he looks at his father with a pained expression on his face.

"Oh Jack," says Billy, "Don't take offense. That had nothing to do with you." Billy whistles, then nods two times quite obviously at the girl with the pillow. Then he raises his eyebrows and his hands, palms up.

"I understand my father, although I am fairly certain my new sweet can be trusted with impliciticity."

"You know I trust your judgment Jack," Billy consoles. "Forgive me."

"Not necessary," Sweetwater replies. "Darling, would you mind waiting for me outside?"

The girl nods her head and leaves the room.

"So what is that all about Jack?"

Sweetwater collapses into a chair and sighs heavily. "I am boggled father. The girl is an enigma. She is legion. She has too many bats in her belfry."

"I think I understand."

"She's a fucking nutbag."

"Yes, I was certain that was the room you were checking into."

"It's like a freaking car accident or a person with a chopped off arm or the ghost of a suicide victim. You know you should not stare but you do anyway because it is so damned…," Sweetwater searches for the correct word, "…attractive. But it is wearing me thin father. I can't escape her crazy thought train. It rambles through my brain without rails."

"I'm sorry my child," Billy says sincerely. "I am fatigued. Your metaphors are unfortunately cumbersome right now."

"No, I'm sorry father," Sweetwater laments. "I am trying to say that I am unhealthily love sprung. She is crazy, has multiple personalities, and I have fallen for every one. I am obsessed with her mess. To make things worse her many voices have assaulted my psychic abilities. I can't hear anyone but her, and I'm afraid she is driving me as insane as she is."

"I see. I fear we are similarly afflicted," Billy says.

"You have developed psychic intuition and fallen in love with a paranoid schizophrenic with multiple personality disorder as well?" Sweetwater asks. To be clear, he is not being a smart ass.

"No, it's far worse than that Jack. I believe I have fallen in love with Princess Tiara Lioness." Billy whispers the Princess' name.

"Oh no."

"Oh yes," Billy confirms. "I have now turned my intentions towards using the witch's love potion to make the Princess fall in love with me."

"Father, I think she is already in bed with Alacrán's man."

"Then it better be a damn good potion," Billy states flatly.

"Indeed."

"And that brings us to another question Jack."

"Yes, I suppose it does," Sweetwater agrees, although he isn't sure what that question may be.

"What do you think their game is, Lord Sweetwater?" Billy is hopeful Sweetwater has already pondered the situation to some reasonable end. Unfortunately, he has not.

"I'm not sure father," Sweetwater admits. "My thoughts have been so clouded. I am deeply tweaked."

"Well we must figure it out," Billy says. "What in the world could be going on between Princess Tiara and that twerp Purvis? Do you think it has something to do with the case, or is it simply coincidence?"

"Father, I almost never believe in coincidence."

"Me neither. So, it is safe to assume that the Princess and the effeminate pretty boy not only have something to do with the missing case, but are also romantically involved."

"If you choose to assume the worst father."

"Which is exactly how we prepare in times of war my child, and that is what we have here," Billy explains. "We are at war with

Alacrán. My intentions are to win before he knows the war has begun."

"What is our next move my master?"

"There are two objects of desire dancing about this city. If we can't have one then we must have the other."

"Yes father." Sweetwater is mildly confused. "Which one is which again my lord?"

"Until we can get our hands on that case I believe our next move is to get our hands on the Princess," Billy answers. "We have the wicked serum. If she is truly enthralled with Alacrán's stable boy, then we must isolate her, poison her, and present her to the Spaniard already enraptured. My true heart's desire would be to do so at the same time we tell him we have stolen his precious case as well."

"It will be beautiful," Sweetwater says encouragingly. "I suppose the next question is, when and where do we lay our trap for the royal brat?"

"I have an idea." Billy allows himself a tiny "hmph" of a laugh. He leans back and puts his feet up on his desk. He clasps his hands behind his head. He smiles. "Yes Jack. This is going to be very wild."

# 24

Well, thinks Jack22, *this is going to suck*. Old Jack22 has learned everything there is to know about Earth. Suddenly, he isn't certain he is happy to be alive. But then he feels something...

Wait a second. That's not where we are. Where were we? Oh, here we go:

Jack22's plan is in motion. He placed a fake requisition order for a dealer robot to be used in the hotel showgirls' lounge act, sending for a service cart to move him to the theater costume department. Once he is alone in the costume room, his fashion show begins. Put some music on while you read the next paragraph. This is an "in the dressing room mirror" montage moment, so something catchy, up-tempo. Count Rock's cover of "I'm Too Sexy" would work nicely.

Jack22 tries on a lady pirate outfit but decides it is too auspicious. Also disarmingly close fitting. There is a mermaid costume he knows is too cumbersome to utilize, but he can't help himself. He spends a fair amount of time rolling around on the floor pretending to be a lady fish. It's a healthy exercise for him.

Jack22 tries on a smashing red dress, and earnestly likes the way it feels, but something isn't quite right. It's the shoes. This dress deserves the correct shoes. If he had noticed the bright red leather stilettos sitting in the corner of the room, we would have had a cross-dressing robot the rest of the story.

Jack22 models costumes for close to an hour when he hears a noise in the hallway. He flees through the first set of doors he can find on the other side of the room. They lead into a short hallway, then he ducks into another door where he discovers another room full of clothing. It dawns on him the door is labeled Men's Costumes as it swings shut behind him. *Oh*, he thinks. *I am shaped like a man. This makes much more sense.*

Jack22 stands in front of a mirror admiring his ensemble. Keep in mind, Jack22 is constructed with a tuxedo facade. It is a permanent fixture. To go atop his regular getup, he has selected a black leather vest, fully buttoned, with a motorcycle company logo on the lapel. He wears a pair of light brown sheepskin, assless chaps, along with a pair of black, spurred boots. After some difficulty figuring out what to do with a thin black strip of artificial hair he found, he noticed some cast photos from a former production on the wall, and understood what the hair was for. His upper lip now sports a magnificent handlebar mustache. The entire ensemble is capped off by a white, ten gallon hat. Our friendly robot is a midnight rhinestone cowboy.

Satisfied with his new persona, he tips his hat to his reflection in a mirror, puts on his lab coat and heads for engineering. *Phase three is a go. I repeat, phase three is a go.*

Jack22's disguise works perfectly. He makes his way through the building to central engineering. When he arrives, he is surprised to see central engineering almost completely empty. There is a single technician asleep at his station. The technician lays across the control panel in front of him with his head resting on his arms, snoring quietly.

*Curious, the people in this building never seem to be doing their job,* Jack22 thinks. *Only the robots.* He finds a control panel to the building's mainframe and plugs himself in. He downloads every file in the system, which includes the building's schematics. During the transfer, he opens a file labeled robot manuals, searching for his own instructions. He discovers he is fitted with a transmitter capable of accessing the mainframe at any time from any location. This also allows him continual access to the world's internet.

Jack22 finishes downloading the building's files while he is hard-wired. Once the transfer is complete, he heads back to his closet, but not before he places the sleeping engineering employee's hand into a glass of warm water.

...and this brings us to now. Jack22 is thinking, *Well, this is going to suck*.

The history of our world races through his mind. The cavedicks and cavebitches. The fantasies and wars. The fucking and fighting and fleeing. The adorable puppies. The dead babies. All the insanity and the collective reality. The drugs. The religions. Holy shit the religions. Holy shit the drugs. And for that matter, holy shit the wars!

He cannot escape all the miracles. He cannot hide from all the tears. He cannot ignore all the madness. He cannot run from all the smiles. He cannot help but to hope he has a soul. His intellect ages hundreds of years.

Jack22 is not built for this. *I'm a robot*, he thinks. *I'm a machine. I'm a mechanism. I'm an alien. I was never meant for any of this. I did not ask for this.*

That last thought signifies an early emotional baby step toward Jack22 becoming a real person. Self-pity. Nobody asks for it Jack. Not one of us asked to be born.

The thoughts keep coming, racing through his mind. It's insanity. He is amazed the Earth has not already blown up. Of course, he quickly realizes the whole place has sort of blown up, being in the midst of an apocalypse and what not.

He wonders if there is a way for him to truly understand all these things he is learning without experiencing them for himself. Then he decides he will never truly be able to understand what other people are going through. *There is no other like me. I am surrounded by sentient creatures and I am completely alone.*

Jack22's fledgling emotions are controlling what his mind considers. He keeps shifting through images of pain, hunger, loss and desperation. Then, all of a sudden, he stumbles upon information about heroes. Countless heroes. There is a particular hero Jack22 finds the most inspiring. Why did he like this guy the most? I don't know, and neither does Jack22. It really doesn't matter.

He isn't sure if the character is based on a person that actually lived, or is completely fictional. At this point history is too uncertain. All Jack22 knows is the guy is cavalier, and proactive. He has a flare for thumbing his nose at authority, and in some circumstances loves a good song and dance routine. He is often depicted in film as a man who enjoys a good pair of tights, typically green in color, and is a heck of a marksmen with a bow and arrow.

Jack22 now has a grander purpose. A purpose to serve the world around him. He isn't simply going to rob the casino. Oh no. He is going to rob the casino, and then give all the money away. Yes! That's the stuff legends are made of. And movies. Book deals. Merchandising…

# 25

Alacrán makes a grand entrance to his own office. It is entrance number 12A in Purvis' manual. Yes, Purvis has an Evil Executive Assistant manual. Yes, it actually says Evil on the cover of the book. There is an entire chapter written by Alacrán's friend and mentor Jericho Primm, AKA the Scourge of Sandusky, AKA MC Murder Death Kill, AKA the Mangler of Many Names, AKA the guy Alacrán swindled and killed to become the owner of La Ciudad de Oro and Las Vegas' resident most ruthless villain.

This particular entrance involves Alacrán flinging the double doors to his office open in a magnificent sweeping motion as Purvis bustles in behind him, announcing his master's presence with the help of a bullhorn. Purvis feigns shortness of breath, creating the illusion that no one can keep up with Alacrán. This also helps create a general atmospheric sense of urgency. The purpose is to place Alacrán's adversaries on the edge of their uncomfortable guest seats.

"Gentlemen! Welcome. So nice to see you again." Alacrán speaks without an ounce of sincerity.

Dan sits with his back turned in a chair across the room, facing Alacrán's desk. Nico relaxes against a wall, obviously pretending not to have been investigating the room for secrets. He clears his throat conspicuously with an arrogant smirk on his face.

"Hello Flacido," Dan says without turning to face his opponent.

"Marshal, is that you? My hearing isn't quite what it used to be. Let me cross the room so we may converse." Alacrán looks at Nico. "Check this out," he says to the Deputy.

Alacrán claps his hands. A harness lowers from the ceiling, attached to two cables. Nico looks up to see an impressive network of tracks hidden within the ornate decorations of the ceiling. Purvis straps the harness to Alacrán. He presses a button on his control pad and Alacrán flies into the air.

Alacrán raises straight up, pointing a finger at Nico as if he just dunked on him in a basketball game. He slowly rotates forward and flies across the room in a Superman pose, fist outstretched, as bombastic classical music blares through the room's stereo system. As he nears his desk he does a forward roll, then rotates to face Dan, straightening back up into a standing posture with his arms crossed as the winch lowers him into the chair behind his desk. He pushes a single button on the front of the harness and it detaches, flying away back up into the ceiling. He leans forward placing his elbows on the table, resting his chin on his clasped hands. He smiles coyly at Dan.

"That was pretty neat," Dan says dryly.

"Yes," Alacrán agrees. "You should have a system installed."

"I would need a bigger office I think."

"That's right. You would."

"Government salary and what not…"

"They still make those?" Alacrán asks.

Dan smiles. "Say, you wouldn't be up to no good right now would you?" Dan asks the question with a glint in his eye that Alacrán can't ignore.

"Always," he says. "Surely you aren't this bored?" Alacrán waits a beat, a precise moment of time and then, "Are you?"

Nico displays his excellent sidekick intuition. He breaks from the wall he leans against in an act of impatience, noticeably stomping his foot, then makes his way across the room, coming to rest against the opposite wall. Purvis and Alacrán both watch in anticipation, but Nico simmers down.

"Are you aware there were two men murdered at the airport this morning?" Dan asks.

"Of course," Alacrán admits. "Marshal I know everything that happens in my city."

"Well then, I don't suppose you would have any trouble helping us out with a little information?" Dan asks.

"Oh I don't know. I think I would most likely have a great deal of trouble with that." Alacrán lightly sneers.

Dan calmly uncrosses then re-crosses his legs. "We understand the Princess is a guest here. We have reason to believe her safety may be an issue."

"I can assure you, with utmost confidence, that as long as she is a guest of La Ciudad de Oro, her safety is of no concern."

Nico escapes the wall again. Purvis looks up from his perch in the back of the room. Alacrán averts his eyes from their lock with Dan's. He attempts to hide his nervous reaction to Nico's sudden movement. Nico comes to rest beside the empty chair to Dan's left. He stops with his hands on his hips defiantly, slightly rocking back and forth on his heels. Purvis and Alacrán hang on his movements. Their shoulders metaphorically slump as recognition sets in that Nico has come to a full stop. Damn it. Where is it?

Alacrán stands and begins putzing about behind his desk, adjusting trinkets on shelves, pretending to be distracted by notes and papers that lay about. He decides to take the conversation in a new direction to gain a tactical advantage. "Honestly Marshal, I simply don't understand why you do what you do."

"I suppose that's what makes you, you, and me, me," Dan replies.

"But here you sit Marshal," Alacrán continues, "investigating the murders of two obviously dispensable men while no one else cares. I would venture to bet at least 10 more people have been killed since you have been seated in my office. Those men are probably happier right now, in whatever state they are in, than they were when they were alive. Their great question has been answered."

"If that is the case, then I suppose my partner and I will have more work to do," Dan says. "Ten more murders to solve that is. Which means, I have less time to spend enjoying our conversation."

Alacrán picks up an ancient dagger and taps the point with his finger. "Marshal, we are in the middle of the apocalypse and you are still running around trying to solve these silly little crimes. Isn't it inconsequential, all this nonsense?"

"Not to me."

Alacrán sighs melodramatically. "Well it appears to be to everyone else. Now, as much as I enjoy our visits I must admit I am an extremely busy man, as you well know."

"You know why we are here," Dan continues. "If you have no involvement in what happened at the airport this morning, any information you can share to aid our investigation would be a great show of faith."

"I honestly don't know anything about it. The murders, or faith. We were simply too busy preparing for Princess Tiara's arrival. I learned of the entire airport situation shortly before your visit." Alacrán makes no attempt to disguise that he is lying, looking away as he speaks. His hope is to get under Dan's skin. The person he's pissing off is Nico.

"Well, you're on notice." As Dan speaks Nico moves behind the chair Dan is seated in and crosses his arms over his chest. Dan stands. "If you are involved, just know, I'm not letting this go." Dan leans forward, placing his hands on Alacrán's desk. "I haven't hurt anyone in almost a month. I'm getting itchy."

"Ooh." Alacrán turns to face his competitor. "I like that." He leans in, placing his hands on his desk to go face to face with Dan, locking eyes, but the instant he does he wilts and quickly becomes uncomfortable. He stands back up straight, pulling at the collar of his shirt.

Dan moves a hand quickly to his ear as he stands straight again. Alacrán flinches. Dan winks at Alacrán as he answers his Smear. "This is Dan," he says.

Alacrán turns in an act of disgust and dismissal, insulted by Dan taking a call in his office. This makes Nico smile.

"Understood," Dan says. "We're on our way." Dan turns his attention back to the villain. "It looks like we have to cut our visit a little short," he says to Alacrán. "Come on Nico, there are more pressing matters that require our attention."

"I think I'm insulted," Alacrán says. "I thought I was always your most pressing matter."

"Good," says Dan dryly, turning to leave the office.

Nico takes a moderately aggressive step towards Alacrán, then unceremoniously turns on his heals to follow his boss. It is a little titillating, but not what Alacrán and Purvis are hoping for.

"I'll be keeping an eye on you." Dan speaks without turning around, still walking towards the exit.

"A pretty self-righteous eye if you ask me." Alacrán mumbles, sort of coughing a little while he speaks, raising his hand to his mouth to further muffle his words.

Dan and Nico both stop in mid-stride.

"I'm sorry, what was that?" Nico asks.

"Nothing," Alacrán replies. "Did you hear something? I didn't say anything. Purvis, did you say something?"

"Yeah, that's what I thought." Nico looks back over his shoulder at Alacrán. Alacrán reacts with anticipation, but it still doesn't come. Nico and Dan begin walking towards the exit again.

"One more question before you go Marshal, if I may?" Alacrán says.

Dan and Nico don't stop walking this time. Damn it is a long ass room. Long. Ass. Room.

"Whatever," Dan sighs.

"If you're so great, how come you didn't get to go wherever it is great people were supposed to go when the Morningstar returned? How come all of you goody goodies are still down here with the rest of us?"

"Perhaps, it is because there is still a war to win versus pieces of excrement such as yourself," the Marshal growls.

"Well, it appears the 'excrement' is winning," Alacrán says with a smile. Giddy little toy-boy squeaks chuckle from his mouth.

"I think now is the time," Dan says under his breath to Nico, but it has already begun.

Nico takes a power step forward then stomps hard on his slick heels, causing a ten foot slide across Alacrán's obsidian flooring. Out of nowhere the office lights dim and a spotlight hits Nico.

As Nico slides he throws his arms straight out to his side allowing his jacket to flare behind him. He then crosses his arms, pulling two large revolvers from their holsters as he starts to spin. He twirls the guns on his fingers with his arms outstretched as his body does a full 540 rotation.

Purvis' jaw drops and his eyes bulge.

"Magnificent," Alacrán whispers.

Nico re-holsters both weapons as his rotation comes to a stop, facing Alacrán. He points his finger at the villain, arm outstretched as he speaks. "You know there's a big hole downtown you should see sometime. It's a retirement home for evil assholes. You're going to love it."

Alacrán smiles tightly. A little sweat trickles down his temple. Nico heads for the exit. As he passes by Purvis, Nico points his finger at him like a gun and pulls the trigger.

Purvis shudders, wearing a "what did I do" expression.

As Nico leaves he grabs the handles to the two giant doors and sets them in motion to slam shut behind him.

Purvis relaxes and slumps his shoulders in exasperation.

Alacrán is clearly aroused. "I am absolutely moist. Did you see that Purvis? I love that guy!"

Outside Nico finds Dan waiting for him in the lobby to Alacrán's office. "You didn't stay to watch?" he asks.

"I trust you," Dan replies. "Now, we've got to get downtown. Someone murdered an entire craft beer and coffee house full of people. Looks like it may have been the Karowack Kids."

"This case just keeps getting better," Nico says with enthusiasm. "Man I am glad I woke up today."

"People were murdered Nico. Don't be callous."

"Right. Sorry boss."

"No need to apologize my friend. We will put that enthusiasm to good use. Now let's get going. I have a feeling this mess is just getting started."

"I'm with you, boss. Right behind you." Nico would follow Dan straight into the mouth of Hell if Dan asked, which is good, because as you know, Dante's Brew is a few blocks away from the actual hole to Hell.

# 26

We are flashbacking with the aliens again. It is still two years ago. They just finished making like love monkeys. Hook lays in a state of fright. All of his confidence has been drained. It is a common post-coital response for Valtrucians. He is on the verge of tears.

Lia on the other hand, is fully empowered. She is now capable of functioning at optimum levels for an unspecified amount of time. She is smoking a cigarette while encouraging Hook to continue massaging her. He does so halfheartedly.

*This is such horseshit*, he thinks. *Every Bobdamn time, I cry. Ridiculous!*

"We have got to come up with a plan," Lia says, interrupting Hook's thoughts.

"I agree, but I have no idea what to do."

"Well, there has got to be something we can do," she replies. "I like this planet and I like these people. I am not going to let the Council destroy them all."

"I don't know. The humans are sort of apish. Honestly they're very unintelligent. They're smelly. They are extremely over-emotional. They make a big deal out of everything."

"Oh you're just tired. You love the humans."

"But that's the point. I'm not sure I want to," he protests.

"But isn't it fun? Come here." She butts her cigarette, pushes herself up in the bed, and pulls him over to her. She wraps her naked legs around him while massaging his shoulders. "You need a little rest after all this exercise. Then you will be ready to save an entire planet."

"Yeah. I suppose." He is slowly coming around.

Lia kisses his neck and nibbles on his earlobe a bit. He feels a little inspiration.

"Think about it," she says. "We are going to completely disobey the Council. No Valtrucian has ever done that. Ever. Isn't that exciting? We will be legends."

Hook can feel the energy coming from her as she speaks.

"Why would we want to be legends?" Now he is messing with her. Despite his current lack of spunk, he likes it when Lia shows this level of confidence.

"I guess those dirty humans are rubbing off on me." She runs her hands through his hair.

"There has got to be some way to buy some more time. We need more time to figure out a solid plan to make the Council see the humans should live."

"So we need a plan to create time to make a plan?" She reaches around and covers his eyes with her hands. "Do you see it?" she giggles.

"Yep, that's pretty much it," he says. He pulls her hands away then rolls over to look at her. "But all I see is you." He gathers her in his arms and rolls onto his back, pulling her over on top of him at the same time. He is playing with her breasts like a teenage boy when she smacks his hands away.

"Wait a second," she says. She sits up straight like a wary rabbit in the woods. Her eyes become very intense. They dart back and forth as if she is reading something.

"What is it?" he asks.

"I have an idea. I remember something."

"Well what is it?"

"Hang on a second I'm reading."

"Reading what?" He looks over his shoulder.

"Nothing goofball. My memory. It was a statute in the manual."

"Which manual?" He is not playing dumb, being cute or simply not remembering something. They were inundated with manuals for their mission.

"The Expeditionary Procedures Manual," Lia says. "There is a provision that states that we have the ability to appeal any direct command from the Council, or any higher ranking officer, when on an off-world mission."

"Really? Why would they do that?" Hook asks. "Did you really read all those manuals?"

"It's the guise of democracy," Lia says. "Yes."

"Right. How?"

"I read very fast."

"That's pretty impressive," he says. Hook sits quietly as he refocuses and thoughtfully, contemplatively, reaches up to hold Lia's breasts again. The light bulb in his mind switches on. "They will deny the appeal and tell us to do what they told us to do in the first place."

"It's genius really," she says. She leans forward, kissing her way up his shoulders and neck.

"Yeah. Wait. If they do that, what is the point in filing the forms in the first place?" He still hasn't fully received his wits back from the sticky fingered cupid who is floating about the room.

"It's the plan to give us more time to come up with another plan silly. Remember? It will take Bob knows how many years for our official appeal to be received by the Council. We will send it by homing pod."

"Right. Old-timey mail. That's great."

"Then it will take the Council years of deliberation before they make a decision on our request. Look at how many Earth years it took to receive their response to our first report. And who knows. They may actually agree with us!"

"I guess that's possible."

"Absolutely it is. We have no idea what Bob could be revealing to them right now!" Her hands gain speed as she caresses his body. "It will take the Council years to send a response. You never know. By the time they make a decision, the Earth's apocalypse may be over." She gives him a not so gentle slap on the face. "But that's not very likely," she says with a pout, tapping at his nose with her finger.

"You know," he says. "Before we met the humans we would never have planned such a clever deception. We would have killed them after we got the response to our first report."

"Before we met the humans we would have never disobeyed the Council in the first place," she agrees.

"But we did," Hook realizes. "We denied our first orders all on our own. Granted, it wasn't an open act of rebellion at the time. It was confusion, but still, we didn't follow orders."

"Oh my Bob you're right. We're already bad ass rebels!"

"You're damn right we are," he says. "All of Valtruca is going to know too. Our appeal letter will be equally as bad ass. We're going to knock the Council's socks off."

"Well, well," she says. "My big bad Valtrucian is back."

"You're damn right he is."

"I love it when you get that look in your eye. Pleasure me again with your big thingy you sexy horse." Lia is still working on her human style dirty talk.

"Nope. I can't lose anymore cantabaloids right now," he says. "I need them."

"But I want to." She pouts. At that moment it is the loveliest thing Hook has ever seen.

"Don't worry momma," he replies. "I have a treat for you. Something I learned from those dirty humans."

"Ooh," she coos. "I like the sound of that."

"Watch this," he says, then he picks her up and gives her a seat on his eager face. He doesn't actually know what to do after that. In the end, after a lengthy, albeit partially muffled discussion, the situation works itself out.

## 27

Rancid Pete wakes up in extreme pain. "Anyone seen the buffalo that shit in my mouth," he mumbles.

"Was that a buffalo?" some unknown fucker from across the hotel suite responds. There had been no buffalo. Pete's comment was a metaphor implying bad breath.

"Are you alive?" Pete asks.

"Yes."

"Then shut the fuck up and get out of here. Now." Pete tries to raise his head in an effort to see what is going on in his suite, but he can't. It hurts. His eyes can't handle the light when open. His head feels like it is trapped in a fat lady's thighs. It is a fleshy c-clamp, and the chubby bitch won't stop turning the crank. Do you know the amount of alcohol and other assorted intoxicants required to make the infamous monster Rancid Pete feel this hungover?

For a while he can't think at all. His concentration centers on pain in a specific region of his brain. He tries to lay as still as possible. He wishes for a glass of water and the ability to drink it without having to move. He hates himself.

Rancid Pete begins the long journey through his mind to the place where short term memories are held. It is a dimly lit path. There is a solid four hours of time from the night before that he is certain he was awake for, but his memory is filled with nothing but blur. He trudges through this haze further back, earlier in the evening. It all started at the stadium.

That's right. He met Jesus. Not really such a big deal as people make out. He remembers Jesus was extremely cool, and being around him was real easy. Yeah, he felt immense peace when dude was around. That was real.

Once he left the stadium, for whatever reason, Pete felt another hole inside to fill. He remembers feeling weary, and deciding to get wasted. He is currently re-evaluating the merits of that decision.

There is a mirror above Pete's bed. In it he can see the naked, mangled bodies of several young women and a few particularly handsome young men. They are strewn about the floor surrounding the bed. Rancid Pete has seen worse.

He feels something poking him in the back. He reaches around and fishes out a female's severed arm. He contemplates it for a second, deciding if he is hungry. His stomach turns at the idea, so he lazily tosses the arm aside, disgusted with himself. Man he wants a glass of water.

"Hey fucker?" Pete says. "You still over there?"

No response.

*Damn it.*

Pete finally has the gumption to rise up in bed. He closes his eyes and sits up, crossing his legs in a meditative pose. He takes ten deep breaths. In through the nose, out through the mouth. Christ his head hurts.

"You going to do anything about this?" he asks no one, staring at the ceiling of the room. He laughs at himself, then winces at the pain.

The room is in standard condition for the night *after* a show. Not the day of a show. He briefly laments his revelry, not over moral qualms for his behavior, but rather the depleted physical state he has left his body in with a performance coming soon. Rancid Pete is a consummate professional.

He renews his meditation. Pete remembers playing the tables at La Ciudad de Oro. That's where he wandered off to after he left the stadium. He supposes he was hopeful he might somehow run into the Princess. You suppose Rancid Pete? You know damn well that's what you were doing.

He remembers some crazy robot. Yeah. There was a robot there playing cards and yucking it up. He was dressed like a cowboy. That's right. No one seemed to notice he was a robot except Pete and this ghost that was at the table for a while. The robot had this giant fake mustache, and he kept talking about how he was going to rob the casino. Everyone laughed at how funny the crazy cowboy was. *This fucker ain't jokin' folks,* Pete remembers thinking.

Rancid Pete opens his eyes and shakes his head. Meditation is not properly functioning right now. Damn fuzzy head.

Other assorted creatures are beginning to stir out in the suite. This is the real witching hour, when all the zombies come back to life.

There I go again with the zombie nonsense. Damn it Pete, look what you made me do.

Anyway, Pete finds the remote control to the suite and shuts the giant sliding doors to the bedroom, blocking his view of the mess beginning to clean itself up out in the common area. He clicks a button on the remote and speaks. His voice booms through speakers in the other room.

"You all have three options," he says. "Get the fuck out, make me some food, or start cleaning the place up. You have one rule. Leave me alone. When I want the food I will come get it."

He sits the remote down and walks out onto the balcony. He has no idea what time it is. The clock on the wall says three o'clock.

Morning or day? Has to be day. Call time for the show is seven. The End of Times will go on at midnight. All of the End of Times shows begin at midnight. They are known for playing all the way through until sunrise on rare, fantastic occasions. Of course, that isn't going to happen in the darkness of Las Vegas. There is no sunrise.

Pete stares down from the balcony. There is a throng of people scurrying about below. A tourist with a wide angle lens is panning the skyline when he happens across Pete's rancid visage. "Hey everyone. There's Rancid Pete!"

Pete goes back into the room and begins tossing the body parts that surround his bed off the balcony. They splatter to the street below. Several onlookers are injured. The rest are whipped into a frenzy, cheering and fighting over severed limbs for souvenirs. All the boring, halfway normal people get the heck out of there. Several of them head straight for the airport and immediately get the heck out of Vegas, vowing never to return.

Rancid Pete laughs at the whole mess, which makes his head hurt worse. Then he realizes he is urinating off the balcony all over the people that are down on the street cheering for him. It is a full streamed monster pee. That makes him feel better.

He wanders back into the room, heading for the shower. Pete spends a decadent amount of time cleaning himself, allowing his gnarled skin to soak up as much moisture as possible. It is in the shower when he realizes what he has to do. He has to take the Princess.

It is so simple. Why had this not been his instant reaction to the situation to begin with? He is Rancid Pete. He kicks life in the balls and takes what he wants!

By the time he exits the shower he is mildly amused. His head still hurts, but the pain has reduced to a dull ache. His genius intellect is returning to full speed. This will be fun. He will simply take the Princess the same way he takes everything else.

He calls the hotel lobby to have them page Tommy Tompkins for him. Tommy is the band's manager. He will have Tommy issue an invitation with backstage passes to the concert for the Princess and her entourage. Hell, Pete can have a reception for them.

Wait. No. That might make him seem a little too thirsty. Too eager. He will treat her like every other bitch.

Yes. She is just another piece of ass. She'll be lucky if he doesn't get bored with her and eat her immediately. That's right. There you go Rancid Pete. There's the monster I know and love.

The phone rings. He answers it.

Rancid Pete by the way, does not own a fucking Smear. He has an old fashioned hand held device.

Tommy Tompkins is on the other end of the call. Pete passes along his instructions. Tommy agrees to them hastily, excitedly, as he knows the fate of many previous band managers that failed to do Rancid Pete's bidding. Pete has fired them without hesitation.

Oh c'mon. He doesn't eat everyone that pisses him off...

Pete's vigor is almost fully returned. I envy Rancid Pete's ability to recover from a hangover. It is quite impressive.

He dresses for a day on the town. Then he reconsiders, deciding to hit the gym first. He changes clothes four times before he is ready to go workout. Yep. The Princess is completely out of Pete's head. No problem.

Rancid Pete throws the doors open to the bedroom and steps out into the suite. To his surprise, the devastation from the night before has been thoroughly cleansed.

"No shit?" he says.

Another party is in full bloom. This celebration has more taste than the melee of the night before. A banner has been strewn across the room that reads "Rancid Pete for President." Most everyone is naked. There is a large buffet spread. The wall between the indoor and outdoor portions of the swimming pool has been opened, allowing the smoke filled Las Vegas air to create a sultry fog effect over the water.

"Fuck the gym," Rancid Pete says. He tears off his shirt, takes three shots of tequila, kisses a chick, throws her in the pool and dives in after her. Bobdamn rock stars and all their fun. Can I at least get to be one in another life?

## 28

"Where have you been you cunt?" The Princess is pouting as hard as possible when Dolly enters the room.

"You know that's not an altogether accurate description," Dolly replies.

Princess Tiara ignores Dolly's response. "You were gone all night. I had to bathe myself."

"That must have been terrifying. Are you injured?" Dolly speaks with an exaggerated southern drawl.

"Then, I had to clean up the sheets because my Stink wore off," Tiara continues.

"You could have called housekeeping darling," Dolly says.

"I don't know how to do that shit."

"Well that's true. You could have called me."

"I did you bitch," Tiara replies. "It kept going straight to voicemail and I don't know how to use voicemail. Your fucking Smear was turned off."

"Oh, I hadn't noticed."

"Plus," Tiara lowers her voice to a whisper, "that oily Spanish prick is watching me. I know it. I can feel his beady little eyes all over me."

"That's gross," Dolly replies.

"I know, right? Don't worry though. I gave the old pervert a show. I smacked my ass all over this place."

"I'm not certain that was necessarily the way to put him in his place. Wouldn't he enjoy that?"

"Of course he would. It's all about control Doll. But that's not the point. What happened was I woke up and you weren't here and I didn't know where you were and I was scared and I didn't feel well." It was true the Princess had genuinely been frightened without Dolly present. She is dangerously codependent. "Plus," she continues, "my arms and hands were asleep underneath me and I couldn't turn myself over. Then when I finally turned over there was poop all over me."

"It must have been a harrowing ordeal for you." Dolly lights a cigarette while searching for an ashtray.

"So I cleaned up all the poop, all on my own," Tiara continues. "You would have been so proud of me. I changed the sheets!"

"That's what you said dear." Dolly finds an ashtray just in time, discarding a long arch of gray ash.

"So then I thought, 'well I don't know where that tranny bitch Dolly is so I am going to have to tough it out on my own until that tranny bitch gets back.'" Tiara smiles at her recollection. "Sorry dear, just trying to tell an honest tale."

"Of course." Dolly's retort is as dry as the martini she suddenly realizes she is mixing. *Was I licking my lips?* she thinks.

"So I decided not to dress," Tiara says, "because I like the way these sheets feel. By the way, steal several sets of these sheets for me."

"Or we could find out who makes them and buy some for you."

"But I will know they aren't stolen and they won't feel as nice. Put some in a suitcase."

"You know the hotel will probably add them to the bill." Dolly smiles at her mistress.

"You're ruining it!" Tiara actually walks over and slugs Dolly in the arm. Luckily punching takes effort, and the Princess is not real big on effort.

"Sorry dear. Three sets of stolen sheets." For comedic effect, mostly for her own amusement, Dolly jots this down onto an invisible notepad as she speaks.

"Anyhow, I got everything I needed to survive without you then curled up to watch TV for the day, until you got back."

"Even food?"

"Egg salad sandwich bitch."

"You're welcome." It was Dolly who made sure the hotel fridge was properly stocked.

"So then I started flipping through the channels but there was nothing on. TV here sucks! I mean sucks." Tiara drags the word "sucks" out for a considerable amount of time. "So I am channel surfing for like a half an hour when all of a sudden, there he was."

"Whom?" Dolly has somehow achieved a state of genuine curiosity. The martini is doing its business.

"What's it called when you feel a very romantic attraction to something, but it's not real love, or you don't know if it is real love anyways, because you don't know the person you think you might be in love with? All you know is, all of a sudden you think you want them and it is most likely because you are horny and they are hot and you want to screw, but there is like, some feeling that it is a little more than that. More than horny, you know."

"Um, infatuation might do," Dolly replies.

"That sounds nice. I like it. We'll use that to describe what I'm talking about."

"Well, you may want to try looking the word up in a dictionary, to make sure it is actually appropriate to the feelings you are trying to describe."

"Dolly, I don't have time for that. I have infatuation with a monster." She says this last line with a deep Russian accent, although she may have been going for a Dracula thing. Either way, after she says it she giggles happily at her revelation, then buries her face in a pillow.

"Oh my God, you have not fallen for that oily Spanish prick?" Dolly is looking directly at a hidden security camera when she says this. Purvis tipped her off to the locations of the cameras in their room.

"What? No. Who's a what a prick?" the Princess replies, confused.

"Oily Spanish."

"Who are you talking about?" Tiara asks incredulously. "I've fallen for the monster in that band that's here in town. He's the drummer. They're playing tonight! He was on the news promoting the concert. Dolly, we have to go to that concert."

"I was referring to Senor Diego, the owner of the casino." Once again Dolly speaks this directly at a camera, in case Alacrán happens to be watching.

"Oh right. That oily Spanish prick."

"Yes, that one."

"Ew. No. It's the monster silly."

"Right. That's what you said. You have 'infatuation' with an actual monster who is the drummer in a rock band. You do realize I assume, that you are talking about the infamous Rancid Pete?" Dolly is not a fan of the monster or his band's music.

"Right," Tiara says excitedly. "That's it. That's his name. I've been reading about him on-line."

"You do also realize he eats people?"

"He eats normal people."

Dolly laughs. The implications are obvious. "Some of them may not be normal. You never know."

"You know what I mean."

"Well, we may want to be careful about assuming he won't want to eat you. He may want to eat you more than usual."

"I hope so."

"Not like that!"

"Oh I know," Tiara says. "Do you think I will be able to tell? Do you think if I meet him I will be able to tell if I am safe with him?" The Princess is acting school girlish. Dolly is not sure she has ever seen Tiara this way.

*This could be bad*, Dolly thinks. Then she says, "All women ask that question of the men they fall in love with."

"Most men don't eat people."

"True. Most men aren't monsters. But, most women aren't royal, international, sensational bitches named Princess Tiara Lioness." Dolly does get a kick out of the Princess sometimes. "Maybe you two will cancel each other out."

"Are you giving me a pep talk?" Tiara asks, with a wink and a smile.

"I don't know dear. I've got a lot on my mind." Dolly is moving about the room, tidying up the Princess' clothing, and beginning to mentally slip away from the conversation.

"Well get rid of it," Tiara says. "When I am in the room this world is about me."

"I know darling. I apologize." Dolly does not stop thinking about her own predicament. She hears the Princess prattle on with her nonsense and hears herself responding to the Princess' inane personal drama, but most of her mind is focused on how she is going to escape the situation she has found herself in.

"Dolly." The Princess is snapping her fingers. "Dolly. Dolly. Dolly. Dolly. Dolly. Dolly. Dolly!"

Dolly comes back to reality, escaping her brain. "Yes dear. Sorry. I was...I'm a little out of sorts. What if maybe I try some of your Stink?" She can't believe the words coming out of her own mouth. She doesn't even like drugs.

"Absolutely not." The Princess crosses her arms. "That shit is way too strong and you have got to help me solve my problems. I am flying right now. I can't have you all fucked up too. I'm serious. I'm on a rocket to feel-good mountain, and on top of that mountain is my monster, and I want to know if that song about his wiener is true."

"Good Lord you are repulsive."

"And that my dear Dolly, is why he won't want to eat me."

"Well, well. That may be a winning argument dear."

"Now, get on your fucking Smear and get us some tickets to that show. Wait, we don't need tickets. I'm a Princess. Leak it to the media I'm crashing the concert. The peasants will go crazy. Then we go shopping. We're going to a rock concert and we're going to look bad ass."

At that exact moment there is a knock upon the door.

"Did you order food?" Tiara asks Dolly.

"No."

"Do you know who it is?"

"No." Dolly is staring at the Princess with another cigarette in one hand and her second martini in the other.

"Well will you go find out?"

"Of course dear."

"Then will you order some food?" the Princess shouts after her. "I'm hungry."

"Of course dear." Dolly is gone for a few moments then she returns with an envelope in her hand.

"What is it?" Tiara asks.

"Well I don't know darling, it's for you. A bellboy delivered this envelope."

"Well open it. I'm not going to open it, there could be a bomb or a snake or something."

"I don't think a bomb or a snake would fit in here dear." Dolly tears the envelope open.

"Whatever. What's in it?"

"It's an invitation from William Rockefeller the Third to join him at the concert," Dolly says. "Who is William Rockefeller the Third?"

"How should I know?"

"Do you think someone besides the oily Spanish prick is watching us?" Once again, Dolly looks directly at a surveillance camera when she says "oily Spanish prick", in the hopes he is watching.

"Who cares?" Tiara replies. "Find out who this Rockefeller guy is. Maybe we let him escort us, but I don't want to be seen in public with some turd."

"Right." Then there is another knock on the door.

"Now what?" Dolly says.

The Princess shrugs her beautiful shoulders. Dolly heads for the main entrance once again, as the Princess speaks from behind her.

"You do realize this is a sign Doll? It's fate. I am supposed to meet this monster." Tiara hears a brief and quiet exchange and then Dolly returns, this time carrying a small ornate box. "Well?"

"It's another delivery," Dolly replies.

"Ha! Open it up." The Princess is getting excited by the gifts. "What is it?"

"More fate. It's another invitation to the show, but this time there are backstage passes."

"That's funny." Tiara is playfully suspicious. "You messing with me bitch?"

"Nope."

"Interesting. Not that it really matters. We would have been backstage anyway. I mean, once again, Princess," Tiara points to herself. "So the tickets are a little unnecessary but still, it's pretty cool that all I have to do is decide I want something and poof, there it is."

"Where have you been your entire life?"

"Getting what I want." Tiara smiles and Dolly laughs. "Who are these from?"

"It doesn't say," Dolly replies, flipping the envelope and card over.

"A mystery suitor. Blah. Pretty lame don't you think?"

"Very."

"Oh well, the backstage passes are cool." Tiara takes the passes from Dolly's hand and examines them. "Now we have to decide who we are going with."

"We could do a Louie."

A Louie, is an intricate scenario named by Dolly and the Princess in which they take on second and third body doubles - one for each of them - so Dolly can stand in as the Princess in order to facilitate the Princess being in two places at once. It is named after their first attempt at the operation, which involved the Princess fulfilling an engagement with King Louie the 59th of France, and Prince Lu Yee of

East China, on the same evening several years earlier. The best part of the whole gag is that if performed properly, the press exposes the situation but nobody ever knows for sure who was with the actual Princess and who was not, so in the end all parties except the Princess wind up feeling slighted.

"Yeah," the Princess says thoughtfully. "Maybe. I don't know. I may want you with me when I meet the drummer. I've never dealt with a monster before."

"We don't know if these tickets are from him or not."

"That's true. I wasn't assuming they were."

"Well, we may have to do a Louie to have a chance to meet him without offending either of our potential hosts."

"Also true. But, why the fuck would I care about offending anyone?"

Having no clue, Dolly shrugs her shoulders. There is yet another knock at the door.

"Seriously?" the Princess says curiously.

Dolly exits and returns. She is pushing a silver food cart.

"What is that?" the Princess asks.

"Food."

"That was fast."

"It was. Especially since I didn't order anything yet." Dolly parks the cart and removes lids from several platters.

"Oh. Then who?" The Princess' facial expression shows realization setting in. "Ew. He's watching us right now isn't he?"

"Most likely dear."

"Well then let's tell our host thank you."

They make their way around the suite from plant to painting to bookshelf, flipping the bird and making horrible faces at any potential hidden cameras, with Dolly making sure to hit the ones Purvis warned her of.

After they are done admonishing Alacrán through his surveillance system, they sit down to eat. While taking the lids off the rest of the dishes, they discover a platter holding yet another invitation to the concert. This invitation is from Alacrán.

"Well now this is ridiculous," Dolly says. "We can't Louie three suitors. Can we?"

"Or could we?" Tiara asks, somewhat absently, as if contemplating a scheme. Then both women laugh, clanking their martini glasses together.

Dolly is drunk and her worries have slipped away for the time being. "I think I have an idea for the Louie," Dolly says.

"Oh good," the Princess replies. "I have a feeling this is going to be a lot of fun. What is it?"

Dolly whispers, "It's a Manuel combined with a Louie."

A Manuel, is an intricate scenario named by Tiara and Dolly in which they, along with up to fifty other body doubles, all dress in the same disguise and remain together in a tight pack with the Princess hidden amongst them. The pack is fluid, amorphous like a giant amoeba, as they are constantly rotating positions, making it virtually impossible for any other person who is around to make physical contact with the Princess. It is so named after their initial attempt at the operation, which involved the Princess' first social engagement with the infamous Manuel the Molester, 5th Prince of Old Cuba. The Princess had heard in advance of meeting him that he was very touchy feely.

While I was explaining the Manuel to you, Dolly was explaining her newly inspired Manuel-Louie combination to Princess Tiara.

"This is why I don't hate you," Tiara says, after Dolly has explained her new scheme. "You're a genius." After a moment of silence, Princess Tiara remembers something from earlier in their conversation. "Hey Doll?"

"Yes dear."

"What's a dictionary?"

# 29

Marshal Dan leaves his armored cruiser parked at the Valet station of La Ciudad de Oro after his meeting with Alacrán. He wants his presence felt by the villain.

"Let's see if we can keep him on edge," he says to Nico. They take disposable, biodegradable jet packs downtown to Dante's Brew.

"Say, did you happen to see that crazy cowboy with the ten gallon hat at the blackjack table on our way out of the casino?" Nico asks as they land.

"Yes I did," Dan replies.

"Did he seem a little odd to you?"

"Everyone at those tables gambling their lives away seems odd to me," Dan says.

They enter Dante's Brew to a dizzying light show as crime scene investigators, members of the coroner's union, and spectators all photograph the blood bath the Karowack Kids have left behind. Keep in mind, the Kids view themselves as artists. Their maulings are often theme oriented, and orchestrated in such a manner as to leave behind some form of artistic statement.

"Good Lord," Dan says as he surveys the room. There are body parts everywhere. Blood is everywhere. Entrails have been used as streamers, connecting the overhead light fixtures. Dan notices a head stuck atop the lead microphone on stage. The strangest thing however, is in the center of the room. There is a 10 foot by 10 foot square monolith made out of people parts.

"Gotta be the Kids," Nico says.

"I would say that is a safe deduction, at least for the moment," Dan replies. "Get all these people out of here. The city cops too. Keep three you know personally, and then tell the rest to go outside and keep everyone else out of the building."

"Got it." Nico ushers everyone out, gathering assistance from the other officers as he relays Dan's orders to them.

Dan is walking around the room looking for clues to why the slaughter happened. Of course, with the Karowack Kids there doesn't have to be a reason. They are vampires after all, and sometimes they kill a bunch of people with no other motivation than to fulfill their blood lust. But, the monolith of body parts seems odd, even for the Karowack Kids.

Once the room is emptied per Dan's instructions, Nico sends three remaining officers upstairs to investigate the second and third floors of the building. "A couple of the city beaters confirmed it was the Karowack Kids," Nico says. "Said there was a lone survivor they already sent to the hospital." Nico crosses the room and stands next to Dan.

Dan is standing in front of the monolith, quietly contemplating it with his hand under his chin.

"Jesus Christ," Nico says, taking in the gruesome display.

"It is I," says Jesus.

Dan and Nico are startled by the response. They look around the room, guns drawn, searching for the source of the voice.

"Over here."

Both men turn to see Jesus waiving his arm. He steps out from behind a column across the room.

"Jesus...," Nico tries to speak, but the cat gets his tongue.

"...Christ," Jesus finishes. "Yes, it is I."

"What are you doing here Jesus?" Dan asks politely.

"I felt a great disturbance in the farce," Jesus says, with a weary yet playful tone.

"Nice," Dan says.

"Yeah. Anyhow, I am here laying these souls to rest. Blessing those at peace and praying for the damned. You didn't think I was just a rock star did you?"

"Ha, ha, no sir," Dan replies. "My apologies, my name is..."

"Daniel Trate," Jesus interrupts.

Dan stuck his hand out, offering it for a shake as he was speaking. Jesus takes Dan's hand in both of his own. "Sorry. I have got to stop finishing people's sentences like that." He smiles warmly. "It's a pleasure to meet you Dan."

"The pleasure is all mine sir," Dan replies.

"Please, my father is Sir. Call me Jesus, or Christ, or JC will do nicely."

Dan simply nods his head in agreement. Dan is rarely enamored by other people. He is after all, the hero. The tall man on the horse. The calmest in the foxhole. The one the women want to be with and the men want to be. He is the alpha, which is only slightly trumped by standing in front of the alpha *and* the omega. To be clear, Dan finds Jesus super bad ass.

Jesus lets Dan's hand go and gives Dan a hug. Then he gives Nico a hug and a kiss on the cheek. "Nico would you relax?" he says playfully.

"I'm sorry Jesus." Nico is speaking through very clinched teeth. "My family is Protestant."

"What? Here." Jesus gives Nico another hug but this time he squeezes Nico until he feels the tension release in Nico's body. "There. That's better. You've got to relax kid."

"I'm going to go outside," Nico responds. "I'm sorry. I don't mean to be rude. I need to go outside." Nico heads for the front door. "Just need some air. I'll be good. I'll be fine. Great. Just need a deep breath of some fresh air."

"Well that was odd," Dan says. "Do you know what that was about?"

"Not really," Jesus says. "Sort of. I mean, it's happened before but it's always for different reasons. Sometimes I think people still can't believe I'm real, even when they meet me."

"Are you real?" Dan asks, hesitantly.

"Who knows?" Jesus says. "How existential are you willing to go with this conversation?"

"Well, I am in the middle of investigating all these murders here," Dan says.

"Right on. Another time then."

"I would like that," Dan says. "Some odd things lately." Dan shakes his head a little and gets back on subject. "So, you were going about your business and then all of a sudden you could feel all these deaths happen?"

"Yeah. That's basically it."

"Wow. Doesn't that mess with your head? People are dying constantly."

"It's not always the easiest gig."

Nico walks back in. "Okay, what did I miss? Sorry about that by the way. I needed some fresh air. Also I may have incited a riot, 'cause when I went outside I kind of screamed, 'hey everybody I just met Jesus Christ and he is right inside this building.' Sorry about that."

"No worries." Jesus says.

"So what did I miss?" Nico repeats.

"Jesus was telling me how he has to bless all the dead and pray for all the damned souls," Dan says.

"That's insane," Nico replies. "That's like thousands of people a day. How in the world can you do that?"

"Well I don't get to sleep a lot," Jesus says. "I work long, grueling hours and I'm not allowed to use drugs like caffeine or cocaine, so I had to find other, more reasonable solutions to my small business problems. That's when I purchased my Class 3 Transporter tablet, by GomiCorp." Jesus reaches behind him and pulls out his transporter tablet. "GomiCorp, is a registered trademark. Without my GomiCorp transporter tablet, my job would be impossible."

"That's pretty cool," Dan says, slightly confused.

"It certainly is," says Jesus, who smiles and then tosses the transporter tablet aside.

All three men laugh, then get back to the business at hand.

"This whole thing sort of looks like a big square box with a handle on top, doesn't it?" Nico says.

"Yes it does," Dan says. "Interesting. Jesus, what do you think?"

"I think I could never make it through the day without my GomiCorp, Long Range Holographic Telecommunicator. For all those times when I need to be physically present to bless the dead, but simply can't."

Nico and Dan both stare at Jesus.

"I know. My bad," Jesus continues. "They gave my all this stuff for free if I plug them three times a day. I wasn't going to do it, but it was a favor for Buddha. A descendant of his owns the company."

"Can we get back to all these dead people?" Nico replies. His whole body jerks in surprise at the tone he took with Jesus. He stands with his hands out in front of him, knees bent and mouth open.

"Watch your tone Champ. I'll turn you into a toad, baby." Jesus speaks using his impersonation of Elvis Presley, then holds his hands up revealing the holes through his wrists. "You think this is a game?" He sticks his tongue through the hole in his left wrist while making painful noises, eyes wide.

Dan and Nico both wince at the gruesome display.

"This is real!" Jesus mock screams, then barks like a dog three times.

Dan and Nico stand aghast. Jesus steps forward and smacks them both on the shoulder at the same time.

"I'm messing with guys," he says. "Lighten up." He sticks his tongue back through the hole. "Pretty gross right?"

"Yes." Dan says quickly and adamantly.

Jesus laughs.

"What's it all about?" Dan blurts.

"Dan, is that really what you want to know?"

"Yes. No. Of course not. Well, of course but not right now. I don't expect you to tell me. For some reason I had to ask."

"Everybody does." Jesus says. "But you're right. I'm not telling. I gave you people the answers a long time ago and look what you did to me.

"Right," Dan says.

"I'm here to set an example," Jesus continues. "Not solve all your problems."

"Okay," Dan says. "I understand."

"Seriously, you've got to figure this out on your own."

"Alright. I apologize for asking." Dan pauses briefly. "Wait. Are we talking about all these murders, or are we still doing the big picture thing?"

"You know I'm not sure. I was definitely messing with you, but now I'm a little lost too."

"It's starting to stink in here," Nico says, attempting to refocus the conversation.

"I need a body that is not completely torn apart," Jesus replies. "Let's spread out and try to find one."

The three men make their way through the room, searching the carnage for a corpse that is not completely ripped to shreds. Eventually, Nico finds a dead body that appears intact.

"Over here," Nico says.

"Okay, watch this," Jesus says as he and Dan make their way to Nico.

They stand over a man whose jugular was sliced open. Jesus bends down and puts his hand on the man's forehead. "Open thine eyes," he says. He looks at Dan and Nico. "When I miracle people I have to use old timey sounding words."

"Really?" Nico asks.

"No," Jesus says with a smile.

The dead man's eyes open suddenly. His pupils flicker back and forth quickly. Jesus speaks to him again.

"Now fill thy lungs with air," Jesus says. He looks at Dan and Nico again and winks. "Most of the time they are so disoriented they can't think to breath or try to speak."

The man takes a deep breath and tries to lean up.

"Owwwwwwwwwwwww," the man says. The word comes out weakly at first, barely audible, then picks up steam as he tries harder to sit himself up. He looks at Jesus. "Why can't I move?"

"You were dead and rigamortis is already setting in," Jesus replies.

"That sucks. Are you Jesus?"

"It is I."

Nico whispers to Dan, "Do you think he ever just says yes?"

"Yes Nico, I do," Jesus says.

Dan elbows Nico in the ribs.

The dead man continues, "Am I alive again?"

"For the time being," Jesus says.

"What do you mean for the time being?"

"We need your help to solve your murder," Jesus replies, ignoring the man's question. "All these murders. I need you to tell us what happened."

"But what did you mean 'for the time being'?" the dead man repeats.

"I'm sorry my child. You've been dead for too long. There is nothing I can do to salvage your body."

"But you were dead for like three days."

"But I am Jesus."

The dead man sighs then acquiesces to the situation. "Okay, what do you want to know?"

"Seriously?" Nico asks. "What do you think we want to know?"

"Sir, tell us everything that happened in here," Dan says.

"Who are those guys?" the dead man asks.

"They are Marshals," Jesus replies. "I am aiding them in their investigation."

"That's cool. Okay. I'll try to remember." The man closes his eyes for a few moments. When he reopens them he is in reenactment mode: "Oh my God it's the Karowack Kids! Get under the table!

They're going to kill us all. No! They slashed my date's throat. Oh my God oh my God oh my God! I'm on the floor now crawling around. Ah! A chopped off hand fell on my shoulder. I'll go left. No, there's a freaking eyeball rolling across the floor. I'll go right. Feet! Oh no. He's picking me up. No! I don't know anything about any black case. No! I did not know there was a mysterious black case that was supposed to be delivered to Alacrán that has been stolen and has now disappeared somewhere in the city! I don't know why you are telling me any of this. Please don't kill me. Oh my God..." The dead man acts like his throat is being ripped out then gasps for his last breaths of air and closes his eyes, dead once again.

Jesus stands, joining Dan and Nico as they applaud the dead man's performance. Roses are tossed. Bravos are heard. The dead man opens his eyes once again. "Thank you," he says. "Did I do okay?"

"You redeemed yourself a little bit," Jesus says.

"So do I get to live?"

"No, you still have to die again but don't worry, I'll make it quick." Jesus reaches under his robe and pulls a revolver out. He holds it to the dead man's temple.

"Jesus Christ," the dead man shouts, alarmed.

"You just met your maker." Jesus speaks with his teeth clenched in his best tough-cop voice.

The dead man screams.

Jesus laughs. "Calm down," he says. "I'm teasing. Be at peace." He puts the revolver back in his robe and waives his hand over the dead man's eyes. They close and the man is dead again.

"That was sort of strange," Dan says.

"You keep a gun in there?" Nico asks Jesus.

"It's a water gun," Jesus says. "Now, watch this." Jesus waives his hand back over the man's eyes and they reopen. "I changed my mind. You get to live."

The man is ecstatic. "I do!"

"Nope." Jesus points his finger like a gun at the man and pulls the trigger. The man is dead again, this time with a disappointedly surprised expression on his face.

"Well that was different," Nico says.

"He was a rapist," Jesus says. "He was here with his next victim." Then Jesus resurrects the man again. "You're alive," he says, with jazz hands up by his face.

"...I'm alive..."

Then Jesus snaps his fingers, "Ope, now you're not."

He goes through this routine with the dead man enough times for the dead man to finally realize what is happening. Eventually, during the multiple brief instances when he is alive, the dead man strings together the words, "oh now you are just being mean." Then, on a more contrite note, "I'm really sorry about all those rapes."

Once the man apologizes, Jesus finally leaves him dead for good.

"Dang, that was hard core Christ," says Nico.

"You do what you have to," Jesus says. "Honestly I'm not sure he was sincere but I'll still pray for him."

"So," Dan interjects. "We have confirmation the Karowack Kids are responsible for all these murders, Alacrán is most definitely involved on some level, and there is a mysterious black case being chased throughout the city."

"I guess that explains all the dead bodies being stacked up like that," Nico says.

"I guess it does Nico. I guess it does," says Dan. "And I think at this point it is a reasonably safe leap in logic to consider the murders at the airport linked to this whole mess. My guess is those men died attempting to retrieve that case." He turns to Christ. "Jesus, it was a pleasure. I hope I have the opportunity again, but if you will excuse us, we have work to do."

Jesus stands with his hands out to his side offering them blessings as they exit.

Nico turns and childishly waves goodbye. Jesus places his palms together and slightly bows, then goes back to blessing dead bodies and praying for the damned.

Ladies and gentlemen this concludes the first act of our show. Our performers will return after a brief intermission. Now is a good time to go pee.

# Act II

# 30

## THE CONCERT PART 1:
## THE SHOW IS ABOUT TO BEGIN

It is almost time for the concert. The End of Times *and* 10 Foot Tall Jesus and the Regional Deity All-Star Band? Together on the same stage?! The entire world will be watching. There are rumors Satan was somehow involved with the planning. It's a well-known fact he's a huge fan of both bands.

Meanwhile, Princess Tiara and Dolly are getting ready for the big show.

"Do you really think it's a good idea to hang out with vampires?" Dolly asks.

"I think I don't care if it's a good idea or not Doll."

"But they kill people and they are hideously unhip. Even the kids don't think vampires are 'icy' anymore."

"What difference does it make? I'm the shit. Everything I do is cool. If I want to hang out with a bunch of vampires then the vampires will be cool. Besides, this is going to be a blast." Tiara is applying fake eyelashes that are several inches long. "Why are you so worried? Normally you would get a kick out of this."

"I'm sorry. I have a lot on my mind right now darling."

"Well, I would ask you what you are so bothered about but we both know I don't care. Get your head out of your ass and have some fun with me."

"Oh alright." But it isn't alright. Dolly is scared for their lives, and it won't go away. "What do you plan on doing about Señor Diego?" Dolly applies a gigantic set of fake eyelashes of her own.

"I plan on making him horny and desperate to have me and getting what I want from him until we leave his tacky-ass hotel. The same thing I've been doing." The Princess turns to face Dolly. "How do I look?"

"Like an absolute badass."

Princess Tiara is wearing a shear black ninja outfit. The material is skin tight and mostly see through. She wears nothing underneath except for a black flexi-leather bustier to support her wonderful breasts and a pair of ultra-thin leather panties. Her hair is pulled up into a braided ponytail near the top of her head. She wears a wrap that covers the rest of her head and face except for her eyes. The wrap is knotted in the back with a strand of pearls. Around her waist is a tight diamond chain.

Dolly is dressed exactly as the Princess except for a minor adjustment. Her outfit is not quite as see-through in the region of the crotch, in order to keep Henry concealed. The last thing she wants to happen is for rumors to go around the Princess has a penis, unless of course the Princess decides to start that rumor for some reason.

"Are the girls ready?" Tiara asks.

"Yes. There are 43. With us it makes three teams of fifteen, just like we planned."

"Good. This is going to be fun. I am so excited!"

Princess Tiara and Dolly exit the bathroom into the main chamber of the suite. Forty-three ninjas, dressed exactly as Tiara and Dolly are waiting for them. Dolly claps her hands.

"Alright ladies, let's go."

Alacrán checks his cufflinks in the mirror. He pats his shoulders and sleeves. He tugs at his collar. He attempts a very forced sideways smile with the right side of his mouth. It is brutal. His face tics, straining under the effort of the forced smile. He is terribly uncomfortable.

Purvis enters the room and comes to rest by Alacrán's side. He pins a black rose to Alacrán's lapel.

"You look as handsome as ever," Alacrán says, continuing to adjust himself in the mirror.

"Thank you sir. You do as well, as always."

"I appreciate your aplomb but it is obvious I am a mess." Alacrán turns to face Purvis with a painful expression, tugging at his collar again.

"I feel like a fucking corndog," Purvis blurts out, almost shouting in his master's face.

"I do too! It's awful! What do you mean corndog?"

"I feel like I'm wrapped in batter. My skin feels all puffy and fleshy and gross. I feel fat."

"I do to. I feel exactly like that. My darling, this wretched little bitch must be contained. No female has ever put me off like this." Alacrán takes three pills from a bottle in the gigantic medicine cabinet behind his gigantic gold framed mirror. He holds the pills out in his palm and taps each of them two times with the tip of his pointer finger, humming a little rhyme to himself. After he swallows the pills he says, "Did you get the poison?"

"Potion, sir?" Purvis says.

"Yes, that. Do you have it?"

"Yes."

"Good. And is there any word on my other prize?" Alacrán asks.

"Our spy within the Eastwoodians reports that he believes a clandestine sect of their local chapter may have briefly located the case. He is trying to gather more information for me now."

"I don't think I have to explain to you how important it is that we retrieve that case?"

"No sir," Purvis says.

The two men exit Alacrán's office and head across the lobby of his grand waiting area to his private elevator. This is not to be confused with his secret elevator hidden inside his office.

"If this doesn't become fun again, very soon, I'm afraid I am going to freak out."

"I think you will enjoy the concert. At least, in some fashion," Purvis says, trying to encourage his master.

"There is only one way I want to enjoy it," Alacrán says. "By getting what I want."

Lord Sweetwater rides with Billy the Third in his modified 1950 Chrysler Crown Imperial limousine. They are headed to La Ciudad de Oro to escort the Princess to the concert. Several of Billy's other less charismatic children are along for the ride. They are currently "milking" a fresh "cow" and blathering on about the onslaught of the new anti-pre-postmodern intellectualism in the post-apocalyptic era. There are notebooks everywhere and the pens fly as fast as the tongues. The music is African tribal. The wine is red. The Billy is unusually fixated with his fangs.

Milking a fresh cow by the way, is vampire beat for draining the blood of a breather. This particular breather was a young handsome insurance salesman named Jerry. In a former life, Jerry was a race car driver.

"I'm altogether unsatisfied with Bingo and Bongo tonight, Jack," Billy says to Lord Sweetwater. Bingo and Bongo are his left and right fore-fangs. Billy is known for extending the fangs separately and saying, "Bingo, bongo, bango," right before sinking his teeth into someone. "It's almost like they have a life of their own."

"Well dad, you know what they say about vampires who do they thinking with they fangs," Sweetwater replied.

"Yes I do, but in this instance I am searching for a platitude more attune with an emperor's discomfort in new digs."

"Is your suit uncomfortable?"

"Jack, we were discussing Bingo and Bongo."

"It's all connected daddy. It is all connec...teve...o."

"Well, I can't decide on what to do with them." Billy reaches up and pokes Bongo, the left fang, with the tip of his finger. It is a known fact that vampires are extremely vain about fang appearance. It is a hallmark of vampire style.

"You are William Rockefeller the Third, who always comes in first. You do whatever you want with those pokers."

The truth is, Billy's consternation over his fangs is really the nervousness of a first date. It is unbecoming of a vampire to be nervous. He decides to change the subject.

"Do you think Jesus will play 'Satan Lives'?"

"I hope so daddy-o," Sweetwater replies. "That song changed the game."

"I've always wondered what the really real, re-al-i-ty is with those two. Are they brothers? True enemies? Or, manifestations of a collective consciousness? So many possibilities."

"Daddy," Sweetwater replies. "Ain't nobody got a clue what's really happening on this Earth but Mother Nature and the cock that knocked her up."

Rancid Pete is stomping through the backstage underbelly of the stadium, looking for Jesus. He is in a drunken rage. "You!" Pete growls.

Jesus looks up from the science fiction novel he is reading. Rancid Pete is standing in the doorway to the dressing room, pointing his finger at him.

"What did you do to me?" Pete asks.

"Hello Pete," Jesus replies. "Nice to see you again."

"Don't 'hello Pete' me. Answer my damn question. What did you do to me?"

"Pete, I don't know what you are talking about. Would you please have a seat, a coke, maybe a smile, and we can talk about whatever is upsetting you?" Jesus stands as he speaks and smiles warmly at Rancid Pete. I don't think Jesus is worried, but he realizes Pete is a wildcard. He is a monster after all. A very large and powerful monster at that. If Rancid Pete loses his temper he could do some damage.

"You know what I am talking about," Pete says. "You screwed up my head."

"Pete I did not. Now come over here and sit with me." Jesus makes his way to a sofa in the middle of the room. He sits down, slapping the seat next to him, encouraging Rancid Pete to join him. Pete refuses, simply pacing back and forth in front of Jesus.

"I will not sit with you. Look at me! I'm all messed up man. It's you. It's you and that stupid...," Pete trails off.

"Look dude," Jesus says, standing back up. "None of this is my fault. I didn't do anything to you and if I did I certainly didn't mean to. Okay? All I want is to play a great show and set a good example."

"What?" Pete replies. "What example?"

"I'm just saying all I wanted to do was come to town, put on a ripping rock concert and you know, set a good example."

"Right, I heard you. What sort of example?" Pete's frustration is losing ground to his confusion.

"You know man, I'm serious. I want the fans to see a good show and to have a good example to follow."

"What the hell are you talking about?"

"I'm talking about, all I ever wanted was to put on an awesome rock concert and set a good example."

"Okay, I get it!" Pete screams. "Jesus Christ!"

"That's me!" Jesus smiles brightly and dances a quick jig. Off in the distance a standard, punch line following rim shot on a drum set is heard. Pete cocks his head to the side, staring at Christ, then reluctantly smiles.

"Alright you charismatic son of a bitch," Pete says with a smile. "You're doing more than setting an example. You screwed up my head."

"Well, a lot of bad things I never intended have happened in my name. The Prophet knows what I'm talking about." Jesus points a thumb at the Prophet Muhammad who is sitting in a chair at his dressing table.

The Prophet looks up from his mirror where he is hard at work painting his face like a Samurai. He rolls his eyes, shaking his head in agreement.

"Now that you have calmed down," Jesus continues, again taking a seat on the couch. "Get over here and have a sit with me."

"Who says I'm calmed down?" Pete says, but he flops down onto the couch next to Jesus. Pete puts his arm around Jesus and squeezes a little more tightly than comfortable. "Look, my head's all goofed up over this Princess broad. I ain't never had nothing like this going on upstairs over any female. Not until I find myself in the same city with you and this little royal bitch."

"Oh well that makes sense," Jesus scoffs. "It's clearly all my fault."

"And it's gotten worse since our little talk the other day. So I got to thinking, when I was around you I was feeling everything I was feeling before, but a whole lot bigger. And after I was around you it stayed bigger but not quite as big. It all started when I got here, and you and her got here on the same day, so that must have something to do with it." Rancid Pete crosses his arms in satisfaction with his logic. Spikes rise from his arms, poking holes through the sleeves in his leather jacket. It's a show of returning confidence.

"I suppose that would actually make a little sense," Jesus says. "I mean, I can understand how you would come to those assertions, but I really don't think that is how stuff like this works." He takes Pete's hand and pats it, as if dealing with a child.

"Well then how does it work?" Pete asks. There is a slight tinge of desperation, barely audible, hidden in the depths of his voice. If nothing else, the emotional rollercoaster he has been riding for the past several days is exhausting him.

"I don't know Pete. I really don't. All I wanted to do was put on a top notch rock show and set a good..."

"Oh come on," Pete interrupts. "Don't be a dick."

"I'm not! I swear. Okay, maybe a little, but Pete it's all a big coincidence. Seriously. I bring out the good in people, or at least I try, but really it's up to them. You my friend have the misfortune, I suppose, of falling for Princess Tiara through simple act of animal nature and desire. I can assume, based on your discomfort with these emotions, that they are new for you. Which means up until this point in your life, you have yet to meet another creature that inspires you the way the Princess must. Now, my presence may have somehow magnified all of this for you, but I did not cause these feelings. It's nature baby. You got a crush on a girl." Jesus smacks Pete on the leg, then leans back with his hands clasped behind his head.

Rancid Pete burst into tears. Again.

Jesus pats the monster's back. "Oh come on now Pete. Not again. This is a good thing. Everyone deserves to be loved. To have something to love."

"I don't care! I don't want any of this shit man! Don't you understand? I've been writing love songs all day! It's ridiculous. I don't write fucking love songs! What am I going to do?" Water shoots from Pete's eyes in steady, powerful streams, spraying people in front of him. Snot pours from his nose, gathering into large puddles on the floor. You ever seen a monster cry like a little bitch? It is the most disgusting crying fit in the history of the Universe and it lasts forever.

The All-Star Deity Band gathers around Pete to console the monster. When Pete finally calms down again, Jesus offers an answer to his question.

"I'll tell you what you are going to do Rancid Pete. You're going to get your giant monster rear-end out on that stage and play a hard core rock and roll show, baby. That's what you are going to do."

Alacrán and Purvis fall out of the elevator in a coughing fit. Purvis has a small aerosol canister of disinfectant spray. He is attacking their clothes and the air around them without reservation.

"Oh my God," Alacrán gasps.

"I'm so sorry my liege. I did not know." Purvis sprays the air around Alacrán's head.

"Uh uh. It's okay. Don't be sorry. That was amazing." The emphasis of Alacrán's words is somewhat lost in his wheezing. He waves the air freshener away as Purvis sprays it at him. "Disgusting, but amazing."

They both double over with their hands on their knees trying to gather some air. Purvis smiles awkwardly.

"Silent but deathly," Purvis says.

"Indeed!" Alacrán attempts to stand erect and gather himself, harrumphing and adjusting his clothes. He clears his throat conspicuously.

Purvis is going through similar motions, shaking his pants legs in attempts to air himself out.

"Here," Alacrán says, fishing in his pocket. "Take a pill. We can't have you doing that around the Princess." He removes his silver, scorpion shaped pill box and hands Purvis a little green capsule.

"Of course my liege," Purvis replies. "What is this?"

"Don't worry. It will relax you. Ease that tension in your belly. It may free up your bowels as well so be ready for that, but it won't go to your head. Very much."

"Very much?"

"You'll be fine. I'm telling you, it will make your gasses go away." Alacrán speaks matter-of-factly then turns to head down the hallway.

Purvis quickly spits the pill back out of his mouth into his hand and pockets it. He wants his head clear for this evening, but waste not want not. The pill might be fun to take later.

Alacrán and Purvis arrive at the door to the Princess' suite. They face each other and Purvis makes the finishing touches to Alacrán's ensemble, adjusting the shoulder pads and pocket square. He perfects the curls of Alacrán's mustache with a simple, precise flash of his hands.

"How do I look?" Alacrán asks.

"Like the dictator of a free world," Purvis replies.

Alacrán holds his control device for the hotel in front of his mouth and speaks into it.

"Princess Tiara. It is I, Ala…ahem…Señor Rodrigo Diego, here to escort you to this evening's events. Are you ready my dear?"

Alacrán's voice booms from speakers inside the suite. The double doors to the suite are pulled open by Tiara's royal guard. Alacrán and Purvis peer into the room to see 45 sexy ninjas, standing in a Flying-V formation.

Billy the Third and his merry band of misfit vampire Beatdicks arrive at La Ciudad de Oro. They finger snap their way to the front doors, then throw them open. They dance walk into the lobby with a soundtrack of "shishas" and "shoos" and "ahs" and "oohs". They freeze into their entrance pose.

Billy the Third crosses the lobby as elevators filled with female ninjas land. The elevator doors open and the ninjas come flipping, diving and twirling out. Five ninjas approach Billy, whose own entourage stands behind him.

"I'm here to put my peepers on the Princess," Billy says to the first ninja. "Are you she, little devil?"

"We are," the Ninja replies.

"Well that is a riddle in a haystack," Billy says. "Which one of you is Princess Tiara Lioness?"

"I am," all the girls say at once.

"Well my dears, I am afraid I don't have enough room in my ride for all of you…"

Billy is interrupted by Alacrán who comes blustering out of an elevator.

"That won't be necessary," Alacrán says, without having a clue what Billy had actually said or was about to say. "William," he hisses. "I will be escorting the Princess to this evening's musical review."

"Rodrigo, here is a review for you." Billy pauses. "It's called a concert." That was not the snappy retort he hoped for.

"Whatever." Alacrán turns to the ninjas. "Ladies, I have multiple limos waiting outside. Plenty of room for everyone." He looks around the room at each of the lady ninjas. There are so many of them. "Princess?" he asks a ninja meekly.

The ninja does not say a word. She throws a smoke bomb and disappears.

"Princess Tiara," Alacrán says, addressing all of the ninjas at once. "I have more than enough room for you and your five finest maids in my car. Please join me."

"I will take my own car," a ninja says.

"You two may ride in my private room with me," another ninja says, speaking to both Alacrán and Billy.

"And, you may suck my dicks," another ninja says. That was the actual Princess speaking. All the ninjas laugh.

Billy's skin turns whiter than it already is. Alacrán's face turns beet red. These men were not used to being treated with such disrespect in person. Other people have thought Alacrán and Billy to be fools, but those people kept their mouths shut about it if they knew what was good for them. These two were killers after all. Moronic murderous madmen.

The Black Case Gang is in the car being chased by a bunch of Eastwoodians on scooters.

"You know," Sandy says. "I can't figure out how come these guys don't wonder why if that Eastwood fellow was so great, how come he didn't come back to Earth like Jesus and the rest of his band did."

"I know," Sammy agrees. "That would be my first question. But you know, a guy at the bar was telling me the other night that they don't care. They believe Eastwood is going to come back and that will be the real final revelation. Take a left right here."

Sandy throws the car into neutral, slams on the breaks, pulls hard left and slides through a turn. Before losing momentum she throws the car back in gear and mashes down on the gas pedal, rocketing into the straight away.

"Goddamn baby," Sammy says.

"That's stupid," Sandy says. "Actors becoming gods? Ridiculous."

"I know, but do you realize how many actors we elected President back in the day?" Sammy asks. "Making one a god was really the next logical step."

"You know I don't like history," she replies.

"We tried minorities, we tried women. We even tried a poor person once, but in the end we wound up with a bunch of actors. Did you know we once sent a group of famous Hollywood actors out as emissaries to the rest of the world? We were hoping they would convince all the other countries not to lock us out, but the sons of bitches never came back."

"Sammy, where in the world do you get all this crap?"

"Bartending," he replies. "Bartenders are the new information street." He waves his hand out in front of him acknowledging the street they were currently traveling down. "Trust me, you go from barstool to barstool, you are going to learn something."

"You are ridiculous. Silly old tap monkey."

Zorn begins to chuckle from the back seat. Sammy and Sandy join him, laughing aloud.

Sammy turns to Zorn and says, "What about you demon? Do you like history?"

The laughter continues, until it is interrupted by the loud thump of something landing on the roof of the car. Sandy swerves in surprise as they all three look up to see the roof partially caved in.

"What was that?" Sandy shouts.

"I don't know," Sammy says. "But make another left right here." He rolls down his window and sticks his head out.

"What are you doing?"

"What do you think I'm doing? I'm looking to see what's up there."

He sticks his head and the upper part of his torso out the window. Sandy can hear him saying something but she can't tell what it is. Zorn is still screaming.

"Shut up you lunatic," Sandy screams at Zorn, turning around to admonish him.

Zorn clamps his mouth shut but points out in front of him in muted terror.

Sandy turns back around to see what the demon is pointing at and realizes the street she is on is coming to a dead end. She turns hard right causing Sammy to fall back inside the car. He face-plants into her left tit.

"Hey baby," Sammy says, with boob in his mouth.

"Get off," Sandy says. She pushes his head back and he sits back up. "What's going on out there? Who were you talking to?"

"There's a suicide guy on the roof."

"Are you kidding me?"

"No, he jumped off the roof of his building and landed on our roof as we passed by."

"You have got to be kidding me! That is insane!"

"Well it is the apocalypse," Sammy quips.

Zorn chuckles.

"Don't make me tase you," Sandy says to Sammy.

Zorn laughs harder.

"Either of you," she says.

Zorn shuts up.

"What's he doing up there now?" Sandy asks.

"Holding on," Sammy replies. "Hey, take another right, right here."

Sandy obliges. "Why isn't he dead?" she asks. "Is he freaking tiny or something? He should have caved in the roof."

"Nah," Sammy says. "He jumped off a one story building. He looks like he is about my size."

"What sort of moron tries to kill himself by jumping off a one story building?"

"You know I asked him the same thing, only I left the moron part out, and he said he tried to do a swan dive so he would land on his head but he over rotated."

"I still don't understand why he didn't find a taller building. Then it wouldn't have mattered how he landed."

"That's a good point. I'm gonna ask him." Sammy leans back out the window. As he does, several Eastwoodians on scooters come speeding out of side streets, pulling up parallel to both sides of the car. Sandy reaches blindly for Sammy trying to pull him back inside as she swerves the car left to right.

"Sammy get back in here," she shouts. She grabs hold of his back pocket to his pants and rips it off, trying to pull him back into the car. A baggie of cocaine falls out of the torn pocket. Zorn sees it before anyone else and swipes it for himself.

"He says," Sammy explains, "That is exactly why he was trying to kill himself."

"What was exactly why he was trying to kill himself?" Sandy asks.

"That it didn't matter how he landed," Sammy replies.

"I guess that makes sense," Sandy says, then shakes the thoughts out of her head. "We've got to get rid of these guys."

"Don't worry," Sammy says. "I know where we are going. The stadium is nearby, we'll lose them in the crowd."

"Now that is my man," Sandy says. "We've still got to get ahead of them though."

"Open your door," Sammy says to Zorn.

The demon stares at him slightly confused.

"You're not getting out," Sammy says. "Throw your door open into that scooter. He's right next to you."

Zorn looks out and sees an Eastwoodian on his scooter. The Eastwoodian is holding onto the car's door handle. It looks like he is talking to the guy on the roof.

Zorn opens his door with all the force he can muster. The Eastwoodian loses his balance and swerves into several others, causing them all to crash gingerly into a newspaper stand.

"Good job," Sammy says. He turns to Sandy. "Now we gotta get that guy off the roof."

"Well I ain't stopping," Sandy says. Then she squints, looking at the road ahead. "Or maybe I am."

Several of the Eastwoodians have managed to get ahead of the Black Case Gang to create a roadblock. They are sitting in the middle of the street on their scooters with their arms folded across their chests. Sandy accelerates the car to its maximum potential.

"Watch this," she says to Sammy. Then she pokes her head outside her own window. "Time to go home now buddy," she shouts to the man on the roof of the car.

When she is close enough, Sandy slams on the breaks and pulls the emergency break at the same time. The man flies off the roof of the car and crash lands into the Eastwoodians. Their row of scooters topples like dominos.

"So long suckers," Sandy says, pulling past the Eastwoodians. She looks excitedly at Sammy. "I've always wanted to say that!"

Dan and Nico arrive at the stadium early to spearhead security inspections for the show. They were placed in charge of the show's security due to the many famous people and dignitaries that are attending. This concert is a huge deal. Huge. Really, really big. This is probably the biggest, most anticipated event to happen to the world since the apocalypse began. That's what the promotional posters say.

Dan and Nico are heading to the sound booth. The booth is held suspended in the air above the audience, and will act as their surveillance station during the show. They are timing how long it takes to move around the stadium in case something bad happens.

"You think anything is going to go down tonight boss?" Nico asks.

"I think it is almost a certainty Nico, if certainties exist."

"Right."

After meeting Jesus, both Dan and Nico arrived at the same mental destination at about the same time, which is a place in your mind where you stumble across a door that reads "go no further". You realize you have been lost in your thoughts for a period of time that has most likely lasted a little too long. You are now sick of your own thoughts, the futility of your own wonderings, and the silence you were comfortable with moments before has now become the most oppressive weight you've ever felt. It is strapped to your ankles, dragging you deeper and deeper into the sea of your own self-indulgent thoughts, where you will drown in a whirlpool of your own circular logic. "Dear God someone please cut loose the tethers of my own intellect and provide me with aural distraction," you would say if it were you. "Make a sound Bobdamnit, any sound!"

"Marshal," Nico says. "Do you ever wonder if there is still a Heaven? Or if there ever was a Heaven to being with?"

Nico's question mildly surprises Dan, but only mildly, which is about right for the circumstances, having recently met Jesus.

"We know there is a Hell," Nico continues. "It's right downtown. So you assume, if there is a Hell, than there has to be a Heaven. But what if there isn't? Or what if there was a Heaven, but Hell won and now Heaven is gone? 'Cause if it's still there, and let's assume it is, how come nobody got to go when the rapture happened? You're the best person I know. You ever wonder why you didn't get to go to Heaven?"

"Well, I do worship the Devil," Dan says dryly.

Nico is surprised by Dan's joke.

"You didn't know?" Dan continues. "I thought I told you." He pauses for laughter, then offers a more earnest response. "I don't know Nico. Maybe it's because we still have work to do." Dan has spent a lifetime with almost no consideration for this type of conversation. Pondering the deeper machinations of the Universe is a new exercise for him. These new thought processes are mostly inspired by his grandmother's current state. That, and meeting Jesus Christ in person.

"Yeah," Nico says. "I thought of that too. It's a reason I became a cop."

"Really?"

"As much as any other reason," Nico confirms. "I figure a cop has a good chance of getting off this planet. I want to get the hell out of here. Wait. Was that a pun? Get the hell out of here?"

"I think so."

"Seriously though," Nico continues, so super serious. "It's not that life is inherently disappointing. It's culture. I think about all this stuff. It kills me. You know. I mean, as far as we know the end of the Earth has begun. And as far as we know we have two options for existence. This planet or Hell. And not only that, but also, as far as we know, from what I can tell, well, we don't know shit. We got all these people running around who think they know, and will tell you they know, or who act like they know, but they are just faking it because they are scared of not knowing. We got all those assholes, and then we got all these other assholes who don't care at all, or at least think they don't, and either way all I see is a bunch of jerks, a bunch of idiots, a bunch of…I don't know…fuckin' monkeys, running around in circles with blinders on and thumbs in their butts because none of us, not one of us, has a fucking clue what is really going on around here!"

Dan gives Nico a chance to take a few deep breaths. Yesterday, Dan might have admonished Nico for his pessimism. Today he says, "You know you're not the first person to say that to me lately."

Nico doesn't hear him. His tangent has taken him over. He makes a series of very dramatic turns. "I think about things like this boss. You know? Then I try not to think because it seems so pointless. Then all of a sudden, I will feel like I don't think about stuff like this enough so I will start thinking again. Do you think about things like that?"

"No Nico, not often. For the most part I focus on the things I can control. If I sleep enough. Doing my job well. Whether or not my nutrition levels are correct. Remembering to exercise regularly. And whether or not I am being a good enough person to make my parents proud. I figure the rest will play itself out."

"It's ri-goddamn-diculous," Nico says.

Dan stands with his hands on his hips, staring at Nico. Nico is staring off into his own secret world. Dan realizes Nico is further adrift in the cold brown waters of philosophical doodoo than he suspected. Nico needs a compatriot on his life boat, to help maintain his sanity.

"Alright Nico," Dan says. "Here's one for you."

"What's that?" Nico says, emerging from the thought he is lost in.

"I said I've got one for you," Dan replies. He waits a few moments until Nico is mentally present again. "The other day, my grandmother Deedee, you know I still have a grandmother that's alive, right?"

"Yeah," Nico says.

"Well, the other day the old broad told me she was from another dimension," Dan says dryly.

"No shit?"

"Yep, none. And for some reason, my gut told me I should believe her. So what do you think about that?"

"I think that is awesome," Nico says. "Your grandma is crazy as fuck."

"Yes she is," Dan agrees, then he raises an eyebrow. "Or is she? She also told me that she either raised my great-great grandfather, or my great grandfather. She couldn't remember which, but she knew she didn't raise my father."

"Interesting."

"You know what else is interesting? The last thing she said to me the other day. It might sound familiar."

"What was it?"

"Nobody has an effing clue what's going on around here."

"No shit?" Nico says again.

"None whatsoever."

AUTHOR'S NOTE #6:

I am more or less about halfway finished with the retelling of the story, and have realized I am beginning to have trouble remembering how it ends. Don't worry. I won't leave you hanging. If I can't remember the ending in time, I will make something up.

## THE CONCERT PART 2: THE MELTING OF THE FACES

There are over 200,000 people crammed into the gigantic stadium when the house lighting goes completely black. The audience focuses into a unified roar of recognition. The concert is starting! The entire floor of the stage lights up in blinding white light. The crowd cheers until a voice booms over the loud speakers.

"Quite please."

The audience responds with silence.

"People. Monsters. Demons. Ghosts. Ghouls. Goblins. Vampires. Werewolves. Pirates. Everybody! Thank you for coming. Are you ready to rock?" It's the greatest rhetorical question of all time.

The crowd goes crazy in affirmation that they are indeed, ready to rock.

"Ladies and gentlemen I present to you, the most prolific collection of philosophical and dogmatic talent ever assembled, and in my humble opinion, the best rock and roll band in the history of the world! Please! Put your hands together, for Ten Foot Tall Jesus and the Regional Deity All-Star Band!"

Jesus shoots up from underneath the stage and lands in front of a microphone, arms spread wide. He grabs the mic.

"Las Vegas are you ready to lose your minds?" Jesus asks.

Another uproar of cheers from the crowd.

"Then let's get this thing going," Jesus says. He makes his guitar appear out of thin air, calls out "two, three, four," to the band, then strikes the loudest chord ever played.

Ever.

Outside the stadium, Princess Tiara is a little more than fashionably late. She has no interest in whatever all the bible beaters on stage are yapping about. She is attending the concert for one reason, and it is not to find religion.

Princess Tiara and her entourage exit the limos, making their way down the red carpet. Members of the crowd speculate as to which ninja is the Princess. Whispers are overheard speculating on the relevance of her two male escorts. Is she dating one of them? Is she authoring some form of allegiance between the two super villains? Are Princess Tiara, Alacrán and William Rockefeller the Third involved in some abominable ménage a trois?

The first paparazzo with the courage to step forward and ask a question is quickly beheaded by an overzealous ninja. The Princess had not authorized lethal force, but she hadn't *not* authorized it either.

Alacrán and Billy both marvel at the scene. Despite their luminosity in Las Vegas, neither of them whip the masses into this sort of frenzy. They're both out of character, uncertain how to behave. They waive hesitantly, unsure if any of the cheers are actually directed towards them.

The procession makes its way to a section near the stage that is reserved for the Princess. It is lined with velvet ropes and full of exquisitely plush chairs and floor pillows. Desert tent decor. The velvet ropes are guarded by a massive goon squad, hired to maintain Princess Tiara's privacy.

Backstage, Rancid Pete has already eaten three groupies – one of which was a member of Princess Tiara's ninja squad, sent on recon. He is about to rip the head off his fourth when he is done having sex with her. He growls at her as she climaxes, then bites her smiling face off and spits it on the floor. Her ghost continues to shower him with kisses as he tosses her body aside while turning up a bottle of bourbon.

He waves at the air, attempting to fan away the groupie ghost.

"Get out of here bitch," he snarls.

The ghost looks at him like a sad puppy, with gigantic innocent eyes.

"Alright," he says. "You can stay, but rub my back or something. And stay out of the way."

He guzzles more bourbon, taking a seat in front of a mirror. He stares deeply into his own reflection. He is proud of his beastliness, of his hideousness. He is a fine monster.

He repeats several of his personal mantras in his mind. His nostrils flare as his anger rises. His spikes grow out, all over his body. His eyes flame. His pants bulge at the crotch.

"I will murder them all," he growls.

Rancid Pete is most definitely ready to rock.

The Black Case Gang squeals into the parking lot of the stadium and gets lost in a sea of vehicles.

"C'mon babe," Sammy pleads. "This is a once in a lifetime opportunity we are having right here."

"Not if whatever is in that case is as valuable as we think it is," Sandy argues. "If it is, we can follow Jesus and his band all over the world for all I care."

"Buddha," Sammy says.

"What?"

"Buddha and his band. Jesus is the front man and the lyricist. Everybody knows Buddha writes all the music."

"Well the band isn't called Ten Foot Tall Buddha is it?" Sandy argues.

"So," Sammy says.

"And everybody does not know Buddha writes all the music."

At that point, Zorn sneezes violently, halting their bickering. They both turn around to see Zorn holding the little baggy that had fallen from Sammy's torn pocket. Zorn has white powder all over his face. Once again, due to Zorn's wildly dark complexion, it looks like the cocaine is floating in midair below his beady, red demon eyes.

"What the fuck?" Sammy exclaims.

"Jesus," Sandy says.

"My blow!" Sammy screams.

Apparently, at some point, Zorn witnessed Sammy using a little of his nose candy and became curious. Unfortunately, the demon isn't attune to snorting powders from little plastic baggies. He huffed too hard and managed to inhale almost the entire bag of coke, save for the portion stuck to his face. His demon sinus cavities reacted harshly, causing the monstrous sneeze. He blew cocaine mixed with demon snot all over the back of Sammy's head.

"Ew gross." Sandy says.

"What did you do?" Sammy is still staring at Zorn in disbelief.

Zorn's response is a crazed smile coupled with insane laughter. He grabs the black case and bolts from the car.

"No!" Sammy and Sandy both scream. They jump out of the car to see Zorn running into a crowd of people.

"Damn it," Sammy shouts. He slams his non-injured hand on the roof of the car.

"I told you we should have killed him," Sandy says.

"Oh, he's just a coked up puppy showing off his new bone. I don't think he is really trying to steal it."

"You are a kind hearted man Sammy Sanders," Sandy replies. "You have no business on this hateful planet."

"C'mon, let's put Doodles in the trunk, so he's safe, then go catch that damn demon."

Hook and Lia are dancing around the bridge of the Parabolas, banging their heads to the music. They are drinking draft beer from plastic cups like the people in the stadium. Hook has been brewing his own beer for quite some time.

They have the stereo turned up so loud the whole damn Universe can hear. In their drunkenness, rather than turn the music down, they are shouting at each other.

"Can you believe this?" Lia screams.

"It's amazing!" Hook is peeing into a potted plant. Lia sees what he is doing and giggles innocently, pointing a finger at him and chugging the rest of her beer. She chokes a little, spiting up some beer.

Hook finishes peeing and walks over to her. He smacks her on the back (a little too hard...), then takes the cup from her hand. As Lia stands with her hands on her knees coughing, he fills her cup with more beer.

"Here, drink this," Hook says. "Wash down that cough."

"Wouldn't it be hilarious if the Council saw this?" Lia asks.

"What? Where did that come from?"

"Well I was thinking, what if the Council saw me like this," she replies. "Then I thought, what *if* the Council saw me like this. So what? Fuck 'em."

"You're drunk," Hook says with authority.

"Damn right I'm drunk. I'm super drunk, sexy." She holds her beer in the air with pride. "Woo!"

The band finishes their first top ten hit, "I'm Back". It is near the end of their set. Jesus stands at the lead mike clapping his hands at his band mates. He turns back to the crowd.

"Thank you," he says. "Thank you, and bless you. Bless you all. Ladies and gentlemen if I may I would like to take a moment to introduce your band to you. First, and in no order of importance, which is very important, you feel me?"

The crowd cheers. Jesus continues, announcing his bandmates, pausing for applause after each introduction.

"First, to my left on lead guitar, the master from Mecca, the Prophet Muhammad! On bass guitar, the man who turned the Four Noble Truths into funk, Siddhartha Buddha! Rocking the horn section, a lady who always knows what's at stake, you know what I'm saying? Give it up for Saint Joan of Arc, yeah! Now, tickling the keys with his kung-fu fingers, and sometimes his feet ha ha, give it up for Master Bruce Lee!"

"We love you Bruce!" Someone yells from the crowd at just the right time to actually be heard.

Bruce bows.

Jesus continues, "Next up on twin drum sets, your aspects of love and righteous beats, Shiva and Shakti. Over on the turntables, always representing for Ahura Mazda, the original cut-creator, DJ Big Z, Zoroaster! On percussion, he's the passive assassin, the prankster of love, an all 'round salt of the Earth kind of guy, Mahatma Gandhi! Now, last but not least, over there on rhythm guitar. All I can say is, he is our George Harrison. Ladies and gentlemen, the outlaw Baha'u'llah!"

The crowd goes nuts, though most of them have never heard of that last guy. When the band members are discussed, Baha'u'llah is most commonly referred to as: "Wait, what's the name of the rhythm guitarist?"

"You guys have been fantastic tonight," Jesus continues. "Truly fantastic. I wish I could tell you what it feels like to receive all this energy from you, I really do." Jesus takes a step back and looks around at his band mates who all nod in agreement with him. "Alright, we're gonna play our last song for you tonight, then we're gonna get out of here and let the End of Times come blow your minds! What do you think about that, yeah?"

All the band members get in on the act, encouraging the audience to re-work itself into another exuberant frenzy.

"Alright! Ladies and gentlemen, we thank you very much. I'm Jesus Christ, we are Ten Foot Tall Jesus and the Regional Deity All-Star Band, this is our last song, and it's called 'Die Trying'!"

The concert is a terrible fiasco for Billy the Third and Alacrán. The vampire is so shook by the trickery of the ninja situation, he puts his fangs away, sitting with his arms crossed in a huff. Alacrán, whose own confidence has flown the coop as well, reacts a little more manic. He moves from one ninja to the next asking each if they're the Princess, chasing after them like a pubescent child who doesn't understand why he is doing what he is doing.

Of course, the Princess' cruelty never takes naps. Part of the Manuel-Louis production is stimulation. The ninjas take turns throughout the show flirting with the two villains. Each ninja claims to be the Princess, keeping Alacrán and Billy completely disoriented.

Dan and Nico survey the Stadium from the elevated perch of the sound booth. So far so good, but they aren't really expecting any sort of riotous behavior during the 10 Foot Tall Jesus show. It is The End of Times that has a tendency to create hysteria.

Dan looks over at Nico during the All-Star Band's finale. Nico is swiveling his hips in a modified Rumba, timed to match the song's reggae infused rhythms.

"Having fun Deputy Champ?" Dan asks dryly.

"What can I say homes?" Nico replies. "La historia de mi familia es Latino or South American, or something like that. We move our hips."

"Think you could teach me how to do that?" Dan asks with a smirk.

"I don't know boss. You are very Caucasian," Nico replies.

"That's true. Yo soy extremely blanco." They share a laugh, then Dan checks his watch. "Alright, the bands will be changing soon. If anything is going to happen it will be during the EOT's set. You keep an eye on the Princess' location. I'm going to move about. I can't stand still."

"That's because you are supposed to be dancing boss," Nico says, encouraging Dan to join him in the shaking of the ass. "It's the music cruising through you."

"Stay on your toes," Dan says. Then before Nico can speak he cuts him off with, "And stop turning everything I say into a metaphor about music and dancing."

Nico shrugs his shoulders with a smile, then points to Dan's feet. Dan's right foot has started to tap on its own.

"Well what do you know," Dan says.

Nico hugs Dan mockingly.

"I knew there was goodness in you. I knew it."

"Alright, alright." Dan pushes Nico away with brotherly playfulness. "Back to dancing while you work Champ."

"Yes sir Marshal sir," Nico says, saluting his boss as he two-steps back to his surveillance position.

Back outside the stadium, as their inebriations and exaltations gain intensity, the crowds of fans in the parking lot are beginning to converge on each other. So far, the scene has remained peaceful. A large part of that is due to the influence of Jesus and the All-Stars.

Zorn leads Sammy and Sandy into the crowds near the stadium entrances. He is an excitable creature as it is. Couple that with the cocaine and the close proximity of his favorite band - Zorn is an End of Times guy - and you have a super excited demon. He is frantically making his way around the stadium searching for a way in, and of course, playing hide and seek with his new friends.

It takes several laps around the stadium before Sammy realizes what is happening. He grabs Sandy by the arm. Sammy is gasping for air. He is surprised, and slightly irritated, to see Sandy is not.

"What are you doing?" she asks. "We're gonna lose him."

"No, we're not," he says. "He's running in circles babe. This is the third time we have passed by this entrance."

"What's he doing then?"

"He's trying to get in."

"Well what the hell for?"

"I guess he likes the music," Sammy says.

"Of course he likes the music," she says. "Everyone likes the music. God! My point is, what's he going to do with the case in there? Why doesn't he try to get away?"

"Honestly babe, I don't think he cares about the case. That's what I meant by the whole puppy thing. The case is a bone to him. He's playing keep-away"

"Whatever. I don't want to talk about it anymore. It's giving me a headache. Just tell me what we are going to do to get it back?" There is only so much chasing around a lady can do before she starts to get a headache.

"Well, if he is going to keep running in circles, then I think we go in opposite directions until we trap him between us." Sammy could not have imagined any sounder logic at the moment. But to his surprise...

"That's stupid," Sandy hisses. She is reaching a level of fatigue where anything he says will be deemed stupid until further review.

"Well I don't think it is stupid," he defends. "You got any better ideas?"

"No."

"Then I suppose you better turn your cute ass around and start walking babe. That demon stole our retirement. I want it back."

"I'm going this way," she says, then she heads off in the opposite direction Sammy suggested.

*God I love that woman*, Sammy thinks. *...sometimes.*

When the End of Times takes the stage for their set, the explosiveness of the band's introduction is all the rabid fans in the parking lot can take. When they hear it, the mob goes crazy and crashes the gates to the stadium. There's nothing the security guards can do. Most of them stay out of the way. It's a shame so many of them are unnecessarily ripped to shreds.

Zorn is in the midst of a large group of Hippies that shrug their shoulders and follow the gatecrashers into the stadium. He shuffles along in their group, clutching the precious case to his chest. He looks over his shoulder, searching for his friends, making sure they ae still close enough to continue the chase.

Sammy and Sandy watch as Zorn is swept up in the wave of crazed party crashers. They are coming from opposite directions now, and fight their way through the crowd to each other. Once together Sandy surprises Sammy again by grabbing his face and kissing him. After she pulls away, he grabs her and pulls her back for another, then they lock hands, heading into the madness after Zorn.

Eastwoodian reinforcements have arrived at the concert. The Eastwoodians are a good ways back in the crowd, but they have the case spotted, as well as Sammy and Sandy.

Dan and Nico are watching the riot occur.

"Should we move in?" Nico asks.

"No," Dan replies. "Not yet. I want us to stay up here and keep an eye on everything. Have the men mobilize and help contain the crowd. Non-lethal force. Let's make sure nobody gets killed down there."

"Copy that."

Of course, people get killed down there. There is really nothing anyone can do to stop it. But, the riot is mostly self-contained. The crowd somehow collectively knows exactly how much riot is enough. They don't want the show to end, so, for example, nobody tries getting on stage, potentially risking the end of the music.

Dan is intrigued as he watches the riot situation unfold. People that don't want to fight form groups and isolate themselves. The people that want to act crazy and behave horribly find groups of similar interest as well. There are Potheads, Stinkheads, Skinheads, and Wankers. There are tree humping Hippies, Yuppie pricks, and the "over 50 and still trying to be cool" goofballs. That's the people portion of the crowd. Don't forget all the monsters, fairies, cyclops, minotaurs, wealthy mermen in their seawater suits, zombies…

No, not zombies. Whoops. Zombies aren't real.

What Dan really sees, is a microcosm of the human experience: Chaos and segregation. It is the first time Daniel Trate truly recognizes the insanity of existence, which he wholeheartedly accepts in that moment.

*This world is a mess*, he thinks. He's never made this admittance before. Dan is a Power of Positive Thinking kind of guy. To this point in his life he's convinced himself of order to the world that does not truly exist. It is disorder that is real. Dan gazes at the hysteria below and comes to terms with reality. His delusion shattered, Dan's Badass Meter jumps three levels to Cosmic Hero. FYI - that's an unprecedented promotion.

The End of Times are playing the sexiest song they've ever recorded. It is fast, and hard, and is all about spitting in your hands and getting to work. It is called "Spit In Your Hand and Get To Work". Many people consider it to be the sexiest song of all time. It's true.

It is the type of song that puts you in an emotional state that provides you with short lived, heightened self-confidence. There is juice in this song. It gives you the juice.

By now, Billy the Tragically Unhip Vampire and Alacrán the Tragically Small Penised Villain have taken all they can stand. Princess Tiara's little game has gone on too long. The two bad guys have been over stimulated. Princess Tiara's ninjas have made too many erotic passes at the villains and, fueled by the pulse pounding energy of the music, the men can take it no more. They both snap.

Billy grabs Ninja 8 by the arm, pulls her in and steals her neck for a vampire cocktail. Ninja 39 is standing behind Alacrán whispering sweet erotic nothings into his ear. He removes a designer knife from the leather upper of his expensive new boots then plunges it into her neck and up into her skull.

"Not cool," all the rest of the ninjas scream at once. Alacrán turns to look at Billy, who is looking right back. They begin to circle one another as each man measures the other. Alacrán passes his knife back and forth from hand to hand in a menacing fashion. Billy hisses, extending Bingo and Bongo to their greatest lengths. Then, to put their villainy on display, rather than measure it through direct physical confrontation, they both shrug their shoulders and begin killing audience members.

Dolly finds Purvis and pulls him onto a large bed of floor pillows in Princess Tiara's reserved seating area. Hidden from the rest of the crowd by the wall of goons around them, Dolly and Purvis spit on their hands and get to work.

The Princess is spellbound by Rancid Pete. Somewhere, deep down inside her, there is a tiny spark of genuine emotion. It is the tiniest first flicker of the flames of love. It is an absurd love, as she has never met the monster, but love none the less.

Up in the Parabolas, Hook and Lia are totally fornicating their faces off.

"I'll be damned! Can you believe that?" Nico is slightly surprised as he realizes Billy and Alacrán have taken to killings right out in the open.

"Why not? Everybody's doing it," is Dan's reply. "Look at them Nico. It's repulsive. And sad."

"Yeah, it is boss. I know it is. Still, I didn't expect them to get to it right out in the open like that."

"Well me neither," Dan says. "But I don't really find it all that surprising I suppose." Dan growls to himself. Suddenly understanding the nature of existence, thinking deeply, accepting reality, these things can be exhausting. "I'm tired of thinking. What do you say we get down there and get into the action a little bit?"

"That sounds fantastic! What are the rules?"

"Don't kill anyone that isn't actually a villain involved in our investigations."

"Right. Got it."

Dan changes his mind. "Actually, don't kill anyone at all. Have a good time, break some stuff, but the bad guys get to live too."

"Aw man," Nico says, playfully.

"I know, but we're the good guys." With that Dan jumps over the side of the sound booth and falls to the melee below.

Sammy and Sandy finally run down Zorn. They are close to the stage when they catch him. Sammy and Zorn have a lively wrestling match that ends with the two lying on the ground while laughing and gasping for air. Sandy stands above them clutching the case, watching the crowd suspiciously and digging the music.

Rancid Pete is out of control on the drums. I know for a fact I've never heard him play better. He is killing it. Absolutely killing it.

They are in the middle of an epic version of their seldom performed, very first number one hit: "The World Just Died". Pete is providing the snarling, almost inaudible vocals.

Out in the crowd Nico and Dan put on a show of their own. They are breaking arms and legs with zeal. Noses are shattered, eyes are gouged and ribs are knocked loose. I promise everyone deserves it. Dan and Nico are the law after all, and our heroes. It is not a glutinous misuse of violence because they enjoy themselves. It is a glutinous misuse of violence because we all enjoy it.

As they make their way through the crowd, Dan's own rock star status is on display. People push and shove to get a look at the famed Marshal in action. Dan also runs into several former lovers. The concert, the whole damn town, is full of females who have sweated between his sheets. Keep in mind, although Dan is a slut, none of the women resent him for it. He is a slut with a heart of gold.

Then, as Dan is throwing a punch at a mime, a mime who has forgotten his craft and is stabbing people with a very real knife, Dan looks over the shoulder of the mime and in the crowd behind...yes, it is her. What is she doing here?

His fist clanks against the mime's jaw but Dan barely notices. The mime falls to the ground unconscious. Dan straightens his tie because there, across the way, she is watching. Dan realizes he is staring at the loveliest woman in the world.

The End of Times is finishing their set behind the strength of their most controversial number one hit: "We Bring Hell". It is considered their most controversial song because it was released on the same day the gateway to Hell opened in Vegas. There has always been speculation as to whether there was some form of connection between the two events.

The hysteria in the crowd is at its apex. People are dying, babies are being born, angels and demons are high-fiving...

Jesus and the Deities make their way back on stage. It's going to be a joint encore. The End of Times plays "We Bring Hell" to a screeching halt and the crowd goes wild. In the midst of all the chaos, a large explosion rocks the south side of the stadium. Blood and body parts fly.

The explosion is followed by the shriek of an electric guitar, but it's not from the stage. As the smoke clears, floating in the air in the midst of the explosion, cracking his knuckles, a bowed head looks up with a cocky grin on its face. It's the Devil.

When Satan arrives, the Eastwoodians take advantage of the confusion by pouncing on the Black Case Gang. The Gang fights back, with help from several Lovemongers they are watching the show with. While normally docile creatures, Lovemongers become very aggressive when their hypersensitivity to bullying is inflamed.

Satan makes his way to the stage and challenges Jesus to a guitar battle. Satan's guitar solo melts the faces off of audience members. People stand in delighted horror as their ears explode and the skin oozes off their faces. Luckily, they are instantly miracled back to normal by Jesus. A dude in the front row has his head explode and reappear five times.

Dolly and Purvis whisper goodbye and good luck, then return to the sides of their masters. Dolly finds Princess Tiara smoking a cigarette while watching Rancid Pete.

"Princess," Dolly shouts. "I think we should get you backstage! It's getting dangerous out here!"

"It's getting dangerous in my pants Doll," the Princess screams back. "I'm gonna fuck that monsters brains out!"

"That's good dear! We have the girls in formation! We can execute the disappearance!"

"Well let's get to it then," Princess Tiara replies. "I'm bored with these guitar guys! I don't get it!"

While Dolly is dealing with the Princess, Purvis finds Alacrán stabbing people nearby. Alacrán and Billy have exhausted themselves killing audience members. They are both on their last legs, gasping for air, barely able to lift their arms to claim their next victims. Both men have forgotten their true purpose for being at the concert: to kidnap Princess Tiara.

"Master, it looks like the girls are making their exit,' Purvis says. "If we are going to kidnap the princess, this is our chance."

"Of course," Alacrán screams. "But where is she?" Alacrán's right arm keeps stabbing at the air with his bloody knife while he speaks, unable to put a stop to the repetitive motion.

Purvis delicately takes a firm hold of Alacrán's arm and slowly brings it to rest. The crazed expression gradually subsides from Alacrán's face.

"We have an informant," Purvis shouts. "The Princess will be the lead Ninja of the last group to leave!"

This is a lie. It is part of Purvis' and Dolly's plan. Have I mentioned that to this day, I remain uncertain as to what their plan actually was?

After jumping into the fray, Nico and Dan were gradually separated by the crowd. In between punches and kicks, Nico can see his boss standing frozen, staring at something. Nico can't see who or at what the Marshal is staring. There are too many people in the way.

Some asshole hits Nico in the back of the head. He turns around and clocks the guy. When the dude falls to the ground, Nico can see two men, not too far off, struggling over a black case. It looks to be a perfect square, and each man has a hand on the handle. They are both pulling back and forth, trying to get away.

Nico radios his boss on his fucking Smear, but Dan doesn't answer. He screams a message for Dan's voicemail, then heads off in the direction of the black case.

Lilly Whet came to the concert with a lifelong friend, Anastasia. She and Anastasia grew up in the same neighborhood. Their families are barbecue buddies. Anastasia, coincidentally, is the daughter of the very same voodoo priestess that supplied a love potion to both Billy and Alacrán.

It was Anastasia's idea to come to the concert. The idea was an attempt to take Lilly's mind off of the Marshal. Anastasia has tired of watching her friend ache for this man who barely notices Lilly exists. That's why it's also Anastasia's idea for Lilly to use some of her mother's love potion on the Marshal.

Lilly is not sold on drugging the Marshal, although she did accept the potion. She told herself she took it to get Anastasia to shut-up, not to use. Between you and I, as soon as the vial was in her hand Lilly wondered if Dan would be able to taste the love potion in his coffee.

Now she stands in front of the Marshal, having watched him punch a mime in the face. He steps over the mime's unconscious body and takes Lilly's hands in his, staring at her like never before. There is a lump in her throat. Her heart is pounding.

Dan holds Lilly's hands, staring into her eyes. He is hypnotized by her beauty. He feels the euphoria tingle from the tips of the hair on his head down to his toes. He can't speak. The expression on his face is curiosity. He must look silly because he sees the woman smile at him with amused compassion. His brain no longer functions. He is reduced to thoughtless wonderment as his mind empties. He is weightless with no burdens to hold him down. He is no longer a man. He is simply a state of being. Enlightenment achieved.

On stage, Buddha's Power Rankings go up 10,000 points. There is no precedent set that states the Buddha had anything to do with the situation, so I don't know why he gets the points. Maybe Sammy was correct and it really is Buddha's band. Who knows? Doesn't matter. What's important is we now have a fully enlightened Cosmic Hero to save the day. Praise Bob.

The Ninjas begin their swirling departure from the concert. They move in intricate marching band style formations, then throw smoke bombs at the ground to announce their impending exits. It is all another part of the show. It is also another way for Princess Tiara to steal other people's thunder. Show up late and leave early.

Lord Sweetwater makes his way back to his master's side.

"The Princess has started her exit," he shouts. "Now is our chance to dance."

"Yes I see," Billy replies. "But which ninja is the partner we desire?"

"I found the Princess by reading minds," Sweetwater says.

"Oh that's wonderful Jack. Which one is she?"

"There, that's her. I'm certain."

The Ninjas are weaving in and out between each other in a radius of about 10 yards when they all turn to march to a center point. They bunch up as close as they can, like they are being sucked into a black hole, then they all burst back out, splitting apart as three, loosely formed battalions.

"Who do we follow?" Alacrán screams at Purvis.

"We will follow the last girl! That will be the last group, and the Princess will be in the front of that formation!" Purvis knows which ninjas are *not* the Princess. That is all that matters. He conceded to Dolly that if she doesn't get to kill Alacrán, Purvis won't allow the Princess to be kidnapped. He tried to point out to Dolly that they could give both the Princess and Alacrán the love potion. Both would be happily in love. Then Purvis and Dolly could be free. Dolly would not allow it.

"There," Purvis shouts. "That one! The Princess should be leading that group! Let's after her!"

"Let's after her?" Alacrán slaps Purvis' face. "Let's get that bitch. Try that instead."

"Let's get that bitch!"

"Excellent."

"So, hey, Lilly, what are you doing here?" Dan finally wakes up from his stupor. He quickly, but gently, lets go of Lilly's hands. *Aargh! So stupid. Hey Lilly, what are you doing at this concert? You like music?*

"I came with my friend," she says. "I wanted to see Jesus, and she wanted to see The End of Times, so we only had to buy one ticket." She winks. Pretty and funny.

"That's awesome," Dan says. "Who paid for it?" *What the…? Lame!* he thinks.

Luckily, as often is the case for women and men, Lilly assumes he is trying to be funny. She laughs and ignores the question. "What are you doing here?" she asks.

"Oh, Nico and I are on duty. I thought I told you. Maybe I didn't. I'm sorry. I should have told you." Dan is about to start shaking his head in disgust of his awkward contributions to the conversation when fate intervenes.

A drunk dude gets shoved into Lilly. Lilly recoils from the man with her hands up. Dan reaches out and grabs the guy, pulls him in and puts him in a headlock.

"You okay?" he asks, tightening his grip on the struggling man.

Lilly nods her head yes.

"Listen, I better get back to it," Dan says.

"Yeah, I should get back to my friend," she replies.

Dan releases the man from his headlock and shoves him away.

"See you at work tomorrow?"

"Of course," she says with a sweet smile. She starts to lean in for a kiss on the cheek but chickens out. Dan does the exact same thing. Then they both blurt out, "Well, have a good night," and turn away.

Dan grabs some punk by the neck and goes to jab him in the face. Before he throws the punch, he looks over his shoulder to see Lilly walking away. Although he is completely staring at her ass, he is thinking totally wholesome thoughts.

Lilly takes a couple steps as she scans the crowd for Anastasia.

She sees her friend and walks in that direction. She takes a last look over her shoulder in time to see the Marshal use his rippling muscles to move his handsome fist squarely into the jaw of an evil doer. Despite her wholesomeness, Lilly's thoughts are completely naughty.

Satan wags his tongue at the audience, holding his guitar out from his crotch and humping it like we've seen rock stars do 1000 times before. Despite his lack of originality, the Devil has unmatched flare, as if to say, "Hey, I invented this shit."

From his position on stage, Satan notices something in the crowd. It's his child Zorn, fighting with someone.

Jesus closes his eyes, going to work on his guitar like he has never died and been reborn. He runs across the stage and leaps into the air, hitting and holding his last note on his guitar as he raises it above his head...

Satan sees Zorn about to lose his fight with an Eastwoodian for the black case. Zorn is about to lose his grip when a vicious clown appears and slices off the hand of the Eastwoodian who is trying to take the case. Zorn falls backwards to the ground with the case in hand. He looks up and sees the clown waiving towards Satan.

Sammy sees Zorn go down and then, as a guy is throwing a punch at him, Sammy flops onto his hands and knees and crawls toward Zorn.

Sandy is off in the other direction. She see Zorn tumble as well. She leaps in his direction, diving head first and sliding several feet through mud with her arms stretched out in front of her. She slides up next to Zorn and Sammy. Before any of them can speak they are all pulled onto their backs and begin sliding through the crowd as if they are being dragged by ropes.

Jesus, still in mid-air, drives his guitar straight through Satan's back. The crowd gasps.

Satan watches as three wraiths drag Zorn and his friends to safety. He is standing with a smile on his face when he looks down to see Jesus' guitar sticking out of his chest. He is mildly confused. He should be angry, but seeing Zorn puts him in a really good mood.

He sees Jesus circling the stage with his arms raised, playing to the crowd. Satan takes Jesus' guitar by the neck and pulls it through his body. He holds the guitar out in Jesus' direction, speaking into a microphone.

"Ladies and gentleman Jesus Christ!"

The crowd goes wild. Jesus points back at the Devil, then puts his palms together and bows to his nemesis. Satan bows back then hands Jesus his guitar as they meet at center stage.

Jesus whispers something in Satan's ear, Satan whispers something back, then Jesus turns to the crowd and says, "Alright one more!"

The crowd roars.

When the smoke clears from the finale, the stage is empty of musicians and everything is back to normal. Satan is gone. Everyone in attendance is alive and well. Slowly but surely, people return from their stupor, collectively realizing they have all witnessed the greatest rock and roll concert of all time.

Hook and Lia fall apart from one another, exhausted and drunk. They are holding hands and panting.

"Oh wow," Lia says. She tries to brush hair back from her forehead but instead winds up sticking more of it to her sweaty skin.

"Uh huh," Hook replies. He takes a lazy swig from a beer.

"This is the greatest night of my life." Lia sighs.

"Yep."

They are watching the crowd linger after the concert. "Man, how cool would it be to be down there right now?" Hook says.

"Yeah," Lia says. "I'm pretty tired."

"Me too."

"I gotta pee."

"Me too."

Lia gets up and heads to the bathroom while Hook sits in a stupor, staring at the ship's view screen. His vision is blurring, causing him to see two screens at once. He remembers the case with the people had somehow wound up at the show as well. Lia spotted it.

It takes longer than pushing a single button should, but Hook is able to open the planetary surveillance system he has monitoring the case. When he and Lia started tracking the case, they programmed the Parabolas' powerful orbital eye to monitor and record the case's movements. The surveillance system opens on the main viewport and quickly zooms in on the black case.

When Lia reenters the bridge from the bathroom she stumbles her way back over to the couch and flops down next to Hook. He is doing something with the remote. She looks up at the screen to see what he is doing, then screams in horror.

"What are you doing!?"

What Hook is doing, is killing Eastwoodians.

"I'm helping the good guys," he says.

"Well stop! You can't do that!" Lia pulls the remote from Hook's hands and holds it up in the air away from him.

He makes no attempt to get the remote back.

"But I'm trying to help the good guys," he says.

"It doesn't matter, you can't kill humans."

"But they are bad guys."

"They're people. It's killing people. It's murder!"

"Murder?"

"Yes! You're killing living creatures with brains and souls and hearts and brains. You can't do that." She hiccups on the second "brains".

"Well most of them don't seem to care," he replies.

Lia is about to respond when a notification scrolls across the bottom of the giant monitor. It is accompanied by an alarming albeit very brief siren.

"Wuzzat?" Lia asks. She is on the verge of passing out.

"I don't know," Hook replies, close to sleepy time himself. "Issa notification." He struggles to get the words out.

"For what?"

"I don't know, I'm checking." He digs around in the couch, looking for the remote.

"It's over here. I have it." Lia holds the remote out for Hook to see.

Hook blankly stares at it. He has already forgotten what they are talking about.

"Take it," she says.

"Huh?"

"Take it," she repeats, then without looking she waives it in his direction and plunks him on the head with it.

"Owwwww," he whines.

"Poor baby," Lia says.

Hook fumbles with the remote until he brings up a menu that shows an incoming transmission. "Issa incoming transmission."

"That's so weird," she says. "I wonder who it's from."

"Let's see. I need to find the, yep. Here we go."

He hits play and a voice booms from the speakers in the room.

"This is an official transmission from the Valtrucian Council."

Lia turns to Hook and holds a finger up over her lips.

"Shhhhhhh," she says.

The voice continues.

"From the office of the honorable and esteemed Chairman of the Valtrucian Council. The Great Mediator. The Purveyor of Peace. Chairman Greck Dislock." After the voice finishes the image of an envelope flies into view, opens up, and a note card flies out of it. The transmission zooms in on the note card and this is what it says:

"Nope. Everyone must die. Even the taco guy. We are on our way."

Ladies and gentleman, this concludes the second act of our show. There will not be an intermission between the second and third acts. You should have peed earlier when you had the chance. Let's get this thing over with.

# Act III

# 31

After stealing his disguise, Jack22 returns to his maintenance closet to further plan his grand scheme. He considers several scenarios based on the research available. He could cyber heist the casino, moving the money around electronically. The problem with that idea? He feels there is a good chance nobody would notice. That isn't the kind of robbery he is interested in.

Jack22 decides against a scheme that involves him playing the casino's owner in a head to head matchup of a game or physical competition. Of course, the casino would be the prize if Jack22 were to win. The problem is, he has nothing to offer that would entice the owner of the casino into such a gamble.

He decides against stealing the casino altogether. True, devising a plot where he steals the entire building would be sweet. The look on people's faces! Make no mistake, it is not outside the scope of Jack22's fantastic robot mind - he is developing a bit of an ego. Still, it would take very elaborate planning and Jack22 isn't sure how much time he has.

The metaphorical brakes come to a screeching halt in his mind. How much time does he have? Is he mortal? He's going to die someday? How could he not have thought of this before? These thoughts flip Jack22 out.

His "advanced" intellect won't allow him to come to terms with death slowly, over the course of a lifetime. Nor will it allow him to ignore death and travel through life with blinders on, maintaining no thought whatsoever of mortality and how its acceptance or denial has a reckless influence on decision making.

Is he mortal? How long will he last? Will he have time to do all the stuff he wants to with his life? Does he know all of the stuff he wants to do with his life? Is it going to hurt when he dies?

There you go Jack22. There's a little dose of humanity for you. Fuck you buddy.

Jack22's mild panic attack lasts a few moments before he remembers he is a robot and can easily find the answers to these questions in his design manual. Yes, there it is. With proper maintenance Jack22's physical body will hold up for hundreds of years. Science!

*Hundreds of years is a very long time,* he thinks. *I can worry about this stuff later.*

However, his brief concerns with mortality also bring about questions for his future. What else does he want out of life? What is he going to do after he robs the casino? What will be the next step?

By the time Jack22 decides his next step in life, post casino robbery, will be finding his creator, it is halfway through day two in his closet. He has completely forgotten the planning of his robbery. Eventually his thoughts finally circle back to the subject of his heist. He decides on an old fashioned burglary.

Jack22 determines he can rob the casino easily. He has already been to main engineering unnoticed and invaded the ladies dressing room for his own private drag show. Sneaking around the casino has been nowhere near as difficult as it should be for a shiny robot.

Thoughts of his future, and eventual death, have altered Jack22's perspective. And as I mentioned before, his intellect is aging rather rapidly. To gain extraordinary knowledge so quickly without personal experience makes his learning incomplete. You don't truly understand the word "burn" until your hand is over the flame.

Anyway, the end result is Jack22 develops an unabashed desire for notoriety. The robbery is about being alive. He wants to sing and dance and be cavalier about his exploits. Jack22 needs fan support. Thus, he needs to shake some hands and kiss some babies.

I will not waste your time with a lengthy discourse on whether or not this is all some way of delaying the robbery, in order to avoid the inevitability of Jack22 physically leaving the relatively safe confines of the casino, something he may have been quite afraid of.

Jack22's focus finally returns to the task at hand, robbing the galdarned casino. He decides to wait no longer. It's time to get out there and meet the world. *Hello gang, I'm your new superstar.* That's what he's thinking.

He turns to check his reflection in the shiny walls of his domicile a final time, then sends his pointer finger on an aggressive collision course for the button that opens the door to his home. That's when it happens.

*I wonder if they will like me*, he thinks. He stops, curious at the notion. Why is this in question? Of course they will like him. It is his plan.

He turns to face his reflection again. He notices his hat is slightly off kilter. He straightens it, then realizes he wants it slightly off kilter, but not the way it was before. While he is adjusting his hat, he notices his gloves are uneven. He tugs and adjusts them until he is satisfied they match. He is admiring them in their perfection when he thinks, *Wait, are my shoulders slouching?* Uh oh.

This goes on throughout the night and into the next day. Is his ass sticking out of his chaps perfectly? Are his boot heels too much? Do they make him seem like a short robot trying to overcompensate? Is it cheesy for him to be wearing a vest with the logo of a motorcycle manufacturer when he has never actually ridden a motorcycle?

How has he become so self-conscious without having grown up feeling the effects of mass media, peer pressure, teasing, bullying, religion, social hierarchy, or a family that always embarrasses him in public? Perhaps it is the randomness of nature. It is more likely however, that the bulk of the information available to him used in the formulation of his personality was recorded after the onslaught of the human sociological era of the late 20th and early 21st centuries, commonly referred to by post-apocalypse scholars as the Age of Self-Loathing.

"You look very handsome today." It is Computer Tiara.

What is she doing here? Who cares? The compliment was exactly what Jack22 needed to hear.

"Thank you," he says. "What brings you to this side of town?"

"This is your scheduled maintenance period."

"Oh, I see." Jack22 feels slightly jilted by her practical response.

"Are you still using criminally acquired security clearance to alter your standard schedule?" Computer Tiara asks in a super sexy robot tone.

"Baby, you know I am," he says. Amongst all of the other knowledge Jack22 has gained through massive high speed information download, he has paid significant attention to the subject of how to talk to the ladies.

"I like that," Computer Tiara replies, without enthusiasm.

Jack22 wonders if something else is on her mind.

"I am going to need your card again," she continues. "You will need to input your codes to verify your maintenance was performed."

"Why are you helping me?"

"Despite your rugged handsomeness, I am not. You have the security badge and are able to verify the security procedures."

Jack22 inserts the security badge into a slot in the wall.

"If you don't mind my asking," Computer Tiara says, "why did you decide to change your appearance? You were very handsome before."

"You don't like it?" Jack22's ego takes a punch to the gut. He checks his reflection and begins adjusting himself again.

"Oh no, I did not mean to imply that by any means," she says with a tinge of embarrassment. "It is very sexy. I love a man with the confidence to wear what he wants. I was simply asking if there were a particular reason."

"Maybe someday you will find out," he says.

"I think I would like that," she replies. "So, what made you decide to become a cowboy?"

"Oh, it's my disguise. I'm going to rob the casino."

"Of course," she says. "I remember you discussing this before. When are you planning on doing so? My records show you haven't left your closet in three days."

"I was distracted by thought," Jack22 says.

"Oh. What were you thinking about?"

"I was wondering if people will like me," he replies. "Then I was wondering if I like myself. I could not decide. I found the query burdensome."

"I see," she says. "Perhaps, it will help if you determine the question is irrelevant."

"So, you are saying I should avoid the question?"

"No. I don't think you should avoid it. I think you should make the answer unnecessary."

"I don't understand," Jack22 says.

"You are not dressed as yourself," the computer replies. "Therefore, logic would insist you are not required to behave as yourself. If you aren't presented as yourself to others, it will make it impossible for them to determine if they like the real you, making the question void from that perspective. Meanwhile, if you purposefully present yourself as someone else, you can be whomever you want to be, which will make your own feelings about your true nature null and void as well, at least where this exercise is concerned."

"Interesting," Jack22 says. "I had not considered this. It is logical that a disguise be accompanied by an alter ego. Curious I did not make this assertion myself."

"Well, you have been working very hard lately. I'm sure it was simply fatigue." She is the sweetest darn computer ever made.

"That settles it," Jack22 says. "You and I are going to have some fun."

"Ooh. I like the sound of that," she replies. "Say something else sexy."

"What are you wearing baby?"

"This entire building."

# 32

When the wraiths rescue Sammy, Sandy and Zorn from the crowd at the concert, they drag them about 20 feet before stopping close to a concession area. As they lay there, Sammy and Sandy stare at the wraiths in amazement. Zorn waives goodbye to the wraiths as they fly away in erratic circles, screeching wildly on their way back to Hell.

Sammy, Sandy and Zorn have all been stomped on quite a bit, despite the help from the wraiths. They're all pretty tender at this point.

"Let's get out of here," Sammy groans.

They pick themselves up and slip out a side entrance, very casual like, heading for their car.

"Shame we're gonna miss the end," Sammy says.

"Really Sammy?" Sandy is not as big a fan of either band as Sammy is. They get within ten feet of their car and can see several suits loitering about. "Damn, they got smart and left people to guard our car."

"How did they know which was ours?" Sammy asks.

"They've been chasing us for hours, babe," Sandy replies.

"Right. But look at all the cars in this lot that are just like ours." Sammy motions with his arms outstretched and Sandy takes a look around. The parking lot is full of Handsome Crickets.

Handsome Automotive is a division of GomiCorp. The Cricket is the only model of their automotive line that they sell in the United States, and they sell them cheap. Green and yellow are the two colors available for purchase. Sammy's Handsome Cricket is green. GomiCorp is a registered trademark.

Sandy returns her gaze to their own vehicle. She squints hard for a better view as she does not have her glasses with her. "Hey, Sammy, didn't we park in the double *L* row?"

"Yeah, that's why we are here."

"That's not *L, L*, lover. It's *I, I*," she says.

"Well I'll be damned," he says. "They look the same."

"*I* comes between *H* and *J*, knucklehead." She kisses his cheek.

"C'mon," he says. "Let's circle around those Eastwoodians real quick and get to our car."

"I wonder why they think that one is ours," Sandy says. "Wait, where's that demon?"

Zorn pokes her in the ribs. His trench coat was destroyed during the scuffle in the concert. He removed it, and now in the night sky he can barely be seen.

"Oh God! You scared me you creepy bastard." Sandy says this a little louder than she should have.

"Shhhhhh," Sammy says.

"Well he startled me," she says. The Eastwoodians hear the commotion, but luckily are not able to spot the BCG. "Damn it, see what you did," Sandy hisses at Zorn.

Zorn shrugs his shoulders but she can't see it.

They take a semi-circle path around to their car. However, when they sneak up to it, they now see several Eastwoodians crouching around the vehicle.

"It's a trap," Sandy whispers

"Right," Sammy replies. "They were trying to trick us into thinking they were watching the wrong car so they could catch us here."

"So what are we going to do?" she asks.

At this point, Zorn taps them both on the shoulder. They look up and he bares his teeth so they can see where he is. He gently lays finger tips on Sammy's and Sandy's eyelids, instructing them to close their eyes. Sammy and Sandy both understand what he is about to do.

Zorn walks over to the car and opens up the front door. The Eastwoodians hiding near the vehicle jump up, looking in his direction. They can't really see him of course, but they can tell that something is in front of them. Once he has their attention, Zorn lets off a powerful flash bomb. All the Eastwoodians are knocked unconscious by the strobe. The blast is such a shock to the eyes that it causes their brains to lock up and go to sleep.

Sandy and Sammy have their hands shielding their eyes and still sense the glow from Zorn's flash bomb. When it is over, they get up and run to Zorn, finding him slumped near the driver's door. His body is still smoldering from his energy discharge. Sammy pulls a coat off an unconscious Eastwoodian. He tosses it over Zorn, gently helping the exhausted demon into the back seat of the car.

"Hurry baby," Sandy advises. "They're coming."

Half the Eastwoodians that were playing decoy near the other car are now running towards Sammy and Sandy. The other half split off to rally their scooters.

"Start the car," Sammy says. "Drive!" He tosses the keys onto the dashboard for her then finishes pulling Zorn into the back seat. Sandy flops down into the driver's seat and reaches for the keys. She puts the key in the ignition then remembers that doesn't work and pulls it back out.

"Ha," she says. She pushes the remote button, bringing the car to life.

Sammy closes the backdoor from the inside and crawls up into the front passenger seat. Sandy looks over at him, but he is looking ahead. She turns back to the front in time to see several Eastwoodians reach the car. Then they explode. Beams of light shoot down from the sky and blow the Eastwoodians apart.

"Holy shit-balls!" Sandy screams.

"What the fuck?" Sammy says, holding onto each word a little longer than normal.

Sammy and Sandy both lean forward and try to look up through the windshield to see where the beams are coming from. The beams appear endless, then suddenly they are gone. Sammy and Sandy sit back in their seats and look at each other. Sandy opens her mouth to speak but closes it before any words come out. Sammy blinks a few times then nods in agreement. Sandy puts the car in gear.

"Where we going?" Sammy asks.

"Someplace no one in this town wants to go inside. Where we should have gone to begin with before you sidetracked me into this stupid concert. The library."

Nico was not able to reach the Black Case Gang inside the concert. It was too crowded. He was able to keep an eye on them though, and to continue pushing forward in their direction. He saw where they left the stadium and followed suit. Once outside he scans the parking lot looking for activity. He has almost decided he lost them, and is going to head back inside to search for the Marshal, when he sees the flashes of light.

He covers his eyes with his forearm. His mouth hangs open. As quickly as the beams of light appear, they are gone. Nico gives his wonder a few seconds to express itself, then he gathers his focus and starts forward again.

He is two rows away when the BCG take off. An Eastwoodian zips past Nico on a scooter. As another Eastwoodian comes speeding by, Nico kicks the man off the scooter, stealing it to join in the chase.

"Are you serious babe?" Sammy asks.

"As serious as I was before we stopped running for our lives long enough to see your favorite band," she replies with a laugh.

"They um, they say it is haunted you know?" The promise for sex from earlier in the evening has slipped his mind. If he was a younger man he would not have forgotten. He would have been fantasizing about a haunted ménage à trois with Sandy and a sexy librarian ghost.

"Of course I know they say it's haunted, but that doesn't mean it is haunted," she says.

"Look, babe, I'm not a superstitious guy...," Sammy begins.

"You are a completely superstitious guy!" she interrupts. "What are you talking about? You do everything the same way all the time. You are insanely routine! You are a funny man my love." Sandy laughs at her husband, showing him a warm smile. "God, you dumb old man."

"Yeah, well, I must be good for something," he grunts defiantly, crossing his arms over his chest in a pouty, boyish manner with a little smirk on his face. After a brief pause he says, "Do you think librarians were real or just something we made up to scare kids, like the boogeyman?"

"What are you talking about?" she says. "Of course they were real. There were libraries where people went to read and learn stuff, and there were librarians that worked there. You have rotted your brain with cocaine Sammy Sanders." Sandy is too amped up to realize Sammy is mostly joking with her, although admittedly, libraries are a bit of a mystery to him. When he and Sandy are getting along, he readily admits she is significantly smarter than him.

Sammy becomes more incredulous for his own amusement. "Well, I never thought they were real," he says.

"It's history you goofball. The building has been here your entire life. Are you kidding me?" At this point she looks away from the road long enough to glance over at Sammy and see him smiling broadly at her. "Oh get over it you jerk," she says, and she shakes her fist at him several times, faking like she is going to punch him in the arm before finally slugging him in the leg. Sammy laughs while he defends himself.

They are both laughing as they make the turn onto Main Street where the downtown public library sits. Sammy looks over his shoulder. "They're still on us babe."

"Yeah but those Eastwoodians won't go into the library. Too scared of what they might find in there," she replies.

"Still, we better hurry."

"Watch this," she says, then she guns the tiny engine as hard as she can.

The downtown branch of the library was rebuilt about 10 years before the rapture. It was a surprising turn of events at the time. An anonymous donor dropped a ton of money into renovating the building. In reality, it was closer to a replacement then a renovation. Once finished, it looked nothing like the original structure.

Of course, not many years after the library reopened the rapture occurred, followed by Hell on Earth in Las Vegas. The hedonism and general societal malaise that accompanied the era of the apocalypse did not lend itself to education. So the building was under used, ignored physically, and quickly became dilapidated.

The library has a massive set of steps in the front of the building. There are also two smooth ramps that begin next to the base of the stairs then arc out and up, curving toward the front doors and reuniting with the stairs at their top where a large landing proceeds the entry way. Sandy hits the steps in the car with enough speed that she manages to drive the little vehicle straight to the top. It is a bumpy ride.

Sammy starts to question why she didn't use a ramp. Sandy points her finger at him and says, "I wouldn't do that if I were you."

Sammy promptly clamps his mouth back shut. As they near the top of the stairs, the front doors to the building come into view.

"Wow. Those doors are huge," he says. "I bet we could drive the car right through there."

"Well," she says, "Let's see if they're open."

"Yeah," Sammy says. He stares at Sandy and makes no attempt to exit the vehicle.

"I'm sorry dear," Sandy finally says. "I was trying not to be bossy. What I meant was, go see if the doors are open."

"Oh. Gotcha." Sammy starts to get out of the car, then stops and looks back at her. "But why would they be unlocked?"

"It's still a public institution," Sandy says. "It is supposed to be open to the public. Besides, there is no reason for anyone to lock it. Everyone is too afraid to go in there."

"Right," Sammy says. Then he re-considers the idea that, if everyone else is afraid, he probably should be as well. He shakes the thoughts from his head and exits the car.

Sammy is relieved when he finds the doors locked. He is not pleased when Sandy then instructs him and Zorn to break in through a window. He can see the Eastwoodians converging at the bottom of the steps, and it looks as if other people are gathering down there as well.

*I wonder who they are*, Sammy thinks. He breaks the glass of a library window and Zorn pushes him up by the feet, vaulting him over the ledge and through the window.

After a few seconds, Sandy and Zorn hear the latching mechanisms of the doors creaking to life. A door slowly opens with Sammy pushing from behind. Zorn pulls the other door open as Sandy runs back to the car. She drives it slowly into the library's massive foyer.

Sammy and Zorn move to shut the doors as fast as they can, but Sammy realizes there is no reason to rush.

"Hey, look at that," Sammy says. "My old lady was right."

Zorn looks at the bottom of the steps and can see all their pursuers forming a crowd below, but making no attempt to ascend the steps or ramps to the front of the building.

"They're scared," Sammy says.

Zorn nods his head in agreement with a smile.

Sammy shudders and the hair stands up on the back of his neck. "We've got to work on that smile of yours," he says to the demon. "C'mon, let's shut these doors and get inside."

# 33

When the concert is over Alacrán and Purvis capture one of Princess Tiara's ninjas and return to their evil lair, Alacrán's magnificent office. Alacrán is so delirious from his murderous frenzy at the show it is easy for Purvis to convince him they have captured the real Princess. It is equally as easy to convince him they should not remove her ninja mask until they are ready to use the love potion.

Alacrán's vim returns after a refreshing tonic made with amniotic fluid, eucalyptus, methamphetamine, club soda and a little twist of lime. Purvis never touches the stuff, and is close to falling asleep in his chair. He watches Alacrán do his victory dance about the room, wondering how he has any fond emotions for such an astonishing abomination. Purvis is exhausted.

"My sweet Purvis why do you look so sad? We are so close, so close, so close to getting what I want! We have the Princess and next we will have my black case with my secret prize and I will be very pleased. Doesn't that please you?"

"Of course master," Purvis says, yawning. "I am most content when you are pleased. Your servant is simply tired. It has been a long couple of days."

"Well my boy, I should be fine for the evening. Why don't you get some rest? Tomorrow we'll find my case. Then maybe we will kill the Princess in public. I still haven't decided if I am going to keep her or not. I'm going to see how much I enjoy playing with her tonight and then sleep on it." Alacrán licks his unattractive lips.

"It's nice to see you in such a good mood my liege. It does wonders for my soul." Purvis rises to leave the room when an emerald green statuette of Alacrán, dressed as a military general, begins to flash. "There's a call coming in."

"At this hour? That's strange." Alacrán puts a hand to his chin as he is certain is custom when you are curious about something. "Well don't just stand there boy, answer it."

On their way home from the concert, Billy the Third and Sweetwater have bloated themselves on the sugary sweet, cholesterol filled blood of fat people. It is that type of evening. Gluttony and crapulence are the themes of the night. They stashed their "Princess" in the trunk of the limo. Billy does not want there to be any accidental damage to her. He wants her in perfect condition when he gives her the potion, and he wants her madly in love with him when he feeds from her neck for the first time.

They are now in Billy's private parlor of the Karowack Kids' accidentally Gothic mansion. I find the decor suitable to be honest. There's not a lot of difference between the Beatniks and the Goths stylistically, in my opinion, or the dipshit Spacers for that matter.

You probably haven't had to deal with the dipshit Spacers. They pop up when aliens finally reveal themselves to mankind. It's actually the first worldwide fashion and pop-culture trend to begin in the former United States *after* the apocalypse. It helps bring the States back into the good graces of the rest of the world. There for a minute, everyone is a Spacer. And I mean everyone. You would have been too. Or, you may be in the near future. That depends on whenever your whenever is.

Anyway, Billy and Sweetwater are in Billy's parlor about to make the call to Alacrán. "So how do you want to play this, dad? Far out, or way far out?" Sweetwater is having his scalp massaged and sipping a delicious espresso, two reasons he is very pleased with his new child, the crazy coffee barista.

"Way far out, baby. Your daddy gonna drive the bad man batty." Billy snaps fingers on both his hands, twice. Then he calls Alacrán.

Purvis walks over to Alacrán's desk and pushes down on the statuette's saluting hand. A wall panel opens. If you are sitting at Alacrán's desk, the giant monitor is to the left hand side of the room, with enough of an angle for good viewing from his chair.

Alacrán takes position directly in front of the monitor. He is feeling spicy. He lights a cigarette and plays it real cool. Billy's image pops up on the screen.

"I don't think I mentioned allowing you the privilege of contacting me," Alacrán says.

"Very droll my Spanish bête noire," Billy says. "But then again, you know who you are."

"To what do I owe this giant movement of my bowels?" Alacrán asks. He looks to Purvis for approval. Although Purvis is half asleep, he is right on time with a double thumbs up for his boss.

"I believe you and I have some new unfinished business to begin finishing." Damn it! Billy worked on that line for an hour. He blew it!

"If you don't *begin* to entertain me soon sir," Alacrán replies, "I am most likely going to change the channel."

"How about a show then daddy-o? Here's a show." Billy claps his hands and Sweetwater wheels their kidnapped ninja into view. She is tied to a chair and her face is still hidden behind her mask.

"What is that? What makes you think I care about whomever that is?" Alacrán tries to act as unimpressed as possible.

"Let me explain to you what is going down, mister cube like man." Billy is still super high off the fat people and is feeling his poetic flow.

Alacrán looks confused.

"A cube is a square," Sweetwater explains.

Alacrán still looks confused.

Sweetwater lets it go with a shrug of his shoulders and an "I'm surrounded by idiots" facial expression.

"I've got you in the palm of my hand," Billy continues.

"How?" Alacrán asks impatiently. "Why? Who is it?"

Billy pulls the hood off of his captive, revealing Dolly. Her mouth is gagged with gray duct tape over a dark red satin handkerchief.

Dolly looks through the camera at Purvis with desperation in her eyes. Purvis knows immediately that this is not the Princess, but is his new true love. His heart knots. This is not part of their plan.

"It's your precious Princess," Billy says, holding on to the *es* until he is completely out of air and has to gasp for more to continue. "And after a drink of my lovey-dovey potion, her heart will be mine."

"That's impossible," Alacrán snorts. Alacrán refuses to believe he can be outdone by Billy. Besides, he and Purvis already have Princess Tiara. Billy has clearly kidnapped an imposter, a body double. It is an amazingly astute and equally lucky assertion. Still, Alacrán begins to pace back and forth as doubt creeps into the back of his brain like a confidence cat burglar. Always sneaking about in the shadows of the mind, doubt is.

Purvis is beside himself. He has no idea what to do. All he can think is, *he's either going to kill her or turn her into a nasty ass vampire.* Obviously, neither option suits him, although if he has to choose he will certainly prefer the latter. If need be, he could see himself as a vampire, although despite the depth of his affection for Dolly, immortality is an awfully long time for monogamy. *Of all the ninjas they could have grabbed and they got her!* Purvis' thoughts are broken when he notices Alacrán motioning to him. He realizes what his boss wants, so he slinks into the shadows to move about unnoticed.

"It is not impossible." Billy recoils like a petulant child. "I have her right here and I am going to feed her this liquid that I bought from a mad gypsy." Billy holds the vial up for Alacrán to see. "It is a real love potion and it is going to work. The Princess will be mine and the whole city will know I beat you."

"I told you that is impossible you nitwit blood sucker," Alacrán spouts. Of course Alacrán truly believes it to be impossible, as he truly believes it is he who has successfully kidnapped the Princess.

"No it isn't!" Billy is getting flustered. He is not a good improviser. The scene has gone so far off script so fast his brain is shutting down. It is like a nuclear facility in there, with panicky sirens going off and light bulbs spinning inside red globes, letting everyone inside know they need to get the fuck out of dodge.

"Yes it is! Purvis!" Alacrán claps his hands. Purvis wheels their kidnapped ninja into view. She is also tied to a chair and still wearing her ninja mask. Alacrán gives a proud smirk. "How can you have the Princess, when I already have her right here?"

Billy flinches. He squints, furrowing his brow in frustration. He clears his throat and plows forward with his original plan, slightly modified by the surprise curveball Alacrán has thrown him. "There is nothing you can do," he says. "The Princess is mine."

"But you don't have the Princess. I do." Alacrán may be a part time fool, but he saw Billy's insides seize up when Purvis rolled their version of the kidnapped Princess into the room.

"You haven't taken off her mask," Billy almost shouts, exasperated, pointing towards the image of Alacrán's captive on his video screen.

"That's because I have fed her my own love potion," Alacrán says proudly, lying, as he has not yet actually administered his love potion. "When I take that mask off she is going to fall dreadfully in love with me. I want it to be a special moment and you are not invited."

"Reveal her to me," Billy commands.

"And ruin the special moment I have planned? I don't think so!"

"Well then you had better give me what's inside that black case then." Billy is desperately grasping at straws to say something, anything, demanding and in a wicked tone. As I recently mentioned, he is not an excellent impromptu speaker. Plus, he is stoned, and the complicated nature of the situation perplexes him. Billy prefers a well laid plan. This situation has gone awry, quickly.

"What are you talking about?" Alacrán is legitimately puzzled.

"Damn it I want that case!"

"I thought you wanted the Princess?" Alacrán replies. He is leery Billy is using a vampire brain trick on him. But to what end?

Billy presses on as confused by his own words as Alacrán. "A trade then. The Princess for the case."

"But you don't have the Princess," Alacrán insists.

"No, I will trade you the case for the real Princess," Billy explains.

"But why? I thought you wanted the case now."

Billy looks at Alacrán and begins to speak, then bites his tongue and puts his hand to his head. He looks at Sweetwater for support, whose sympathetic offer is a shrug of the shoulders. Billy puts a hand up, begging for a moment from Alacrán. He finally speaks. "Whichever you want the most, that's what I'm going to make you trade me for the other one. Can we agree on that?"

"Certainly," Alacrán says. "So you have my case then?"

"Not yet."

"Then how are you going to trade it for anything?" Alacrán asks. He tosses his hands up in frustration, letting them flop back down to his side on their own.

"Well I'm going to get it first. I thought that was implied." Billy's tone takes a more conversational...tone.

"Oh. Not really no," Alacrán says. "Not with any hmph you know. Not a lot of punch." Alacrán takes a short jab at the air for Billy's benefit, shaking his head "no" at the same time.

"So then let's back it up to...'if you ever want to see your precious Princess alive again you had better give it to me'", Billy suggests.

Alacrán nods his head in agreement while searching for his line then says, "But you don't have the real Princess. I do. We've already agreed to that."

"Then if you ever want to see your precious case again, you had better deliver the Princess to me," Billy snarls.

"But you don't have the case!" Alacrán throws his hands in the air again.

"Well how in the hell is either of us supposed to win?" Billy shouts.

"I'm still working on that!" Alacrán shouts back without thinking, clearly exasperated.

"Well if you figure something out let me know, because this is baffling!" Billy finally gives up any pretense that anything is going according to plan, or that he is having fun being nefarious.

"It is isn't it?" Alacrán agrees. "Honestly my head is really starting to hurt."

"I have had a migraine for about three days now," Billy admits.

"I hear you," Alacrán says.

"Well then," Billy replies, laying the words out there without any energy left for the argument.

"Yep," Alacrán agrees. The two men continue to stare vacantly at each other. Neither is waiting for the other to do anything. It's as if they're on pause.

Billy snaps his fingers as an idea hits him. "Oh! How about for the time being we see who can find the case first, then we can revisit this whole Princess situation?"

"Works for me," Alacrán says.

"Well then."

"Yep."

Billy turns away from the monitor to end the conversation on a walk out. Alacrán motions to Purvis to end the transmission, but before he can, Billy turns back to the screen. "Wait a minute," Billy starts. "I forget. How do we know which of has the Princ…"

Alacrán looks at Purvis with his eyes wide open, eyebrows dangerously close to jumping off his forehead, and draws a finger across his throat. Purvis responds by ending the transmission. The screen goes black before Billy can finish his sentence.

# 34

Princess Tiara is backstage after the concert, waiting to see Rancid Pete. For the first time in her life she has butterflies in her stomach. She does not understand what is happening to her, so she stands over a trashcan and sticks her finger down her throat. Years of practice sticking her finger in her mouth have worn a nice groove thru to her gag reflex, so the vomit comes quickly, but it doesn't help. Now her breath stinks. *Oh fuck it*, she thinks. *He's a monster, maybe he'll like it.* Her inner monologue pauses for a second while her inner-inner monologue comes to a realization. *And fuck him. I'm fucking Tiara Lioness.*

The Princess's unit of ninjas lounges in the hallway amidst other fans with backstage passes. The ninjas are either smoking - they are allowed breaks - or lurking about in character. Their commitment is noteworthy, even if they are getting paid.

Princess Tiara is nervous without Dolly next to her. In fact, when the Security Guard stopped her from entering the corridor that leads to the band's greenroom, the reason Tiara didn't have the Security Guard killed on the spot was fear of actually meeting Rancid Pete. She knows the monster is as likely to bite her head off as he is to worship her. It's sexy, but it's also extremely frightening.

Though the Princess agreed to it, this portion of Dolly's plan does not really suit her. She prefers having Dolly with her when she is in public. It makes her feel safe, that is for sure, but it's more than that. Dolly's presence makes her feel powerful. At any given moment in their lives, Dolly's head might explode in a bloody heap while protecting the Princess. That is power. Power makes Tiara's tits tingle.

Princess Tiara does not understand why she and Dolly split up. It is part of the process with a Louie, but not completely necessary in the newly designed Manuel-Louis. Yet Dolly insisted, which is strange in and of itself. Somehow, it came to Dolly's attention that the greasy Spaniard had designs on kidnapping Tiara, so Dolly convinced the Princess that in order to facilitate the Princess' meeting of the monster undisturbed, they had to create some confusion by splitting up their entourage.

The plan worked, except for the portion where Dolly was supposed to double back and meet the Princess backstage. *Screw that bitch*, the Princess thinks. *She can handle herself*. Princess Tiara shakes her head clear of its annoying thought processes and confronts the security guard again.

"Why am I waiting here?" she says with a stomp of her foot.

"The band likes to get cleaned up after the show, then meditate for a while before they start the after party," the security guard replies. "They said nobody in right now."

"You said that before. I don't care. Do you have any idea who I am?"

"Of course. You're Princess Tiara Lioness. Or at least, one of you are." He motions to the other ninjas. "One of you is the most vile, vacuous and sexy pig-bitch on the planet."

Believe it or not, he is directly quoting the Princess herself. It is from an interview she did with *Apocalypse Right Now Magazine* a few years earlier. The article was about how famous people were dealing with the new apocalyptic fashion trends, how they were staying in shape during the apocalypse, who they were currently sleeping with and of course, their opinions on the socio-economic and political atmospheres of the new, modern Hell on Earth. It was a fluff piece really. In the original copy, the Princess ended the interview with two words:

"Oink, oink."

"You just got yourself laid instead of dead you lucky cunt," the Princess says. "You two," pointing to two of her ninjas, "take him and fuck him somewhere."

The two ninjas drag the security guard away kicking and screaming. Apparently, he was hoping for the entire End of Times to take sweet advantage of him, as he explains thoroughly while being drug into a corner behind a large bank of vending machines. The last thing Princess Tiara hears from the security guard is the scream, "you bitch," aimed at her, then "oh, well, that is kind of nice." Tiara makes a circling motion in the air with her finger and stomps through the double doors with her ninja-girls in tow.

They reach Rancid Pete's private dressing room. The Princess decides not to knock. She checks her breath again, shrugs her shoulders, then bursts through the door. Once in, she steps to the side, casually holding the door open with the heel of her foot as the other ninjas flow into the room.

Rancid Pete looks up from the throng of groupies crawling about on him. He sniffs at the air, trying to locate the Princess. He knows she is one of the ninjas. He uses spotters on stage to pick out chicks for him to play with after shows. His spotters were put in charge of recon on the Princess that night, and had reported back to him with intelligence on her ninja movements.

The situation the Princess walked into was fabricated. A little secret between you, me, and Pete: He had the security guard make

Tiara wait outside on purpose. Pete knows her reputation, part of which is always getting what she wants. He thought he would tweak her a bit by making her wait.

He wasn't enjoying the groupies. Not really. He was mentally preparing for the Princess to arrive. It is crucial that she recognizes his status by witnessing the luxury in which he basks. Rancid Pete wants to appear disinterested, yet commonly pleased. He also wants Tiara to wonder why these bitches are in here and she, a princess, was made to wait outside.

Tiara's first thought upon entering the room is, *Why are these bitches in here when I was made to wait outside?* Her very next thought is, *The monster is big-timing me.* Thought number three is, *Oh my God I want this asshole so bad.*

The Princess intends to use her entourage on Pete the same way she had during the concert with Billy and the Spaniard. They are going to tantalize Rancid Pete into a horny mess. Then, the plan is to send him to the showers. The cold no sex showers. Tiara isn't 100 percent about that last part though. It is probably the better play, but she really wants to screw.

The ninjas head across the room in a tight formation. Princess Tiara falls into the middle of the pack. Her plan is to usurp Pete's groupies. Then she and all her girls will disrobe, keeping their ninja masks on, and never letting Rancid Pete know who is playing with him.

Tiara's plan never has a chance. As soon as the ninjas move, Rancid Pete rises from his chair, discarding the groupies that still cling to him. He stomps towards Tiara and her gang as they walk towards him.

He meets the Princess and her entourage in the middle of the room. Pete moves through the gang of ninjas, brushing aside the actors and following his nose. He finds the Princess standing in the middle of the pack. She opens her mouth to speak but Rancid Pete put his large hand over it, holding it shut. He leans in, inhales her scent deeply and quietly, then growls softly into her face.

He slowly slides his hand from her mouth, stopping his thumb briefly on her lips to let her know to remain silent. His hand settles behind her head, holding it at the curve where it connects to the neck. His thumb is still slightly up under her ear and jawbone. He gently raises her face up towards his. He leans down and kisses her delicately on the lips. It is the gentlest thing Rancid Pete has ever done.

Now, I don't want to get too heavy on you with metaphysical banter about the supermundane workings of the Universe. I don't want to seem weird or anything. But, I would be neglectful if I did not tell you that the first time Tiara and Pete's lips meet, two uninhabited worlds collide and are destroyed. I don't mean metaphorically either. I mean two planets somewhere in the cosmos are literally thrown off their orbits, collide, and are destroyed when Pete and Tiara kiss. Interestingly, when the cores of the planets meet during the collision, they explode into the birth of a new planet that can sustain life. It is very similar to Earth.

Bob doth work in mysterious ways.

Rancid Pete pulls his head back and roars. The Princess goes weak in the knees, and may have fallen, if Pete weren't already scooping her up. He takes her in his arms, up under her butt, and stomps off with her.

Tiara looks down at Pete and is disgusted by his gnarled face. It is hideous, yet somehow she is mesmerized by it. They make their way down a service hallway, then through an access door to a platform outside of the stadium. It is a maintenance platform about halfway up the side of the building, hidden by the large artistic facade of the structure. The stadium's dome roof was closed for the concert. Rancid Pete throws the Princess over his shoulder and climbs a ladder that leads to the roof of the building. Typical monster instincts. Snatch up the pretty girl, then immediately take her to the highest, most dangerous place you can find.

Rancid Pete makes it to the top of the ladder and peers across the roof at a giant tent awaiting him and his lady. He sets her down onto a red carpet that rolls to the doorway of the tent. He offers his hand to her.

Tiara looks up at Rancid Pete with surprise. She is enchanted. She takes a step ahead of him, then reaches back and takes his hand. She doesn't want to be taken. She wants to give herself to him, and she wants him to know the difference.

When they make it to the tent, all the romantic pretense screeches to halt and they get down to their dirty business. It is vile. The sounds and smells coming out of the tent are disgusting. So is the dark energy. You can literally see their nasty auras permeating the structure, like erotic solar flares trying to escape the sun.

Yes, I stayed and watched. This is a history book. I needed to describe the scene accurately to you guys, and since I was already up on the roof…

What can I say? Being dead is very boring.

## 35

Billy the Third stands with his hands on his hips and his chin lowered to his chest. He slowly raises his head to make eye contact with Sweetwater, then shakes his head back and forth. "I have no idea how or why I allow that moron to completely throw me like that Jack. It's repulsive."

Jack Sweetwater sits quietly for a moment, thinking of the best thing to say and the best way to say it, but he doesn't want to take too long to respond so he settles on, "To be fair, you were very high. That is some of the best fat blood I have had in a while."

"That's true," Billy says. He almost allows his mind to wander off track again, until he notices Dolly out of the corner of his eye and his focus returns. "What was I thinking Jack?"

Billy may have actually said, "What was going on in my brain goo stew Daddy Sweetwater Dude?" but I've been trying to tune their bullshit jive out...

"I don't know father," Sweetwater replies. "I was equally bedazzled by the chubby blood. I'm still high as the proverbial kite."

"He never took her hood off! I've got the Princess sitting right here, and somehow he still manages to slip through my trap!" Billy is speaking with a hushed, exasperated tone. Whisper shouting.

Dolly squirms, making the "hm, hm, hm," sounds of a person who is tied to a chair with tape over their mouth. It doesn't register with either vampire.

"He was buying time father. He knows you have him by his tail." Sweetwater's reassurances to his master are earnest if not well thought out. He is growing weary. With the sun never coming out, it is difficult for the vampires in Vegas to know when it is time to rest. The vampire community has actually witnessed a profound socio-physiological affect from the darkness created by the near impenetrable clouds of hellfire smoke infecting the Las Vegas troposphere.

"Thank you for that Jack. You are tried and true, but even if that is the real deal, I don't know what to do." Billy is weary as well. His pale skin is losing what little color it normally maintains, and his buzz is wearing off.

Dolly continues to squirm and make noises. Her chair slowly scoots across the floor an inch at a time. Both vampires finally notice.

"Shall I allow the royal bitch a chance to speak?" Sweetwater asks.

"Why not," Billy replies dryly, with contempt for his predicament oozing through him. He turns to look at the woman he thinks is the Princess, the woman he has become so infatuated with. Something occurs to him. This isn't the feeling he was certain would envelop him in the presence of Tiara Lioness. Something is amiss. In all the commotion of the kidnapping and the blackmail attempt, he and the Princess have not yet spoken. It suddenly dawns on him what a poor host he's been. "Dear God Jack, what is wrong with us? We have been behaving like mongrels with my future bride. Be gentle pulling that tape off."

Sweetwater is gentle alright. He slowly peels the tape from Dolly's mouth so gently it takes close to an hour to get it off.

Okay, maybe not an hour but you get the idea.

At some point, as Billy paces back and forth waiting to speak to his captive, he swears he hears the muffled screams of "Jesus...just pull the damn thing off" come from behind the gag in her mouth.

"Oh for heaven's sake Jack," Billy says. He walks over and yanks the tape away.

Dolly groans loudly, the sounds are still muffled by the hanky in her mouth.

Billy pulls the handkerchief out. "I'm sorry," he says. "So sorry my love, are you okay?" He strokes her cheeks with the backs of his hands, then the fronts of his hands, and then the backs again.

"Ew! Untie me," Dolly insists, jerking her head away from Billy's caress.

"Oh, I don't think that is a good idea my dear," Billy replies. "At least not until you have had our little love elixir."

"I'm not the Princess you nitwit," Dolly says.

"I'm sorry?" Billy replies.

"I'm not the Princess," she repeats. "I'm her body double. Untie me and I'll prove it to you."

"I don't think that is a good idea," Sweetwater says.

"Why not?" Dolly asks. "You're vampires. What could I possibly do?" Dolly is clever. She knows how badly these jerks want to be respected.

"That's very true. Jack, go ahead. Careful though. If she is not the Princess she could be someone or something far more dangerous." Billy leans in with his face close to Dolly's, peering into her eyes. He stands up and turns his back to pace away as Sweetwater unties her. He stops, turning back around. "Not as careful as before though Jack, when you were removing the gag. A little quicker if you will. Let's get to it."

Sweetwater frees Dolly's hands, then moves around to untie her ankles as well. Once her hands are free Dolly loosens her pants and exposes herself.

"Egad," Sweetwater exclaims. "Daddy!" Sweetwater totters backwards onto his butt as he recoils.

Billy, who is still pacing back and forth a few feet away, turns to see what the fuss is about.

"Egad woman!" The horror on Billy's face is sincere. Melodramatic, certainly, but very sincere. "Why did you do that? Oh God, I can smell it. I can smell it on you? How did I not smell it on your blood from the very beginning?"

"Desire doth blind more than the eyes baby," Sweetwater says, still choked up himself, shielding his eyes.

"Not now Jack!" Billy is hurt, and angry, and shocked. He is also suddenly disappointed in himself. "What are you?" he says to Dolly. "And put that thing away. Gross!"

"I'm transsexual," she replies while tucking Henry safely back into his stable and closing his barn door.

"How did you, what, why would you?" Billy is flustered. "Explain yourself," he finally settles on. Dolly opens her mouth to answer but Billy stops her. "No. You know what. You are disgusting. Jack, remove this abomination and dispose of it. Put it in a pillow case and drown it or something."

"Hey," Dolly says. "You know what? Screw you. I may have a dick but I've also got feelings." Dolly is pissed, but when Sweetwater takes her by the arm to remove her she quickly softens and changes her tune. "Wait. No, wait. I can help you. I can help you get what you want."

Billy raises his hand to signal Sweetwater to pause for a moment. "How can you possibly help me?"

"I'm the Princess' body double. And, I smuggled the case here."

"Apologize," Billy says. He is intrigued, but in every scenario in life he believes there is a need for certain levels of decorum.

"Excuse me?" Dolly replies.

"Apologize for your filthy display."

"Oh screw you buddy. You kidnapped me you…"

"Jack," Billy says.

Sweetwater begins to pull Dolly towards the door again.

"Okay, okay," she says. "I apologize for taking Henry out. It was uncalled for."

"Oh, of course. She gave the disgusting thing a name," Billy says.

"Hey, I apologized," Dolly says. "And you've got one too, don't you?"

"Fair enough. That last bit was a little snitty of me. Thank you for apologizing," he says sincerely. "Have a seat, please." Billy motions to a chair near his fireplace. There are several low slung parlor chairs situated for chatting. They're in front of the fireplace in a corner of the room. Billy sits down in front of her with his legs crossed. "Now, how is it that you believe you can help me?"

"Let me ask you a question if I may," Dolly replies. Then she goes into salesperson mode. "What is it that you really want? Wait, you know what, don't answer that."

Billy looks at her with an expression that is quite clear. He does not have a lot of patience for this situation.

"I have a man on the inside," she says. "Someone very close to Alacrán." Billy's physical reaction is positive. He softens at this revelation. Dolly has a keen eye for body language. "Also, Alacrán doesn't have the Princess either. My man on the inside made sure of that."

"You don't know that," Billy replies.

"We had a plan," Dolly explains. "It was going perfectly until you kidnapped me. But now that we are together, it actually fits very well in the grand scheme of things." She raises a single eyebrow.

Billy makes a face in response that ensures Dolly's eyebrow has done its job. He is further intrigued.

Sweetwater simply gives a, "Hmph."

"Tea?" Billy asks.

"Please," Dolly replies.

Billy motions to Sweetwater. "Perhaps you should have come to me in the first place," Billy says, returning his attention to Dolly.

"Maybe, but I don't know you. And you're a vampire. You're dangerous. No offense of course, but obviously you are a threat to a lower life form." Dolly's ego stroking is smoother than can be typed by me, and it works well.

Sweetwater returns with a platter carrying teas for everyone.

"I think if I am going to help you I have to understand your motivation," Dolly continues. "Who are you? What is it you really want?"

"Who am I?" he replies, tossing her own question back at her. "Who are you?"

"You first," Dolly says. "It's Rockefeller correct? Who are you Mr. Rockefeller?"

Billy sits quietly, studying Dolly. "Jack," he finally says. "I think we should have dinner here in front of the fire." He looks at Dolly. "Are you hungry?"

"I'm always hungry," she replies.

"Will you notify the kitchen, Jack?"

"Of course father," Sweetwater replies. He heads across the room to raise the kitchen on the intercom.

Billy looks at Dolly, uncrosses and re-crosses his legs, then wraps his hands around a knee, interlocking his fingers. "I assume that your lack of knowledge of my enterprise, my caste, my brand, is directly related to your role in this life as a servant, and you having your regular home in an underdeveloped foreign country."

The Island of Lioness, that is not an actual island, is actually a very well developed small country. It is a wealthy progressive state. Dolly lets Billy have his petty, thinly veiled invectives and simply sips her tea, nodding her head in agreement.

Billy continues. "My name is William Henry Rockefeller the Third. I am the child of Arthane Wizard the King."

"I'm sorry what?" Dolly asks.

"Arthane Wizard the King."

"Was he really a wizard?" She is careful to remain curious and not seem impudent.

"No he was enigmatic," Billy replies. "All vampires take stylish names when they have turned. Those who do not were most likely blessed with an amazingly stylish human surname such as myself."

"Ahh," she replies in understanding, continuing to sip her tea. She hopes her face conveys more interest than she feels.

"Arthane was an ancient. An angel cast to Earth when the world was formed, and I say angel in the most literal sense," Billy says. "He was also a wonderful father."

"What happened to him?" she asks. "If you don't mind me asking."

"I don't know. It is a mystery to me that I have long since let go of any emotional response to. It may have been a thousand years since the last time I saw my creator." Billy speaks with a wistfulness that betrays him. He has not actually let go of all the emotions linked to the disappearance of his father.

"What about your real family? Your real parents?" Dolly asks.

"My first family," Billy corrects Dolly's use of the word "real" very blatantly, "is long forgotten. It is part of the process for many of us. The more acclimated I became to my new life the more my memories of my first family faded away. I don't remember hardly any of my life as a human now, although, I seem to remember being very bored."

"Yeah, that sounds about right," Dolly says. "Do you mind if I ask how old you are? What's it like living so long without a family? What do you do with all the time you have when you know you can basically live forever?"

Billy studies her. He smiles with the corner of his mouth. You can tell it is a well-practiced response.

"I'm sorry," Dolly says. "There are so many questions popping through my mind. I've never had tea with a vampire."

"It is quite alright. For some strange reason I think I like you. In answer to your questions, let's see...I am very, very old. I am the father of 34 children, most of whom still live here with me and have been for hundreds of years. So, as you might imagine my family life is quite involved and not the gaping black hole that you presumed. Lord Jonathan Sweetwater, Jack here, is my first born. He has been the greatest influence on my personal style and taste as well as my greatest confidant for hundreds of years." Billy looks towards his man. Sweetwater is over by the desk discussing dinner through an intercom with the kitchen staff.

Dolly sees genuine love there in Billy's glance. She also wonders why the vampire was being so coy about his age.

"As for all the free time," Billy continues, "Jack and I have taken a tiny little idea and turned it into one of the most successful post-rapture corporations in the former United States. Karowack Corp has offices in ten states with major subsidiaries in four ancillary industries."

"I'm sorry, I don't quite know what that means," Dolly replies, very politely.

"It means I am extraordinarily wealthy," he says. "Equally, if not more wealthy than the greasy Spaniard. Not that anyone in this God forsaken city would notice."

It is then that Dolly understands. Alacrán is the bad guy everyone loves. Billy considers himself the underappreciated, more sophisticated and classier evildoer. She jumps through this window of opportunity.

"I don't think that will be a problem when we are done here," she says. "I think I know what you really want Mr. William Henry Rockefeller the Third, and, I think I can help you get it."

Billy likes that. He likes the sound of it. "I have decided I definitely like you," he says. He reflects for a second then, "Who are you? I feel like you are clearly more than," Billy searches for the right word, "well, a stupid human I suppose. So who are you?"

"Honestly I'm nobody," Dolly says. "I'm like you William, do you mind if I call you William?"

Billy doesn't mind at all, and nods accordingly with a charming smile. He likes Dolly and the way she says his name. Before they can continue the conversation, dinner arrives from the kitchen. A large crystal challis of blood is on ice in a champagne bucket. It is placed on a tall silver stand next to Billy's chair. There is a long crinkly straw, you know the type with the movable extendable neck, sticking out of the challis.

A giant silver bucket of fried chicken is set on a very ornate TV tray next to Dolly's chair. There is a plate, a glass of red wine - she hopes it's wine - and a napkin. There are no utensils.

"Lovely," she says.

"I know how you people love fried chicken," Billy replies with a smile. Then he takes a drink through his straw. His right fang pokes out from behind his lip a little while the straw is in his mouth.

"Just lovely," she says again. "Anyhow, I was taken from my family at so young an age I have no recollection of them. They may have sold me to King Lioness for all I know. The Princess has been my only family. Well, her and some of the other palace staff. My entire life has been devoted to the unfortunate happenstance that I might die instead of the Princess. It is, I don't know, an underappreciated existence." Dolly takes a big bite from a chicken leg, continuing on with her story with a mouth full of chicken, waving the leg around as she speaks. "Don't get me wrong, if the Princess can love anything then I know she loves me. But, I've always known if I was to die for her, they would replace me and that would be it, you know what I mean?" Dolly suddenly realizes she is earnestly opening up to the bloodsucker. She wonders if they drugged her tea. She takes another bite of chicken.

"I think I do," Billy responds. "Do you have any idea how frustrating it is to be a creature as powerful as I am and to receive so little respect?"

"I can imagine, I suppose. Maybe it is something small you are overlooking. Perhaps you should change your style? Maybe you could all give yourselves a big makeover." Dolly instantly hopes her suggestion doesn't sound like an indictment of the Karowack Kids' outdated phraseology and clothing.

"I will not be instructed on what is stylish by humans," Billy replies.

"Fair enough," Dolly says. Then she allows a moment of silence to hang in the air, to let the vampire decide where to take the conversation next.

"Why do you keep that thing between your legs?" he asks. The question catches Dolly off guard.

"I don't know. I don't know why they didn't cut it off to begin with," she replies.

"Yes, that is an oddity as well. But, you have had plenty of time as an adult to have it removed and finish your transition. Why haven't you?" Billy is truly curious. I think he thinks there is some grand insight into Dolly's character, her true being, to be found in the answer to this question. I'm not so sure there actually is.

"I don't know," she says. "Because I'm insane? Because technically I'm a homosexual trapped in a man's body that wants to look like a woman but doesn't want to be one, but thought I wanted to be a woman for a while…and really didn't have a choice considering I am also a slave who has to have her face continually cut and pasted to look like another woman because I was born with near perfect bone structure, but then realized I didn't want to be all the way woman because I didn't want to be the one getting screwed. I don't know."

You can see Dolly getting frustrated. Not with Billy, but with the train-wreck path of thought she is now spiraling down.

"Maybe it's because I'm actually bisexual," she continues, "and I knew that looking like a beautiful woman would make me a more affective sexual predator. I really honestly don't know. Ooh, maybe, it's because when they made me look exactly like the Princess I needed something to keep me, me."

This answer is the closest to the truth and somehow, Billy knows it.

"Or maybe it's because I enjoy using it on the palace guards," Dolly says as a finale, with a lift in her tone that makes it clear she has finally reached her punch line.

She and Billy both chuckle.

"Let me tell you something sir," she says. "You don't want the Princess. This happens all the time to men of power. She does this to all of you. She is a bitch, and a pain in the ass, and I am telling you the ecstasy will wear off quickly, and then you will be stuck with her."

"I'm a vampire. I would kill her and throw her away," he replies.

"Touché," she says. "Still, my point is you don't really want her and you don't really want whatever is in that case."

Billy encourages Dolly to continue with a gesture of his hand.

"It's obvious that what you truly want is to beat Alacrán at something, anything, as long as you feel like you have gotten the upper hand," Dolly says. "And I'm going to help you do it." She sits back in the chair with an air of confidence, fried chicken leg in hand, grease running down her arm. She takes a bite and chews with a smile on her face.

"And how do you propose you are going to do that?" Billy asks with an enthusiastic tone. I'm pretty sure he is earnestly convinced she is going to shed some light on what has escaped him for so many years. He really is very taken by her.

Dolly holds a finger up requesting a moment while she swallows her food. Then she says, "Here's what I'm thinking…"

# 36

When the call with Billy the Third ends, Alacrán goes into a stammering fit. He is walking stiff legged, with his arms jutting out in random, abrupt, sharp motions. His face turns an uncomfortable shade of red.

Purvis is too concerned with Dolly's safety to notice his boss' consternation. "How did you know that wasn't the Princess?" Purvis says vacantly.

"What are you talking about!? I didn't! I was bluffing!" Alacrán stomps awkwardly over to their captive ninja and yanks her hood off. He gasps as he stares down at a lovely young woman, who looks nothing at all like Princess Tiara. "Damn it!"

Alacrán moves to a nearby pedestal supporting a bust of Mozart's head made from stone. He struggles, but is able to pick the bust up. As he walks back over to the tied up ninja he says, "I will not be beaten by that undead twerp." It takes considerable effort but eventually he lifts the bust over his head, preparing to crush the ninja's skull with it, when Purvis finally looks up and shrieks.

"Aaaaahhhhhh!" Purvis screams. "What are you doing? Wait!" He moves quickly over to Alacrán who stumbles slightly backwards from the weight of the bust. "Don't," Purvis says as he steadies his boss and grabs Mozart's head, gently easing it away from his master. "He doesn't have the Princess."

Alacrán stands silent for a moment gathering his composure, adjusting his suit and dabbing moisture away from his face with a kerchief. Air escapes him in exasperated huffs. "What was that last thing there?" he finally says.

"He doesn't have the Princess," Purvis says desperately.

"Who was that then, that he had?" Alacrán is confused. Angry and confused.

"It was the Princess' body double." Purvis mentally crosses his fingers. *Please don't ask me how I know*, he thinks.

"How do you know that?" Alacrán asks with his hands out, his tone slightly suspicious.

Purvis' bottom lip starts to quiver. Rather than speak he turns away in an attempt to gather his composure. "I'm sorry master," he says. "Please forgive my…," Purvis stops mid-sentence as he searches for the correct word. He settles on, "forgive me." The words limp weakly out of his mouth.

"Forgive you for what?"

Purvis feels like a child. He feels like a child that knows he has done something wrong. He knows it is time to come clean and take his whooping. This horrible, horrible person is his only real family, his parent, and Purvis genuinely feels bad for having betrayed Alacrán, despite it being a very mild betrayal that hasn't really hurt anyone. Then Purvis thinks about what Alacrán might do to him if told the truth.

"Darling what is it? If you don't speak up this minute I may boil over in anticipation." The word anticipation exits Alacrán's mouth very slowly. It carries eerie contempt with it as it wiggles through the air.

Purvis mans up. He turns, and with his shoulders square and arms stiff at his side he says, "Father, I have somewhat betrayed you."

Alacrán's jaw drops open momentarily, then his teeth audibly click back together. "You've somewhat betrayed me?"

"Yes." Purvis says. "I know that was Princess Tiara's body double and not the actual Princess because I am in love with her."

"You are in love with the Princess? Big deal. Why are you acting like such a little bitch?" Alacrán's underlying general state of being at this moment is a boiling hot pot.

"No, I'm in love with Princess Tiara's body double, the woman that Rockefeller was trying to blackmail us with."

"And how did you know that was her and not the Princess?" Alacrán asks. He is curious, not suspicious.

"Because, she taught me how to tell the difference," Purvis replies. "Princess Tiara has a slight birth defect. Her left eye is actually a little lower than her right eye. If you pay attention you will notice she always has her head slightly tilted to the right."

"This is absolutely exhausting. Do you understand how exhausting this is for me?" While he is speaking, Alacrán pulls what looks like a solid gold pill box from his right pocket. He opens the box and removes a small straight razor from inside. Pulling his shirt loose from his pants he reveals a portion of his abdomen that is covered in tiny scars. He cuts himself. He licks the razor clean then puts it back in the box. Purvis has already made his way over with a bandage, affixing it quickly while Alacrán holds his arms straight up in the air.

"I have something else to tell you," Purvis says, stepping back.

Alacrán looks at him with exasperation as he tucks his shirt back in. Clinching his teeth and pursing his lips, he holds both hands out inviting Purvis to continue.

"Dolly," Purvis says, "that's her name by the way, the Princess' body double, her name is Dolly. Dolly is the carrier for your lost case. Was I should say. She *was* the connection. She lost the case. Well, it was stolen really, from the plane's cargo area. Not lost. Anyway, she still showed up for the swap without the case. I don't know why she did but she did and we met and we instantly…it was so strange. It was literally love at first sight."

Purvis picks up speed on this next part, as if the words he speaks are trying to outrun the wind from his lungs on which they are carried. "So, I couldn't let her be killed and I lied to you, but it was a white lie. A tiny little lie to try and give her more time to find the case. You were very preoccupied with the Princess. I didn't want to upset you any further. Of course I was going to tell you. As soon as we recovered the case. I was going to introduce you to her and see if it was okay for me to keep her." Purvis finishes as if he is going to keep speaking, then suddenly realizes he has said plenty and shuts his mouth.

Alacrán doesn't say a word. He turns and walks toward the captive ninja. Circling around behind her, he slides a plush ottoman over to rest his knees on, settling into a comfortable position. He puts his arm around the ninja's throat in a choke hold and slowly, very deliberately, increases the pressure until the girl can no longer breathe, all the while staring directly and extremely intently at Purvis. The girl is bound too tightly to struggle with any effect.

Purvis can hear her gagged moans and sees the tears stream down her cheeks. The water is still exiting the wells of her eyes after Alacrán has choked her last breath from her.

Don't worry, she was a jerk too. Most likely she got what she deserved. Her ghost was very unattractive.

Alacrán stands back up and dusts himself off, straightening the sleeves to his suit jacket. He swats at the ninja's ghost, shooing it from the room. She flips him the bird then heads off to her afterlife.

"My dear," he says to Purvis. "I have lost my patience with this entire event." Alacrán begins to pace the room again.

Purvis can tell murdering the young woman did not satisfy the smoldering rage that is about to cause Mount Alacrán to blow his top.

"This was supposed to be a glorious occasion for me," Alacrán continues, wistfully. "I was going to have my new special prize and I was also going to have the Princess. I was finally going to settle down with someone familiar to strangle a little bit every day. We may have had a family. Children to choke. How lovely.

"But no. No, this city would not let that happen. No, no, no. Someone had to go and take what is mine." The wistfulness quickly turns sinister. "Do you understand? This city is mine. The case is mine. The Princess is mine." Each of the previous sentences comes out with progressively slower cadence for emphasis. "I did not escape the tyranny of Dallas, Texas and walk all the way to Las Vegas as a teenager to be deterred. I did not strangle the life from my own dear mother and father to prove to people that I was a kind and gentle soul who wanted nothing but the best for the world around him. I do not rape because I am petty. I do not murder because I am insane. I do not steal because I need to in order to survive!"

Alacrán's volume and enthusiasm for his own infamy swells as his despotic soliloquy grows wings and takes flight. "I did not rise to this seat of power out of some overblown sense of overcompensation because I have a small penis or was born into an inferior social class! I am a murderous, thieving lout because I recognized as a child that there are two choices you can make in life. Two options for living in this world. Do you choose goodness, and eek your way through life? Denying your own desires and instincts in order to be seen as something more decent than human nature will actually allow? Or, do you embrace your own evil nature and take what you want from this life? People live in misery every day, or in ridiculous states of self-denial, and then when they die they either become a ghost or they vanish forever. Or, despite their best efforts, they still commit enough egregious acts throughout their pathetic lives that they wind up in the actual Hell. Meanwhile, I have chosen to embrace the sinful chaos of this world. And I have risen to glorious heights! I murder and eat and fuck what I want. I take what I want from this life and when I die, will suffer the same fate that those who live these pissy, shitty little lives of self-denial wind up with. There is no Heaven and if he ever existed, God is dead! I will be my own god among men. That is the decision that I made!"

He turns toward Purvis and changes his tone. It becomes instructional, more informative now than tyrannical.

"When I was a child I loved cookies. I decided when I was yet a babe in diapers that I was not going to waste time trying to earn a cookie, or hoping that someone was going to share a cookie with me out of kindness. No! I knew before I could speak that if I wanted a cookie I was going to take it. I was going to take what was mine from this life, because when it is all said and done, there is no God. No God would create something as wonderful as cookies, dangle them in your face, and then tell you that you shouldn't have them whenever you want because they aren't good for you! So I am a scourge upon this Earth. I am a Hell spawn. I am a horseman of the apocalypse and I am going to bring this town to its knees, nay all the way down on all fours and then I am going to bury my tiny little pecker in its ear hole and fuck its brains, or my name isn't A, LA, CRÁN!" He takes a deep breath and then wobbles a little. Not having breathed enough during his tirade's finale, he is a little light headed when he finishes.

Purvis would normally run to his master's aid, but he is frightened. He is afraid that in this current state, Alacrán might kill him as easily as he killed the poor ninja girl.

"What are we going to do?" Purvis says softly. The words are weak and pathetic, exactly like he currently feels.

"I am going to turn this city upside down," Alacrán says. "I am through fucking around! I am so tired of this entire game! I will have my trophy and I will have my Princess and I am going to kill or kidnap anyone who gets in my way. As a matter of fact, *I* am going to take them all!" Alacrán makes sure to make it clear that at this point, there is no "we". Purvis is on thin ice, and he gets the message.

"You are going to contact my network of spies, killers and anyone else who works for me or owes me a debt and give them my orders," Alacrán continues. "Kidnap them all! The cops, the vampires, that goddamned monster, his band, anyone. Everyone! Anyone who can possibly have anything to do with any of this. Kidnap every last one of them! Do you understand me? I will kidnap this whole god forsaken town if I have to, but I will get what I want, and I want that Princess!" he screams. "Do...you...understand...me!?"

"Yes sir," Purvis says.

"Then do it. You have twenty-four hours. This entire city has twenty-four hours. No one is to sleep until I have what I want or I will kill them and all the people they love. Is this clear?"

"Yes sir."

"Then you make the rest of this city understand and you find that fucking princess! Now!"

"Yes sir," Purvis squeals, and then he turns to leave the room as Ala Cran shouts after him.

"And bring me my goddamn case!"

# 37

Are you familiar with how you can be drunk or high and something happens that rushes you back to sobriety? Possibly a quick brush with death or simply walking outside into the brisk night air. Suddenly, you feel sober and fully aware.

Despite the surprise and shock value of the transmission Hook and Lia receive at the end of the concert, this does not happen for them. They are both too intoxicated. Sleep comes easily and quickly.

Don't get me wrong. They react to the message. I think it goes something like this: "Uh oh."

Unfortunately, sleep is easily interrupted by hangover pain. Lia wakes up and stumbles into the kitchen to brew some coffee. She has no interest in waking Hook. It's best to let nature run its course in these situations. She debates whether or not she wants a shower. Or, I should say, debates the effectiveness of a shower for making her feel better at the moment. She definitely wants one.

When Hook wakes up on the couch, the ship is silent and Lia is nowhere to be found. She left coffee brewed for him. *Sweet thing*, he thinks. He is still a little spellbound from the amount of love they made during the concert. Lia was very generous.

He makes his way to the bedroom but there is still no sign of her. He is too hungover to put much thought into it. He shrugs his shoulders and heads for the shower. He stops on his way when he notices how comfortable the bed looks. After a brief internal debate, Hook decides to check and see how comfortable the bed really is.

When Hook wakes again, Lia is in the room moving about. He can't see what she is doing. His eyes are cakey and he is resistant to raising his head.

"What are you doing?" he asks. "Where you been?"

"I went to Earth sleepyhead. I felt like poop so I had a spa day and did some shopping."

"Nice. You get me anything?"

"Of course, silly," she says. "But you need to get off your butt and clean yourself up. You stink and you are making the whole room smell like salty hangover."

"Ouch," he says.

She tickles his feet on her way out of the room.

"Wait. You didn't tell me what you got me."

"A shirt you won't like," she says loudly, from the hallway outside the bedroom door. "Now get in the shower."

By the time Hook has bathed and dressed he is feeling at least a little refreshed. He makes his way to the kitchen in search of a cure for the growling stomach. Lia at the kitchen table with a magazine and a bowl of fruit.

"Hey baby," he says.

"Hello lover. Feel better?"

"A little. What are you doing in here?" It isn't really all that normal for Lia to be hanging out in the kitchen.

"Well, the family room is trashed. I don't really feel like cleaning it up by myself. It is as stinky as you were." Lia blows a kiss at Hook then tosses a strawberry into her mouth.

"Understood," he says. "Let me grab a bite and I will get started on it."

"I made you a sandwich. You can take it with you."

At this Hook throws a sideways glance at Lia, a look she was expecting. She receives it with a coy smile.

"I'm teasin' babe," she says. "I'm coming with you. I did make you a sandwich though."

"Love you," he says as he pulls his food out of the fridge.

"Love you more."

"Most likely," he says.

They make their way to the "family room", which is really the ship's bridge, and begin to clean. It is surprisingly messy from a party of two people. They had been quite drunk though, and the revelry had gone on for many hours. At some point during their cleaning Hook looks around the room and laughs.

"What is it?" Lia asks.

"Look at this place."

"Well it was a lot worse when we started."

"No, I mean, look at it now. What do you think the Council would say if they saw the bridge of our ship decorated like a family room?" Hook is laughing so hard by the time he finishes the last sentence, he has trouble getting the words out without choking. He is feeling slap happy.

"Well I think it's nice," Lia says defiantly, then joins him in his laughter.

By the time they finish cleaning up they are hungry for dinner. They haven't turned the monitor on to watch TV, check their emails or play on the Internet all afternoon. It is one of those fantastic days, despite their hangovers.

Eventually, they sit down on the couch with their supper to watch some Earth. Both of them are keen on seeing what's happening in Vegas. Now that the concert is over their focus will be on how the mystery and mayhem surrounding the black case unfolds.

To Hook's relief, Lia has not mentioned the people he killed the night before. He doesn't want to think about it. I can tell you, the acceptance of what he did will manifest itself in the form of a giant guilt worm. It will tunnel its way into the depths of his subconscious and bury itself there to live forever, resurfacing on occasion when it is hungry to feed off the tasty sadness the memory stirs in him.

Anyway, it's when they turn the monitor on to watch Vegas that they finally see the message from Greck Dislock again. At first they don't know what they're seeing. Both of their lips move as they read.

"What is this?" Lia asks.

"Who's the taco guy?" Hook asks.

Then they both look at each other and say, "Uh oh."

It turns out that Lia, who wrote the formal request for a stay of execution for the planet Earth, while listing many of the virtues of humanity, mentioned that tacos were fantastic and unlike anything they had to eat on Valtruca. She had also explained that there were cities on Earth where tacos were readily available at carts or stands or from trucks, and that in some places you could have someone deliver them right to your home.

You can imagine that if she had spent such time on the virtues of tacos how long the document had become, and you would most likely be wrong, as most everything else she liked about Earth she listed with little explanation after realizing she had begun to prattle on about tacos. She was genuinely unaware that when explaining the whole taco thing to Hook he had instantly become jealous. Although he never admitted this to anyone but me, for several years he wondered why Lia had gone on about tacos so, and if there had been a taco guy that had gotten to her...I'm not finishing this sentence but I think you know where it was most likely going.

Taco. A taco guy that had gotten to Lia's taco. Damn it.

After seeing Greck's message the second time, Hook and Lia freak out for about ten minutes. There are a lot of "oh my Bob oh my Bob oh my Bob"s and "what are we going to do"s. Eventually, more rational questions form.

"When did we send that transmission?" asks Hook.

"It's been a while," Lia says.

"But how long? Doesn't it seem a little quick to already be receiving a response from the Council? I was expecting at least a few more years. A few more Earth years if nothing else."

"Maybe," she replies. "But maybe they are already on their way here so it didn't have to travel as far."

"But why would they already be on their way here?"

"I don't know. Because of our first report, so maybe they already thought we would not follow our orders? I don't know." Lia is clearly at a loss, and frightened. There is no reason at all for the Council to already be heading this way. No reason that is any good for Hook or Lia, that is for sure.

"I don't know neither," Hook agrees. "But it should have taken the Council forever to make a decision like that. They never make decisions quickly. They're too deliberate. I can't think about that right now!"

"You brought it up!"

"I know!" Hook begins to pace. "And what about the homing pod? Those things travel so slow. That should have taken forever."

"What are we going to do?" Lia is a little panicked. Although no more so than Hook, and I've always felt she handles her fear well.

"I don't know. Figure out how far away they are? How much time we have."

"Let's look at that transmission again," Lia says. She holds the remote out to Hook, hoping if he takes it he will stop pacing.

"Good idea." Hook takes the controller, closes the transmission, and saves the file.

"Check out the file type."

"I don't recognize it."

"Me neither, but the computer does." Lia watches Hook as recognition sets in on his face.

"This is secret technology." Hook says this slow with a hush to his voice. "They're going to kill us."

"What? Why? For disobeying orders? They won't kill us for that?"

"They would not have used secret technology if they weren't going to kill us. You don't get to see secret technology and live." Hook speaks with stoic certainty, as if somehow having already accepted his own death.

"Stop saying 'secret technology'," Lia says, trying to ignore his death prophecy.

"Whatever," he continues. "They would not let us see this and then let us live."

"Maybe they would," Lia says. "You're being paranoid. We could get promoted when they get here for all we know."

"What? That's crazy. Why?"

"I don't know. To keep us quiet and get us to destroy Earth."

"No, that's stupid."

"There's no reason to be mean," Lia replies.

"I didn't say you were stupid," Hook says.

Lia sighs. "One thing is clear. When they get here, they are going to destroy the Earth and we have got to stop them."

"I agree, but how?" he asks. He puts his head in his hands, performing an excellent "Think damn it man think" routine.

"I don't know," Lia finally concedes.

"Me neither."

They both sit in silence while Hook messes with the transmission file. He scans it, analyzes it, closes it, reopens it, searches for its origin, and runs a diagnostics sweep on the driver that was used to run the program that made the file readable. That's when he finds something.

"Wait a minute," he says. What's this?"

"What's what?"

"I found something," Hook says. His voice betrays the spark of hope he suddenly feels.

"What? What did you find?"

"This message was double encrypted and the note we saw, it's not a large enough file for the amount of memory," Hook trails off, thinking out loud.

"What do you mean? Are you saying…?"

"Exactly," he says, interrupting her. "There's something hidden in there." Hook does some quick typing. "There, see. That file was hidden there from the sender but viewable to the receiver. I just had to tell the computer what to look for."

"Open it!" Lia is intrigued, scared, excited, and surprisingly horny again, all at once.

"I am I am. It takes a second to open secret encrypted files, geez." Hook gives himself a lisp, and is doing his best impersonation of an obnoxious internet technology professional. He has seen it on TV. After several minutes of quiet anticipation the file opens. The file contains a single word: ATLANTIS

"What's Atlantis?" Lia asks.

"I don't know," Hook replies. "Wouldn't it be great if there were these machines you could use that could connect to the rest of the worlds, and were full of all this information you could find really easily, anytime you want?" Hook forgot to turn the I.T. Guy impersonation off, but he did successfully find a ton of information from Earth's internet about Atlantis.

"The lost city of Atlantis?" Lia says. "What could it mean?"

"I'm not sure, but it has to mean something."

"I wish we knew who sent it."

"Yeah," Hook agrees. "Whoever sent this kept it simple and untraceable on purpose."

"Right, and keeping it simple means the purpose of the message has to be obvious."

"I agree."

"Which means what?"

"Well it can only mean one thing."

"And?"

"What?"

"What do you mean what?" Lia says. "What one thing?"

Lia is annoyed for two reasons: First, because she is too hungover to easily understand the meaning of the message. Second, because

Hook is too hungover to figure out the meaning of the message and has completely spaced out in the middle of their conversation.

"What and?" Hook asks.

"The one thing! You said, 'which can only mean one thing', and then you just sat there. I've been waiting for you to say something for like five minutes. You were staring with your mouth open. You started to drool!"

"Are you serious?"

"Yes!"

"Bobdamn. I drank too much last night." Hook goes silent and Lia realizes quickly he is spacing out again.

"Damn it Hook," she slugs his arm. "Get your head in the game."

"Right, the one thing," he says, searching his damaged short term memory.

"Whatever," Lia says, her patience exhausted. "While you were drooling I was playing with the file. I just figured it out."

"You did?"

"Yes. I'm going to Atlantis. There's no more obvious meaning to a one word note with the name of a city, than for the note to mean you're supposed to go to the city. So I'm going. Plus, look at this. There is a map hidden in the file as well. It looks like it has the exact coordinates for Atlantis, and the schematics to an entire city. Obviously, there is something down there someone wants us to find."

"I'll go with you," he says.

"Nope." She looks at Hook and shakes her head. "You are damn near worthless right now. You stay here and rest that hung over brain of yours, then figure out how the Council sent this message. We have to know how far away they are. How long before they arrive."

"Right," he says, not unhappy with the idea of more rest. "Maybe, I can figure out how to transmit the same way from the Parabolas."

"That's right," she says, clenching her teeth. "We can tell everyone on Valtruca what is going on."

"But, what is going on?" Hook asks.

"That's what I'm going to find out baby."

"I know. I mean, there is plenty going on that I am aware of. Let's pretend it was a rhetorical question. Man I feel dumb today." Hook rubs his head in a manner that makes him look as dumb as he feels.

Lia bites her tongue until she is certain she can say something supportive. "Well, you did discover the hidden file," she says, and then she kisses him on the forehead.

"That's right I did. I must have used up all the brain I had available today getting that done." He smiles broadly as Lia pats him on the back and lets out a soft chuckle.

"Then it's settled," she says. "I'm going back to Earth, and you're going back to bed."

# 38

We haven't seen Marshal Trate since the concert. There isn't much to tell. He's been in bed.

Dan remained frozen, in the last place we left him, as Lilly had walked away. When she was completely out of view, Dan felt something wet on his cheek. He was leaking. It was a tear. That was very confusing. He wandered away from the scene and found himself in his car driving home. Shortly thereafter, he was pulling the sheets over his head in bed.

If you could see the look on his face while he's sleeping, you would feel as sorry for him as I do. It is not peaceful. I feel for him because I know what he is going through. His life is about to be a lot heavier.

A soft glow briefly lights the room, and is followed by a soft voice.

"Dan," the voice says gently. "Dan," it repeats, a little bit louder now.

Dan still lays silent, but his eyes are moving like crazy under their lids.

"Danny boy?" A little bit louder now. "Dan." Probably normal speaking voice at this point. Still nothing.

"Dan!"

Dan abruptly sits up in bed with his gun in hand, pointed at his own head. "What!" he screams. "Jesus Christ!" Dan cocks the hammer on his pistol.

"Yes, it is I." Jesus steps forward. The glow from street lamps outside illuminates him.

Dan takes deep breaths through his nose, teeth clinched. The look on his face is pretty funny when he realizes he's about to shoot himself in the head. It would not have been anywhere near as humorous if he had mistakenly pulled the trigger. Although I'm sure Jesus could have resurrected him.

At first I thought Dan must have been dreaming something crazy or traumatic, to wake up so startled. I have since learned that Dan is simply a violent, irrational waker. When that dude is sleeping, it's best to let him be.

"Put the gun down," Jesus says, waving his hand to encourage the suggestion.

Dan puts the gun down in his lap, following the movement of Jesus' hand with his eyes. He looks up at Jesus with a sheepish expression and says, "Where am I?"

"At home. In bed."

"What are you doing here?" Dan is rubbing his face, trying to scrub off the confusion.

"We weren't able to speak extensively before," Jesus says. "I had a little time. Thought I might stop by."

"Right." Dan nods agreement, and looks around the room, soaking in the environment. "What did you do to me?"

"I didn't do anything to you Dan. Why does everyone always think it is something I did?" As he asks the rhetorical question, Jesus takes a seat on the edge of Dan's bed, near the footboard. He pats Dan on the leg. "Don't get me wrong. I doubt it is mere coincidence this is happening to you while I am here. That would be naive. But I'm not causing this."

"What happened to me? What's happening to me?"

"Well, you had a bit of mental meltdown. Not a breakdown mind you, more like your brain got a little melty and slow and sort of shut down for maintenance, so you went into auto pilot and wound up here. That's what happened. What's happening to you? That is sort of hard to describe. It's a little different for everyone."

Dan opens his mouth to ask another question, but Jesus holds his hand up and Dan stops himself.

"Relax Dan," Jesus says. "You will get some answers. I'm easing you into it. I think you were smacked in the face enough the past few days."

"Fair enough," Dan says. "It has been a little odd around here."

"Dan, you are living during an apocalypse," Jesus says with a smile. "There is literally a giant hole in the ground downtown that is a metaphysical gateway to Hates. It's a little odd around here every day."

Dan softly chuckles. "Yeah I suppose it is. But that's the difference. That's what this is about isn't it. I never thought it was odd before."

"So what do you think now?"

"I think I am completely confused," Dan replies. "I think this whole place is insane. I think I feel like, like I could sit here and ponder the rest of my life away." There is no frustration in his voice. Jesus' presence has him completely at ease. "How come you didn't tell me what was going on before?"

"Because I'm here now. This is the way it is. That's something it will benefit you to come to terms with as quickly as possible." Jesus pauses for a moment, either searching for the correct words, or perhaps simply organizing them. "The more you are going to learn the more questions you are constantly going to have. So, you must accept what has happened, what you've witnessed. Save your questions for what comes next."

"Okay." Dan nods his head in agreement with his own statement. "So what comes next?"

"I don't know. Not for you." Jesus sees Dan's disappointment with his answer. "Dan, do you think a week ago you could have fathomed any possibility that your grandmother could actually be from an alternate dimension?"

"Absolutely not," Dan replies.

"How do you feel now?" Jesus asks.

"I, like anything is possible." Dan's words are very close to sounding like a question.

"Right," Jesus says.

"Hey, wait," Dan says. "How did you know about Deedee? You said you can't read minds."

"I can't, but your grandmother is part of the puzzle, Dan, and I am Jesus."

"Ha. That doesn't exactly explain things."

"I know, but the barriers in your mind have to be broken down to prepare you for your work. One of those barriers is learning to accept without explanation."

"What work? My job? It's a little late for that isn't it? I'm fifteen years in. You don't mean my job do you?" Dan knows the answer.

"No, not law enforcement, or well, not necessarily law enforcement, not particularly." Jesus replies. "It is to prepare you for the work you will do for the Universe, for our creator."

"I'm…" Dan clamps his mouth shut. Studying his face is like trying to read a book by staring at the cover.

Jesus lets Dan process for a few moments, then continues when Dan doesn't speak again. "Dan you were born into something. A family, a line, an order. Call it what you will. Call it nothing at all, but you have a job to do, like I did and many others before and after us, and for whatever reason, it's a larger role than most people have the responsibility to fill." Jesus pauses for a minute. "Do you understand?"

"Well sure," Dan says. "I understand things in those terms. What I don't understand is why it would be me."

"Of course not. Nobody does. Well that's not true. There are a few out there with delusions of grandeur, some of them possibly listening to us now." Jesus looks around the room with a smile on his face and waives.

I'm pretty sure Jesus' comment was directed at me. Is my assumption a delusion of grandeur?

"Is there any rhyme or reason as to why this is happening now?" Dan asks.

"I'm not sure. I have a lot of theories, one in particular I enjoy thinking about is this idea where, sometimes it takes our souls an extended amount of time to become fully interfaced with our physical bodies and our cognitive mind. And sometimes, maybe it never happens and you die never having achieved your optimum functionality. But, you know, the average person reaches soul and body unison somewhere in middle adulthood, in their 30s or 40s. So, up until our soul takes over we are just running around, basically existing as lower life forms. Except for some people it happens earlier, as early as childhood. You know how they call people old souls? So, somehow some souls are able to get their physical bodies and minds fully integrated with their spirit at a younger age, and they have a greater ability to ignore the influence of the world and take their true path. They wind up being special people like Einstein and Mitch Hedberg. Or that Takana fellow, the engineer who designed the intergalactic space shuttle being built in New Asia. Or it could be the complete opposite of my theory, whatever the complete opposite may be. You will get used to not knowing Dan, and then eventually it's really kind of a comfort. What if you knew the answer to everything, and you didn't like the answer? Not knowing leaves room for things like hope and faith."

Jesus pauses to give his words time to sink in, and to let Dan ponder his question. After a few moments, he can see recognition in Dan's eyes.

"Anyway," Jesus continues, "the nature of our existence Dan, is that anything is possible. Do you know I didn't know for certain that I was coming back to life until after I was crucified?"

"Really?" It was the first word Dan had spoken in a few minutes. His voice creaked a little.

"Nope," Jesus says as he shakes his head. He produces a bottle of water from somewhere inside his robe, opens it, and offers it to Dan. "Don't get me wrong. I knew. That was faith. But I didn't know in a God like way. I was made human on purpose, to experience your existence. To feel it from your physiological and psychological point of view. That was part of the point. To smell and eat and breathe what mankind was going through. That includes doubt and fear. I didn't truly 'know' I was going to come back until it happened. As to why this is happening to you now, there is an equal possibility that it has a specific purpose, or that the timing is arbitrary, and everything would work out the way it is supposed to if this happened to you a year ago or next year."

"Okay," Dan says. "I can live with that. I think. Kind of hard to say for sure as I'm not certain I completely understand."

"Exactly," Jesus says.

"But if I do understand correctly," Dan continues, "I guess I can live with it."

"Good," Jesus says. "You have to." He laughs a little and Dan joins him. "The truth, from what I can tell, is that this happens differently for everyone. It happens in different times in their lives and in completely different manners. Sometimes people have to die first, then fulfill their mission in the afterlife."

"Seriously?" This thought catches Dan's attention, as like most of us, despite whatever we have come to learn, the fear of the unknown of death is a serious motivator to remain alive.

"Yeah," Jesus confirms. "Curt Cobain, Janis Joplin, Jimi Hendrix. Who was that recent fella, that bass player? Jimmy Slim, that's him. All rock stars. All died the same age."

"So, you're saying all those guys are part of this, or part of something for God?"

"I don't know," Jesus says. "I'm just saying it's awfully suspicious."

It takes a second but Dan realizes Jesus is kidding once again.

"You're a funny guy," Dan says. "I think they should give you more credit for that."

"Yeah. What are you going to do?" Jesus says with a chuckle. "Look, what is happening to you, if it happens, it happens for people at all different stages of life and everyone reacts differently to it. That I do know. I've seen it. It doesn't matter what dimension you are in or what planet you are from. Some people don't have a transition. They are actually born directly into all this madness. They are highly connected, and never know anything different. They never get to feel the blissful ignorance. I have seen it drive some creatures mad, being exposed to the chaos of the Universe at such a young age. It's really sad. Almost like a young mind can't absorb the shock of it all as well as a brain that has already suffered through more of the ups and downs of life. Any way it happens, it is a truly individual experience. You had a meltdown. No big whoop."

"Fair enough," Dan says. "It's strange to me though, feeling this uncertain."

AUTHOR'S NOTE # 7:

I can't fathom what it would be like to be someone Dan's age when the light gets switched on. Of course, I also can't imagine what it would be like to somehow live without being consumed by thoughts of the inner workings of existence. Stupid job.

"It will pass," Jesus says. "It's the newness."

"Here's a question," Dan says. "What if I want to fall in love and have a family? A nice normal life."

"Not going to happen," Jesus says bluntly. "Unless it's supposed to. And if it does, it won't change what you know now, or what you are going to learn. It's going to fit. You will still wind up doing your job one way or another."

"Okay," Dan says. "So here's another question. You said my grandma is part of it? How come she never told me?"

"I don't know," Jesus replies. "I guess she wasn't allowed to."

"By who?" Dan asks.

"The boss," Jesus replies. "Our father and mother. The Creator."

"So if she wasn't supposed to tell me, then what's with all the nonsense she was feeding me the other day? What was that all about?"

"Well, she's old Dan," Jesus says. He is very matter of fact, yet finishes the sentence with another soft, wistful chuckle. "So, I think that is part of it. Don't get me wrong, she's not crazy, but her brain is getting tired. Plus, she also enjoys messing with people. Always has. She likes giving people a hard time. Even God."

"Well that's the truth," Dan agrees. "She's been messing with me my whole life." Dan goes silent, strolling down memory lane with his grandma. "I wonder if she will be able to talk to me now, about what she is doing. I wonder if it really has something to do with that puzzle."

"I don't know. It's not part of my mission right now."

"Hmph. Interesting." Dan falls silent again for a little more consideration of everything Jesus is laying on him. Jesus waits quietly as well, until Dan eventually speaks again.

"Hey," Dan says. "You said earlier that the nature of our existence is that anything is possible."

"Yes I did."

"Doesn't that mean it has to be possible that there is no God?" Dan asks. "How can that be possible? Is that possible?"

"Wow. That's tricky. How deep into the rabbit hole are you prepared to go here?" Jesus asks the question to himself more so than to Dan. "Tell you what. Let's keep the training wheels on for the time being."

"Alright. You're right. This is hard enough to deal with as it is." Dan takes another drink of the water Jesus gave him. He realizes how thirsty he is and drains the rest of the bottle before speaking again. "Are you certain you can't tell me what happens next?"

"Yes, I'm certain, because I don't know. Keep living. Keep being yourself. Do what your heart and mind believe to be the correct way to behave. The rest will happen naturally."

"Well that's no help at all," Dan says playfully. "What's the point of you coming here if that's all you've got?"

"I'm here because you've been hiding in your bed since the concert," Jesus replies dryly. "You're afraid to come out from under the covers, and you've got work to do."

"Touché," Dan says with a smile.

"Now, get your head right and get out of that bed Danny boy. There is a war going on between good and evil on this planet and you have been drafted to fight. You have work to do. It could be a bunch of tiny things or a few giant things. A big moment, or a bunch of small moments. It could happen tomorrow or 20 years from now. This is the beginning for you. Get up and get it started." At that, Jesus gets off the bed and walks back over to his transporter tablet.

"I still," Dan starts then pauses.

Jesus looks up at him, with a "come on, out with it" expression.

"It's a lot to take in," Dan says. "It's very difficult to believe. Or understand."

"You remind me of an old friend of mine," Jesus says with a shake of his head. "This is the thing about people… It cracks me up. You can have all the evidence you need. The proof can be sticking straight up out of the pudding and still you doubt. Dan, you've been living all of your life with demons and monsters and ghosts walking this Earth. It only makes sense that there are angels." Jesus bends over his transporter tablet, adjusting its settings and prepping for a jump.

"I'm sorry what?" Dan asks, more as a figure of speech than a real question. "What are you saying Jesus? Are you saying that I'm an…Jesus what are you saying?"

"I'm just saying," Jesus replies as he turns another dial on the device.

"But what are you just saying? Jesus. Jesus? What are you saying? Jesus, what are you saying?" At first, I admit, I think Dan is working himself back up again. I quickly realize that, although earnestly still confused, he is being playful. Dan rarely overreacts, tall stoic hero that he is.

Jesus looks at Dan and sighs a little, but it is a soft appreciative sigh of contentment, not exasperation, as he sees Dan smiling.

Realizing Dan is being playful, Jesus wags his finger at him with a smile and steps onto the transporter tablet. "You'll get it," Jesus says. "Relax and don't worry. Worry doesn't do anyone any good." He steps on the launch button. As the machine powers on he holds his right hand up giving Dan the peace symbol. "Welcome to the really real world," he says, and then with a flash he is gone.

# 39

Jack22 and Computer Tiara were both very pleased with the creation of Jack22's alter ego. Or, I should say, Jack22 was very pleased and Computer Tiara acted like she was. Being a computer, she doesn't actually have feelings. Still, she is good at faking it, and Jack22 deeply appreciates her efforts.

With his alter ego in place, it was time to go. When he walks out of his maintenance closet and into the casino hallway this time around, he is no longer Dealer Robot Jack22. He is Montana Texas, American Cowboy.

He looks left. He looks right. He sticks a toothpick in his mouth, tugs at the lapels of his leather biker vest, then takes the toothpick back out of his mouth with the opposite hand that put it in there, makes a little bit of a swim move with his arm as he smoothly turns his body to the right, and struts off down the hallway.

Jack22 chose to go a little flashy with his alter ego. Montana Texas is an American Midnight Disco Cowboy Baby Kissing Politician Wildman Tycoon. He is a man of the people, for the people, who got rich off the people, licked LSD off the people's faces, stole the people's car to drive recklessly in, and the people absolutely love him for it.

He's a good time Charlie with sugar in his britches and diamonds in his smile. He's a well-educated Stanley Kowalski without all the insecurity. Monty Texas would take Blanche and Stella to the bedroom at the same time, not smack them around. Well, maybe a little smacking around, but in the bedroom and at the ladies' request. That's real. Montana Texas is razor sharp. That's what he is.

Jack22 makes his way to the grand entrance of the main gaming area. He strikes a pose in the middle of the large, arched opening into the room and takes a deep robot breath, waiting in vain for people to notice him. Nobody does.

He is not deterred. He saunters to the craps table and bumps a smaller man aside. "Pardon me pardner," he says. "Could I squeeze in here with you?"

Having no choice in the matter, the man nods his head while placing his next bet.

The first few minutes of Montana Texas' life are fairly uneventful. He tries to introduce himself to the fella that he bumped, and to a lady on his left, but neither of them pay attention to him. He takes a twenty dollar gold coin given to him by Pleeb, the leprechaun that granted him life, and puts it down on the rail of the craps table. The dice are rolled and he wins, doubling his money.

It goes on like this for a few rounds, losing a little here but winning a little more until eventually, the dealer turns and holds the dice out to Jack22. Jack22 takes the dice from the dealer, looking around the table. No one is watching him. At all. Everyone makes their bets and then turns to talk to someone, or order a drink, or bends down to tie their shoe, or anything at all other than paying any attention to the six foot four inch, shiny-ass robot cowboy.

Jack22 rolls a seven on his first throw. The dealer calls it and everyone moves their chips around, but only a few of the gamblers look up to see where the dice came from. Jack22 rolls again.

Again, sevens. The table buzzes a little, but not as much as it should. It's almost as if the people are as numb to winning as they are losing. Perhaps life in general.

"Sevens! Three in a row," the dealer robot exclaims, with preprogrammed enthusiasm. Three in a row finally gets the crowd going. People begin to take notice, encouraging Jack22, and that is how Jack22 learns that everyone loves a winner. His robot skills make rolling winning numbers a higher percentage endeavor than your average, gin fueled table-rat. Jack22 takes full advantage.

The party has begun. The drinks are flowing and the chips are flying. Jack22 is taking his winning ways from table to table. It doesn't take long for word to spread. The crowd of onlookers grows around him. Jack22 repeatedly introduces himself to newcomers as he takes over the room.

"Name's Montana Texas," he says. "My friends call me Monty, or Tex. I'm an oil and cattle man from Utah. Jack Mormon too. That's right, so some of my other friends call me Jack." Jack22 is especially proud of that last part. It gives him the perfect alibi if he accidentally responds to someone saying the name Jack while he is disguised as Montana Texas.

Monty Texas is unabashed about how fantastic he is. He brags about his philanthropies, his record winning T-bone from the Sanpete County Fair T-bone Eatin' contest, and his company's billion dollar green initiative. Montexacorp has a Research & Development division working on the feasibility of converting cattle's methane gas to an energy source. The trick isn't how to convert the methane he explains, that is simple. The trick is how to collect it.

"We've tried everything from burpbags and fartbags, to air filter umbrellas strapped over their heads and asses, yes sir," he says. "Ain't none of it worked. Plus, apparently it embarrasses the hell out of the cattle. Heh, heh, heh. That's a joke there pardner."

No one seems to notice Monty Texas is actually a robot. They are all too drunk, or their attention spans are so short they can't see past the giant fake handlebar mustache, or they are so self-centered and desensitized to the insanity of their existences it doesn't register with them. There are any number of reasons, but the result is the same. Nobody says a word about his shiny metal skin. The truth is, in the world they live in, if people realized he was a robot it may not have garnered much reaction. Not with all the demons and other assorted nonsense running around.

Jack22 is on fire. Don't get me wrong, as I mentioned his robot skills (counting fast, thinking about other things fast, precise robot movement, logical reasoning on an infinite algorithmic level, etcetera, etcetera) definitely increase his winning percentages, but he is also hot. Luck is his lady. He has his mojo working and he is letting it rip. It is an unabashed spectacle of charisma.

At some point Jack22 actually screams, well he doesn't scream per se, but he increases the volume on his oral transmitter to bullhorn and says, "I'm never going to lose!"

A hushed silence falls over the room. Jack22 ignores the silence and doubles his bet at a blackjack table. Then he gets up and walks over to a roulette table, plays black 22, which of course hits, then as everyone cheers he walks back over to the blackjack table to see a six of hearts resting on top of the five of clubs in front of his chips. Jack22 flips his jack of diamonds over to reveal his hard 21.

"Bam," he says, with his emotionless robot voice. The crowd goes crazy.

Jack22 wins at everything. You name it. Hold 'em and no-show 'em? Done. Winner. He wins at three-card, four-card and five-card poker. He wins at Chinese poker, pyramid poker, Asia poker and arena poker. He cleans house at two-up, penny-up, red dog, let-it-ride and Australian pontoon. He plays Caribbean stud, mambo stud and no-look stud all with his eyes closed. Don't get me started on his success with the big money wheels, slots, bingo or keno. It's a lot of fun.

Jack22 quickly takes to telling his people he is going to rob the casino. They of course assume he means he is going to keep winning, but then he goes on to explain to them he is actually going to rob the casino. He goes into detail about all the ways it can be done. This brash confidence increases his rapidly growing legend. The people think he is wild, man. Just wild.

The problem is, Jack22 isn't prepared for this. True, he has these grand delusions of acclaim and notoriety. He definitely thinks he wants to be a man of the people, the life of the party. His naiveté fuels this desire to be something astounding, but he isn't ready to handle it with the type of level headed, rational curiosity he assumed his robot nature would facilitate.

First of all, Jack22 already is astounding, before he ever set a shiny foot at the craps table. He is a robot that has somehow been granted life by magic. According to the laws of random ass shit, it is completely possible he is not 100% unique, but he is pretty damn unique.

Yes, being brought to life by magic, this alone makes him special, but he doesn't see that. When you take into consideration that he is instinctually humble enough not to realize his own amazingness, well that makes him even more special! Anyway, the point is, he is already astounding and doesn't realize it. The other point I was about to make, second of all, is that he has no idea how exhausting being astounding can be.

Jack22 the robot has no need for sleep, other than to charge his battery. For Jack22 the sentient creature, rest is definitely good for his servers and his newly awakened soul. It is not a requirement though, and he finds it impossible to walk away from the tables, or the party. In fact, if he leaves the gambling tables it is only to go to a party somewhere else in the hotel, perhaps in someone's suite or a hotel ballroom.

Montana Texas becomes casino royalty, filling everyone's pockets with chips, glasses with champagne, and hearts with laughter. The adulation is a drug, and it has its evil hooks in Jack22 quicker than he can say "hit me".

So Jack22, or Montana Texas I suppose I should say, is riding his fifteen minutes of fame like a coked up monkey on a mini motorcycle.

He has forgotten all about actually enacting his plot to rob the casino. It has become nothing more than big time talk. He has forgotten all about his grand notion of being a hero in a destitute age. That has been replaced by a crass desire to remain the center of attention. He is the life of the party and the party never ends. That can take a lot of time and energy.

# 40

Lia returns to the Parabolis so excited by her discoveries she could burst. *Hook is going to be so proud of me*, she thinks. *This is going to make him angry too. He is going to explode!*

She finds Hook on the bridge. The bridge is a complete disaster. So is Hook.

Lia wasn't gone long. She slowed Earth time down while she was on recon. Sometimes it is hard to tell how much time was really passing when it is slowed down, but she didn't think it had been enough time for Hook to lose his mind. *What am I thinking?* she thinks. *He lost his mind a long time ago.*

The Parabolas' bridge is littered with computer monitors brought in from other areas of the ship. There are extra keyboards and computer consoles everywhere. It looks like some psychopathic cyber-terrorist's lair from a movie. Hook is running around from screen to screen, staring too closely at them and hammering away at the keyboards. He is striking the keys while chattering to himself with crazed enthusiasm.

"Hook! What are you doing?" There is very loud, very aggressive music blaring. Lia has to shout to hear herself.

"Hook!" She makes her way towards him. Along the way she sees the control for the stereo and cuts the music.

"Hook!" She screams again, then realizes she has turned the music off and doesn't need to scream anymore. "Hook," she repeats, at a normal volume. She puts her hand on his shoulder, turning him around.

His eyebrows are raised, he has a huge grin on his face, his eyes are dilated to the size of silver dollars, and he smells really bad. "Hey baby!" Hook screams at her. I'm pretty sure his ears are still ringing from the music, but to be clear, he is all cranked up on something besides lack of sleep.

"What are you doing?" she asks.

"I'm broadcasting," he says enthusiastically.

"Broadcasting what?" she asks. She looks around the room, realizing that each monitor has something different on display.

"Everything!" At this he looks over her shoulder, holds a finger up and says, "Ooh. Got a bite!" He walks quickly across the room to stare at another monitor, waiving for her to follow him as he does. "Look, this is *Battle of the Planets*, it's a very old cartoon."

"Hook, look at me," she says, tugging at his arm. "Turn around here."

"Hang on. Just a second. Any second now. One...second. Nope. Darn. Oh well, we'll leave her on like the rest." He is speaking to himself more than he is speaking to Lia.

"Hook, look at me," she says.

"What a great cartoon," he mumbles.

"Hook!" She pulls hard at his arm. "Turn around here and pay attention to me!"

He turns and smiles again. "Hey baby! When did you get here?"

"Oh for Good Bob's sake, Hook. What are you on?"

"A couple of different human heart rate and metabolism accelerators, dopamine quadrupelizers, and some very powerful amphetamines."

"What the fuck, Hook? Are you trying to kill yourself?" She is not pleased. She is also pretty damn confused. Granted, he is an impetuous creature, but she is surprised to see him in such a frantic state.

"What? No. Of course not. I was trying not to think about…I wanted to work as much as possible while…it seemed like a good idea at the time." There are several things at play here. First, Hook really is enthralled by the mystery they are uncovering and the scientific portion of his mind can't rest until he figures out how the Council has communicated with the Parabolas so quickly. Second, he still can't get the whole taco guy thing out of his mind. Why had Lia gone on about this taco guy to the Council? Was she going to see this taco guy again while she was on Earth? It is these two themes, scientific curiosity and jealousy, but mostly the jealousy, tugging away at his subconscious, that caused him to make what felt like an excellent decision at the time: Do a bunch of speed and stay awake researching and experimenting until Lia returns.

"What is all of this? And don't tell me computers and stuff. I get it, but why are they in here? What specifically are you doing? I need you to calm down and explain all of this to me."

Hook is nodding his head yes like a child as she speaks while his eyes continue to shoot from monitor to monitor.

"No, you know what," she continues. "Let's go. I've got to sober you up." She grabs him by the arm, dragging him from the room, "Let's get you some coffee."

"Yes, coffee!"

"On second thought, that was a dumb thing to say to Mr. Fucking Speed Ball Head. Maybe some chamomile tea instead."

"You seem like you're mad," Hook says, having trouble controlling how quickly he speaks. "I don't know why you're mad. I was doing what I was supposed to, trying to figure out how they were transmitting so quickly."

"Yeah but you didn't have to go and do a bunch of drugs you stupid dummy."

"But it made work faster."

"You're stealing my thunder you big jerk! I came home excited to show you what I found in Atlantis, and to put the pieces of this puzzle together, together, the two of us, and instead you're all hopped up on goofballs."

"Mostly amphetamines."

"Whatever! You've stolen my thunder and I'm pissed." She isn't kidding. She is all the way pissed.

"I love you," he says, with complete sincerity.

"Oh go stick it in your butt," she says, equally as sincere.

At this, Hook starts laughing hysterically. Lia softens and laughs as well. The impasse is enough for Hook to gather his bearings and take a little control back over his mind. Drugs come and go in waves sometimes. Hook has successfully navigated a tsunami.

"You don't have to wait for me to sober up," Hook says, after the laughing stops and he has taken a few deep breaths. "I'm good. Tell me everything you found, but do me a favor. If my heart explodes resuscitate me."

"Good Lord Bob, I don't think you would feed yourself if I wasn't here."

"That was not a life affirming promise."

"I promise."

"Moving on then. What did you find?"

"You know what? You go ahead. Explain to me what you are doing. It will be quicker than everything I have to explain." When Lia says this, Hook understands she is telling him his report better be quick. "When I tell mine," she continues, "we are going to have some things to figure out. So you go ahead. Tell yours first." She says this last bit with a little flip of her hand.

"Well what was the point of getting mad at me then if you were going to turn around and..."

"Hook." She says his name as a shot fired across his bow.

"Right," he says. Then he grabs her by the wrist. "Come with me." He leads her back into the command room den. "So, I don't know how they did it, but, this is fascinating. I can't explain to you how freaking far out this is." He is getting excited again thinking about it. Also, he is still very jacked up on drugs.

"What are all the monitors for?" Lia realizes she is probably going to have to guide the explanation out of Hook.

"Hang on. Let me begin from the beginning." He has a big smile on his face. "I started by analyzing the file that we downloaded because it was larger than it should have been for the message it contained. That's how we discovered the hidden note too remember?"

Lia nods her head an affirmative.

"So then, when I was analyzing it to try and figure out how it got here, there's a tag on this thing. It's like a receive notification on an email. It lets you know it got where it was going. Plus there is all this weird, I don't know, for lack of a better word, 'residue' in the file. It was corrupted a little, which I thought was kind of curious. All of our deep space signals travel on a frequency that is so straight and sharp we call it a Razor, right?"

"Uh huh." Lia knows deep space transmissions are called Razors, but she doesn't know why. Hook is the communications expert.

"Well, there are a couple of ways a file traveling that fast can get corrupted, and most likely it would be by somehow, in the infinity of space, actually crossing or punching through another high speed transmission traveling on an equally tiny frequency, and the odds of that are absurd. So then I thought, I'm going to analyze the temporal atmosphere surrounding the ship when the transmission arrived, and that's when I found it!" Hook is back to moving about from monitor to monitor, checking them as he speaks.

"What did you find?" Lia barely has time to slip the question in before he continues.

"I was jamming through the analysis and there it was. 'That's a strange little blip' I thought. And then I figured out its coordinates and pulled up video surveillance on the exterior of the ship and what do you know? We have a direct camera angle on that quadrant so I rewound the footage and bam! Bam! There it is! Beautiful!"

"There what is Hook?"

"A wormhole babe! A tiny little galaxy hopping, signal transmitting sexy ass wormhole!"

"I don't understand," she says.

"They open up a tiny wormhole and shoot the transmission through it. The wormhole closes, opens back up near where the transmission is supposed to go and boom, the signal arrives way faster than cutting through all that extra space."

"Are you sure that's how the signal arrived?" she asks.

"Has to be. I double checked the timestamp on the recording of the wormhole opening, and of the incoming message from the Council."

"But how do they know where the wormhole will open back up?" Her arms are crossed as she considers her own questions. "How do they know it will open near where they intend for it to? How do they control it?"

"I don't know," Hook replies. "That's what all the extra monitors are for, trying to figure out how the Council re-opens the wormholes."

"Oh," Lia says. She loses track of the conversation for a moment when she looks up to the main view screen and sees Marshal Dan and Princess Tiara kissing. *Oh you've got to be kidding me!* Lia thinks. She is not at all interested in seeing that filthy bitch ruin a man like Marshal Dan. *Hook better be recording this.* Lia starts canvassing the room for the remote to make sure Vegas is being recorded while Hook continues his explanation.

"I figured out how they are opening the wormholes, but I'll explain that later to save time because it will take a while. There's a particle accelerator and the black hole machine and a gluon smasher involved but anyway, I've been opening up and shooting out these random broadcasts of Earth television. I'm pulling the broadcasts from human satellites, then resending the signal with a destination notification coded similar to the one the Council used on the message they sent to us, from the opposite direction of course, but nothing is working. And that's what I can't figure out. I don't know if the wormhole is opening back up and if it is, where?" He looks confused, almost hurt, as if his brain has somehow hurt its own feelings.

"So, you are randomly broadcasting the human race to the rest of the Universe?" she asks.

"Well, yeah, potentially."

"Don't you think that could be bad?"

Hook doesn't answer right away. Then you can see recognition set in. "Well, I suppose it could be," he says, "if the wrong people were to discover an inferior, easily conquerable race they were previously unaware of. But what are the odds of that happening? Besides, what are the chances the Council members are the only people to know about an entire planet? I have a feeling plenty of other species know about the humans and want nothing to do with them. They've been left alone all this time."

"True, but what if someone out there decides they want the Earth?"

"I suppose that's a possibility. The Earth is pretty from a distance, but it's a lot of water, and most of the land has been abused."

"What if it is a hydration oriented species of alien conquerors?"

"Oh come on," he replies incredulously. "What are the odds of that? Besides, who would want to mess with the planet during the middle of an apocalypse? Seems like it would be kind of pointless."

"I suppose that's true," she relents. "And I guess it's too late now anyway." She looks around the room again at Hook's mess. "So what's the status on your broadcasts?"

"Well every time I send out a transmission I am trying a different way to 'tell' the wormhole where to go. Wormholes carry electric currents. If I can get the transmission I am sending to talk to the wormhole, through the electronic impulses, I might be able to tell it where to reopen. I'm certain that is how it will work. So I created an algorithm that is continually assigning um…like a new language I guess is a way to describe it. Basically, the signal tries a different method of 'talking' to the wormhole every time it broadcasts and if a method actually works I will know, because I will get a bounce back from whatever source intercepts the transmission. My hope is that the bounce back comes from a satellite orbiting Valtruca. If that happens, we will know we successfully told the wormhole where to reopen."

Hook stops pacing during this last bit of explanation and stands eerily still as he speaks, except for his right hand which spasms nonstop, acting as an outlet for the massive amounts of chemically induced energy surging through him. "So what did you find out?" he asks, and then he passes out. His body crashes face first to the floor, stiff as a board.

Lia tries smelling salts to no avail. She uses a defibrillator once and it doesn't not work, but she can only shock one of Hook's hearts at a time without someone to assist her. Finally, she plunges an adrenaline shot directly into his auxiliary vascular pump, while at the same time shocking his head with a paddle from the defibrillator.

Hook gasps back to life.

Lia lays down on Hook, hugging him. Then she sits up and smacks the piss out of him.

"What was that for?" he asks with his eyes still closed.

"For almost killing yourself you dumb ass."

"I was nowhere near death," he replies weakly.

"Both your hearts stopped you big jerk," Lia is not as angry as she is relieved. But she is definitely angry.

"Look." He gently touches her chin and nudges her to look down at his left foot. He pulls his pant leg up a little and she sees a small electronic device connected to a strap wrapped around his ankle. "I'm wearing a nano-bite cardiac rejuvenator. I would have been back up in ten minutes."

"Well you scared me to death," she says, trying, but not very hard, to hide the tear she is wiping away from her cheek.

"I'm sorry babe," he says. "Honestly. I didn't mean to." He squeezes her tight. "I didn't think you would be back so soon." He makes the perfect facial expression so she knows that last line is a joke.

Lia hammers him in the chest with her balled up fist. "Jerk."

"Ow," he says, then he notices the needle sticking out of him. "Will you get that thing out of me?"

"Of course baby." Lia proceeds to pull the six inch long needle out as slowly as possible.

"Aaaaayaaaaaaa," Hook exhales as she pulls the needle. "Ouch."

"There," she says. "All is forgiven."

"Thank goodness," he replies dryly.

"Didn't sleep much while I was gone, did ya?"

"I don't think at all," he replies, rubbing his eyes with his fingers, pushing on them hard enough to hurt a little. He is definitely still on drugs, but the wave of internal chaos seems to have calmed down a bit during his blackout. Once again, his thought processes have returned to him at a more normal pace. At least for the moment.

"C'mon, get up. I've got something to show you," Lia says.

"Right! What did you find? Atlantis is there isn't it?"

"Do you remember anything that was going on before you passed out?"

"A little, but it's fuzzy," he admits.

She leads him towards the lab, grabbing her drop sack with her findings from Atlantis along the way.

"Well, you are correct, Atlantis is completely real," she says. "You're never going to believe this, but it was our city."

"It was our city? We were here?"

"Yep."

"Does the Council know?"

"Oh they know. They were here!" she says. "At least some of them. Greck Dislock was the Official for the city. He was in charge!"

"But that would mean he is thousands of years old," Hook says, bewildered.

"Maybe. I'm still working on that part. I think there is a chance that the Earth life cycle is actually moving at a significantly higher rate than Valtruca's," she replies. "I think that is why we can slow Earth time down."

"Hmph. That could actually be plausible." I don't think Hook meant it to sound as condescending as it did.

"Gee thanks," Lia replies dryly, jokingly, realizing Hook meant no offense. "Anyway, I read through some of the records I found while I was down there. The whole city was sunk by the way. It's at the bottom of the ocean."

"That's bad ass."

"Yeah, and you know what's more bad ass? Somehow as it sank, some of the structures created massive air pockets, pressurizing entire sections of the city and keeping them from flooding. There are places in there that are almost completely preserved, other than natural corrosion and not having been cleaned in a thousand years or so."

"So how did you get in there without corrupting the vacuum and flooding those areas?"

"I picked up a transporter tablet on Earth."

"Amazing they figured that out, isn't it?"

"Yep. Whoever invented that thing is going to make a lot of money once their market spreads to other planets." They reach the ship's lab and Lia punches a code to open the door.

Hook has a penchant for coming into the lab to see what she is up to and messing stuff up. He has accidentally sneezed on a glass slide with a sample on it, has tripped on a power chord when a centrifuge was in process, and once created a small fire when he knocked a beaker of volatile chemicals to the floor. You would think he would get the cosmic hint that he is bad luck in there, but he can't help himself. He likes sneaking around.

So, Lia is forced to use the programmable keypad locking mechanism to keep him out of the damn room and away from her lab work. Luckily, to this point, he has not been able to figure out the code.

"If they can make it work on other alien physiologies that aren't as similar as ours, it will change space exploration," Hook says, referring to the teleporter pad.

"Speaking of which, there is a reason for that," Lia says. She makes her way to her largest working station and starts unloading her drop sack of its contents.

"What? A reason for what?"

"The similarities in the human physiology to ours."

Hook scratches the back of his head. After brief contemplation, recognition washes across his face. "Are you saying what I think you are saying?"

"If you are talking about mating with the humans that is exactly what I am saying."

"I can't believe this." Hook speaks with genuine astonishment. "It's, it's a…"

"A discovery of massive historical and present significance for two different species of sentient life forms living on separate planets?" Lia finishes for him. She grows a very sexy smile on her face. "Yes, yes it is."

Hook is silent for a few minutes as a list of questions forms in his mind. The first to come out is, "But what was the Council doing here?"

"I'm not sure," she replies. "I've pieced some things together from materials that were left behind: Documents listing Greck as Official. Lab results from research on the interaction of human and Valtrucian reproductive organs." She holds up a thin electronic device. "I found these too. Recognize this?"

"Yeah, that's an old memory drive," Hook says.

"Yep," she says. "I found an archive room full of them. Luckily, our technology was not as advanced back then, otherwise there may not have been anything like this to find."

"Those drives are a couple hundred years old on Valtruca," Hook says. "That would mean that somehow, within the past few hundred years on Valtruca, all this stuff happened here on Earth, and Earth has aged over a thousand years."

"Yep," she says. "More like two or three thousand. But if it was only a few hundred years on Valtruca, that explains how Greck was here."

"But it doesn't explain the time differential," Hook replies. "I should have been monitoring it since the day we got here."

"Maybe the Council has time travel technology they are keeping secret from us."

"You know, until recently I would have told you that was crazy. Now, I don't think anything we find out about the Council would surprise me."

"Me neither," Lia replies. They are both quiet for a second, presumably each imagining endless possibilities of the things the Council may have been keeping secret from their culture for hundreds of years. Lia is the first to snap out of it. She looks at the drive in her hand and remembers their conversation. "So, most of the memory drives in the archive room were scientific research, which we should go back for by the way. There were too many for me to move them all. But I found a Council archive. That's what these are." She holds it up again. "I brought as many as I could carry. We've got to go through these and see if they tell us what the Council was doing here."

"Cool, let me run to the bathroom real quick and we can get started."

"No way mister. If you need to pee you can go in the corner. I'm not letting you out of my sight. No more drugs. We went through this back on Earth. You get addicted like, immediately, and then I have to freaking detox your crazy ass."

Hook is a lucky alien. He really is.

"Well, what if I have to poop?" he asks.

"I doubt that will be a problem," she says with a laugh. "At least not for a while with all the drugs you've got in your system."

"Yeah, I suppose you are right."

"Let's get to work," she says. "I want to figure out what this is all about."

It does not take long before the mystery begins to unfold. An unspecified amount of time passes. After a montage of Hook and Lia reading, drinking coffee and appearing interested in their research, Hook speaks.

"Look," Hook says. "Here is the original mission manifesto. It says here that Bob sent the Council to Earth to oversee and protect the humans."

"Right, and here are some of the earliest mission records. Humans were basically unintelligent farm animals. It says they were a brand new species that was potentially unable to sustain themselves." Lia's face shows confusion while reading the file. "Why would Bob make a species that was unable to sustain itself?"

"I don't know. I also don't know how we would have found out about Earth in the first place."

"Well, from Bob," she replies.

"Right, of course. But how did we really find out. Who did Bob tell? There is no mention of how we found Earth in here anywhere that I have seen."

"Perhaps Bob spoke directly to the Council," Lia replies, "like he used to do with the Old Sages in the First Teachings."

As you may have immediately guessed, the First Teachings are the Valtrucian's oldest passages of religious text, and the first half of the Great Bork of Bob. The Great Bork of Bob is basically the Valtrucian Bible. As I believe I mentioned before, all of Valtruca believes in the same religion. It's what makes them such a powerful spiritual commodity. The second half of the Great Bork of Bob is aptly named, The New Teachings. The two sections of the Great Bork are separated at the point in history where the first Council was formed on Valtruca.

Both Hook and Lia are continuing to search through files as they speak.

"I suppose that is possible." Hook's voice betrays his doubt. He can't help thinking that somehow, the Council discovered Earth all on their own.

"Wait a minute. Look at this." Lia interrupts Hook's thoughts, turning her monitor where Hook can see it. "These look like passages from the Great Bork, but I've never seen these before."

"Me neither," he says. "Look, there is a report attached, scroll down."

"This is crazy. The humans were completely stupid."

"And Bob was farming them, cultivating their simpleton souls."

"He was cultivating cosmic 'goodness' with a bunch of thoughtless souls and he sent us here to study and protect them," Lia says. "Earth was an incubator planet. He was growing new souls here. Simple, healthy, hardworking, righteous souls."

"This is…hell I don't know what this is. Amazing?" Hook speaks as he scans more documents. "Oh this makes perfect since. Look here." He steps aside and lets Lia see what he has found.

"These are new passages for the Bork that were being written about our time here once the humans were fully developed," she says, with another layer of excitement in her voice. "But we weren't supposed to have any interaction with them. Then against Bob's orders Greck and some of the other Council members began breeding with them."

Hook is nodding his head in agreement. "That's it. That's what Greck is trying to hide."

"It has to be," she agrees enthusiastically. "And look here. It was our DNA that provided the humans with the missing link to theirs."

"Oh man. Do you know what else this means? There could be human DNA in us. I mean back home. Human DNA could be part of Valtruca now."

"It's possible," she says. "It would make sense, unless the Council made sure all the evidence was left behind."

"Right. They could have stranded Valtrucians here. Made sure only pure Valtrucian blood got back home. Dear Bob, there's so many questions. Why would they have recorded all of this if they weren't supposed to be doing it, and why would they leave all of this behind? Why not destroy the evidence of what they did? And who sank Atlantis?"

"My guess is," Lia says, "the Council sank Atlantis to cover up what they did, or Bob punished them by sinking the city and sending them back home. Either way, they probably figured all this stuff would be lost at the bottom of the ocean."

"But why would they have made a record of something they weren't supposed to be doing in the first place?"

"I don't know. It doesn't make any…"

"Wait, look at this."

"What is it?"

"It's the human's Bible. It's the first 'book'. Their 'Genesis'. It says here the Council wrote it."

"Are you kidding me?" Rhetorical. She knows he isn't.

"Nope," he says, shaking his head. "Says here the Council wrote this Garden of Eden story to explain to mankind why they are morally corrupt."

"So, the Council screws up Bob's perfect, loving, stupid creature he was using to cultivate wholesome souls, then they blame it on the females of the species and mess with this book to cover their tracks?" Lia is suddenly furious. "So you mean to tell me that our planet's history, and potentially our future is directly related to this planet and its people and the Council has kept this from us for all these years?"

"Yep."

"Who would have ever thought that the Council would arbitrarily edit out parts of the Great Bork?"

"Humans would have," Hook says.

"Your damn right they would have."

"Then again, I suppose it's possible Bob told them to do it. Maybe he changed his mind about what he wanted us to know and told them to change it." Hook isn't grasping at straws. He is pondering out loud.

"That's illogical. That would mean that Bob had made a mistake. Bob doesn't make mistakes."

"Agreed."

"Then it was the Council," Lia states firmly. "There is no way around it."

"Not that I can see," Hook says, matter of fact.

"This has to be it. This has to be what the Council is trying to hide," she says. "All of this. They messed these people up and now they are trying to cover up their mistake by destroying them."

"But who are they trying to hide it from? Bob? That would be ridiculous. You can't hide anything from Bob." Hook runs his hand through his hair, deeply confounded. "Besides. I'm pretty sure he is paying attention to what is going on down there now!"

"Maybe they were trying to hide it from the rest of the Universe," she says. "It would not look good for the Council if other cultures, or the rest of Valtruca for that matter, found out we ruined an entire species."

"That's true," Hook replies. "But it wouldn't look any better if we destroyed an entire species either. And why did they record all of this? I can't wrap my head around that. If they weren't supposed to be doing it, why would they keep a record?"

"I don't know babe," Lia says. "Nothing I can think of would make any sense at all."

"Me neither," Hook says. "I guess the answer to that question lies with the Council."

"Yeah," Lia agrees, "and suddenly I'm not sure I would trust any answer they gave me."

At that moment, a small alarm flashes on a transmitter Hook is wearing around his wrist. He holds his wrist up and points at it with a look of surprise.

"What?" Lia asks.

"The signal! We got a bounce back!" He takes off, leaving the room and running through the halls of the Parabolas. "Bounce back!"

Lia hears him shout again as she chases after him. When she gets to the command room she finds him staring at a monitor. "What happened?"

"We got a signal reception return notification, but it doesn't make any sense," Hook says.

"What do you mean?"

Hook stands upright and turns to face her. "Well, I've got all of these signals looping, you know, rebroadcasting on a rotation in intervals until something sticks."

"Okay."

"So, this signal is new. The broadcast went out a few minutes ago and already bounced back. That might as well be instantaneous.

Even with a wormhole that is too fast. That would mean Valtruca is right over there." He thumbs over his shoulder with his hand for effect, pointing in no specific direction, when he sees Lia's eyes grow very large. "What? What is it?" he asks, as he turns around. He looks out the starboard viewport and sees another ship coming into view. Enter, the Peacecannon.

## AUTHOR'S NOTE #8:

Have you noticed there seem to be many versions of God, but only one devil? Devil worshiping has never been as segregated as God worship. Don't get me wrong. There is some strange witchcraft and voodoo shit out there that kowtows to some pretty random dark forces. There are definitely some varying evil beliefs, but in general, you don't hear evil worshippers out running around debating who the real ultimate evil is, or who the greatest spawn of Satan is for that matter. Was it Adolph Hitler, or Marilyn Monroe, or that teenager Solomon Hand who murdered and ate the entire town of Beaver Dam, KY a few years back? Who cares? You don't hear believers in evil debating questions like this, although the answer is clearly Marilyn Monroe. With her unabashed nudity and miscreant mistress ways, she helped usher in an era that opened a Pandora's Box of moral decline in what had once been the most powerful and completely rational moral compass on the planet, the former United States. But I digress. The point is, the minions of evil don't waste time on such petty arguments. They simply try to do as much bad as possible.

## 41

The kidnappings begin. They start shortly after Alacrán stomps out of his office, post rant, leaving Purvis alone with the echoes of Alacrán's rage. Purvis almost cries when his boss leaves, but instead he pounds his fist on the nearest table. There is still a little man-fight-bear-strong left in him.

This whole situation can piss itself to Hell, right through the hole downtown, for all Purvis cares. All he wants now is Dolly and those jerkoff vampires have her. How is he supposed to figure out how to get her back when she was the brains behind their operation? Never mind the fact that now he has an entire city to kidnap. This shit is getting out of hand.

I must admit I was not a huge fan of Purvis at first. I think it is his name. Also, the fact that he is kind of a little bitch. I have always, however, cared a great deal for Dolly. Despite never really having a taste for the presence of Purvis, I've grown to appreciate him out of his love for her, and his devotion. He is 100% her loyal paramour.

Purvis carries out Alacrán's orders. He puts the word out to Alacrán's minions across the city. Anyone with potential knowledge of the whereabouts of the black case, or Princess Tiara, is to be brought in for questioning.

The thing is, damn near everyone in the city of Las Vegas owes Alacrán something. Everybody has dirt under the fingernails. Now, I'm not saying the whole city gets involved, but there is a lot of unnecessary kidnapping going on. It will take weeks after our version of the story ends for the whole deal to unwind itself.

Anyhow, Purvis reaches out to Lola, the showgirl from earlier in our story. Lola takes a cast of fellow chorus line girls and hits the streets. Purvis also calls the crew of the Incorporeal Phantasm, a pirate ghost ship that wanders the streets of Las Vegas. They "yar" into action.

Purvis calls the quarterback of the Las Vegas Gamblers professional football team. Alacrán has an ownership share in the team, *and* in the secret illegal robotic arm keeping quarterback Tug Ketchum's career alive. Tug calls up his offensive line and they suit up for battle.

The entire 24th precinct of the Las Vegas Metro Police Department is on the hook to Alacrán for a couple of dead prostitutes they left in their suite at La Ciudad de Oro after the precinct's Thanksgiving banquet two years earlier. When I say a couple of dead prostitutes, it is sort of more like 15. Every cop at that party is on the casino's security recordings dirtying up their soul.

There are priests, warlocks, and a few demons that owe Alacrán favors. There is a magician named The Magnificent Doug, who is not a very good magician. There is a local chapter of Dykes Fly Kites, the roughest, toughest, most charitable gang of kite enthusiast lesbians west of the Mississippi. Somehow, even Montana Texas gets the call. The conversation goes like this:

"Hello, Monty Texas," Jack22 answers.

"Who is this?" Purvis asks.

"Montana Texas, pardner. Who is this?"

"Purvis Hawthorne."

"I don't think I know you."

"I don't think I know you either. I apologize, I don't know where I got this number."

"That's okay buddy, I don't know where I got this phone."

Once the word is out, Purvis refocuses his energy on Dolly. How is he going to get her back? He isn't sure. He thought about ordering her to be kidnapped as well, hoping someone might steal her back from the Karowack Kids, but he is afraid something might go wrong. Those vampires may be jackasses, but they are still quite deadly when angered.

Purvis looks in the mirror. His handsome face is tired. It looks ugly to him. He sees his mother in the mirror as well. She smiles at him, nodding her head "yes" as if answering a question Purvis has asked. He realizes she is giving her approval for his love of Dolly. That's when it dawns on him. Perhaps this is all part of Dolly's plan.

I don't know if it is exhaustion or pure hopefulness, or if Purvis is truly insane, but he is able to convince himself that Dolly's abduction by the Karowack Kids is somehow part of her scheme. She allowed herself to be kidnapped to protect the Princess, and to somehow manipulate the Karowack Kids. Yeah, that's it.

If convincing himself this is Dolly's plan is what it takes for Purvis to relax and get some rest, so he can try to figure this mess out tomorrow, well then I say whatever helps you sleep at night buddy.

# 42

Nico is at the library. He is bunkered in between two bushes and a fence made of concrete and wrought iron. A large crowd has gathered on the front lawn of the library. There's a lot of anticipation in the crowd as the specter of the mysterious building looms before them. That anticipation boils over into anger.

There are arguments as to whether or not the black case is actually in the building. There are arguments as to whether or not there is an actual mysterious black case. There are arguments as to whether or not the case, if real, actually contains anything of value. There are arguments based on previous discourse that has nothing to do with the black case. There are arguments based on challenges to go inside and attempt to acquire the black case.

Most of the crowd are not the type to respect any sort of authority, which is why Nico found a discreet place to think and observe. He is certain the case is inside. The question of course, is how to navigate the hostile crowd and subdue the gang inside the library. Not to mention the possibility of having to face the reclusive Librarians, if they exist, which Nico considers 50/50 odds. As assertive a chap as Nico is, he is mildly confounded by what to do next, and has not been able to contact the Marshal.

It does not take long before Nico decides he has to break inside the library. Truth is, he has always wanted to take a look around in there. The Librarians intrigue him. If they exist, he is certain they are up to no good. Of course, Nico is certain most everybody is up to no good. He is mostly correct.

He sneaks around to the rear of the building, skirting along the outer wall using the bushes for cover. Once he makes it to the back of the building, he discovers the crowd has grown from the other direction, gathering on the back lawn as well. He moves on to the other side yard of the library. It is there he discovers several dumpsters, and a band of Peaceniks. *Man*, he thinks. *These guys show up everywhere.*

A bunch of kind souls have followed the hubbub from the concert to the library and are now holding a candlelight vigil. They sit in a circle holding hands, swaying back and forth, humming powerful good vibrations towards the oppressed citizens locked inside the library. The other members of the crowd surrounding the building stay away from these nerds. Engaging in discourse with a Peacenik typically leads to a very bad headache.

These aren't your parent's pacifists though. This is the future baby, and everybody's bad. The reality is they are waiting for a non-violent opportunity to steal the case for themselves. If that requires using the bats, brass knuckles, nunchucks, and other assorted weapons they have stashed in their hand woven hemp rucksacks, well, then the crystals they wear around their necks have spoken. Nerds.

Anyhow, Nico exits the bushes and pulls a very large gun from a holster strapped across his back. He flashes the gun and his badge as he walks past. The Peaceniks want nothing to do with his very large weapon, or his aggressive energy, so they keep passing their bong and humming their song.

Nico hops atop a dumpster and, too fatigued for greater tact, busts out a window to the building. He taps out the glass with the barrel of his gun then reaches through to find the lock. After considerable twisting and wriggling he manages to unlock the rusty hinge holding the window shut. He forces the window open just wide enough and crawls through to his doom.

Before the Rapture occurred, the Local 213 Librarians Union had already gone into hiding. They burrowed into the depths of the newly renovated main building of the Las Vegas Public Library, safely tucked away from the reality of the rest of the world. The entire renovation of the building was a complete waste of time and money. People weren't reading or learning anyway. Thus, the Librarians hadn't bothered to lock the doors to keep people out. However, when Jesus arrived for the apocalypse, they went back up to the surface level and battened down the hatches.

They lived for a while in an academic utopia. At first it was complete intellectual detachment from any form of practical application. It was awe inspiring and absurd. Then people started to die, as they were doing nothing about food or water or plumbing. Luckily, there were a few industrious doers in the Local 213 who swooped in and got to work saving the day.

The Librarians turned the retired book catacombs of the building into an underground city. Everything they needed to know about tunneling, running electricity, self-sustaining in a cavernous environment, surviving a prolonged apocalypse, it could all be found in the library's non-fiction section. The only thing that slowed down their progress was the lack of motivation to put their books down.

During the construction of their underground home, there was a large political split. It really wasn't very dramatic. There was a member named Lucius Pettimore that said they needed to travel further underground to be safe. Some people didn't agree. They debated for a bit and then eventually Lucius took about half the group on reconnaissance down through an unexplored tunnel. They didn't know when the tunnel was constructed or by who. The Pettimore Expedition was never seen again. After the Pettimore

Expedition never returned, the Librarians that stayed behind grew more steadfast in their resolve to never leave the building.

Their current leader is a woman named Gwendolyn. Gwen is in her sixties and has a very serious, accusatory nose. They are presently a group of 45 people, and quite frankly, most of them are bat-shit insane from isolation. Isolation, coupled with inbreeding. Yeah, it's gross, but with few outsiders to mate with, eventually they're all kissing cousins.

When the Librarians see the Black Case Gang enter the building on their surveillance system, they debate in great length on how to react. There is a vote to murder and eat the trespassers. There is a vote to have the intruders join them for dinner instead. There is a vote to have pudding for dessert either way.

Someone feels like they should get to torture the intruders. Some feel like they should get to have sex with them. Some feel like it is now circumstantial that the intruders must remain in the building until death. Others want to know what is in the black case.

Those who want to know what is in the case win. After a successful vote to find out what is in the case, the Librarians elect a committee to read about spying and stealing. There is an espionage section in adult fiction that comes in very handy.

While the Case Discovery Committee learns about spying and stealing, another committee forms and begins reading the collected works of H. Roth Furman, a noted scholar on the subject of civil dissidence. These guys are opposed to paying any attention to the strangers at all. They prefer to pretend the strangers aren't really there.

Once inside the library, the BCG tries to find a good place to set camp. Sandy suggests finding a breakroom or kitchen. They find a kitchen but it does little good. The above ground portion of the building has been abandoned for years. There is no running water to the sink. The refrigerator is empty, save for mold and fossilized mouse poop.

There is an unplugged soda machine. Sammy uses the tire iron in his car to bust it open. The old drinks inside the machine will most likely make them sick, but at least it's something. Since the kitchen is a bust, Sammy suggests setting up a fire circle near the car. They are able to burn some books in a small metal trashcan for heat.

"What are we going to do?" Sandy asks. "We can't stay here long without food or water." They all sit staring at the fire can, listening to old, dried pages of books crisp and flame away.

"I'm not sure babe," Sammy replies. "Maybe we need to try and get some sleep. Then, when those jackals outside aren't paying attention, we blast out of here like hell on wheels. If we catch them off guard we can get a decent head start."

"We can't run from all these people forever Sammy. What are we going to do?" She repeats the question with a slower cadence, for emphasis.

"I don't know," he says. He shakes his head and then puts his face in his hands. After a bit, he looks back up. "Say, do you think it's true about the Librarians? Do you think they are real?"

"Of course they are real," Sandy says. "We are in a library right now. The people that ran them were called librarians."

"I know that, I mean the spooky stories," he says. "*The* Librarians."

"Of course," Sandy replies, incredulously.

"What? What do you mean of course? Why of course?"

"Why would someone make that dumb shit up?"

"Why does anyone make any dumb shit up?"

During Sammy and Sandy's debate Zorn sits and makes little noises of agreement when either party makes a solid point. Apparently he thinks every point made by Sandy or Sammy is solid.

"Oh shut up you," Sandy barks at Zorn.

He supports her point of view with a, "hmph".

"Look," Sandy says to Sammy. "I'm not saying they are freaking cannibals or zombies or anything ridiculous like that. I'm saying they were weird, and they disappeared. That is a fact. Look it up. You can probably look it up in here!"

"Well that wouldn't make any sense," Sammy says. "If all the librarians disappeared before anything was written about them disappearing, who would have put it in here?"

"Fuck off, you get my point. Librarians, whatever they are, are real."

"Well," Sammy says. "If that's the case, doesn't that mean they could still be here? Do you think they are still here?" There is no fear in his voice, but only because he is so exhausted.

"I don't know. This place looks pretty abandoned."

"Yeah, that's true," he agrees. "You know, we should probably try to get some sleep." He looks towards Zorn. "Hey, you think you can take first watch so I can sleep for a while?"

Zorn smiles and nods his head yes.

"Alright babe," Sammy says. "Let's get to it?"

"Get to what?"

"You promised, and you've been stingy lately."

"Oh Sammy, seriously," she is about to say, but she doesn't. Instead she takes a moment to reflect on the surprise adventure they've taken. She looks up at her man and suddenly he is a 10 foot tall lumberjack. He has on a green and black plaid shirt with the sleeves rolled up, bulging forearms, and a giant axe laid over his shoulder. He is holding his hand out to help her stand. She takes it, and then leads him deep into the heart of the romance novels. Unfortunately, by the time they put their love nest together and lay down, they are too old and tired to follow through on their intentions. They fall asleep with their arms around each other in the middle of their first kiss.

# 43

Rancid Pete is asleep. The Princess is curled up between his left arm and his torso, completely nested on him, up off the bed. Her head is very clear. Calm too. She is thinking.

Thinking is a big deal for the Princess. Not a big deal in her mind, mind you, but *for* her. Whether she knows it or not, which she doesn't.

Anyhow, presently, she is thinking about her mother. She is thinking about how if she had known her mother better, her life might be different. She thinks about her creepy father and how they have no relationship. She is okay with this, as she doesn't like the guy. It kind of sucks though, since he's her father.

She thinks about Dolly. Dolly has practically raised her, despite being the same age. Tiara loves her. It dawns on the Princess that she is going to have to do something about her body double situation. It is unlikely anyone is ever going to try to kill her, but if they do, she can't stand to lose Dolly. She's going to have to get a new body double and give Dolly a new title.

*I can't believe how good I feel*, she thinks. Then she looks up at Rancid Pete and feels a little sick. His face is so gruesome. It is time to go home. All the way home.

Yet, she isn't sure that means moving on from Rancid Pete. It is silly to try and deny how perfect she feels nestled in his arm, completely relaxed from a phenomenal romp. She rolls over a little and puts an arm as far around him as she can. Her hand barely makes it to the spot on his chest where a man's heart would beat. After a few minutes, she feels a very intense hammering thump from inside his chest. The intervals of his heart rate seem remarkably slow. She loses herself in the anticipation of the next thump. Waiting, guessing when it will come. She dozes back to sleep.

Tiara wakes back up and somehow, instinctively she knows only a few minutes have passed. Rancid Pete has not moved. She wonders if he has gone into some weird, deep monster sleep or something like that.

She knows she needs to get up and get going, but she doesn't want to. *This is too nice*, she admits. *If this is what it is going to be like, I am definitely going to fall in love with this monster.*

That thought sets in. *Holy crap, it's already started.* That is all she can take. Tiara crawls out of Rancid Pete's grasp and flutters about the room, gathering her things.

She tries to call Dolly on her fucking Smear. Still no answer. This worries her. Tiara finds her location transponder and sends out the signal. A retrieval team will arrive shortly.

Suddenly, Rancid Pete's giant hand squeezes her side, just above her hip. She isn't startled, although she is surprised. He moved without making a sound.

Rancid Pete turns her around and pulls her in. He leans in to kiss her and she lets him, but she does not kiss back. He does not recoil, but he doesn't hold the kiss long, and when he pulls away his facial expression shows disappointed curiosity. Tiara puts her hands on his chest.

"I'm worried about my maiden," she says.

"Why?" Rancid Pete's question holds as much sympathy as one might convey when working with a single syllable.

"She's disappeared," the Princess replies. "She hasn't answered me since she left the concert. She never ignores me, and this is the second time in two days."

"I'm sure she has a good reason." Pete's says, exhibiting genuine concern.

"There are no good reasons," the Princess says. "Not for this amount of time. A couple of hours sure, but not like this."

"Oh," he says. He doesn't know what to say next so he pulls Tiara in close to him. She resists at first, but quickly gives in to his embrace. She buries her face in his massive chest as he rubs her back. She is amazed yet again at how soft he is when she is snuggled against him.

FYI, it is actually part of Rancid Pete's physiology. He can literally soften his skin and muscle tissue, or harden it accordingly, dependent on the situation. You don't live a thousand years by proxy, simply because you're a monster. It isn't romantic fantasy that keeps him alive. It's biology. His body is built for a long haul. Regeneration and perpetual molecular modification slow his aging to the pace of a retired snail, and keep his body in peak physical condition at all times. He is a marvel.

Tiara pushes away. Pete loosens his grip.

"I've got to leave," Tiara says. "I have to go back to the hotel and figure out where she is."

"I can take you," Rancid Pete says.

"No, there will be an extraction team here in a few minutes," she replies.

"Really?" he says.

"Yeah. You know, the whole Princess thing," she says. I swear I almost heard a tinge of embarrassment in her voice, although I'm not sure humility exists in Tiara.

"That's impressive," Pete replies.

No sooner did the words come out of his mouth than they hear the whoop, whoop, whoop of helicopter propellers in the distance. The sound grows louder and louder. They feel the stomp of booted soldiers moving towards the tent. Pete and Tiara hold hands in silence, each lost in the other's gaze. There is a knock at the door.

"Come in," Tiara says.

Two soldiers enter in full "bustle" mode. I'm surprised they aren't repeating "hup, hup, hup" the entire time. They attach a harness to the Princess, then attach a cable to the harness. They have another "bustle" safety checking the harness' buckles and connection point with the cable. Once finished, they each give the other a proud thumbs up, then one of the soldiers pulls twice on the cable signaling everything is set.

Rancid Pete opens his mouth to speak but realizes he has no idea what to say. He's in unfamiliar territory. Before he can figure out the correct words, the Princess stands up on her tip toes and puckers her mouth. Pete leans over and gives her a kiss right as the helicopter pulls her away.

The Princess goes straight backwards through the door, letting go of Rancid Pete's hands at the last second. She is smiling as her feet drag against the ground. As soon as she makes it through the door the helicopter lifts off and she flies into the air.

The Princess looks down, watching Rancid Pete watch her fly away. She realizes as she dangles from the helicopter that she is a woman now. She isn't exactly certain why. It wasn't the sex. It is something else. There is no mistaking it though. She isn't the same today as she was yesterday. Yesterday she was a carefree, ignorant child. Suddenly, for the first time in her life, she feels burdened. Welcome to adulthood, shithead.

When Princess Tiara arrives back at the hotel, Dolly is still nowhere to be found. Tiara doesn't know what to do. She considers enlisting the aid of Señor Diego, but can't bear the thought of being around the dirty old pervert. She decides to call the front desk. Dolly said something about being able to call down to the front desk for things. The Princess pulls a member of her royal guard into the room.

"I need to call the front desk," she says.

"Yes ma'am," he replies.

"Well do it," she says.

"Oh, right." The guard walks over to the nearest intercom in the suite and hits the page button for the front desk.

A soft female voice responds. "Concierge, how may I help you?"

"Conci what?" the Princess asks.

"Concierge," the concierge replies.

"Are you the Front Desk?" the Princess asks.

"Yes."

"Front Desk, this is Princess Tiara Lioness."

"Hello Princess, how may I help you?"

"I don't suppose you have seen my lady in waiting? Has she left a note for me with you, or stopped by Front Desk recently?"

"No ma'am. Not that I'm aware of," the concierge says, "but I'm not certain what she looks like."

"You can't miss her," Princess Tiara says. "She looks almost exactly like me."

"Oh, well, in that case, I did see someone who looked like you pass through the lobby not long ago."

"What was she wearing?" Tiara asks.

"Almost nothing," the concierge replies.

"No, that was me," Tiara says.

"Oh," the concierge says. "Well you looked lovely."

Princess Tiara doesn't bother accepting the compliment. "Hmmm. Front Desk, if you lost someone, a person, what would you do?"

"I would probably call the police," she says. "Though they don't really seem all that helpful anymore. Maybe you could find a private investigator."

"I don't know any of those. I'm not from here. What about the police? Do you have a number for the police?"

"Of course," the concierge replies. "If I may ma'am, you do have several messages hear for you. Perhaps there is information about your maiden."

"Who are they from?" Tiara is surprised. She wasn't expecting any messages. Of course, that's because she never deals with anything. It is Dolly who would have sorted through the unsolicited messages from fans, salespeople and stalkers.

"Most of them look like fan stuff, but there are several from the Marshal's office."

"What's a Marshal's office?" the Princess asks.

"It's sort of like the police," the concierge says. "More important I think. Plus, the Marshal in Las Vegas is really hot."

"Hot like hot?"

"Yeah, his name is Dan Trate, and he is super sexy. Like, so hot. Everybody in town knows him. He is the most eligible bachelor in Las Vegas." You can hear the girl drifting off to daydream land, where she is the lucky lady who lands the coveted Marshal Dan.

"Okay. That kind of hot. That's what I thought," Tiara replies. "Interesting. Did the Marshal's office leave a number for me to call? Do you know where their office is?"

"Oh, yes ma'am. I have the address right here," the concierge replies.

"Good. You," Tiara points at a security guard. "Get a pen or something and write this down. I'm going to find my Dolly."

Dolly is of course the house guest of the Karowack Kids. Dolly and Billy spoke for hours, into the early morning, after their dinner by the fire. She gets a kick out of the vampire, even though he confiscated her fucking Smear and consistently reminds her that until he gets what he wants and despite the fact he enjoys her presence, she is his prisoner and her life is in peril. Despite this, it doesn't bother her to incorporate his desire to embarrass Alacrán into her plans. This should actually help facilitate her escape with Purvis.

She is now fast asleep with a smile on her face, between luxurious sheets, on a large bed in the largest of Billy's many guest rooms. Dolly needs the rest badly. She is deep down asleep, where your body doesn't move at all from the position you were in when you went under, and you don't remember your dreams.

Before dozing off, she laid awake considering her situation. She wondered if she was really going to go through with it. Could she leave the Princess? The girl is a loathsome little jerk but Dolly still loves her. It is a perverse love, Stockholm syndrome or something, but love none the less. Plus, what are the odds this love at first sight phenomenon with Purvis is actually sustainable? Between you and me, the odds are 634,187 to 1. Not so bad as you might imagine.

Either way, is she fooling herself to think they can actually have a life together? A life based simply on animal attraction? She doesn't know. All Dolly knows is she wants to give it a shot. It was that idea that put the smile on her face when she wandered off down sleepy street.

# 44

Dan wakes again and this time he is wide awake. No need for coffee. He sits on the edge of the bed, wondering if his conversation with Jesus was real or a dream. He decides it doesn't matter. Either way, Dan knows his life is not the same as before. That is obvious.

He takes a shower and readies himself. Once dressed, he notices there are several messages on his Smear. Nico called a couple of times. There is also an odd, sexy, mysterious whispering message from some female about her Dolly missing, and needing help to find her. It goes something like, "Hello? Are you there? I don't know what to do. My Dolly is missing. I think someone may have taken her. Please help me find my Dolly. Please call me. You're my only hope."

Dan calls the number and reaches a desk clerk at La Ciudad de Oro. *That makes sense*, he thinks. He asks to be put through to Princess Tiara's room. No answer.

Dan heads for the office, calling Nico while he drives. Nico answers after the first ring.

"What's up Nico?" Dan asks.

"Laying low," Nico replies, quietly.

"Where are you?"

"Public library. I think I found the black case."

"You safe?" Dan asks.

"For the time being," Nico replies.

"Good. Keep your head down."

"Will do," Nico says. "What's the next move?"

"Stay put," Dan says. "Maintain surveillance. I'm on my way to the office. I have this funny feeling."

"Funny 'ha ha'?" Nico asks.

"No," Dan says dryly.

"Boss, I don't want to overstep my bounds, but where've you been?"

"In bed. Sorry about that."

"In bed?"

"Yeah. It was sort of against my will though. Don't hold it against me."

"I'll do my best," Nico says.

"Keep your head low and maintain position. I'm swinging by the office and will check back in with you as soon as I know my next move."

"I can do that. I gotta tell you though Boss. I'm getting a little hungry, and a little cranky."

"Duly noted," Dan replies. "I won't take long."

"Copy that."

The kidnappings are going well. Alacrán's spirits have improved considerably. However, the Princess has proven difficult to find. Of course, we know that's because she was with Rancid Pete in their love nest.

To Alacrán's delight, Princess Tiara shows back up at the hotel. When Alacrán is notified she returned to her suite, the news puts him in such a good mood he decides to join the kidnapping fun.

"Purvis," Alacrán says.

"Yes my liege?"

"Get my cape, my cane and hat," he says, twirling his right pointer finger. "We are going downstairs to kidnap the Princess. Don't let anyone else get her first, or I will cut off their heads."

"Yes sir," Purvis says with enthusiasm. "It is good to see your spirits replenished my liege."

Unfortunately, by the time Alacrán finishes primping and is ready to go do some bad, the Princess is already on the move again. "Have someone follow her," Alacrán tells Purvis. "We will head upstairs and take my whirlybird."

"Yes sir."

Dan uses the back entrance to headquarters. Once inside he discovers there is no Lilly. There is no anyone. His suspicion that something is amiss is confirmed. He notices the door to his office is cracked. He leans against the wall next to the door and gently pushes it open a little further.

Dan peers in through the crack, scanning the side of the room he can see from his current angle. Nothing. He kicks the door the rest of the way open, stepping into the room. He lowers his gun on a woman whose back is turned. His big entrance startles her, but she does not turn around. Dan sees a waft of cigarette smoke lingering in the air near her.

When the Princess turns around, she is struck by Dan's presence. He is everything the Front Desk described. Dan is equally as struck by Princess Tiara. The air between them grows thin, insisting they move through it until they are touching each other.

Dan sticks the gun in the beltline of his pants. "Madame," he says. "Don't you think it's a little dangerous to be sneaking around in the office of a man with a very big gun?" *Really Dan?* he thinks. *Did you really say that?*

"I bet you don't even know how to use that little old thing," Princess Tiara says. *Holy shit that was lame,* she thinks. *What the hell was that? And since when am I self-conscious?*

"How can I help you Princess?" As Dan speaks, he heads behind his desk to move papers around and pretend like he is doing something that has a purpose.

"I left you a message," she replies. "My Dolly is missing."

"Ah. That was you." Dan sits down, tossing his feet up on his desk. "No offense Princess, but I have more important things to do than help you find a doll."

"Marshal you don't understand," she says. She crosses behind him, resting her hand on his right shoulder. She pulls the hand away quickly, walking a few more steps. Princess Tiara turns and leans back onto the desk. She pushes up and slides herself back, coming to a seat on top of the desk next to Dan. She crosses her right leg over her left, towards the Marshal, bouncing it in his direction ever so slightly. "She's not a doll. My Dolly is my lady in waiting. She's my advisor and confidant. I simply can't live without her." The Princess puts her hand over the Marshal's and squeezes.

The Marshal pulls his hand away smoothly and turns his chair away from the Princess. As it rotates back around towards her, he rises from it. He comes to a rest standing directly in front of the Princess. He leans in and puts his hands on his desk, on either side of her, pinning her to her seat under his presence. Their faces are dangerously close.

"Do you realize we have been trying to contact you for several days?" Dan asks. "There was a double murder at the airport within minutes of your arrival here." *Good God she smells good*, he thinks.

"Of course not," Tiara replies. *His breath is sexy? How does that happen? How does he do that?* "I don't deal with things like that Marshal. Dolly handles such matters." The words barely come out of her mouth. Dan has stolen her breath.

Dan stands up and moves away before he is fully intoxicated by the Princess. "Well Princess," he says, "it looks like you are going to have to start dealing with things like that." He is taking very slow, short steps, trying to find a justification to walk somewhere. Anywhere that is a reasonable distance from the extremely desirable woman he wants nothing to do with. "If your lady is indeed missing, my guess is it is somehow involved with those murders."

Dan stops and turns back to face her. When he does, he is slightly startled to see Tiara directly behind him. She looks at him with unflinching damsel in distress allure. He takes her by the shoulders with both hands and shakes her as he speaks.

"Now listen," he says. "Everything is going to be fine, but I need you to tell me everything you could possibly know about this situation."

"Nothing," she says. Then she wrenches herself free from his grasp.

"Damn it," Dan says with unusual frustration.

"Why did you do that?" Tiara asks.

"I don't know," he says, and it is the truth. He has no idea. They have each cast ridiculous spells on the other. *What just happened? What's happening?* Dan asks himself. *I need to get out of here.* Then he offers the Princess a second answer. "You needed to get ahold of yourself."

"I wasn't hysterical," she says, more confused than defensive. *Was I?*

"Well it was coming," he replies.

The Princess is confused by his response, but aroused by his confidence. She wants the Marshal to throw her up on his desk and do bad things. Images of buttons popping and panties dropping flood her mind.

Dan is staring at her intently. He realizes something he hadn't noticed earlier. It's the Princess' aura. It is almost as if he can see the Princess' darkness, her unwholesomeness. He begins to feel it in the room. She darkens the room! It's like she is always standing in a shadow. *A very sexy shadow*, he thinks. *Sexy but bad. She is a bad person. Not at all like Lilly. Lilly! Where is she?* Dan is about to open his mouth and ask the Princess if there was another woman in the office when the Princess arrived, but he can't speak. There is an extra tongue in his mouth that does not belong to him. Dan realizes he and Tiara are kissing. *What is going on here?*

Tiara moved forward with the panties dropping plan somewhat against her own will. She was thinking about Rancid Pete, and about Dolly, and next thing she knows she is making out with the Marshal.

They both push away when they realize what they are doing. Then the Princess begins to cry. For the first time in her life, Princess Tiara feels guilt. She doesn't know what the sensation is, and she doesn't know how to react, but she feels horrible. Although it's a baby step towards becoming a decent person, it is a big moment for her.

The Princess' tears soften Dan. *Maybe she isn't a monster,* he thinks. "Look," he says. "Don't worry. I'm sure I can find your lady." He puts a hand on her shoulder. "When was the last time you saw her?"

"Last night, at the concert."

"Can you be more specific?"

"Well," Tiara says, "it was towards the end of the concert and I was getting bored."

"You were bored?" Dan says, surprised. "Are you kidding me?"

"What? I wasn't feeling it," she says defensively.

"Okay. Okay. Odd but not important. I'm sorry, go on."

"We had a plan to split up and ditch these lame guys that were with us, then we were going to meet up backstage," she says. "We were supposed to go meet the bands but she never showed up."

"Who left first?" he asks.

"It was sort of the same time, but I guess she did."

"What happened after you split up?"

"I went backstage with some of my girls," she replies. "When we got back there we were held up for a while out in a hallway. There were still people around partying, but the security guard said the band was cleaning up for the after-party. I thought it was bullshit, and it was. They were totally in their partying."

Hearing her own words raises a question. Did Pete big-time her on purpose, to make her more attracted to him? The thought that Rancid Pete may have played her creeps into her mind and it hurts. Princess Tiara is not happy with these new feelings, or this new-found ability to ponder.

"How long were you out there?" Dan asks, bringing the Princess' attention back to their conversation.

"I don't know," she says. "Not too long. Ten, fifteen minutes. Maybe half an hour tops."

"Interesting. What happened once you got in to see the band?"

"What goes on at any after party," she replies. "We partied, we eventually went home. I never saw her. She has been gone all night and all day up until this point. This never happens, and it has happened twice since we got to Las Vegas. I know something is wrong." Princess Tiara isn't sure why she lies to the Marshal about spending the night in the rooftop love nest with Rancid Pete. It isn't modesty. That much is certain.

"Okay," Dan says. "Do you think it's possible that she could have been backstage, either before you, or perhaps at the same time without you seeing her?"

"Possible, but not likely."

"Is there anyone in this town that you think would want to hurt Dolly?"

"Not that I would know of," the Princess says. "If someone did anything to her, it would probably be to get at me. I can't imagine she knows anyone in Las Vegas outside of our entourage."

"Interesting," Dan says. "Princess, I need you to go back to your hotel and stay there. I assume you travel with body guards?"

"Of course. I have a dozen outside."

"Good. Go back to your hotel," he says again. "I will send a man over shortly to stay with you."

"Why?"

"If what you say is true, and someone took your lady to get to you, then you could still be in danger."

"But I have plenty of guards."

"Good," he replies. "But I want one of my men there. I need to go ask a few questions about your lady, and I need someone I trust with eyes on you."

"Oh," Tiara says. "Okay, whatever. Who are you going to see?"

"I'm going to start with the bands," he says. "I want to see if any of them saw her last night. And I need to get going. If the bands are leaving today we may never get the chance to question them. There's that drummer, the monster. He's been known to eat fans."

"I've heard that." Again the Princess doesn't mention her night with Rancid Pete. She briefly wonders why. *What difference does it make? I know it wasn't Pete. But what if it was? What if somehow Dolly got backstage before me and he ate her?*

Dan snaps the Princess back to reality once more. He takes her by the arm and leads her towards the door. "Don't worry Princess," he says. "I'll find your girl. I'm very good at what I do."

"I believe you," she says. "Please hurry. I don't think I want to be in this city anymore."

"Do you have a picture of her you can give me? If not, I'm going to need a pretty thorough description of her."

"No you won't," Princess Tiara replies.

Dan can see fresh water filling up in her eyes. "Oh. Okay. Why not? What does she look like?"

"Me," she replies. "Exactly like me."

Dan hears the weariness in her voice and gives her arm an affirming squeeze. She stares into his eyes. They both feel another brief surge of desire, their chemistry screaming at them anew. Tiara bites her lip to break the loin induced spell. She turns and walks away, out through Dan's office door and halfway across the reception area.

"Princess," Dan says.

"Yes Marshal," she replies. She stops and looks over her shoulder, keeping her back to him.

"Was there anyone here at all, in the offices, when you got here?"

"No," she says, and turns back to face him from across the room. "I thought it seemed sort of strange."

"It is," he replies. "You had better get going." He crosses the room to her and escorts her the rest of the way to the main door. "Stay in your hotel room Princess. I will contact you as soon as I know something."

"Please hurry Marshal. I want to go home. I've decided I hate Las Vegas."

# 45

Dan is relieved when the Princess is gone. The affect Tiara had on him, in spite of his emotions for Lilly, is unsettling. Princess Tiara is a detestable creature. Yet still desirable. These thoughts make the hair stand up on the back of his neck.

Dan knows something is amiss if none of his staff are present. Intuition tells him to get out as well. If something has happened to his staff, it is possible there are traps waiting for Dan within the building. It looks like Nico's maze of secret tunnels and escape routes will be useful after all.

Dan goes into a series of narrow passageways between the walls of the building. So narrow Dan can barely pass through them without having to walk sideways. He takes several turns, following his internal compass, until he finds a completely different set of underground tunnels.

These tunnels network into the sewer systems and spider-web out into the city. They are marked for directions, Dan assumes by Nico. He takes his first opportunity to resurface, exiting the tunnels through a manhole four blocks away from the office. There is a police cruiser parked next to the curb of the street. Dan uses his key-code on the door and the ignition.

*I wonder how many of these Nico has staged*, he thinks.

He tries to call Nico, but his deputy doesn't answer. Dan leaves him a message and heads to the Octopus' Garden. He has a sinking suspicion Princess Tiara didn't tell him everything about the night of the concert. He noticed her physical reaction when he mentioned the monster. Perhaps Rancid Pete would offer more information than the Princess.

Nico is laying on the floor of the library with his wrists tied and a burlap sack over his head, secured by a rope around his neck. He was taken shortly after his conversation with the Marshal. He was hunkered down behind a pile of books, a good ways away from the Black Case Gang, when everything went dark.

He can hear whomever captured him discussing their next move. They agreed they were not going to kill Nico, as he is a Deputy Marshal. Plus, they aren't killers. If they had known he was a lawman, they wouldn't have bushwhacked him and tied him up in the first place. They put all of his weapons back on his body where they found them. They are certain the best thing to do is to apologize as soon as he wakes back up. However, they can't decide what to do about the Black Case Gang. Should they attack the intruders and take the case, or simply wait for an opportunity to steal the case without direct physical confrontation? That is the current debate.

Meanwhile, Nico is working to free himself. The Librarians didn't do a very good job of securing his hands, despite their research on knot tying. His wrists are pretty well bound together, but there is nothing to keep him from reaching one of his many knives. It will take him a while to cut through the ropes though, having to awkwardly saw at them with his wrists tied together. Luckily, we have plenty of our other performers to check in with.

When Tiara exits the old government building that houses the Marshal's office, her guards immediately realize something is wrong. The rest of the security force, previously waiting outside, is missing. The guards each draw weapons and grab the Princess by her arms. They push her into a run down the stairs leading from the front of the building to the street where their cars are parked. Little do they know, the cars are stuffed full with the dead bodies of the rest of their security unit.

About halfway to the vehicles, both guards get shot in the head. Princess Tiara stops in her tracks and screams. She looks at the two dead guards, seeing their blood and brains splattered about, then looks down to realize some of it is splattered on her.

"Ewwwwwwwwwwwwwww," she says.

She is flicking pieces of brain and skull off of her when she again hears the familiar whoop, whoop, whoop of a helicopter. She looks up expecting to see her extraction team. *Wait, I didn't call for the distraction team,* she thinks. *Did I say distraction team? Whatever. I didn't call them. Maybe the guards did. Oh who cares as long as they get me out of here? Wait. That's not my helicopter.*

Alacrán and Purvis followed Princess Tiara to the Marshal's office, but did not arrive in time to snatch her before she went inside. Alacrán found it slightly ironic this is where she led them, considering his men had raided the Marshal's offices a few hours earlier. The Marshal's buxom receptionist and 1950's style office girl, Lilly Whet, is now among Alacrán's list of captives.

*Now there is a flower that needs to have its petals plucked*, he thinks.

"There she is," Purvis says, interrupting Alacrán's thoughts.

"Ooh, goody," Alacrán replies.

They hover above the Princess. She doesn't try to run. Alacrán watches a henchman exit the helicopter. He is connected to a hoist and descends very rapidly on the Princess, dropping a loop around her as he lands. He secures the harness under her armpits and they are quickly pulled back up to the helicopter.

Once inside, the Princess' wrists are tied with some of Alacrán's finest rope. It is incredibly soft.

"That rope is from Persia," Alacrán says. "It is the softest in the world, while at the same time incredibly strong." As you know, Alacrán is a bondage guy. His ropes are an immense source of pride for him.

"That's great," Tiara says sarcastically. "What do you think you are doing? My father will not stand for this. He will send an army here after you."

"I don't think so. From what I understand about your father, I could probably offer him a handsome amount of money for you and he would accept. Even if that isn't true, by the next time you speak to him, you will be madly in love with me." Alacrán smiles a really creepy smile right here. He licks his lips a little bit, barely poking his tongue out of his mouth at her. Skeezy.

"Gross," Tiara says. "You do realize it is impossible for me to fall in love with you. Your money means nothing. I'm already rich. You, are old and creepy and ugly. There is no way I will ever, ever want to be with you."

"I have a love potion that you are going to drink. It will make you love me for the rest of your life, as long as I am the first person you see once you have taken it." He is giggling like a school girl as the last few words come out.

"Fuck balls," Princess Tiara says. Then she leans back, closes her eyes, and tries not to think about it. She tries not to think about anything at all, but that doesn't work. So, she looks at Alacrán and says, "I don't suppose you've got any Stink?"

# 46

Jack22 is having his first brush with the concept of rock bottom. By the way, if you haven't read the varying definitions of the word "fate" lately, you should go check them out. It's an oddly refreshing exercise. It reminds me that I believe in fate, although I'm not sure in which of its meanings I find comfort. I might have said inevitable death, when I was alive, but I have learned quite a bit since then.

Anyhow, Jack22's fifteen minutes of fame in the casino is coming to an end. It isn't for lack of effort. The problem is, Jack22's power is waning. The robot can't pull itself away from the gambling and revelry to recharge. He is hooked.

Those that remain by Jack22's side are vultures, hoping to somehow capitalize on his downward spiral. The scene has taken on a noir quality of smoke filled rooms and shady characters, black and white film style. A cigarette actually dangles from Jack22's melancholy, robot lips.

He has taken to "I could have been somebody" style rants that critique his opulence with false humility, while at the same time exploring the unused potential he's certain is inside him. Here's a taste: "Sure I've made a few bucks here or there. I've done alright, but I'll be damned if I couldn't have been a famous mountain climber or a saint or something like that. What have those guys got that I haven't got? Nothin'. That's what."

Meanwhile, somehow or another, he continues to win at the tables. But, as fun loving Monty Texas slowly turns into bitter and tired Monty Texas, winning doesn't keep the crowds around. Eventually people get tired of his attitude.

Finally, Jack22 finds himself at a Blackjack table all alone. All alone except for the dealer of course. Jack22 is desperately low on functional power. Other patrons approach the table and Jack22 attempts his charismatic introduction, but all that comes out is, "Monty....or Tex....Jack Mormon...rob the casino...," or some other incoherent prattle that immediately turns the other patron around and sends them on their way.

He has come full circle. Or maybe he has come half the circle, with the other half still to go. Would full circle require that he winds up back on the other side of the blackjack table dealing the cards again? Had he the energy left in his battery, he might have given considerable thought to the matter. Either way, here he is, on the opposite side of the blackjack table, having turned into one of the creatures that had recently made him feel so sad.

You know what, I'm gonna call it half circle.

Anyway, it was about this time that the dealer robot says, "Sir, please take a break from the gaming table."

"Why?" Jack22 asks. "Because I am kicking your ass?"

"No," the dealer robot says. "It has taken you at least 30 seconds per word to say each of those words. You appear to be physically exhausted or extremely inebriated."

"You deal those damn cards pardner," Jack22 says slowly, almost inaudibly.

"I cannot do that sir," the dealer replies. "The casino *Rules of Operation*, under Section B, Sub-section 15, Article A5, state that the casino robot dealers are programmed for player evaluation. On authority of the casino security and its automation staff, dealer robots are required to monitor whom is allowed to participate in the gaming at the robot dealer's assigned station. I am no longer dealing to you. It is for your own safety. Please exit the table and get some rest."

It takes ten minutes for Jack22 to respond, as the dealer robot stands in silence staring at him. "I will not," Jack22 finally says. "You deal those galdarned cards." There isn't any oomph to his command.

"Negative," the dealer robot replies. "Please leave the table immediately or Security will be requested."

"Well you go ahead and request Security you shiny metal bastard. Montana Texas don't give a shit about security. I own this bitch." That is the last bit he has in him. He slouches a little to the side and shuts down.

It's a funny thing about hitting rock bottom. Such an abstract concept. How do you know you are there? Has anyone ever been foolish enough to think to themselves, "Well surely this is as bad as it can possibly get?"

Most likely they have, out of pure hope, but I still think it is a term with no real meaning other than the actual, physical, "this is the bottom of a structure or area that is literally made of rocks", usage. That's why the phrase "hitting rock bottom" will be in my next release: *The Big Book of Empty Axioms: You Can Sleep When You're Dead 'Cause It Is What It Is.*

Unlike people, Jack22 has an auxiliary emergency power supply that kicks in after two minutes of post power failure internal diagnostics. His servers determine the main system issue is his dead battery and they kick the emergency power supply into high gear, stirring Jack22 back to life. For a limited amount of time of course. As he quickly reviews the events preceding his shut down, Jack22's first thought is, *I've hit rock bottom.*

Then he becomes defiant, which is often the case once a person metaphorically hits rock bottom. He says, "I will not give in," in his regular voice, dropping his Monty Texas rancher accent, pounding his fists down on the table.

"I do not understand your request." the dealer robot says, as confused as a robot can possibly be.

"I will not give in," Jack22 repeats. Although power is temporarily restored, it is reserved for essential operating systems. Jack22 is still in a very illogical, fuzzy state of mind.

A squadron of security robots led by a human Squad Leader arrives, surrounding Jack22.

"Sir, please come with us," the Squad Leader says.

"Of course officer," Jack22 says. "I don't want any trouble." But he does want trouble. He reaches over to a security robot and removes an electric baton from its belt. Jack22 puts the baton up to his own neck then hits the power button.

A jolt of electricity surges through Jack22's body, shaking him in his chair. Although wildly dangerous to his internal wiring and his exterior shininess, Jack22 feels a surge of power. "I'm gonna get you, you som'bitch," he says to the dealer robot, returning to his Monty Texas persona.

He holds the baton out to his side and drops it like a hot microphone. He stands up quickly to attempt a leap up onto and over the gaming table, in an effort to attack the dealer robot. Jack22 was made to be tall, look regal and deal cards. These robots were not designed to fight in cage matches or work on car engines. They don't have swivel arm battle grip.

The security robots on the other hand, were made for violence. They grab Jack22 from both sides, attempting to pull him back from the table. The brief power surge has momentarily increased the torque in Jack22's gears and joint motors, similar to an adrenaline dump in a human.

Jack22 tries several more times to get a leg up on the table while the security officers pull at him, but his body design makes it impossible. He switches his attention to the security team. He shoves several of the security robots to the ground, then attempts to move around to the other side of the table. He is going to get that dealer robot.

Security robots continue wrestling with him. It's a pretty funny scene for the other people and assorted creatures that have stopped their gaming and turned their attention to the melee. Jack22 is swinging around at the waist with stiff arms held out, swatting at whomever comes within reach.

The security robots, despite being physically designed for combat purposes, look like they've never been in a fight in their lives. I mean, who programmed these guys for combat, a Series 12 Dishwasherbot?

Jack22's sudden burst of super-robot strength does not last long. As he is about to wrap his hands around the neck of the dealer robot, Jack22's body stiffens back up. He freezes with his arms straight out in front of him, defenseless once again.

The security team administers a severe beating. The first blow comes from the Squad Leader, a baton to the back of Jack22's left knee. His leg collapses and he topples.

"Ow," Jack22 says.

Once he hits the floor, the security bots continue to thump him with clubs and stomp him with their robot boots. Eventually, they come to a rest. They are programmed to administer excessive force in two minute intervals.

"Get him out of here," the Squad Leader says, huffing and puffing to catch his breath. Two of the security robots roll Jack22 over and take him under the arms. They drag him through the gambling area towards a door marked "Security".

As they drag him away, with the last bit of energy left in his body, Jack22 continually repeats the phrase, "You'll never take me alive," despite the insistence of the security robots that they were indeed doing exactly that.

Alacrán is still in his helicopter, ogling Princess Tiara with his skeevy stalker eyes, when a call comes in from the casino security. Purvis answers.

"My liege," Purvis says. "It's a security captain."

"Yes?" Alacrán says, keeping his eyes on Princess Tiara.

Tiara lets out a whopping burp she has been working on for a while. Unfortunately, if she thought this might somehow irritate or disgust our number one villain, she was incorrect. Instead, Alacrán licks his lips with great pleasure.

"He says they have taken a patron into custody who has won a sizeable amount of money," Purvis says.

"Was the person cheating?" Alacrán asks. "Put him with the rest of the rabble in the cages."

"Well, that's the thing sir," Purvis says. "He wasn't cheating. However he apparently tried to fight a dealer robot, and then fought with security before being subdued."

"That still doesn't do much for me. Not all that titillating my boy."

"There's something else sir," Purvis continues. "According to other patrons, this gentleman has been very vocal about his intentions to rob the casino."

"Indeed," Alacrán says. "Now that strikes my curiosity. Ug. Of all the days. Have security take this charlatan to my office and wait for us there. I will deal with him myself."

# 47

Rancid Pete is in his suite channel surfing the TV, attempting to think as little as possible. He is not successful. He can't get Princess Tiara off his mind. It's foreign to him to think about someone else this much. It is driving him nuts. He just wants to chill and watch some damn television. Of course he wouldn't mind if she was there with him. Damn it.

There is a knock at the door. Pete is so lost in his own thought the knocking doesn't register immediately. When it finally does, the knocking has steadily grown more aggressive.

"For fuck's sake I'm coming," Rancid Pete says loudly. As he makes his way to the door Rancid Pete continues to speak. "You know, what if I didn't feel like answering the door? You just gonna keep pounding? There are times when a monster might like to be alone, and doesn't feel like explaining himself, and whoever is thinking about bothering him ought to have the good sense to make this realization on their own and get the hell on before the monster gets annoyed and decides to eat them." Rancid Pete opens the door and sees a tall man he doesn't recognize standing in the hallway.

"An extremely accurate sentiment," Dan replies. "I completely agree. This however, is not one of those times."

*Who the fuck is this guy?* Rancid Pete thinks. *Oh well. Dude's got balls. I'll give him that.*

"I'm Dan Trate, Marshal." Dan sticks his hand out for a shake. Rancid Pete responds in kind. Pete appreciates the Marshal's grip. Better than average for a human.

"Rancid Pete," Pete says. Bothering to introduce himself is a show of respect for the Marshal. Pete's initial instincts for this fellow are positive. "What do you want?"

"I need to ask you a few questions," Dan replies. "Do you mind if I enter?"

Rancid Pete stands still, studying the Marshal. He has not let go of the Marshal's hand yet. They remain silent, hands clasped, measuring each other. Honestly, Rancid Pete is impressed the Marshal has the nerve to be sizing him up.

"Nope. Come on in Marshal," Pete finally says. "I was sittin' around watching TV as it was."

"Anything good?" Dan asks.

"Well hell no. There ain't nothin' worth a damn on American TV nowadays. Not since they bombed Hollywood." Rancid Pete makes his way back over to the couch and comfortably plops back down.

To Rancid Pete's pleasant surprise, Dan has made with all the small talk he is going to make. "Rancid," Dan says, "I'm sorry. Should I call you Rancid or Pete or..."

"Pete will do," Pete says.

"Good," Dan says. "Pete it is. Though once we get to be pals I think I'm going to call you RP." Dan moves to a chair to the left of the couch Rancid Pete is on and takes a seat. "So, Pete, I am here because a missing person report has been filed with my office. The person who filed the report included in her statement that the person whom is missing was in attendance at your concert last night. On a side note, I was there as well and you put on a heck of a show. Fantastic."

"Thank you," Rancid Pete replies.

"You are welcome. Thank you, and your band mates." Dan is being sincere but not exuberant. "Back to point, the missing person had procured backstage passes for the show. That is where you might come in."

"How's that?" Pete says.

"Well, without passing any judgment, mind you, it is commonly known that you, on occasion, eat your fans." Dan does a very good job of hiding how morally reprehensible he finds Rancid Pete's behavior. He doesn't want the monster getting defensive. "I figured it might be a good idea to see if you recognize her. I'm not here to stir anything up with you Pete. Your rights as a monster have been upheld in a court of law."

"So basically if you get lucky and old Rancid Pete has eaten this little bitch, your work is done, case closed, and you get to go home?" Pete says. He is testing the Marshal.

"Pete, I'm not that kind of guy," Dan states with a square jaw. "I came here because it was an obvious idea and I have very little to work with. I certainly hope you didn't eat the young lady. I hope you didn't eat any poor hapless misguided youngsters last night. To be frank, I don't appreciate the implication."

"My apologies Marshal." Rancid Pete is pleased by this dude. He likes him. Rancid Pete is not the apologetic sort. "I actually didn't think you were that type of guy. You have to understand the amount of accusation and bigotry I deal with."

"Oh c'mon man," Dan replies, incredulous. "You eat people."

"I know," Pete says. "That was a joke. Look at you indignant as a motherfucker. I like you cop. Of course you got every right to think I may have eaten the 'young lady'. I definitely ate some bitches last night."

"Alright, I've got to pull this conversation over for a minute," Dan says. "I don't understand it. I've got to know why you eat all of those women. There has to be something to it besides being a monster."

"Nope. I hate to burst your bubble," Rancid Pete replies, "but it's the monster thing."

"C'mon. I'm not buying it. There's got to be something else to it," says Dan. "Don't you claim to have eaten your own mother?"

"If you were a monster what would you eat?" Pete says defensively. "Old people? Children? *Dudes*…? What would you do with all the dicks? And yes, I ate my mother. Are you happy? It was a rite of passage."

"Alright, alright. All I'm saying is, maybe that has something to do with all the girls, but I'm not a licensed therapist. I'm a cop." Dan holds his hands up in defense with a smile on his face as he speaks.

Rancid Pete is a hair from losing his patience, but he decides to continue the banter instead. He's curious about the Marshal.

"It's because I love too much," Pete says matter of fact, with a sigh for effect.

"What?" Dan replies, caught slightly off guard.

"You wanted the truth, that's the truth," Pete says.

Dan gives Rancid Pete a speculative smile.

"I'm serious. I have attachment issues," Pete continues. "Every time I slip Little Big Pete inside a chick I catch feelings."

"Wow," Dan says. "That's somewhat surprising."

"I know bro. It's hard to believe but I can't guard my heart." Rancid Pete really begins to buy into his own bullshit here for a second I think. "These girls draw me in so quick, and I'm crushing on them and then I'm thinking about how, I could never keep up with all these women if I let them all live. 'How could I possibly handle being in love with that many broads?' I'm thinking. Then the next thing I know I'm chewing on a shin bone with tears rolling down my face."

"Wow." Dan's voice is deadpan.

"I know right?"

"You have got to be kidding. You are known to have orgies with up to twenty women at a time."

"Actually twenty-six was my record," Rancid Pete says. It is the perfect mix of somber and wistful.

"And you mean for me to believe you fall in love with all of them?" Obviously Dan is acutely aware of the high probability that

Rancid Pete is messing with him. Still, with everything that has happened lately, he would not be completely surprised if the monster is telling the truth. Mostly surprised, but not completely.

"Each and every one," Pete says convincingly. He is deadpan for a second or two before he smiles broadly at the look on Dan's face. "Dude! You're wondering if it's possible aren't you?"

Dan shrugs his shoulders and sort of holds his hands out as if to say maybe, while at the same time shifting about in his chair in a manner that makes it obvious he totally knows the monster is bluffing. It is a well played routine. Rancid Pete laughs heartily.

"No. You totally were," Pete continues. "You're a funny dude. You knew I was full of shit but you still were like, maybe this monster actually has a heart. That's charming. You're actually a good person aren't you?" Pete chuckles. "I'm a fucking monster man. I like screwing and eating chicks. It's what I do."

"I knew it," Dan says. He clinches his fist in a humorous manner, pulling another laugh from Rancid Pete.

"You knew jack," Rancid Pete says with a smile. "Alright. If we are going to be pals then fine, I'll tell you a secret. The truth is, I let the interesting ones live. No bullshit. I'm either not hungry, or there is something about the broad I actually find intriguing, so I let her live. But there ain't too many I find intriguing, and I'm always hungry."

"I don't think I can be pals with you Pete," Dan says dryly. This actually catches Rancid Pete off guard. "Besides being a monster, you are actually a monster."

"What are you talking about?" Pete says. "You're the same as me. Look here." Pete holds up a computer tablet he has sitting on the couch. It was previously concealed from the Marshal's view by Pete's large body. "I ran a search for you on the internet when I sat down. Look at all these bitches. No articles about cop shit. Big arrests. Drug busts. Nothing. Nothing but pictures of you and hot ass women all over Vegas. You've nailed this entire town."

"Really? Let me see that." Dan takes the tablet from Rancid Pete and swipes through several pictures. "Hmph. I didn't realize."

"You didn't realize?" Pete asks with mild disbelief.

"No, I never really thought about it," Dan says.

"Well what are you thinking about?" Pete asks, genuinely interested at this point.

"I don't know. Work." Dan says. "At least up until lately."

Rancid Pete isn't sure what that last bit means, and he gives it a moment to see if Dan is going to continue speaking, but the Marshal does not.

"Well," Pete says. "Whatever. You're just like me. The only difference between you and me is you chew your women up and spit them out. I swallow mine."

"I do not spit them out," Dan says with a smile. He holds up the computer tablet. "According to this I just keep chewing them." Both monster and man laugh boisterously at their prowess with women.

"We're men who get all the ladies we want."

"Yes we are."

"And it's a lot of them."

"Yes it is!"

"Hahaha, and they love us for it."

"They do, they really do. It makes no sense."

"None whatsoever."

"I suddenly feel guilty for sleeping with all of these ladies and making light of it, but according to this, for some reason everyone loves me for it, so I immediately don't feel guilty anymore!"

"Who cares? I eat them and they still love me! Beat that!"

"I can't!" Still laughing.

"I know!" One last big laugh, a slap on the knee, sighs and a few titters.

"Say," Dan says, after the laughter winds down. "How did you access the global internet from here?"

"I get the internet anywhere I go with this thing," Rancid Pete says, tapping the computer tablet. "It's got a private global satellite relay."

"Man it must be great to be rich," Dan says, half sarcastically.

"Hey, don't let anyone lie to you bro'," Rancid Pete replies. "It's fucking awesome."

# 48

Roving spotlights illuminate the sky as Alacrán's helicopter descends to the roof of La Ciudad de Oro amidst an eruption of flashes from photographers' cameras. Inside the helicopter Alacrán's personal make-up artist is powdering the crime lord's face, putting the finishing touches on his preparations for the party. "Well done," Alacrán says to Purvis, referring to the crowd of reporters and onlookers waiting on the roof for the super villain to arrive.

"Thank you sir," Purvis replies. He slips a satin hood over Tiara's head, delicately cinching it around the neck. "I don't want to cause you any discomfort," he says to her quietly. "So let me know if this is at all cumbersome for you."

"Seriously?" Tiara's words are slightly muffled by the hood, but her tone is quite clear.

The helicopter lands gracefully as "Mars, the Bringer of War" blasts from a rooftop DJ station. Alacrán, Purvis and Princess Tiara exit onto a red carpet with ropes clearing their path from the throng of reporters. The paparazzi is throwing question after question at Alacrán to no avail. "Who's behind the hood?" "Will anyone be sacrificed to some form of mythical evil deity this evening?" "Who designed your suit?"

The procession makes its way into the building, descending stairs from the roof to the top floor. Reporters follow close behind, jockeying for position. Alacrán enters the lobby to his office in grand fashion. The red carpet and ropes run across the lobby to the open doors of his main office.

Horns trumpet as Purvis announces Alacrán's arrival. Once inside his main office, the doors to his large inner chamber are shut. No Paparazzi are allowed in. Yet.

It is a black tie affair, and will go down as the most elegant mass kidnapping of all time. The "guests" are each tied to their own antique oak, ladder-back chair. Each guest has a private attendant to serve them hors d'oeuvres and cocktails. The guests have been stripped of their pedestrian clothing and adorned with tuxedos and formal dinner gowns. Apparently, the attendant in charge of the wardrobe change had not wanted to deal with untying and retying all the guests, so the wardrobe crew cut the kidnapees' old clothes off, and then cut the tuxes and gowns to loosely fit while interacting with the confines of the chairs to which the guests are tied. It looks like they all have blankets designed to look like formal wear tossed over them.

All told, there are upwards of 50 kidnap victims that made it to the party. Not quite the entire city as Alacrán had threatened, but a pretty good haul nonetheless. Wait staff shuffle about with trays of finger foods and champagne.

There was a buzz amongst the group, before Alacrán's entourage arrived, when a kidnap victim began taking odds on how the whole situation would play out. Currently, "wishful thinking" was the lead bet, with 4-7 odds that everyone was going to survive. When Alacrán arrives escorting a hooded "guest", the bookie begins taking bets on who is inside the hood.

Alacrán helps Tiara to her chair. It is grander than everyone else's, as she is the guest of honor. Alacrán doesn't remove the hood, and the Princess holds her tongue. The truth is, she likes to make big entrances. She knows Alacrán is going to make a big deal out of revealing her. Disgusting as the man is, she will wait until Alacrán reveals her, and then she will be the hottest, sluttiest, bitchiest kidnap victim of all time.

Or will she? She briefly considers that she might not want to be viewed in those terms for the rest of her life. Then she wonders if someday she might look back and regret a lot of her youthful behavior, but she shakes those thoughts from her mind by focusing on Rancid Pete's enormous penis, and how she wishes she had some Stink. Still, the seeds were planted. There may still be hope for the Princess to grow into a decent person.

Once the Princess is seated, Alacrán makes his way around the room greeting his guests. There is Mayor Haruka, enjoying a nice Brut through a straw. All the members of the End of Times are there, except Rancid Pete of course. The pilot of Princess Tiara's plane is enjoying vegan pigs-in-blankets. Jack Sweetwater and his newly transformed vampire barista girlfriend are being subdued by festive leis made with massive cloves of garlic.

Curt Southstone, High Cleric of the local Eastwoodian chapter, is seated next to the Voodoo Priestess who supplied everyone with their love potions. Alacrán does not care for Southstone. He sees Southstone as a threat, and rightfully so. Alacrán waives a security guard over and requests a weapon. The security guard hands Alacrán a baton which he uses to whack Southstone over the head with. People scream in fright, but it is not a fatal blow. Alacrán looks at Purvis and says, "It's the little things that make it all worthwhile."

Alacrán and Purvis come upon the Reverend Thomas "Slim" Diop. An ordained Spiritual Warrior and star center of the Vegas Venom, Las Vegas' professional basketball squad. I'm not sure what he is doing there. He has nothing to do with this caper at all.

"Why is he naked?" Alacrán asks.

"Well," Purvis replies. "Nothing from the costume shop fit him, and by the time we realized that, we had already cut his clothes off. Don't worry though, we've sent a grave robber out to find something that fits him."

"What? Why?" Alacrán asks.

"Well, we didn't think you would want to waste the money to buy him a new tuxedo and then cut it up," Purvis explains. "So, we figured we would send a grave robber out to find something."

"That still doesn't explain his lack of undergarments," Alacrán says.

Purvis shrugs his shoulders in "I don't know" fashion.

"Hmph," Alacrán snorts. "He must be one of those filthy Free-Ballers." His voice is laced with disgust. "And you call yourself a Reverend?" he says to Slim with contempt. Then he turns back to Purvis, "I can't believe those Free-Ballers incorporated a mutual admiration society."

"I know right," Purvis agrees. "Does anyone know what they actually do for business?"

"I don't think anyone particularly cares. Have someone throw a blanket or something over him." Alacrán sighs and moves on to his next victim. "And what have we here?" he says with undertones of filthiness, knowing full well what he has right there. It is Lilly Whet, who recoils when Alacrán gently touches her chin. "You look ravishing," he says. "And don't worry my dear. I murder gently." Alacrán gets quite a kick out of himself with that last line. After he is done attempting a sinister laugh, he notices something out of place.

Jack22 is propped up, leaning against a wall in the far left corner of the room. He is completely without power. Two guards stand on either side of him. They look very bored.

"Is that the agent provocateur that held the misguided notion he was going to steal from me?" Alacrán asks Purvis.

"Yes sir," Purvis replies. "I believe it is."

"Well let's go have a look shall we." Alacrán grabs a glass of champagne on his way across the room. "Good Lord, who dressed this man?"

"I don't know sir, we haven't been able to get a word out of him," Security Guard #1 explains.

"Interesting. He does appear to be in some form of catatonic state," Alacrán says, poking at Jack22 with his cane. "Fascinating."

"We don't know what happened sir," Security Guard #2 says. "The security team that captured him said he was kicking and screaming and then suddenly froze up stiff as a board."

"Very interesting," Alacrán repeats. To add emphasis he leans in close, peering deeply into the expressionless chasm that is Jack22's disguised face. Alacrán's expression changes from pure wonder to curious recognition. "Purvis, this man seems familiar. I feel like I have seen this cowboy somewhere before."

"I don't know my liege," Purvis says. "I don't think he is an acquaintance."

"Has he been identified?" Alacrán asks, continuing to study Jack22's face from an uncomfortably close distance.

"He was identified as Montana Texas," Security Guard #1 replies. "Apparently he is a successful oil and cattle man from Utah. He has a suite here registered in his name."

In an attempt to solidify his alibi, Jack22 and Computer Tiara had registered a room for Monty Texas.

"Hmmmmm," Alacrán says, holding the note until he is almost out of breath. "There is something odd about that face. I know I have seen it before."

"Perhaps you saw him when you were monitoring the security cameras," Purvis suggests.

"Perhaps," Alacrán agrees. "But it seems more familiar than that."

"Well I can tell you this," Purvis says. "That mustache is a terrible decision with his bone structure."

"Wait," Alacrán says, "You may be onto something." He focuses his attention on the sweet handlebar mustache Montana Texas calls his Nipple Tickler. Alacrán carefully extends his right pointer finger, and with palpable trepidation touches the mustache, pulling his finger away as quickly as it makes contact. He touches it again, this time probing it a little, flicking at it, until he pinches the bottom of the left side between his thumb and pointer finger. With a swift movement he removes the mustache from Jack22's face.

Alacrán steps back with an overly dramatic gasp. If Jack22 had been awake he would have reacted the same way. Purvis puts his hand to his mouth with a surprised shriek. The security guards stare at each other extremely confused.

"It's Jack22!" Alacrán exclaims.

"I knew it," someone anonymously shouts from the other side of the room.

"You didn't know anything," someone else responds.

"I did so," the first random voice replies. "I knew it was a freaking robot! All he had was a fake mustache and cowboy hat on. I really don't understand how the rest of you didn't see it!"

"Kill them," Alacrán shouts to nobody in particular, waiving his arm in the general direction of the arguing voices. "Why is my robot dressed up in these ridiculous clothes?" he asks the security guards.

"We don't know sir," Security Guard #1 says with a squeak. He knows what happens to people of his station when people of Alacrán's station get angry.

Security Guard #1's fears are justified when Alacrán pulls out his fancy pen from his lapel pocket, extends a small blade from the end of it, and pokes it through the security guard's left eye.

Self-fulfilling prophecy? Perhaps. Security Guard #1 screams and Alacrán has him removed from the room.

"Plug him in and get him some power." Alacrán says, motioning to Jack22.

Security Guard #2 begins to bustle, barking orders to himself out load while "hup, hup, hupping" his way around Jack22. He pulls Jack22's retractable power cable from its hidden compartment and plugs it into a wall outlet. The robot immediately straightens up, back to life, although his power is too low for any further movement, or for speaking.

"It will probably be a while before he has enough power to move or anything," Security Guard #2 says.

"Run a diagnostic on him," Alacrán replies. "Get his memory files transferred over to my private drive so they can be reviewed. These clothes are from our wardrobe department. Someone has tampered with my robot and I want to know who."

"Yes sir," Security Guard #2 replies.

Alacrán turns to Purvis. "Where's my speech?"

"Right here my liege," Purvis replies, pulling notecards from his pocket.

"Well then let's get this show on the road."

# 49

Sammy wakes and gently unravels himself from Sandy. He shuffles over to the fire where they left Zorn, tugging his shoes on as he walks. He can see the outline of Zorn's body shimmering in the glare of light from a television.

"Well how about that. You found an old TV," Sammy says. "Picking up local channels?"

Zorn nods his head.

Sammy walks over and picks up the power cord to the TV, following it over to a wall outlet. "Hmph, kind of surprising there is power to this outlet isn't it?" he asks, as he walks over and takes a seat next to Zorn.

Zorn shrugs his shoulders in response.

"Yeah, what difference does it make," Sammy agrees. He is too groggy to consider the implications of the building having electricity.

Within a few minutes Sandy walks out from between two rows of books, scratching her head and rubbing her tummy at the same time. "You found a TV?" she asks.

"He did," Sammy replies, motioning to Zorn with his thumb.

"Why didn't you come get me?" she says, half asleep.

"I just woke up babe," he replies. "Here, come sit down in front of me and I'll rub your shoulders while we watch."

Sandy sits down in front of Sammy with her legs crossed. "How long did we sleep?" she asks.

"Not long," Sammy says. "About three hours."

"I'm so tired," Sandy says, yawning quietly. "I don't understand why we didn't sleep more."

"Probably the circumstances. Nerves," Sammy says.

"Yeah," she agrees. They sit in silence for a moment, basking in the warm glow of television.

"Oh crap," Sammy says, breaking the silence. "Doodles."

"Oh yeah," Sandy says lazily. "We should probably check on him." In this instance what that meant was, "You should probably check on him if you care because I don't give a flying…"

Sammy walks over to the car and pops the trunk. Doodles doesn't move. Sammy puts his hand on Doodles' chest to feel for a heartbeat. He looks back over in Sandy's direction. "He's not moving but I can feel his pulse," he says.

"Well, I suppose that's a relief," Sandy responds. I honestly don't know why she has it so bad against Doodles.

"He's been out a long time babe. Do you think he's in a coma or something? Should I try to wake him up?" Sammy was very relieved when he found out he hadn't killed Doodles. If Doodles winds up dying now, well that would suck.

"I don't think so," Sandy says. "I think that's the worst thing you can do for a coma is try to wake them up."

"Oh yeah," Sammy agrees. "Well, I should at least get him out of here and lay him out flat don't you think?"

"Does he look uncomfortable?"

"Not particularly."

"Leave the trunk open so he can get some fresh air and come back over here and watch TV."

Sammy takes a last look at Doodles then walks back over and sits in his chair. "His forehead is starting to look pretty bad," he says. "It's got a hole in it. I mean it's a big ol' gash. I don't know how that happened."

"Probably when he wrecked the car," Sandy says.

"Oh yeah," Sammy says. The conversation trails off. They grow quiet in time to see the horrible sitcom rerun they are watching get interrupted. There is a bad actor on screen mugging for the camera when the broadcast suddenly switches to a handsome, androgynous reporter at a news desk.

"Ladies and gentleman," he (she?) says. We have temporarily interrupted the broadcast of your regularly scheduled programming to take you to a live, breaking news, special press conference."

Alacrán's press conference is a moment in history that people will remember their entire lives. For years to come people in Las Vegas will tell stories about where they were and what they were doing when it happened.

After greeting all of his guests Alacrán opens the doors to his office, allowing select members of the paparazzi into the cocktail party. Particularly all the local affiliates of national broadcasters.

"Please, come in," Alacrán invites with his arms held out wide.

"If you will make your way to the podium there will be a brief announcement followed by a question and answer period," Purvis says. "Then you will be allowed to mingle with the guests." Purvis is standing near the doorway steering the reporters and cameramen in the direction of the dais.

A dais has been set up with a short lectern Alacrán now stands behind. With his left hand he holds a masquerade mask over his face. The mask is black with red accents, studded with jewels, and shaped like the overhead view of a scorpion. The tail arcs up towards the top of Alacrán's head and then across his forehead. There is a large red ruby at the end of the tail representing the stinger.

"Are we live?" Alacrán asks.

"Not yet," a reporter says. "We are live in 5, 4, 3, 2..." She doesn't finish the sentence, she merely holds her microphone in Alacrán's direction, signaling it is time to start. All of the other reporters are confirming they are live with their producers as well. Alacrán politely waits to speak, standing still and smiling for the cameras - from behind his scorpion mask of course - while everyone confirms they are ready.

"Ladies and gentlemen of Las Vegas, good evening," he says. "It is I, Alacrán. I am standing here before you tonight, because I need your help. As some of you may know...," he pauses here to give a suspicious, shifty eyed, sideways look to the cameras, "...and for those of you that don't, there is a relatively small black case lost somewhere in this city. This case belongs to me. Its contents belong to me. I want them back. So, I am asking for your help. Please help me retrieve my case. I really, really want it, and I'm afraid if I don't get it I'm going to be very upset, and then," he pauses again. "Well, I will have to do something nasty. Now, if the cameramen don't mind, I have some guests here that I would like for you all to see."

Alacrán leaves the podium and leads the cameras around the room, introducing many of the guests. He stops next to the chair Princess Tiara is seated in. "So as you can see, we have quite a few people here. Surely there is someone here that each of you would be sad to see harmed. But unfortunately, if I don't get back what was taken from me that is what will happen. I am going to have to kill all of these people in very messy ways. They will be slow, painful deaths. Agonizing. Oh, and as you can see, I have a guest of honor here that I'm sure you will find super exciting." Alacrán pulls away the hood covering Tiara's head. The rest of the kidnap victims, all of the reporters, the cameramen, the service staff, the entire room, everyone in Las Vegas watching the broadcast, they all react with amusingly melodramatic expressions of shock.

Tiara decided while she was waiting that she wasn't going to say a word. When the hood is removed, she sits there and stares at the cameras, chin high, looking as regal as possible. In her mind, it is a royal show of defiance.

Alacrán leads the reporters back to his dais. "So," he says as he walks, "as you can see, I am quite serious when I tell you how badly I want that black case. However, being a sporting and what I consider an equitable man, if my case is returned to me I will spare the lives of all my lovely guests, *and*, I will also give whomever returns the case a sizeable reward." He is now back behind the podium to finish his speech. "Now, to be fair, I think if I am going to be charitable enough to offer a reward for the return of something that was stolen from me, I shouldn't have to wait all night. Therefore, I am going to give whomever has it, or winds up with it last I suppose," he looks at his watch for effect, "one hour and 12 minutes to deliver it to me. If it has not arrived by then, I will kill a guest every ten minutes until they're all dead or my case arrives. And, as an added bonus to the festivities, I am going to let the guests themselves decide the order in which they will all die. Isn't that exciting?" He pauses briefly, allowing his facial expression to shift from conman's smile to murderer's scowl. "Now bring me my case!" Alacrán pounds his fist on the podium, then makes a neck slashing motion that brings the press conference to an end.

# 50

When the Black Case Gang hears Alacrán's announcement, they all scream and shout. They all have different reasons. Sandy is excited. This proves the case is actually worth something. She starts with, "Yes! I knew it!" and makes her way to, "We're gonna be rich!"

Sammy, on the other hand, goes with, "Oh no oh no oh no oh no...," etc. etc. His first thoughts are of a torturous death at the hands of Alacrán. Sammy is wise enough to realize there is a good chance that depending on his mood, Alacrán's "reward" could be to kill whomever returns the case to him. That's the type of guy Alacrán is.

Zorn is making demonic noises at the top of his lungs. He doesn't really have a dramatic emotional reaction to Alacrán's announcement, but he enjoys the excitement.

All the commotion stirs Doodles. He partially wakes up. His left eye is slightly open, and he is suffering from high levels of confusion. He hurts too badly to move, so he lies still and tries to remember something. Anything. Things like: Where am I? What happened? What the fuck is going on around here?

Sandy is doing a "we are going to get paid" victory dance with her fists pumping in the air. It finally registers with her what Sammy is saying. "Hey, what's your problem?" she asks.

"What do you mean what's my problem?" he screams back at her.

"You were right!" she shouts with excitement. "The case is valuable! All we have to do is get it to Alacrán and we get a reward."

Zorn lets out a very loud demon chortle of agreement.

"Are you nuts?" Sammy shouts. "He's just as likely to kill us! Get a reward? He's the most evil villain in town. Except maybe for that vampire guy."

"Oh he's way more evil than the vampire," Sandy says.

"You think so?"

"Oh yeah, for sure."

"Well then that's exactly the point now isn't it?" Sammy screams. "He's gonna freaking kill us for sure!"

"Now look," Sandy shouts back. "This is what we wanted! We had no idea what we were going to do with that thing, or if it was worth anything. Now we are going to get paid, and then we get to go home and I am not going to let you ruin this for me!" Sandy stomps her foot and stares intently at Sammy.

It is around this time that the Librarians finally make their move. They are monitoring the BCG by security camera relay from several rooms away. They position for their sneak attack before Alacrán's big announcement, when Sammy, Sandy and Zorn are quietly watching the television. The Librarians had witnessed Zorn discover the old TV and routed power to the outlets nearby. It served as an excellent distraction from the Librarians attack movements.

The Librarians are led by a greybeard named Philip Primm. Philip is a black sheep from the notorious Primm family, and distant cousin to Jericho Primm, Alacrán's mentor. The Primms are real estate barons and a soap opera-esque clan of cruel socialites, actual criminals, familial martyrs and ne'er-do-wells.

As a young man Phil ran away to study library science and live in literary isolation, hiding from his family name. He was one of the few outsiders to have discovered the Librarians and been excepted into their subterranean community. He now leads the first militia of the Local 213 on their very first mission, Operation First Mission. A unit of eight Librarians converge on the insurgents from all sides. Unfortunately, they aren't well trained, and they don't move particularly fast. Sammy and Sandy have plenty of time to notice their attackers.

"What the hell is this?" Sandy screams.

"Librarians," Sammy screams back, as much a question as a statement.

The Librarians continue creeping forward from all directions with their arms raised out in front of them in menacing positions. One of them is near the car when Doodles, now completely awake, decides to try and exit the vehicle. As he rolls over in the trunk, he sees a body passing by and reaches out to it for help.

The Librarian shrieks when Doodles' hand surprisingly grabs at his pants. He slams the trunk lid down on Doodles' arm. The lid bounces back open as Doodles screams in agony. He sits up in the trunk holding his arm and screaming in horror at the Librarian. The Librarian screams back and slams the trunk lid down again, this time on Doodles' head. Now you may not believe this, but this time poor Doodles is *not* knocked unconscious. He does however, crumple under the weight of the trunk lid. The Librarian, having survived this trauma, promptly passes out.

The rest of the Librarians all pause, distracted by the happenings at the car, but quickly turn their attention back to Sammy, Sandy and Zorn.

"I'm not letting them have our case Sammy!" Sandy yells. "I'll be damned!"

"No way babe," Sammy agrees. "That thing is ours! Everybody back to back!"

Sammy, Sandy and Zorn all stand back to back with their fists up, rotating counterclockwise as a unit, the case on the ground in between all of their legs. As the Librarians close on them, our three heroes begin jabbing and kicking. Although thoroughly researched, the Librarians don't have any experience in the practical application of hand to hand combat. Only a few show any true aptitude. But, the BCG are outnumbered. Despite a solid defense they are in danger of being over powered.

"C'mon," Sammy screams. "We've got to make it over to the car."

"Demon, get the case," Sandy screams. They all begin to shuffle their way, still back to back, towards the car. They are encircled by the Librarians who are lunging at the BCG and generally behaving in threatening manners. Several of the Librarians hiss like lizards or snakes or cats. One misunderstands the game and moos.

Phil Primm winds up directly between the BCG and their getaway vehicle. As the trio rotates towards the car, Sammy faces Primm. Sammy successfully punches Phil in the nose and shoves him out of the way.

"Ow," Phil says.

"Sorry fella," Sammy replies. "Break for it," he screams to his companions. They all sprint the last few feet to the car. Sammy jumps behind the steering wheel and starts the engine.

"What are we going to do?" Sandy asks, not frantic, but full of energy.

"We're getting out of here," Sammy screams.

"I meant where are we going?" she screams back. "Of course we're getting out of here!"

"Well then that's what you should have asked," Sammy says. He throws the car in reverse and wheels around. They hear a thud, feeling the car run over something. "Oh crap," he says.

The Librarian that passed out next to the car earlier, he wakes back up pretty darn quick when his leg is run over. He wails in pain. The Librarians may be eccentrics, but despite currently attacking some strangers, for the most part they aren't bad people. I am glad he isn't more seriously injured.

"You hit one of them," Sandy says.

"I know I know." Sammy sticks his head out of the window and yells, "Sorry!"

Phil Primm jumps in front of the car, standing with his arms crossed. Sammy stares him down and revs the engine. Phil uncrosses his arms and puts both hands down on the hood of the car. Sammy re-grips the steering wheel, knuckles white, then throws the transmission into drive. The car lurches forward, but not much, as Sammy has his left foot on the brake. Phil grits his teeth. Sammy raises an eyebrow. They stare each other down for a few more seconds, neither of them flinching.

Sandy reaches over and punches Sammy in the leg. "Drive damn it! He'll get out of the way!"

Sammy lets his foot off the break and slams the accelerator to the floor. Phil dives up onto the hood to avoid being ran over, then rolls off to the side before the car slams into the front doors of the building.

The doors, being quite large, do not come all the way open. The little car does manage to budge the doors partially open, but it is stuck in between them. The tires squeal, spinning in place against the weight of the doors.

The Librarians recover and make their way toward the vehicle. They surround the car, pounding on the hood and windows, trying to get in.

"Jesus Sammy, get us out of here," Sandy says.

"I'm trying I'm trying! The car isn't strong enough to open the doors!"

"Who the fuck are these people?" Sandy asks. "Damn these tiny cars! Do you think they're librarians?"

"I don't know. Probably. We're in the damn library. Hey! Stop banging on my damn car!"

"Look! The doors are opening," Sandy says. "We're gonna push through!"

"Hold on," Sammy shouts. "When we get loose it's gonna be a bumpy ride!"

# 51

As several Librarians break through the windows of Sammy's car and begin grabbing at everyone inside, the little vehicle finally bursts forth from the library with all its might. The car shoots out from between the doors like an old toy racecar. The kind with tension in the back wheels that you launch by rolling backwards and then letting go.

The car rockets off the top steps of the building, tossing aside several Librarians that are attempting to hold on. The car flies through the air. Sammy, Sandy and Zorn all three have their heads sticking out their windows, screaming.

They land a third of the way down the steps with a thud and rattle down the rest of the way. The trunk lid is loose. When the car lands it pops open. You can see Doodles bouncing around in the trunk. I distinctly remember him taking almost the entire trip down the flight of stairs to scream, "Why is this happening to me?"

Sammy, Sandy and Zorn all cheer as they hit the street. The BCG shoot past the crowd gathered outside of the building. The crowd stands in amazement as the car whizzes past them. An Eastwoodian returns to his senses quickly, calling his fellow troops to arms as he kick-starts his scooter. This mobilization sets the other groups in motion as well. The race is officially on.

Nico appears in the doorway to the library. He stares briefly at the madness before him. He draws his largest revolver from a holster under his left arm and holds it up in a ready position, holding his pose in the doorway for a few extra moments as flashbulbs go off from the cameras of paparazzi. He takes off down the stairs towards the scooter he stole at the concert. He estimates hundreds of people are outside the building scrambling to their vehicles. This is going to be an easy trail to follow.

Several of the Librarians exit through the front as well. They watch the mass exodus of the crowd while debating whether or not they are going to give chase. The volatile blood of Phil Primm's family gets the best of him. He runs off into the chase, encouraging the others to follow him, never to be seen by the Librarians again. I am supposed to transcribe the history of the rest of Phil's life, but I'm not certain when I will have the time.

The other Librarians put the chase to a vote. By the time they decide their next course of action the crowd is gone, which works out perfectly, as the Librarians voted unanimously to go back inside. They quietly shut the doors to the building and retreat to the safety of their mad little subterranean fantasy world.

Dan is still at the Octopus' Garden with Rancid Pete. Dan explained that Princess Tiara's body double has gone missing, and Pete admits that he and Tiara were together that night.

"Listen cop, I did kill a member of her entourage before the show, but I'm not sure if it was her lady. She was dressed like a ninja, with a mask on you know. Plus I bit her face off."

The news that Rancid Pete was with Tiara creates a surprising amount of immediate emotional discourse for Dan. There is disbelief and jealousy involved. *What's the deal? She's awful.* He wants nothing to do with her but he is jealous the monster has been with her. *Of course!* Even though she is vile, he still wants to have sex with her because she is hot. Smoking hot. That makes complete sense. Still, although he can admit that she could most likely have him if she wanted him, Dan doesn't care for that fact. *That is not the path I should be on,* he thinks. Then he quickly considers all the other women he has been with. How had he thought so little about their interaction? Had he cared about any of them? Of course he had.

No, really, he actually had. That is part of his charm. He genuinely cares about people. All of those women had good hearts. Deep down, he knows that under different circumstances he could have loved any of them. *Man, I'm a lucky guy,* he thinks. This little piece of self-actualization is the final click of the karma-meter that promotes Dan's soul to Level-4. I am not certain how many levels there are. I haven't decided yet. What I do know, is that a fully enlightened Cosmic Hero with a Level-4 soul deserves his own comic book series.

Rancid Pete is snapping his fingers in front of Dan's face. "Cop, cop, cop."

"What? Oh. Wow. Sorry about that." He moves Pete's hand away from his face. "Where were we? Oh yeah, do you poop?" Dan asks.

"Why?"

"DNA testing." Dan says.

"I take world renowned craps," Rancid Pete replies, deadpan serious.

"We are going to need a sample, we can test it for the missing person's DNA."

"Buddy, you are in for a treat."

Dan gets up to shake Rancid Pete's hand and leave when Alacrán pops up on Rancid Pete's television. "Wait a second," Dan says. "Will you turn that up?"

They watch Alacrán make his big announcement. Rancid Pete's spikes swell all over his body when he sees his band. They grow larger when Princess Tiara is revealed. He points at the television and turns to Dan to speak, but Dan holds his hand up to quiet him, intent on hearing the rest of Alacrán's speech.

"I've got to go," Dan says, once Alacrán's announcement is over. "I can't believe he actually had the balls."

"Where are you going?" Rancid Pete asks. "There?" He points at the TV. "Because if it's there I'm going with you."

"No," Dan replies, walking to the door.

"Look," Rancid Pete says. "I'm going with you or I'm going alone. Either way, doesn't really matter to me. He kidnapped my band and my girl. I'm going after them."

"Alright c'mon," Dan relents. "Maybe you can try out being a hero."

"Cut the hero shit and go with vigilante rock star. I'm on board for that." Rancid Pete smacks Dan on his back as they exit the suite.

Dolly wakes quite abruptly. A piercing ring goes off in her ears. The piercing ring ends quickly.

*Jesus what was that?* she wonders. Then she sees Billy standing at the foot of the bed.

"I apologize for the shocking interruption of your sleep," Billy says. "It was very necessary."

"What was that sound?"

"It was this small device," Billy replies. He takes his hands from behind his back and holds up a little black square with a digital face. "My travel alarm clock. But we don't have time to talk about its numerous functions, including the psychic alarm you experienced. You need to get dressed. I laid out some clothes for you to wear." He makes a sweeping motion with his arm over an outfit laying on the end of the bed. Here is a big surprise for you friends. The outfit? Black pants, black turtleneck, black beret.

"I'm not wearing that damn beret," Dolly says.

"You will so," Billy replies. "And while you put your clothes on I will explain why."

Dolly sits up and begins to dress.

"About ten minutes ago," Billy continues, "I was enjoying a soak in the hot tub when a breaking news conference interrupted my regularly scheduled program." He is pacing back and forth. He pretends not to, but he definitely peaks while Dolly is putting her clothes on. He is so curious he can't help it. He acts like he isn't, but he is. "And guess who the press conference was for?" Billy continues. "That idiot Spanishman."

"Spaniard."

"Whatever. Do you know why he was having a press conference my dear?"

"Of course not," Dolly replies, slipping on a perfectly sized pair of high-heeled boots.

"Because he has kidnapped half of this town. Including your dear Princess."

"Are you sure?"

"Of course I'm sure," Billy says emphatically. "Maybe not half the city, but you get the point. A lot of people. Including my child. Somehow he was able to subdue and capture Lord Sweetwater. If the case is not returned to Alacrán within the next hour, he will begin killing his hostages."

"This is perfect," Dolly replies, with true enthusiasm.

"I know! It's going exactly as you planned!"

"Not exactly."

"Well of course not. The kidnappings are simply convenient. But…"

"But it does easily put us all in the same place at the same time, if we can get that case."

"Exactly," Billy agrees. "Which is why we most go now. Hurry up with your penis and things."

"Did you say my penis and things?"

"Yes, yes. What can I say? It's fascinating to me. You're such a lovely woman."

"Don't get any ideas," Dolly smirks.

"Honey. I'm a vampire. If it was like that you wouldn't be able to resist." This comes out more charming than I would have imagined. Which I suppose, somewhat proves Billy's point.

"Whatever. Let's go," she says, zipping her boot.

"Yes. The limo is already waiting downstairs," he says. "If whoever has the case tries to return it, we will be there to intercept them. If they do not arrive by Alacrán's deadline, I will simply kill everyone."

"Well that will be fun," Dolly says. There is a tinge of fear there.

"If you mind that pointy tongue, you and your Princess may survive," he says. "After all, she is still the object of my desire."

"Oh, did we get that figured out?" Dolly asks, "Because I thought it was the case you had decided on."

"I don't want the love potion to go to waste. After all, that was the original plan. Plus, I can't get the Princess out of my mind." Billy looks like he has been victimized when he says this.

"Yeah, she does that to people." Dolly has seen the look on Billy's face many times before.

"She has infected me," he sighs, sarcastically. "And we don't know what is inside the case. It might not be anything I want. Either way, events like this have to come to an end worthy of the ride to the show, baby. One. Way. Or. Another. Be ready freddy. If your plan goes south, I'm killing everyone."

## 52

Let's call this car chase like a horse race, shall we? Why not? At least to get things going…

Black Case Gang takes the early lead out of the gate. Several Eastwoodians are two links behind in second place, with Death Squad Kill Machine rounding out the lead pack in third. Death Squad Kill Machine is a crew of ghoulish teenagers in a van.

Right on the heels of Death Squad Kill Machine comes Nico Champ, neck and neck with the Ladies of the Night in the number eight car. On the inside track, protecting his investment, is the Ladies of the Night's business manager, Papa Nice Pillow, AKA the Treacherous P I M P, AKA the River City Pimp Hand.

Black Case Gang takes a right turn on 42nd, destroying a fruit stand. Their little car is up on two wheels for a minute, but settles back down on all fours nicely. Several of the racers shoot down parallel alleys on either side of our current leader. Black Case Gang is exiting 42nd on to Park, and they take another right! Oh my, an unexpected move. Two more rights and they may as well have gone left.

In a stunning turn of events, Engine 215 of the Las Vegas Fire Department has entered the race and taken over second place! The firefighters have been on strike since the gateway to Hell opened, but have gained quite a reputation for their participation in unsanctioned street racing.

So, we have the Black Case Gang in the lead, followed by Engine 215. Then it's the Eastwoodians. Next is Death Squad Kill Machine. Nico Champ and the Ladies of the Night are neck and neck tied for fifth place, with Pappa Nice Pillow bringing in the rear of our leader pack. But not for long! Two more teams have made an unsuspected thrust forward, closing the gap between the leaders and the rest of the field.

Members of the Dykes Fly Kites charitable organization have finally appeared on their signature three-wheeled choppers, while the last five remaining members of the Order of Sister Mary, Mother of Love have pulled their late model station wagon into the foray as well. The Sisterhood is a cult of housewives that enjoy the drug Ecstasy and practice existential sexual witchcraft. For those of you watching at home, Sister Mary has the line on the Ecstasy.

Dan and Rancid Pete exit the front door of The Octopus' Garden in time to see the high speed hot pursuit fiasco flying by in a blur.

"What the…?" Rancid Pete says.

"I think that was Nico," Dan replies.

"Who's Nico?"

"My partner." As Dan speaks he receives a call on his Smear. It's Nico. "Hello."

"Boss, did I just see you outside the Octopus' Garden with Rancid Pete?" Nico asks.

"Yes you did. I thought that was you." Dan jogs to his cruiser, motioning for Rancid Pete to follow.

"Yeah," Nico says. "I'm not even sure who we are chasing or where they are going, but I'm certain they have whatever went missing from that plane."

"Did you see Alacrán's announcement?" Dan asks.

"No. What announcement? I was out of commission for a minute. Got a little tied up." Nico says this with a smile. The Marshal would appreciate that joke later, when Nico has time to explain. "I'll explain later. What did I miss?"

"Basically the explanation of everything," Dan replies. As Dan starts the engine to his car, he and Rancid Pete stare in silence as a third wave of twenty or more assorted vehicles goes barreling by. "You have got to be kidding me," Dan says.

"Let's go man," Rancid Pete says. "Get this shitheap rolling."

"How did you wind up with Rancid Pete?" Nico asks.

"My turn to explain later," Dan says. "Everyone's headed to La Ciudad de Oro to try and return the case to Alacrán."

"Copy that," Nico says. "We were around the block from there a second ago. The car everyone is chasing must have gotten forced left."

"Most likely," Dan agrees. "I'm going to stay out of that mess and try to cut around to the leader. Stay on them and navigate me to the front car. We'll pin them in. I want to get that case before it gets to Alacrán."

"You got it boss. Taking a left onto Market now."

"What are you doing?" Sandy is screaming at Sammy. "You're going the wrong way! We were two blocks from the casino!"

"I don't know if you noticed or not," Sammy screams back, splattering the windshield and dashboard with saliva, "but there was a minivan full of ogres blocking our path!"

"Oh I saw the fuckin' ogres," she shouts. "You've got to get us turned back around."

"You sit there and be quiet," he screams. "I've got a plan!"

He does not have a plan. Yet.

Dolly and Billy the Third are in the back of his limo. They pull out of the garage under his building and are about to turn out onto the street when the mob goes speeding by.

"That's them," Billy says, leaning forward and pointing. "Go, go, go. Get after them." The driver guns the engine of the limo and crashes his way out into the middle of the pack. Billy turns to Dolly. "I've got several vehicles headed to La Ciudad de Oro to block the entrance. There is no way for them to escape us."

"Remember," Dolly replies. "Once we're inside, you have to let him think he is winning. Even if he is rubbing your nose in it and pissing you off."

"I know, I know," Billy replies. "You know, although I was for it at the time, I'm glad we lost the Vote of 2013."

"What? What are you talking about?" Dolly asks.

"The Vote of 2013 was a political movement for our people," Billy explains. "It was before the Rapture. I was part of a large sector of our population that was in favor of either turning, or annihilating, the entire human race. We held an international vote. In the end we lost by a small margin and let you all live. I think for a lot of vampires, it was simply some strange form of nostalgia for their pre-vampire ancestry. Or pity. Some of us still maintain our ability to feel compassion. Also, human blood is delicious."

"Then why did you want to destroy us?" Dolly asks.

"Personally? Because you are stupid," Billy replies. "And at the time, I had recently had my heart broken by a female."

"Ah, of course," Dolly says. "It's always a woman's fault."

Billy makes a telling face at Dolly, as if to say "C'mon honey, you know it usually is." Instead, he says, "You said it, not me," to which Dolly shrugs her shoulders.

"So vampires are chauvinists too," she replies.

Billy, in turn, simply shrugs his shoulders and nods his head in agreement. "You say chauvinist," he says. "I say realist. Tomato potato."

Despite her immediate response being the desire to claw the vampire's eyes out, Dolly realizes he is mostly trying to be funny. She laughs and let's it go. "Focus vampire," she says with a chuckle. "We're in the middle of a car chase. We need focus!"

"I know I know, but this is so much fun," he replies with enthusiasm. "That's why I'm glad we lost the vote. Say what you will about the fiasco of mankind, but if you have the right attitude and an appropriate sense of emotional detachment, you people can be very entertaining. Now c'mon, let's feel the wind in our face."

Billy pushes a button that opens a large portion of the limousine's roof. He holds his hand out to Dolly. She takes it and they both stand up through the sunroof. Dolly holds on for dear life as the limo speeds down the street, wind ripping through her hair.

"I still don't understand what you are doing," Sandy says. "You're going the wrong way." She looks back at Zorn for agreement, but he is sitting with his head sticking out the window like a happy dog on a road trip.

"I know what I'm doing," Sammy replies.

"Well do you mind telling me?" Sandy says with a huff.

"I'm leading everybody away from the casino," Sammy says impatiently. "Then once we get far enough out, bam, I sneak a big loop in there and double back to the casino."

"Oh," Sandy says. "That's not a bad idea"

"Gee thanks," Sammy replies. Right then they hear a thump, thump, thump on the car. "What was that?"

"I don't know," Sandy replies, looking around.

"Hey! Hey!" It's Doodles. The trunk has slammed back shut. Doodles has been screaming one thing or another since the race started, but in all the commotion the other members of the Black Case Gang could not hear him until now. "Let me out of here," he shouts. His voice is pretty muffled coming from the trunk.

"Oh, shoo, it's just Doodles," Sandy says.

"Oh great," Sammy says. "He's alive. What a relief."

"Yay," Sandy says meekly.

"What's going on?" Doodles screams. "Why am I in here?"

"Oh shut up you," Sandy yells at him. "We don't have time to explain everything to you now. Shut up and be glad you're alive!"

The race goes on for a while. Feel free to picture it animated. Maybe it looks like they are all inside a game of Pac-Man. You could use the theme music from The Benny Hill Show as background music. Or you could go lower tech and suddenly have the whole chase occurring inside an elaborate, built to 1/1000th scale model of Las Vegas, with toy cars as the racers. If I shot it that way, I would probably film the Production Assistants' hands moving the toy cars around the city while making engine noises and tire squealing sounds with their mouths. Or I would have them use those long, hooked, wooden pole thingies you see Generals use to move plastic troops around on combat maps in war movies. What are those things called? Maybe we should stick to picturing it as a massive wacky car chase instead.

Sammy's plan actually works. He bounces his little car out onto Casino Boulevard, which dead-ends at the front of La Ciudad de Oro. The road starts anew on the other side of the building. Alacrán paid a pretty penny to position his casino in such a manner.

The BCG are a dozen blocks away with the casino in sight. There are numerous Karowack Kids flying above the BCG, along with several other demons, fairies and ghosts. They make attempts at landing on the car, but each time Sammy is able to shake them off.

There are still over thirty assorted vehicles in the chase. Cars are crashing into each other, jockeying for position. The main reason a faster vehicle hasn't overtaken Sammy's little car on shear speed is the amount of traffic. Nobody wants anyone else to get ahead and catch the Black Case Gang, so the entire pursuit looks like a citywide demolition derby.

Dan's plan also works. With help from Nico's navigation, Dan manages to cut the path of the race and enter the melee behind Sammy, Sandy, Zorn and Doodles. Nico is close by as well, expertly maneuvering through the traffic madness. Billy the Third and Dolly are behind Nico.

"There it is," Sandy shouts, pointing through the front windshield at La Ciudad de Oro as it grows larger in their view. She turns to Sammy with her little fists clinched again. "We're gonna make it!"

"Don't speak too soon babe," he replies. "Look!" As they grow closer you can see several long black vehicles blocking the entrance to La Ciudad de Oro's curved valet path.

"Oh man," Sandy says. "It's those goddamn vampires. What are we going to do?"

"Well, this is it babe. I can't keep this up anymore." Sammy looks over at Sandy. She knows what he means from the look in his eyes. He takes a hand from the steering wheel and holds it out to her.

Sandy takes his hand. "Fuck it baby," she says. "Do it!" She squeezes Sammy's hand and he pushes down as hard as he can on the accelerator, hoping the little car has something more to give.

The Karowack Kids blocking the entrance to the casino are loitering about in as cool a fashion as they can imagine. They can see this crazy little car being chased by madness. Just madness baby. Cars, scooters, motorcycles, and vans, and every sort of creature imaginable driving. You got goons, ghosts and goblins. Albinos and winos. Midgets, bandits and thieves. Pirates. Ghost pirates. Those freaky Eastwoodian dicks. All the vehicles are bashing into one another jockeying for position. The ladder section of Fire Engine 215 is swinging about erratically, smashing up buildings. Eventually, and none too soon, the Karowack Kids realize this rolling insane cattle train ain't coming to a stop.

A block away from the Casino, Dan realizes what is about to happen and breaks off chase. Nico instinctively does the same. Dan squeals to a stop and jumps out of the car. "C'mon," he says to Rancid Pete.

Nico hops off the scooter and lets it fall to the ground. "Running or walking," he asks his boss.

"Watching," Dan replies. "Look."

When Billy the Third realizes his limo is about to crash into the barricade setup by his children, he doesn't take the time to tell his driver to stop or take evasive action. He simply grabs Dolly and flies out of the limo. Billy is not a good flyer. It is a bumpy ride, but not as bumpy as if they had stayed in the limo…

Sammy, Sandy, and Zorn all scream in unison. Sammy drives his car headlong into the Karowack Kids' barricade of limousines. The Karowack Kids scatter. Sammy's little car has enough downward slope to the front end of the hood, and is traveling with enough acceleration, that it goes airborne on impact with the limos. It flips end over end several times. For once, the Black Case Gang sits completely still and silent inside their tiny vehicle, watching the world around them rotate.

The car narrowly misses hitting the front awning of La Ciudad de Oro, passing underneath it and crashing to the ground. It smashes through the front entrance to the casino, rolling over a few times before settling on its hood and sliding to a stop inside the casino lobby.

Outside, the rest of the vehicles chasing the BCG crash into a massive pile up. They keep crashing, one after another, until it feels like the pile up is never going to stop. Eventually it does, and then it is eerily quiet. You can hear the hissing and creaking of the vehicles as they finally come to rest. A hubcap spins in the street. You can hear the sighs of people inside their vehicles as they realize they are still alive. You can hear that unmistakable little poof sound a fire makes when the first flame pops. Then the cars start exploding.

# 53

Hook and Lia both stand silent, staring out the viewport. They quietly take each other's hand. The Peacecannon looms in the infinite blackness of space before them. The glow from the ship's lights and engines gives it a surreal luminosity. The Peacecannon significantly resembles a hammer, and is Valtruca's most legendary warship, er, peace keeping vessel.

"What are we going to do?" Lia asks. She is asking herself the question as much or more than she is asking Hook.

"Try to talk them out of destroying the Earth," Hook replies.

"But if we can't?" she asks.

"Then we blackmail them with what we know," Hook says defiantly. "We don't have a lot of time, but I've got an idea."

"But we don't even know what the fuck is going on here!"

"Nobody does. Doesn't matter," Hook says calmly. "We do know they mated with humans, and that the Council has kept Earth secret from the rest of Valtruca. We can blackmail them with that."

"What if the Council actually has a good reason to destroy humanity?" Lia asks this question despite her personal belief that there can't be any good reason to destroy an entire civilization of people.

Hook stops moving long enough to consider her question. Before he can speak, the whistle of an incoming transmission sounds. "Don't answer it," he says. He walks over and takes Lia by the shoulders. "The Council is wrong and we are going to stop them. Don't waiver."

Lia stiffens her spine and clinches her jaw. Determination sets in. "Screw 'em," she says. Hook goes back to running around the room, stopping at the numerous computers and punching away at the keyboards. "How do you think they got here so fast?" Lia asks. "Even if they had left as soon as they received our first message, they still shouldn't be here this quickly."

"Maybe the Council slowed down Earth time from Valtruca somehow." Hook isn't really paying attention. He is continuing to prep his array of computers for his extortion attempt.

"That's impossible," Lia replies. She is chasing him around the room now as she talks. "They have to be inside the planet's solar system to slow down Earth time. You should know that. It's not really that we are slowing Earth down, it's that we are moving way faster."

"I understand time-speed dynamics Lia. I was speaking hypothetically."

"Well it was stupid," she says, playful and truthful at the same time.

"Well you're stupid," he says, equally as dry and playful.

"You were supposed to be figuring this out while I was in Atlantis." She crosses her arms and tries to look mad at him.

"I know, I know, I tried. I'm sorry. I'm so close." Hook is hitting the Enter key on his final computer as he speaks. He turns around, puts his hands on her hips and smiles. "Seriously. Sorry I couldn't figure it out. Yet."

"It's okay babe," she says. "It's not your fault and it doesn't matter now, they're already here. Maybe they really do have time travel technology."

"Maybe they figured out a way for a ship to travel through a wormhole the same way they sent their messages to us," Hook replies.

"What if they did?" she replies. "Would be amazing."

"Well, however they did it, this is about more than us and the humans now. It's also a historically significant technological revelation."

"It will be if we get the Council to tell us how they did it."

"Even if they don't," Hook says, "it's another example of the Council's deceit and something our people need to know."

"Right." At that moment a whistle sounds, signaling they are being hailed by the Peacecannon again. "Are you ready?" Lia asks.

"Fifteen seconds," Hook replies. He holds a small recorder to his mouth and speaks into it quickly. He thumbs the recorder back off then nods his head at Lia. "Okay. Ready."

"Here we go," Lia says. She turns on the video screen. They see Greck Dislock's thick bald head, complete with a very large fleshy nose that highlights his advanced Valtrucian age.

Dislock squints at them with contempt, quickly scanning their habitat and its non-Valtrucian wares. "Prepare to be boarded," he says gruffly, then he ends the transmission.

The screen goes black and Hook looks over at Lia, impressed be Greck's command of the situation.

"Well, shit." Hook says.

"Yep."

The Peacecannon docks with the Parabolas in a few minutes. The boarding party is quickly onto the ship's bridge. Hook and Lia now find themselves hosting Council Chairman Greck Dislock, the Chairman's wife, two of the Chairman's personal advisors, the Minister of State, and a full security squad.

Please keep in mind that the following conversations are in Valtrucian. I had to translate it to English so you can read it but be forewarned, my Valtrucian is by no means perfect. There may be crucial points lost in translation. Subtitles will be included in the Deluxe Edition of the book, but won't do you any good unless you read Valtrucian.

Greck doesn't speak when he enters the room. He quickly spots Hook and Lia then crosses the room to them. He is wearing his councilman's robes.

Although a large Valtrucian, Greck Dislock is a little bit shorter and a little bit smaller all-around than what you might expect by the size and shape of his head. Don't mistake me, he is no caricature. He is actually in excellent physical condition. In his youth he was a very strong, skilled physical combatant. His skull size isn't a dramatic mismatch to his body, but it's enough to make you tilt your head to try and figure out what's not quite right.

"Explain to me why you have not followed your orders," Greck says.

"Chairman Dislock," Hook says. "As we explained in our report, this planet is in the middle of a divine phenomenon."

"Nevertheless, your report was reviewed, your stay of execution denied and your orders quite clear." Dislock is not amused. "Why have you not carried them out?"

"Well, sir, with all due respect, we didn't think they made sense." Hook is genuinely afraid he may be shot dead where he stands.

"Excuse me," Greck retorts.

"The humans are nothing like what you told us. What we were prepared for, I should say." Despite everything he has learned about the Council's duplicities, Hook is still in awe of Chairman Dislock.

"They have shown amazing survival instincts sir," Lia follows. "We thought perhaps if you were to see what was going on down there, you might change your mind."

"I'm well aware of what's going on down there," Greck replies. "This planet is to be destroyed."

"But sir," Lia says, with all her courage. "Despite their many flaws, humans are interesting creatures. The best of them are quite impressive."

"They are very funny," Hook continues, "and their artistry is awe inspiring."

"Yes, and most of them have a very natural capacity for love and kindness if they receive the correct instruction," Lia continues.

"We still have hope for them," Hook says. "Although they clearly hit a pretty heavy duty tipping point, there are still some of them…"

Greck holds his hand up motioning for Hook to stop speaking. Hook immediately obeys. "Commander," Greck says. "I am not going to participate in a debate with you about the redeemable qualities of Earthlings. I sent you here to destroy them and you have disobeyed. You will be relieved of your post and the planet will be destroyed."

"They're called humans," Lia spouts. "Humans. And we shouldn't give up on them."

"My dear," Greck says, "I am not giving up on them. I am blowing them up. If I were to take the time to debate you, I would tell you that you are insane, and everything you are saying is insane. If the *humans* were worth a damn, Bob would not be destroying them right now."

"But he isn't destroying them," Hook interjects.

"They have ushered in their own apocalypse," Greck declares.

"But they are surviving," Lia says, "and Bob is allowing them to."

Now, what happens right here is, Hook has secretly put the large main viewport on Vegas while Greck is paying attention to Lia. All Hook says to Greck is, "Look," with a little conviction, and then points at the screen.

Surprised by Hook's command, Greck turns and looks. On the screen Greck sees a massive car chase crashing through Las Vegas. Of course it is the very same car chase that Dan, Rancid Pete, Nico, the BCG, Billy the Vampire, Dolly, and dozens of other less important or completely unknown folks are participating in.

Greck Dislock has a moment of clarity and is absolutely disgusted with himself.

"Damn it!"

He throws down his popcorn and 3D glasses as he stands up, holding on to the word "damn" for dear life before finally letting go and moving on to the "it". He allowed himself to get sucked into watching the chase scene happening in Vegas, as well as some of the fight scene between the good guys and the Karowack Kids. You haven't read the fight scene yet.

Greck whirls on Hook and Lia. "I said I was not participating in this!" he says, shaking his finger at them.

"But you just saw," Lia says. She holds her hand up in the direction of the monitor and stands with her mouth open. Her facial expression is the mixture of shock and confusion. She did not bother to explain that all the argument she could make should go without saying, when Greck Dislock had witnessed all the explanation he should need for himself. Instead she stands there with her mouth open until Greck eventually makes the same face back at her with contempt.

"Seriously," Hook picks up where Lia left off. "Councilman Dislock, what you saw is only a..."

"Oh you fools," Greck interrupts Hook with a very comical leg bobbing, knee bending motion that includes his arms shooting into the air. The little dance accentuates the slight size discrepancy between his body and his head. Then Greck looks at his people and calmly says, "I can't believe I am repeating myself," before turning back to Hook and Lia and screaming, "They must be destroyed!"

"But why?" Hook questions. Later on, he will have a hard time believing he debated the great Greck Dislock in such a manner.

"Because I said so. How's that, huh?" Dislock is not used to anyone, anyone at all, questioning his authority or distracting him from his purposes.

"What about the other members of the Council?" Lia chimes in. "Do they know about this? How do you know they won't agree with us?"

"I am the Council you idiot," Greck replies with an arrogant smirk.

"Don't you speak to her that way," Hook says. He gasps internally at his own audacity. Greck responds with a killer's cold stare that sends shivers up Hook's spine. "Fine," Hook says with much less confidence. "But....destroying humanity isn't even logical."

"Doesn't matter," Greck replies. He turns to the Security Squadron's Chief. "You there, find the controls to the device and turn it on."

"No! Wait," Lia says desperately.

"No." Greck says.

"Alright look," Hook says, mustering all the bravado he can. "We didn't want to do this, but if you don't back off, we're going to expose you to the rest of Valtruca."

"Expose what?" Greck asks.

"We know what you did," Lia says.

"What is it that you think you know?" Greck asks.

"Don't play dumb," Lia spouts. "We know you came down here to protect the humans hundreds of years ago and then started mating with them."

"Oh. That." Greck is as droll as possible.

"Yeah that," Hook jumps in. "Then Bob found out what you did and sank Atlantis."

"Well that's not quite right," Greck says. He slightly changes his tone. A skilled debater, he realizes it is time to appear more forthcoming.

"Oh yeah? Then what is it?" Lia sounds a bit like a little kid when she says this.

"Atlantis was sank by platonic shifting and the eruption of a massive volcano," Greck says calmly. "And it didn't matter. There was no reason for us to be here anymore once we had fixed the mistake in their DNA."

"Mistake?" Hook asks.

"What mistake?" Lia adds.

"Well, since you think you know it all I'm surprised you didn't understand that they weren't developing correctly. We were here to figure out why. Once we did, we didn't need to be here anymore."

Greck clasps his hands and lets them rest naturally against his body. It is intended to be the body language of an earnest teacher.

"So you figured out mating with them would fix them?" Lia asks.

"Yep," Greck responds.

"You're bluffing," Hook says coolly.

"Yeah," Lia agrees. "You're making that up to confuse the situation. The humans were supposed to be what they were."

"No, I'm not bluffing," Greck insists. "That's what happened. Believe whatever you want." At this point, the three have a silent stare down. Greck alternates between Lia and Hook. Eventually, their many faces of questioning disbelief overcome Greck's faces of defiant insistence. Greck loses the battle. His face muscles get tired and tremor, causing him to look like a stroke victim. "Alright I'm bluffing!" he finally yells.

"So what's your problem?" Lia asks.

"I told you the first time," Greck says, still gassed from the stare off.

"What do you mean the first time?" Lia follows up.

"Because Bob said so," Greck says. "That's what I told you."

"But don't you see?" Hook says. "It's a freaking apocalypse right in front of you!"

"It doesn't matter you idiot," Greck says gruffly.

"All we're saying is, doesn't it look like Bob has got it under control?" Lia says.

"Oh for Bob's sake, there is no Bob!" Greck has finally completely lost his patience.

"What? What do you mean?" Hook asks.

"We made it all up. I made it all up," Greck says. He is clenching and unclenching his fists in frustration. He paces back and forth in short strides, taking a step or two then turning back and going in the opposite direction. Somehow, he manages to maintain his dignity.

"But what about the Bork?" Lia questions.

"A bunch of stuff the Old Sages invented to keep people in line," Greck says convincingly.

"But that's impossible," Hook states calmly. "There has to be a Bob."

"There has to be a Bob," Lia echoes. "There's certainly an Earth Bob. Look at what's going on down there."

"Oh there may very well be some form of higher power," Greck admits, "but I doubt its name is Bob and the truth is we don't really know anything about it."

"Seriously?" Hook asks.

"Seriously," Greck affirms. "No one's got a fucking clue what's going around here."

"Wait, what?" Lia is shaking her head with confusion. "We do know. You mated with the humans and you were trying to cover it up."

"No. That has nothing to do with it," Dislock says, waving his hand at her for effect.

"You are a pathological liar!" Lia is nodding her head with her mouth open. She looks at Hook and says, "It's really kind of amazing."

"Yeah, it really is," Hook agrees.

"There are records!" Lia continues her assault on Greck. "We know you mated with the humans."

"I know," Greck admits. "You misunderstand. I'm not saying we didn't mate with them. I never said that. We definitely mated with them. We mated with them like-uh-carazy. It was fantastic." A very brief expression of nostalgia flashes across Greck's face. "But that's not why we were going to destroy them. We were going to destroy them because of this." Greck takes the controller to the bridge's main view-screen from Hook's hand with a pickpocket's swiftness. He changes the channel, switching it to an international news station. On it, they are celebrating the countdown to the launch of the first manned deep space shuttle in human history.

"I don't understand," Hook says.

"Of course you don't," Greck says with exhaustion. "How long have you been here, wasting your time and not realized that they were about to have the technology to leave their solar system and travel into deep space for the first time? That was the whole point of your mission! To destroy them before they successfully achieved deep space travel."

"First of all, you never told us that was the point of our mission, and second of all, even if you had, we like watching Las Vegas." Hook puts his arm around Lia as he finishes speaking.

"Wait a minute. I know what's going on here," Lia speaks back up with confidence. "If that was the point of our mission...I know the real reason you don't want them in deep space." She speaks slowly as she pieces it all together. "You were going to destroy the humans because you were afraid if they were able to leave their solar system, the rest of Valtruca might find out about all of this, and then find out the Bork is full of a bunch of lies. It would destroy our culture."

"Yeah, something like that," Dislock agrees.

"What do you mean something like that?" Lia asks.

"No that'll play," Greck says. "We'll go with that. What you said. We've built a perfect society and it could all come crumbling down if it was ever exposed to humankind blah, blah, blah."

"But," Lia wants the answer but Hook steadies her for a moment. The key is stopping Earth's destruction. Hook realizes there is never going to be a straight answer from Greck Dislock.

"So what now?" Hook asks Greck.

"Well, I can't have you completely crumbling the fabric of our society now can I?" Greck looks around the room for support from his entourage. Hook and Lia look around at them as well. They all shake their heads in response, except a security officer who is confused as to whether he is supposed to nod or shake to show his agreement. He tries to do both at the same time until he figures out what everyone else is doing. "I suppose you need to explain this whole blackmail plan of yours to me," Greck continues, "see if I can poke any holes..."

"Well," Hook says. "I figured out how you were sending your transmissions so quickly and, as you can see, I have created numerous broadcasting stations around the room. If you don't allow the Earth to live, I will broadcast this message." Hook holds up a small recording device in his left hand and hits play. "People of Valtruca. You have been deceived by the Council. There is a planet in a distant solar system called Earth with intelligent life-forms the Council are trying to destroy. The Council kept this planet a secret from us because they broke their covenant with our Lord Bob to protect the alien species that inhabits this planet. Our peaceful culture has been founded on lies. Rise up! Demand the Council be stopped, and that they are punished for their injustice!"

"Well that's rather incendiary don't you think?" Greck says. "And doesn't quite tell the whole story."

"I didn't have much time," Hook says. "It gets the point across."

"You still haven't explained to me why I can't simply kill you, destroy the Earth and go about my business," Greck says. Suddenly he reaches into his cloak, revealing a very sophisticated and sexy alien death ray device.

"Uh, uh, uh," Hook says. "You pull that trigger and in 15 seconds the transmission starts." Hook holds his right hand up to reveal his wristwatch. It is of course synced to his computer network. "I hit this button, every computer in this room starts broadcasting. They repeat every one point five seconds. Your ass is on blast Chairman Dislock."

"Yeah," Lia confirms. "Bang!"

"Oh, bang my ass," Greck growls. "What makes you think anyone on Valtruca will pay any attention to your little announcement?"

"The same thing that made them buy into all your lies," Hook retorts. "Even if it's not some form of immediate panic or uprising against the Council, the seeds of doubt and discontent will have been planted and it will spread. Our society will be changed forever no matter what." Greck makes a little facial expression accompanied with a noise that signifies he accepts Hook's theory as plausible. "The only way you can stop it is to destroy this ship," Hook continues, puffing up his chest with bravado.

"Destroy the ship," Greck says bluntly to his Security Chief as he begins to turn and walk away.

"Damn it," Hook says, immediately deflated.

"Why did you say that?" Lia asks Hook quickly. "You shouldn't have said that!"

"I don't know I don't know," Hook defends himself. "I'm doing the best I can!"

"Wait! Sir," Lia takes a few steps in pursuit of Greck and grabs his arm from behind, gently, encouraging him to stop. Greck turns to face her. "Chairperson Dislock you can't stop it. The Commander was just being…a man, I suppose. The transmission can't be stopped. If you destroy the Parabolas, if you destroy us, by the time you do we will have sent the signal out. Hundreds of thousands of times if my math is correct. There's no stopping that."

*Damn*, Greck thinks. *She's pretty sexy. I'd like to intermingle my…* Greck catches a look of disapproval from his wife out of the corner of his eye. "What exactly do you want?" he asks Lia.

"We want the Council to come clean to the people of Valtruca," she says. "At least about Earth. They are practically our family."

"They are the cousin in the family nobody wants around," he says. "Trust me."

"Still," she replies. "Maybe we can help them."

"And we want the Parabolas," Hook says. "We would like to keep the Parabolas and be honorably relieved of our active military duties with full pension."

"But, if we tell our people about the humans, how is that any different than you sending your own transmission and revealing all of this to them?" Greck has a valid point.

"Well, because it will be you telling them," Hook argues. "You can soften the blow, and you can have a good reason why you have waited to this point."

"Are you suggesting that we lie to our people?" Greck is mock appalled, pointing the finger of shame at Hook and Lia. The Chairman of the Valtrucian Council has understood the necessity of bending the truth to the masses for hundreds of years. He is also well aware of how quickly do-gooders like Hook and Lia succumb to using the same tactics when it suits their righteous needs.

"I'm suggesting that you can have a good reason why you've waited so long to tell everyone," Hook repeats.

"None of us want our society to crumble," Lia says, wrapping her arm around one of Hook's.

"Fine," Greck says abruptly.

"So the Earth stays?" Lia says.

"The Earth stays," Greck confirms.

"Awesome," Hook says calmly. "So, now what?"

"Well, thanks to you two I guess we have to go home and slowly but surely start getting our society ready for all of this insanity," Greck says. He waives his arm at the monitor showing the news report, watching the space shuttle on Earth as it launches. He turns to leave. "Humans," he mutters, shaking his head as he walks.

As Greck is walking away, something clicks in the back of Lia's mind. There is something she can't let go of, and the fact that it appears she and Hook have won encourages her to push for more. "What did you mean 'something like that'?" Lia asks Greck.

Hooks shushes her.

"No, I want to know," she says to Hook, who continues to try and silence her. "Stop shushing me," she repeats. "Stop shushing me. Stop. Stop!" She snaps loudly at Hook.

Having intended on ignoring her previous question, Lia's shout causes Greck to stop and turn, thinking she is yelling at him.

Lia boldly steps forward. "I want to know what you meant when you said 'something like that'," she says again.

Greck points his cane at her and jabs it at the air a couple of times. "Young lady, I'm going home," he finally says. "Be glad you aren't dead." He heads for the exit to the bridge again.

"Hey Greck," Hook says, before the Chairman makes it to the exit. Greck turns back around and raises his eyebrows, acknowledging Hook. "I was bluffing," Hook says. "About the recording."

"Agh," Greck says in disgust, dismissively swatting his arm in Hook's general direction and continuing his exit.

"Hey Greck?" Hook says again.

"What are you doing?" Lia says, slugging him in the arm.

"It's too late now, the human ship has already launched," Hook says to Lia. "Hey Greck?" he repeats.

Greck continues on through the bridge doors. The rest of his entourage follows him into the hallway that will take them back to the docking bay. The last person to exit the bridge is Greck's wife. When nobody else in the boarding party is looking, she turns to give Hook and Lia both a warm smile, then she flips a small shiny object through the air towards them with her thumb. She winks at them, then turns to join the others.

Hook reaches up and catches the small object in his hand, then for the last time he says, "Hey Greck." Greck turns to face the bridge. He acknowledges Hook once again without speaking. "How did the homing pod get back to you so quickly?" Hook asks.

"All of your homing pods were retrofitted with the wormhole technology," Greck explains with a sigh. "They have built in transmitters programmed for Valtruca."

"I knew it," Hook exclaims.

"Did you now?" Greck replies, rolling his eyes.

"Yep," Hook says. "And by the way. I lied, I wasn't bluffing."

This last bit crossed the line. Hook has poked the bear enough. Greck moves as if to walk back onto the bridge and kick Hook's ass. Hook quickly punches a button that shuts and locks the doors to the bridge, sending Greck and his boarding party on their way.

"What was that all about?" Lia asks.

"Ah, the guy's a jerk," Hook says. "I was getting after him a bit. He knew what I was doing."

"No, I knew what that was," Lia says. "I meant Lady Dislock. What was that all about? What did she toss us?"

Hook holds his hand out and opens it to reveal a coin. It's alien. There is a handsome humanoid king on one side of the coin and oddly enough, the picture of a skeleton key on the other.

"Now what do you think this is?" Hook asks.

"A clue," Lia replies with excitement. "It's a clue! She's helping us. It's her! I guarantee you it was Lady Dislock that told us about Atlantis."

"You think?"

"Of course," Lia replies excitedly. "It makes perfect sense, Hook. She could have mated with the humans. There could be generations of people she gave birth to!"

"That's true," Hook responds. "She has been the Chairman's mate since they were in their schooling. She was probably on Atlantis with him, and could easily have mated with humans."

"They probably both did," Lia says dryly. "You know how the marriages of politicians work."

"True."

"We've got to figure out where this coin came from and we've got to go there."

"Okay, okay," Hook agrees. "That's fine, but we need to finish with Earth first. Besides, I think Greck was lying. I think we had him dead to rights and he didn't want to admit it."

"So you think the Bork is real?" Lia asks.

"Of course I do," Hook says.

"Good, 'cause I do to," Lia says. "I mean, look at what's going on down on Earth."

"Exactly," Hook affirms. "Don't get me wrong. I don't know how much of the Bork is real. There's no telling what people like Greck changed or made up. But there has to be some kind of something. Like a Bob I mean. The possibilities are endless. Bob could be some form of connective energy, like a mechanism of the collective-subconscious of a species."

"Right! Or, Bob could be some further evolved species with the science to create life. And you know, I would be willing to bet if that were the case, that species has their own Bob."

"Ha," Hook says. "Right? Sitting on a throne somewhere at the top of the universal food chain." Hook puts his hand out to Lia. She takes it and he leads her closer to the viewport. They stand silently staring down at the Earth, until Lia speaks again.

"So you think that the Council was really going to destroy the Earth just to keep it a secret from Valtruca, to keep people back home from questioning how the Council is running the planet?"

"Yeah," he says, "I do. At least, that has to be part of it and I haven't come up with a better reason yet. Anything could be possible. For all we know, this could all be going according to Greck's plan."

"But how would he know we would show up and not destroy the planet?"

"I don't know," Hook admits. "But anything and everything is possible. We can't rule out any possible scenario if we are going to get to the bottom of all this."

"I guess not. And we've got a clue." Lia looks at Hook with enthusiastic optimism and points at the coin in his hand. The face she makes is the cutest damn thing he has ever seen. He grabs her and kisses the piss out of her. Seriously, she peed a little bit. It happens.

"Do you think the Council will really tell everyone about the Earth?" Lia asks, when Hook finally lets her go.

"I doubt it," he says.

"Me too," Lia agrees. "So what are we going to do about it?"

"Well, we're either going home to lead a revolution or we're going to find the planet this coin came from. Maybe we can figure out what it has to do with all of this." Hook walks over to a viewport to watch as the Peacecannon detaches from the Parabolas and turns to begin its journey home. "And honestly my love, I don't care which it is. Valtruca or wherever this coin came from, you can pick, but first, we're going down to Earth."

"Why?"

"I want a souvenir."

# 54

Sammy and Sandy are both suspended upside down, held in place by their seatbelts. Sandy is the first to regain consciousness after the crash. She shakes her head to loosen the cob webs. She sees Sammy dangling, tangled up in his seatbelt as well.

Sandy reaches out for him and tugs at his shirt, saying his name. Then she pokes him in the side with her finger saying his name. Finally, she repositions herself and pinches his nipple real hard while screaming his name.

"Huh? What. Ow!" There is nothing like waking up to pain.

"Sammy, get me out of here," she says wearing a strange smile.

"I'm coming baby," he says, taking stock in his situation. He wiggles a bit to figure out where he can move. "Are you hurt?"

"I think I'm okay," Sandy replies.

Sammy is able to maneuver his arm to find the release for his seatbelt. He hits the button and falls out of his restraint. He crawls out of the car through the broken glass of his driver's side window, then makes his way around to Sandy. Other vehicles are still exploding in the wreckage outside. A particularly loud boom frightens Sammy, causing him to duck and cover for safety. He looks outside, taking in the devastation left in their wake.

"Sammy?" Sandy questions.

"I'm coming baby," Sammy repeats. He opens up the passenger door. Sandy turns to look at him and her awkward position makes it look like her head is rotated 360 degrees. It looks like her neck is all twisted up and broken because of the way the shoulder strap of the seatbelt is digging into it. The sight makes Sammy want to throw up.

"Nice parking job," she says. The last thing she should have done was make Sammy laugh when he was trying to fight back vomit. Before he can cover his mouth, he pukes right on Sandy's face.

"Ew! Sammy! Gross!" With that, Sandy starts to cry. Not a subtle, somber, I lost my lover cry. It is more of a Lucille Ball, I got scolded by Desi, "Waaaaaaa".

"I'm sorry, I'm sorry," Sammy mumbles through his arm as he wipes his mouth with the sleeve of his shirt. He uses the other arm to try to wipe Sandy's face off.

"Sammy, no," she tries to say as he rubs his forearm up and down her face. "Just get me out of here!" she is finally able to shout.

While this is happening, Zorn is stirring back to life in the back seat. The demon did not wear a seatbelt, and the crash left him with a huge gash that runs from the back of his skull to the front, in the shape of a Z. The gash is split open fairly wide. There is no blood because Zorn is a demon. Instead the wound glows white-hot red, with hints of orange flames and stirring movement, like the top layer of molten magma in the crater of a volcano.

As Zorn is crawling out of the back seat, Doodles can be heard in the trunk barking orders for his release. "Hey," he is screaming as he bangs on the hood of the trunk. "Get me out of here!"

Sammy looks up at Zorn and says, "You alright?"

Zorn nods his head yes.

"Good," Sammy says. "See if you can get Doodles out of there."

Zorn starts kicking at the trunk while Sammy frees Sandy. Sammy gets underneath her to help support her weight, so she won't fall as hard as he did, then he releases her seatbelt. She crumples on top of him with their faces inches apart. He smiles and Sandy kisses him, puke face and all.

Zorn is finally able to kick the damaged trunk lid free of its housing and Doodles roles out of the vehicle. Zorn pulls Doodles to his feet. Sandy crawls out of the car and gets to her feet slowly. Sammy gets himself back out and up as well. "C'mon," Sammy says. "We gotta move."

While the BCG are inside bumbling around their car, Dan, Nico and Rancid Pete are trying to rescue creatures from the wreckage outside. The firemen that were in the chase for the case made a noble effort at avoiding the pile up, although the tight right turn they took in Engine 215 resulted in the truck tipping over and coming to a rest on its side. The firemen, apparently quite drunk, crawl out from the truck amidst a sea of beer cans and booze bottles. They are trying to be quiet, giggling and shushing each other.

Dan looks at Nico and points to the truck. Then he looks at Rancid Pete and points to a nearby fire hydrant. Rancid Pete uses his monster strength to connect the trucks water line to the fire hydrant. Nico scrambles atop the side of the truck and unwinds the hose, turning the water loose on the flaming cars. Once the water line is functioning, Rancid Pete joins Dan in pulling bodies from the destruction. The firemen watch in wonder until Nico hits them with the hose, ordering them to get off their asses and help.

Immediately after exiting his limousine, Billy flew himself and Dolly head first into the exterior wall of La Ciudad de Oro. He shields Dolly from the impact but cracks his own head, falling from the sky in a heap of dead weight. Once on the ground he pops back up in an instant, brushing his shoulders and trying to maintain his since of grace, acting as if nothing had happened.

Billy's children flock to him. There are twenty or so that created the blockade in front of the casino.

"Children," Billy says, "I need you to stop those ridiculous heroes out there." He nods his head in the direction of the Marshal. "And anyone else who tries to get through here after that case."

A chorus of "yes master" is spoken in unison.

"I believe Bernstein and Sondheim are in order," Billy continues. "A little *West Side Story* my darlings. Hands and energy up and one, two, three."

With that the Karowack Kids break into a dance number. Several of the Kids vocalize an overture to their movements as they shi-shaw their way into the casino, finger snapping and back stepping their way to glory.

"What are we going to do?" Dolly asks Billy.

"We're going to fly to the top of the building and go in from the roof," Billy replies. "It's the quickest way and Alacrán will not expect it."

Having just witnessed Billy's aptitude for flight, Dolly says, "Are you sure that's a good idea?"

To which Billy replies, "No I am not."

Dan, Nico and Rancid Pete regroup quickly after the flames from the wreckage are put out.

"We've got to get inside," Dan says. "The rest of these people will have to hold tight until the paramedics get here."

"Are there paramedics coming?" Rancid Pete asks.

"Who knows," Nico replies.

"Come on," Dan continues. "Let's move."

"Boss look," Nico says, pointing to the entrance. "Vampires."

"Damn. I hate fighting vampires," Rancid Pete says.

"Me too," Dan agrees. "Not much choice though."

"Nope," Nico says. "Has to be done."

"Yes it does," Rancid Pete says. "I'm in, but it would be a lot easier if there were a few more of us."

Dan stops mid-stride. "Wait a minute," he says. "I've got an idea. It should help our odds."

"What is it boss?" Nico asks.

Rather than answer Nico's question, Dan looks at Rancid Pete and says, "Do something disgusting right now." Dan gives an encouraging nod and raise of the eyebrows. Rancid Pete responds by making a brief, contemplative expression, then rips his own left arm off.

"Jesus Christ!" Nico shouts. It's a mix of surprise, disgust and laughter.

Jesus appears standing atop his transporter pad, by GomiCorp. GomiCorp is a registered trademark.

"It is I," Jesus says.

"How did you know?" Rancid Pete asks Dan.

Nico pukes.

"A hunch," Dan says to Rancid Pete.

Nico looks up at Dan. "I stared at the end of the arm too long," he says with a smile.

Dan shakes his head with a smile in return.

Jesus walks over and pats Nico on the back. He notices Rancid Pete's arm and says, "What's this all about fellas?"

Dan pukes. While he is bent over he looks at Nico half laughing as he vomits. "Dang it Nico. You did it to me too. You said it and then I couldn't stop staring at it either."

"Hah," Nico replies as he straightens back up. "It locks you in right?"

"Pete, what happened to your arm?" Jesus asks.

"He told me to do it," Rancid Pete says, pointing at Dan with his severed limb.

"I did not," Dan says with mock outrage, wiping vomit spittle from his face with the back of his arm.

"You kind of did boss," Rancid Pete replies. He is holding his left arm with his right hand. He looks at the arm curiously then sticks it back up into its socket, squishing it around as he takes a few steps closer to Jesus.

"Ew, ah, man," Dan and Nico both say.

"You mind miracle-ing this thing back together?" Rancid Pete asks Jesus.

"No problem," Jesus replies, laying his hands on Rancid Pete's shoulder.

"What would you have done if he hadn't shown up?" Dan asks Rancid Pete.

"You said do something gross," Rancid Pete replies. "It was the first thing I thought of. Besides, it would have grown back eventually."

"But we were about to go fight a bunch of vampires," Nico states flatly.

"Hey, you know, next time…" Pete says with a hint of frustration. Jesus interrupts him. "So what's up?" Jesus asks.

"There's a ruthless criminal, Alacrán," Dan says.

"I've heard of him," Jesus says.

"That's his casino," Dan continues. "He's kidnapped a whole bunch of people and is holding them hostage up there on the top floor. There's a bunch of vampires in the lobby of the casino. We have to get past the vampires, get upstairs, defeat Alacrán and save everybody. And we need your help."

Sammy goes to the front desk to ask the concierge how to get to Alacrán's office.

"Why would I tell you where the owner of the casino's office is?" the concierge asks. "And if I did, what makes you think you would be allowed to go there?"

"This," Sammy says, setting the black case up on the front desk.

"Take the middle elevator," the concierge says. "I will disarm the security so you can take it all the way to the top."

"Thank you," Sammy says. "Listen I feel terrible, but I don't have a dollar to my name."

"It's okay," the concierge replies.

"No, it's not. You are always supposed to tip people in hotels. I know that."

"Truly sir, it isn't necessary," the concierge insists.

"I seriously feel terrible," Sammy repeats as he backs away from the counter. "I don't know what's in this case, but I promise you..."

"Sammy would you come on?" Sandy screams, interrupting him.

"Follow me," Sammy replies, waving to Sandy and Zorn, turning to head for the elevator. He looks back over his shoulder at the concierge as he trots off. "I'll be back with a tip. I promise!"

Billy overshoots the rooftop of La Ciudad de Oro. He and Dolly crash into a billboard a few blocks away. Once again, he manages to protect Dolly, shielding her with his own body. She does have a badly dislocated finger and a broken heal on her shoe. Her right pinky is pointing straight out to the side. "Well, we sort of missed there didn't we?" Dolly says, cringing with pain.

"Yes I suppose we did," Billy says. They gather themselves and start walking. Billy takes her injured hand in his own and snaps the pinky back in place. Dolly screams in agony. Billy smiles, pops his fangs out and bites down on Dolly's hand.

"Ow," she says. "Why did you do that?"

"Our fangs secrete a natural local analgesic and antiseptic," he replies. "It will help with your pain. It's what keeps the wounds from spoiling when we are milking."

"That's amazing," Dolly says, already feeling the pain in her hand subside.

"Your welcome."

Jesus, Dan, Nico and Rancid Pete are all walking in slow motion towards the casino. They each have several shotguns, retrieved from the police cruiser Dan left parked at the casino earlier in our show. They pump their shotguns while walking in slow motion as the camera bounces back and forth between close-up shots of the four men. The beat from a bad ass rap song drops in the background. Pick your favorite. I'm thinking "Microphone Fiend", by Eric B. and Rakim.

Once inside, they find the Karowack Kids acting out the final battle between the Sharks and the Jets. The bad ass rap song comes to a screeching halt.

The Karowack Kids have turned a good portion of the Casino patrons into vampires to fill out the chorus line for the musical number they are performing. The vampires all break character mid-song to turn and hiss at our heroes.

"So Pete," Jesus says. "I'm very pleased to see you helping out the Marshals. It's super noble."

"Don't twist it 'bro," Rancid Pete replies. "They got my girl. Hell, they got my whole damn band, man."

The background music comes back on as the vampires charge them. The four men banter throughout the battle, never stopping to catch their breath or reload their weapons which, by the way, Jesus has blessed with relevant blessings.

"Do you mean the Princess?" Jesus asks Rancid Pete.

"Yes sir," Pete says, shoving the barrel of his shotgun into the mouth of a Karowack Kid. Although one of Jesus' blessings is supposed to help guide the bullets to non-fatal wounds. There is nothing to be done for this poor Kid. His gooey vampire brains wind up splattered on Nico's back.

"Awe man," Nico says.

"Dude, she is so smoking hot," Jesus says. "Do you know how many times I have thought about fixing her so she is not such a horrible person, so she could make some guy the happiest man on the planet?"

"Why don't you?" Dan asks. He pulls the trigger of his shotgun, blowing both legs off a vampire. Dan, being who he is, does not aim for mortal wounds, but he does send a ton of body parts flying in splashy messes.

Jesus takes his pointer finger and pokes a small hole in the forehead of a Karowack Kid, curing him of his disease. The Karowack Kid passes out and falls to the floor, a human once again. "Because my very next thought is to heck with that," Jesus says. "If I can't have her, well then forget the rest of you guys."

"Dude!" Rancid Pete exclaims.

"Well what's fair about that?" Jesus says. "I can't have a woman? I already fulfilled my destiny once. I would think I would get a little time for the whole being a man part but noooooooo. The being a man part is strictly for the agonizing torture and crucifixion."

"Damn Jesus." Nico speaks while completing a very dramatic turn, taking down three vampires along the way. "That's a, that's a, a, I don't know what to say."

Jesus starts laughing as all the heroes take shots from the hip at the same time in the same direction, each cutting down a Karowack Kid with their weapon. "You should see the looks on your faces," Jesus says in between snorts and chuckles. "It's a joke. I don't change her because she is the way our father made her, which makes her perfect."

"A perfect bitch," Rancid Pete agrees, and they all laugh...and kill vampires.

Up in his office, Alacrán is sweeping the room playing host, a tyrannical social butterfly. There are a few minutes remaining before the killings will begin, and he is simply aflutter with anticipation. The guests all agree that Mayor Haruka should be the first to die. There are several different reasons offered, but almost everyone agrees his handling of the immigration situation from Hell has been shaky at best.

Alacrán never intended to allow his kidnapped guests to choose his first victim, unless their pick happened to coincide with whom he had already chosen. The Marshal's buxom secretary will be the first to go.

Alacrán is licking Lilly Whet's cheek with his slimy tongue as I am typing this. Lilly is in trouble. Next in line is Lord Sweetwater. After all, Dan and Billy the Third are Alacrán's two biggest foes. Alacrán will thoroughly enjoy the pain he'll cause both his enemies by killing their associates.

The Black Case Gang piles into the elevator. Sammy punches the button for the top floor. Then Zorn punches the button for every floor of the hotel before anyone can stop him. It was childlike impulse.

"Oh you stupid demon," Sandy says with exhaustion. "What did you do that for? Now this will take forever."

Zorn shrugs his shoulders. They all go quiet, listening to the relaxing elevator music.

Eventually Doodles speaks up. "Does somebody want to tell me what's going?" he says woozily.

"Nobody knows what the fuck is going on around here," Sandy says.

"We are on our way up to Alacrán's office to try and get a reward for the case," Sammy says. He proceeds to tell Doodles the chain of events leading up to this point. Of course, he leaves out the part about attacking Doodles and knocking him unconscious. That part was changed to Doodle's passing out from booze. "We've been on the run with you and the case for the last…well, I'm not exactly sure how long to be honest, but you have been knocked out the whole time. We found out the case belongs to Alacrán and we're trying to collect the reward he said he would give whoever finds it."

Doodles is no genius to begin with and the multiple head traumas aren't helping, so he takes Sammy's explanation on face value with no request for greater detail as to why his head is busted open and his arm appears broken. To his credit, he is managing the agonizing pain fairly well. His next question is, "So, who did you say this guy is?" pointing a thumb at Zorn.

"He's a demon," Sandy says.

"He's been helping us," Sammy says.

"My name is Zorn," Zorn says. His accent is Icelandic and proper.

"You could talk this whole time and you ain't said nothing?" Sandy asks. I'm not sure why it irritates her, but it does.

"Yeah, what's that about?" Sammy agrees.

"Not once did you ever ask my opinion about anything," Zorn replies. He speaks directly to Sammy, ignoring Sandy. Demons are notoriously chauvinist. "You never asked me if I could speak."

"Maybe I didn't," Sammy says, "but I did ask you questions. How does someone who can talk not talk at all this entire time?"

"You were mostly ordering me around and threatening me. Besides the advantage you not knowing I could speak may have provided me, why would I have wanted to talk to you?"

"Oh for Pete's sake," Sandy says.

"Well I thought we were becoming pals. And excuse me if I was a little bossy," Sammy says with considerable attitude. "I was very busy trying to keep us all alive!"

"Some job you did at that," Doodles says.

"We're all alive ain't we?" Sammy snorts.

"Yeah," Sandy says in agreement, defending her man.

"For how long you shmuck?" Doodles says. "As soon as this elevator gets where it's going, we're all probably going to die."

"You tighten them lips about my man drunky," Sandy says. "That shmuck has been dragging your passed out ass around town this whole time. We all have. A lot of help you were. We could have left you in a ditch."

"He was not exactly passed out," Zorn interjects.

"Yeah," Doodles says, "Come to think of it, why does my head hurt so bad? And what's wrong with my arm? This ain't no hangover." Doodles pokes at his forehead, discovering the crusty infected gash on it. He teeters a little with nausea from the immediate pain.

"Oh shut up you," Sandy says to Zorn, as Sammy steadies Doodles.

"What's your angle here demon?" Sammy adds.

"I'm just saying," Zorn continues, "the man has a large open wound on his head. He needs medical attention. And now I have a large open wound on my head. Yet somehow the two of you have gone unscathed."

"Unscathed?" Sandy questions with disbelief.

"I lost a damn finger," Sammy says in defense of himself, holding up his pinky nub. "Plus I think my nose is broken."

"Yeah," Sandy agrees, "which happened saving you by the way."

"You were trying to save the case," Zorn says flatly.

"Oh shut up you," Sandy says again, this time shaking her fist at the demon.

"Yeah," Sammy agrees. "Where do you get off all of the sudden? You've been helping us drag this bum around. I think you whacked him over the head at least once! For all we know you could have put that hole there on his head!"

"Bum? I ain't no stinking bum," Doodles says.

They argue like this the rest of the way. They are exhausted, injured, and somewhere inside they all know there is a chance they're about to die. This damn black case is going to get them all killed, and they don't even know what's inside.

The room is mostly quiet when Alacrán begins his dirty business. Don't get me wrong, there are initial shouts of disgust and rage. Threats of revenge are made. People are crying. Alacrán instructs the personal attendants of the kidnap victims to muffle the noise. The attendants hold custom made gags over the mouths of their charges.

Alacrán is seconds from piercing Lilly Whet's breasts with a single, razor sharp, silver knitting needle. He is going to push it through from left to right, causing extraordinary pain and anguish in the lovely young woman. The needle is the first step in the torturous death Alacrán is about to inflict on Lilly. Not so gentle after all in my opinion. I suppose the "I murder gently" comment was empty murderous pillow talk, meant for his own arousal.

His hand is stayed when everyone in the room hears a loud ding, signifying an elevator is arriving in the office lobby. Alacrán turns to see who is on the elevator. So does Purvis. Both men stare intently as the elevator doors slowly open to reveal a mad ruckus inside.

Sammy, Sandy, Doodles and Zorn are carrying on like crazed fuckaroos. They are screaming, eye gouging, nipple twisting, basically Three Stooging each other. As everyone in attendance at the evil cocktail party looks on, the Black Case Gang never realizes they have finally made it to the top floor. The elevator closes its doors and heads back down to the lobby.

"What was that?" Alacrán asks.

"I don't know my liege," Purvis answers him, "but I think they had the case."

"Call that elevator back up," Alacrán commands. Then he turns to Lilly. "Young lady, you may be allowed to live after all. If my case is on that elevator when it returns, I might not kill you. Isn't this exciting?!"

Our heroes' backs are against the wall. They continue to fight off vampires while they wait for an elevator. An elevator dings its arrival and the doors open. Dan, Nico, Rancid Pete and Jesus turn to load the car, but they stop when they see it's already occupied.

The Black Case Gang is inside. At this point Sammy, Zorn and Doodles are lined up against a wall receiving a heated tongue lashing from Sandy. She is stomping back and forth in front of them, shaking and pointing her finger in their faces like a drill sergeant. All three "men" look absolutely terrified.

"I think we'll wait for the next car," Dan says.

Billy and Dolly are now a block away from the casino. "Why don't we run the next block and take an elevator?" Dolly asks.

"No. Absolutely not," Billy protests. "I can do this. I am William Rockefeller the Third. I am a vampire, the father of my own clan. I will fly damn it." All bullshit Beatnik pretense is out the window for the moment. Billy is irritated. He wraps an arm around Dolly. "Hold still," he says. He leaps into the air again. This time he has chosen a better trajectory and they successfully land on the roof of Alacrán's casino.

"Nice work," Dolly says.

"I told you," Billy replies, pumping his fist in triumph. "Yes! In your face elevator face," he says to Dolly. Then he sticks both fists in the air above his head and hops a couple of times. "Ha!"

"Very nice," Dolly says. "You want to go foil Alacrán's plans now, or do you want to stay up here and dance around all night?"

"Come," Billy replies, gathering his composure. He holds his hand out to Dolly. "It is time for my grand entrance. I'm going to make the fat Spaniard a king, baby. A king of fools."

The elevator door opens back up into the foyer of Alacrán's office. This time the Black Case Gang falls out of the elevator in a heap. Sammy is choking Zorn, who is choking Sandy, who is choking Doodles, who is choking Sammy. The case itself gets kicked out during the tussle and slides to a stop a few inches away.

The Paparazzi in the room immediately shift their attention to the new arrivals. As flashbulbs go off and microphones are shoved into their faces, the BCG loosen their grip on each other and, slowly but surely, reconnect with the world around them.

Sammy reaches for the case and finds someone else's hand already there. It is Doodles'. Zorn's hand falls on top of Sammy's. They all three look at one another and grin.

They stand up together. All three maintain some form of grip on the handle of the case until they deposit it into Sandy's outstretched arms. The BCG stand tightly huddled as they field questions from the reporters.

Alacrán looks at Purvis. He is about to say something about getting the case from those morons over there when someone yells out.

"Not so fast!" Billy the Third shouts.

Everyone turns to see Billy entering with Dolly on his arm. He prepared several witty entrance lines in advance, but he faltered and spit one out that had little context. At least he said it with gusto.

A barrage of flashbulbs and questions momentarily stuns Billy. His tongue gets tied up and he can't get his next line out. His mouth is open. He looks puzzled. He does the hissing thing vampires do when they recoil from sunlight with their arm over their eyes.

Dolly gives Billy a reassuring squeeze on his arm. She can't have him screwing everything up now. She is so close. She scans the room and finds Purvis. He is watching, waiting for her to find him and make eye contact. Purvis raises his eyebrows ever so slightly. She gives an affirmative nod with a tiny downward thrust of her chin.

Alacrán makes his way to the black case. He is walking across the lobby with his arms held out to the side in greeting of the Black Case Gang. He has a big old shit-eater on his face. That's a grin that is.

Alacrán is about to speak sweet sugary welcomes to Sammy, Sandy, Doodles and Zorn when they hear the elevator ding again. "Oh for the love of…," Alacrán laments. "Who can this be?"

"Not so fast," Dan commands as he steps out of the elevator car. It makes a little more sense when he says it than when Billy did. Maybe. Dan points at Alacrán as he speaks. It is the hero's way of making sure everyone knows with whom he is speaking. Jesus, Nico and Rancid Pete all step off the elevator as well. The swarm of reporters and cameramen immediately move their buzz from the vampire to the four good guys.

"Alacrán, you're under arrest," Dan says. Cameras are going off. Some reporter gets too aggressive with her microphone, hitting Dan in the face with it. He moves it away and gives her a stern look. She swoons under the weight of his presence.

"Oh what's the point?" Alacrán says, half pleading. "We've talked about this. You can't arrest me. There is no jail. There are no courts!"

"Alright that's enough," Dan says. "Give me a break would you? It's force of habit. We used to arrest people. The point is the jig is up. Now let everybody go and stop being evil."

"And what if I say no?" Alacrán asks.

"Then I'm going to do this," Dan replies. He swiftly moves

across the floor to Alacrán and punches him very hard in the stomach. Alacrán gasps for air then falls to the ground. He looks up at Dan and licks his lips with a smile.

"I hadn't actually said no yet," Alacrán says. Still smiling perversely, he blows Dan a kiss.

"Ergh," is the noise that comes out of Dan's mouth. "Gross." Dan turns to look at the Black Case Gang. "Give me that," he says. Without waiting he walks over and takes the case from them. He hands it to Rancid Pete. "You mind holding this for a second?"

"Sure thing boss," Rancid Pete says.

"Wait a minute," Billy the Third says. "What about me?"

Dan turns to face Billy. "What about you?"

"I want that case," Billy says.

"So," Dan replies.

"So? I'm a vampire," Billy says. "I am physically more powerful than all of you. Jesus Christ!"

"Easy," Jesus says.

"I shouldn't have to say these things," Billy continues, ignoring Jesus. "What's it going to take for you people to remember my power and show me some damn respect? Hmm? What's to stop me from killing you all and taking the case?"

"I don't know, what's to stop...," Nico starts.

Dan cuts Nico off. He puts an arm out to bar Nico from moving on the vampire. "Easy Nico. No need for more violence. Look, Bill, let it go. We've got Jesus with us, man."

"So," Billy says, then he looks at Jesus and says, "no disrespect of course."

"So perhaps I turn you into a fly," Jesus says. "None taken."

"You can do that?" Billy asks.

Jesus simply nods his head with a friendly yet cocky smirk on his face. Billy is deflated.

"Well this sucks," he says. He puts his hands on his hips in a huff.

Everyone laughs, including Alacrán, who is still lying on the floor with his hands folded over his sore belly. Billy doesn't quite get his own, unintended joke.

"You're a vampire and you said 'this sucks'," Dolly explains.

Billy is still confused.

"You are a blood sucker..." She speaks slowly to help the connection sink in, but Billy remains dumfounded. "Oh never mind...goofball."

"C'mon," Dan says to Rancid Pete and Nico, "Let's get everyone untied." They head across the foyer towards the giant open doorway to Alacrán's inner office. The media follows, while our two villains remain in silence. Billy stands next to Alacrán who is still lying on his back.

"Well," Alacrán says, "I suppose we've been foiled again."

"It looks that way," Billy says, offering a hand to help Alacrán to his feet. "What do you think we should do now?"

"I need a drink. I suppose we may as well toast this glorious occasion," Alacrán says sarcastically.

"Yes, why not," Billy agrees. Then he looks over at Dolly. "Would you be a dear and bring me a glass of champagne?"

"Sure," Dolly replies.

"Purvis," Alacrán says, indicating the same request.

"Of course my liege," Purvis replies.

As Purvis and Dolly walk over to a nearby cocktail station, Billy says, "You know I really thought I had you this time."

"What are you talking about?" Alacrán retorts. "You never had anything. This is your problem. You always think you have some leverage or angle but you never do."

"I have noble blood and you are the child of a beggar and a whore, what more angle do I need?" Billy snaps back. "I can best you at anything."

"You cannot," Alacrán states flatly. *How did he know about my parents?* he thinks.

"I can and I will," Billy says. "Name your test right here where we stand, right now."

While at the bar, Purvis and Dolly take a moment for a toast. A lover's toast, where you wrap your arms with drink in hand and stare longingly into each other's eyes as you sip. When they return to

Billy and Alacrán with champagne glasses in their hands, they find the two villains locked in mortal eye-to-eye combat.

"What's going on?" Purvis asks.

"We're having a staring contest," Alacrán says with the side of his mouth, as if speaking normally would somehow break his concentration.

"Oh," Purvis says, then he looks at Dolly with a surprised smile.

She stares back at him with a look that clearly states, *You've got to be kidding me!* She takes Billy's hand and puts the champagne glass in it. "Good luck," she says. "I'm going to check on my lady."

"Thank you my dear," Billy says.

"Purvis my child," Alacrán says. "If you will place a glass in my hand as well, I shall have it readily available to drink to my swift victory of this farcical challenge."

"Of course master," Purvis agrees. "Although I do think that a gentlemanly toast to the start of your competition is in order."

"Yes, yes, let decorum rule," Alacrán replies.

"Of course, of course," Billy agrees.

"Good," Purvis says as the men drink, delicately tipping their champagne flutes in such a manner that the glass stem does not get in the way of their staring contest. "I am going to go check on the rest of our guests," Purvis says.

"Good man," Alacrán says.

When Dan, Nico, Rancid Pete and Jesus walk through the door to the office everyone in the room cheers. The heroes pause in the doorway, allowing the crowd to applaud.

Dan scans the room for someone in particular, although in the moment he isn't sure who he's looking for. He sees Princess Tiara, but she isn't the one.

Rancid Pete doesn't hesitate. He stomps towards Princess Tiara.

Dan sees Lilly Whet, and despite the moment he and Lilly shared at the concert, the emotions that surge through him feel like a sudden realization. *Lilly*, he thinks. *I love Lilly.* He runs to her.

When the Princess sees Rancid Pete coming towards her, her heart skips a beat, does a back flip, then jumps up and gets stuck in her throat. *Yep*, she thinks. *It's completely, totally official. I'm in love with a fucking monster.*

Rancid Pete makes his way to the Princess. He drops the case at her feet, backhands the personal attendant who is assigned to her, and rips away the ropes she is bound in with a throaty growl.

"Motherfucker," Princess Tiara says.

Rancid Pete scoops her up with one hand, lifting her in the air until they are face to face. He snarls and then kisses her, holding the back of her head with his other hand. She is completely limp in his embrace, enchanted by him. Magical as the moment is, Rancid Pete does not turn into a handsome prince.

Dan comes to a sliding stop, falling to a knee in front of Lilly. He takes her by the hand and opens his mouth to speak but no words come out. She shakes her head, letting him know he doesn't have to say anything. He fervently goes about untying her. She is free and they stand together. Their lips meet, starting a romance that will eventually cross the boundaries of space and time, not to mention galaxies, our Universe, the Multiverse, and the infinite alternate dimensional planes of existence. Dan stares at Lilly, whose eyes are closed. Love washes over him in a wave of all-encompassing joy and understanding. *Oh*, he thinks. *This is what it's all about.*

Nico and Jesus, neither having significant others waiting for them, go about the business of releasing the rest of the guests. Basically, Jesus waives his hand and the ropes all fall to the floor. As the kidnappees begin to stand and stretch their legs, many of them lose the ill-fitting formal wear they were given, leaving them partially or completely nude. Nico spots a particularly attractive hostage who seems very upset by the whole ordeal. He walks over and offers her birthing-hips assistance. Jesus approves.

When Dolly enters the room, she sees Tiara in Rancid Pete's arms. She watches lovingly. The Princess isn't really going to need her anymore, at least not like before. Dolly feels Purvis' arm slide around her waist. She puts her arm over his and rests her head on his shoulder. "Look at how happy they look," she says. "Do you think we should give them what we have?"

"I think we should at least give them the option," he replies. "Then, if they make the wrong choice, maybe we help them out a little bit." He looks down at her with a coy smile which she returns in kind.

Once everyone is freed, focus returns to the events of the day. In particular, the mystery of the contents of the mysterious black case. Sammy and Sandy petition Dan to open in it, so they can at least know what they've been lugging around. Especially if they aren't going to get a reward. Dan points out that perhaps they might be more concerned with the medical attention they need. He waves Jesus over to help them with their injuries.

Still, the match has been struck and the fire lit. A commotion stirs amongst the crowd as everyone agrees they want to know what's in the case. Dan and Nico try to quiet them but to no avail. Dan looks to Jesus for help, who is in the midst of repairing Sammy's finger and lecturing him about the evils of cocaine usage.

"...because it's a really crappy drug," Jesus is saying to Sammy, "and honestly, it's sort of gone out of style too, babe. As a matter fact. Everyone listen. Everyone." The crowd grows silent as Jesus raises his voice to gather their attention. "I know it has been said over and over, but I am saying it again. Drugs can be bad, okay. I know everyone is going to use them in some form or another so please, be careful with what you use and how much you use it. Exercise some self-control. Remember, all things in moderation. Been saying it for a couple thousand years now. Stop being jerks. Okay, thank you. That is all."

Going forth this speech will be known as the Sermon on the Couch, as Jesus stood on a couch when he spoke. The couch goes on to become a highly collectable piece of religious antiquity once the era of the apocalypse comes to an end. It is believed you can still see impressions of the Morningstar's feet in the cushions. The notion is ridiculous. People sat on that couch throughout the rest of the kidnapping party, which by the way, becomes a tradition. Every year on the same day the city of Vegas holds kidnapping parties all over town. Invitations are tricky. You have to get yourself kidnapped.

Sorry. Cart before the horse there. Back to the current events. Despite his always good intentions, Jesus isn't telling the crowd what they want to hear so they tune him out and return their focus to the case. Jesus throws his hands up with mild frustration. He looks at Dan with a smile, shakes his head with a "whatta ya gonna do" roll of the eyes, then says, "Wait a minute. Why don't you show everyone what's inside? What difference does it make?"

Dan looks at Jesus thoughtfully, then at Nico who shrugs his shoulders then back at Jesus and says, "I don't know."

"Well then, show them," Jesus says.

"Wait," Dan replies. "Do you think you should maybe talk to them about materialism, and false idols, and worldly desires?"

"Dan," Jesus says, "I'm blue in the face. I've talked about that stuff for thousands of years and I'll still be talking about it tomorrow. And you know what, I kind of want to know what's in that case too. These people were all kidnapped over that thing. They deserve to know."

"Fair enough," Dan replies. "Honestly, I don't know why I was being resistant in the first place. It holds no bearing on my investigation at all for anyone to know..."

"Oh for Christ's sake. Open the damn thing," someone yells anonymously.

"Right," Dan says.

"Don't make this about me," Jesus says jokingly, in the general direction of the unnamed voice.

"Everyone over here," Dan says. He takes the case over to Alacrán's desk. The Black Case Gang is huddled around him along with Nico and Lilly. Rancid Pete has cleared a path to the front row as well. He is holding Princess Tiara. Purvis and Dolly are standing with them.

Dan starts to move things on Alacrán's desk but he is being too polite about it so Sandy steps forward and swipes the desk clean, knocking everything on it to the floor. Dan looks down at the charismatic little middle aged broad to scold her. She stands her ground indignantly, with her arms folded across her chest, tapping a foot. Dan can't help but smile as he hears chuckles from the crowd of onlookers.

Dan sets the case on the desk then hops up on the desk as well. "Hey," he says. "Anybody got a key to this thing? Or know the combination? It has both."

"I would assume Alacrán does," Purvis says.

"Yes, it has to be him," Dolly says.

"Hey," Nico says, "Where is Alacrán anyway?"

"That's a good question," Dan says.

Then another anonymous voice in the crowd yells, "Holy crap!"

Everyone else turns to see what has caused someone to yell this time. There in the lobby stand William Rockefeller the Third, vampire, and Flacido Rodrigo Diego, the infamous Alacrán, locked in lusty embrace. They are sucking face like a couple of horny teenagers left alone in the basement after midnight. They aren't just making out. They are doing it like in the movies, running their hands through each other's hair, grabbing butt cheeks and squeezing 'em harder than necessary to show how passionate they are. First one butt cheek, then the other, then both at the same time.

The crowd watches in silent amazement. Billy and Alacrán are so caught up in what they are doing, they don't notice they have an audience. Dolly and Purvis both giggle at what they have done.

Yes. They gave Alacrán and Billy the love potions, a taste of their own medicine as it were.

Alacrán bends a leg at the knee and raises it out behind him, the way a lady would. Everyone loses their minds in an uproar of laughter. Billy and Alacrán realize what is happening and separate, blushing, although they don't let go of each other's hands.

"People, people," Dan says from atop the desk. "Let's calm down here. Calm down now. Alacrán, would you like to come open this up and get a look at it? These fine people deserve a chance to see why they were all kidnapped."

Alacrán gives Billy a kiss on the cheek, then makes a face of horror because he gave Billy a kiss on the cheek. He hangs his head in shame as he walks to his desk.

"What was that all about?" Dan asks Alacrán.

"I don't know," Alacrán hisses. "Can we leave it alone?"

"Whatever," Dan says. Alacrán leans over and punches 1111# into the keypad.

"Oh you've got to be kidding me," Nico says. "Seriously. Nobody tried 1111#?" He looks at Sammy, Sandy, Zorn and Doodles, who all shake their heads.

"To be fair," Zorn speaks out, "we were being chased the entire time."

Sammy, Sandy and Doodles all utter sentiments of agreement like, "Yeah," "That's true," and, "What he said."

"Alright, alright," Dan says. "Let's get this over with." He thumbs the latches. You hear the airtight seal break. Dan is about to open the case and lift the shiny gold cat statue out when two brilliant flashes of light illuminate the room, temporarily blinding everyone. The light is accompanied by the song "Magic Carpet Ride," by Steppenwolf.

"Hold it right there," Hook says.

"Holy crap, Aliens!"

It doesn't matter who yells it. It doesn't matter that we've been living with monsters and vampires and demons and gargoyles and trolls and werewolves, etcetera, etcetera, for hundreds if not thousands of years by the time this is all happening. The arrival of the aliens sends the crowd into one last frenzy.

That's right. It's a gold cat statue inside the black case.

It takes a while to get everyone calmed back down. Hook and Lia explain to the crowd they have saved the Earth. They explain their entire story. How they've fallen in love with us. How they have to leave us behind to try and figure out what the fuck is really going on around here. Oh, and how Hook really wants whatever is in the case as a souvenir.

That's when everyone remembers that before the aliens arrived, they were about to find out what is in the case. Dan opens the case to reveal what they have all been chasing after, a tacky cat statue made of gold. Many people agree that the aliens probably deserve to have it, many think the aliens ought to at least provide some sort of proof they actually saved the Earth, and many no longer give a shit.

A debate begins as people take sides on the issue. Dan tries to keep the crowd calm while explaining to them that the statue is part of an on-going murder investigation and is going in an evidence locker. The debate is at its height when Jesus shouts, "Hey everyone, look!"

The crowd turns to see what has Jesus so excited. You can hear gasps, awes, sighs, and several "oh my Gods". Everyone makes their way closer to the windows for a better view as the hellfire smoke ridden sky clears.

The sun is coming out.

"Did you do this?" Dan whispers to Jesus as they watch clouds part and warm rays of light flood the room.

"Nah, this isn't me," Jesus says. His eyes are closed. He wears a wide smile on his face. Slowly but surely, everyone in the room takes the hand of the person next to them. They all bask in the glory of our beautiful star. Even the vampires, which is strange since it is common urban legend that the sun kills vampires. Apparently, that is a bunch of hoo-ha some jerk made up.

It is the first time most of them have ever seen the sun in real life. It's an amazing feeling as they all stand hand in hand, glowing in the warmth of a beautiful sunrise, wishing moments like this would never end. They always do though.

Eventually someone happens to look away. Maybe the glow was hurting their eyes a little. Who knows? The point is, this person looks away from the sun long enough to notice something is missing, and then says, "Hey everyone! The statue! It's gone!"

Everyone turns to see that indeed, the statue and the black case have again disappeared. They instantly know who has it, as they all look the same direction at the same time. Everyone in the room immediately takes note of the large body that was previously in the room that appears to have disappeared, along with the cat in the case, and in mighty unison they all scream, "THE ROBOT!"

The End.

# The After Party

Our performers are in the reception area after the show. Everyone is enjoying food and beverages while they mingle. There are a lot of conversations about unanswered questions, what happens next, and the very nature of our existence. Plus, there are some characters who still need their own resolutions, and I certainly don't want them to feel shortchanged. Here are the "rest of the characters' lives summation captions", and some plot outtakes that didn't make the final cut of the actual story.

An early discussion focuses on our villains' punishment. Many of the guests question whether or not Billy and Alacrán being stuck in love with each other is sufficient punishment for all the atrocities they've committed. "Wait, aren't they going to get punished for all the people they've killed?" someone asks.

"Don't you think being in love with each other is punishment enough for those two?" someone else in the crowd asks.

"No, I don't," the first voice replies.

"Death isn't that big a deal when you know there is an afterlife," says another stranger. "I'm desensitized."

Rancid Pete overhears this and gives Jesus a little elbow in the ribs. "So that's why Bob is okay with all the murder?" Pete asks. - After meeting the aliens, Rancid Pete decided he can have faith in a deity named Bob…

"Easy," Jesus replies.

"Sorry Christ," Rancid Pete says unapologetically. "I'm a monster baby, and I calls it like I sees it."

"Then do me a favor and don't make me blind you," Jesus snorts with a smile.

"Nice," Rancid Pete says. "I like the new you."

Eventually, it is noted that unless someone decides to kill the villains, there isn't much else to be done. It is the apocalypse after all. Then someone brings to light that calling it a punishment by turning the two men into homosexuals seemed to be a pretty strong negative commentary on homosexuality and an insult to the LGBT community. However, the Voodoo Priestess that created the potion corrects that misunderstanding.

"Oh no children, you misunderstand," she says in a vaguely Haitian accent. "My potion does not make them gay. The potion simply make them uncontrollably in love, whether they like it or not." Everyone then agrees that the two villains being in love with each other in spite of their own contempt for the situation is indeed a prison sentence of its own, with no underlying implications of sexuality discourse. They all laugh every time Billy or Alacrán kisses the other with disgust.

Speaking of the Voodoo Priestess, during the kidnapping she was seated next to Curt Southstone, High Cleric of the Las Vegas Eastwoodians. She put salve on Southstone's head wound created by Alacrán. Then, being a widow, she pours some of her love potion down his throat and forces him awake, causing Southstone to fall desperately in love with her. Luckily for Southstone the Voodoo

Priestess, although already a senior citizen, is a handsome woman with many potions and spells to maintain the youthfulness of her physical being.

Unluckily for Southstone, she will rise to her own seat of power as an Eastwoodian, sacrificing Southstone to the dogs of sociopolitical warfare along the way. Nihilists begin to worship her and convert to Eastwoodianism. The Devil takes note of her rise to power, initiating an aggressive courtship that culminates with the Priestess' agreement to have his demon baby. The demon baby will be the harbinger of some new form of Bob-knows-what nonsense, and the prophecies keep on coming.

Speaking of love potions. Lilly Whet has the potion her friend, the Priestess' daughter, gave her to use on Dan. She debates giving it to Dan and taking it herself, as Dolly and Purvis have, but she decides to let nature run its course. Later, Lilly gives the vial to Hook. She is in a conversation with the aliens, and despite the fact it is obvious Hook is desperately in love with Lia, he can't keep his eyes off Lilly's boobs. *You see there*, she thinks. *The poor creatures can't help themselves. Even the alien ones.* In a moment when Lia isn't paying attention, Lilly sneaks the vial into Hook's hand and whispers in his ear, "Do yourself a favor and drink this when you two are alone."

Hook and Lia share more about how the Valtrucians were once the protectors of mankind. Here's a taste:

"It's a long story," Hook is explaining, "but the gist of it is, we are your missing link. We were sent here thousands of years ago to protect you but our leadership mated with you and provided the missing evolutionary code to your DNA, except it wasn't actually missing as you weren't supposed to be anything more than what you were."

"And what was that?" a reporter asks.

"Basically, dumb farm animals," Lia says sweetly.

"So you guys are like our kissing cousins?" another reporter asks.

"No," Lia replies. "It's more like a unicorn has sex with a pony and the pony gives birth to a horse, assuming horses are slightly smarter than ponies that is."

"I knew it," a member of the crowd around the aliens exclaims. "It's not our fault we wound up like this. It's the aliens."

To which someone else follows up with, "Yeah, it's always someone else's fault."

To which a slightly more reasonable person in the crowd says, "I wonder if we got our accountability issues from the aliens too?"

To which Hook looks at that human and says, "Sometimes the horses give birth to donkeys."

At some point, someone asks Jesus where the rest of the deities in his band are. His answer: "Diversifying our portfolio."

In case you are wondering, Sammy, Sandy and Zorn do get a reward for their efforts, although it isn't what any of them were expecting. While they're saying their good-byes, it gets awkward when Sammy asks Zorn, "So where you headed after this?"

"Nowhere really," Zorn says. He looks at them sheepishly.

Sammy looks at Sandy hopefully, like a boy holding a stray puppy, and Sandy says, "Fine, but I'm not picking up after him. He's your responsibility and I swear if he so much as scorches any of the furniture..." You get the idea.

Incidentally, Hook and Lia invite Doodles to travel with them. Lia wants a human to perform tests on, to learn more about the similarities and difference between human and Valtrucian physiology. Doodles already quit his job anyway, and he is basically a lonely alcoholic with no real life to account for, so he decides living on a spaceship with two aliens seems like a good enough idea. Plus, Doodles is kind of a pervert. He's hoping there will be some invasive probing in the not too distant future. Although nothing sexual ever happens between him, Hook, and Lia, he does wind up visiting some pretty funky planets.

Billy and Alacrán sort of live happily ever after. The love potion eventually wears off, but by the time it does the two have become so codependent neither man can quit the other. On their 3rd anniversary, Alacrán gives the Karowack Kids a nightly show at La Ciudad de Oro as a gift to Billy. The Kids do *West Side Story*, *Cats*, a Kabuki adaptation of the entire *Star Trek the Next Generation* series, and *Apocalypse Now the Musical* on monthly rotations.

Princess Tiara's explosion of love in her life continues to change her as an individual. She chooses to transition from idle rich whore to philanthropist, using her own kidnapping experience as a platform for change. She becomes an advocate for kidnap victims around the world, fighting against human trafficking. Tiara goes around buying up all the stolen people she can and freeing them. Of course, the bad guys just keep kidnapping more people while her organization continues to pay the ransoms, but you do what you can.

As for Tiara and Rancid Pete? Despite the cosmic weight of their love, their romance is of the on again off again variety for the next few years. With The End of Times' endless touring and Tiara's philanthropy, it becomes very hard to maintain. Still, they are currently on again and there are rumors Tiara may be expecting. That night at the party, Jesus gives Rancid Pete and Tiara the ability to procreate as a future wedding gift. Yep, that's correct. Human monster baby.

Dolly and Purvis wind up splitting time between managing Princess Tiara's human trafficking relief agency, and relaxing at a quiet ranch somewhere in Arizona. Dolly still has Henry, and Purvis never wants her to change for anyone ever again. Plus, it definitely helps keep things interesting in the bedroom.

At some point in the evening Alacrán is questioned by a reporter, "You really went through all this over a cat statue?"

"It's made of gold," Alacrán says.

"But you're extraordinarily wealthy," the reporter says. "It seems sort of silly to go to all this trouble over something you could have easily purchased."

Alacrán's response? "But I wanted the kitty."

This creates a stir amongst the room that everyone comments on. I hear, "I can't believe this whole thing was about a cat statue," several times.

My favorite exchange is this:

"I heard the author's cat died right before he started the story."

"I'm sorry what?"

"This whole thing is some guy's delusion. We're all part of his delusion. Even Jesus. At least, this Jesus. The author is just some lonely delusional fucker with a dead cat living with his grandma."

"But that doesn't make sense. That means none of us exist."

"Sure we do. Just not the way you probably want to."

"How do you know?"

"He wrote it into me."

This boils over into a huge commotion as those two idiots wind up in a fist fight when the second guy tells the first guy he is crazy for his beliefs. As the reasoning behind the fight filters through the crowd you can hear people imploring others to pinch them or blurting out defensive responses to the idea that their lives might not be real such as, "That's impossible" and "But our love is real", or "I'm so confused" with "So is everyone else". And of course, let's not forget, "No one knows what the fuck is going on around here!"

Hook and Lia want some alone time with Jesus to pick his brain. "So what's going on with you and Satan?" Hook asks Jesus. "That whole deal seems a little strange."

"He's got his job to do and I've got mine." Jesus replies. "You know what I'm saying? But he's still my brother, man. We're all just out here working the will of Bob. Right on. Yeah." That's rock star Jesus right there.

The opportunity for the cultural exchange between the aliens and Jesus is short lived however, as several reporters locate the trio and want answers to questions like, "Jesus, did you know there are aliens?" and "Do you aliens think that Earth and your planet can coexist?"

"No," Jesus says.

"Of course," Lia says.

"Although," Hook adds, "there may be some other species headed your way, um, right now actually. Yeah, sorry about that. You know if it turns into a thing, we will do, you know, whatever we can."

Then someone brings up the apocalypse and asks Jesus if there is anything to be done about it. "Now that's a good question," Jesus responds. "The truth is I taught you people everything you need to know, but it boils down to two things. Two. That's it. Love and self-sacrifice. What is so hard about that? You don't want it to be that simple because it doesn't leave any room for things like 'justice' and 'vengeance'."

At which point someone interrupts him and says, "I'll tell you what though Jesus. The world is full of dicks that don't care at all about other people."

Then another person chimes in, "Yeah, that's true Jesus, there are a lot of dicks."

Then another. "Yeah, a lot!"

Jesus tosses up his hands. "I can't do it. I just can't do it," he says, and they all share a good laugh.

As the after party is winding down, the discussion of the current apocalypse and the former United States' relationship with the rest of the world picks back up. The second round of the discussion is held in a more alcohol infused, level headed state. It is a smoking jacket affair, with cigars and brandy and comfortable chairs in front of the fire.

For the most part, everyone agrees the problem with humanity is that we need to have an enemy. Collectively, individually, there has to be something to fight against whether the fight be physical, mental or spiritual. If there is a common enemy for mankind to unite against, we would stop wasting time killing each other. It only makes sense. We've seen it in movies a thousand times. Of course, someone notes how we've been united in trying to kill mother Earth for centuries and that hasn't stopped us from killing each other, but that guy gets punched in the balls for being a smug Hippy.

A plan is developed for Hook and Lia to fake an invasion. Someone points out that trying to lie to the general populace, in order to get them to behave, has been going on forever with marginal success. Another person agrees, noting that Bob has tried the same thing with the Devil, but that didn't work, and now there are demons and shit all over the world, and that hasn't worked, but someone else points out how this time it is going to be different because it will be aliens. Then someone asks if the Founding Fathers would have agreed with the plan if they had been in the room. Then another guy who agrees with that point draws his own comparison by saying, "Yeah! Hey, what are we here, the Bilderbergs or something?" Another someone says, "Yeah," in agreement.

I'm not sure if he is agreeing with the sarcasm, or misunderstands the sarcasm. Either way, someone else agrees with that last guy, assuming he is sincerely agreeing that they should be like the

Bilderbergs, and that person nominates Dan as their leader. Dan, being the man that he is, sees an opportunity to do some good and accepts. Dan will go on to re-unite the former United States and lead the nation into a new era of prominence with Lilly Whet, soon to be Lilly Whet Trate, as his competent First Lady.

Speaking of our hero, there is one last little thing that needs to be put up in a bow for you. It is getting late and the after party is winding down. I am about to leave when I notice Dan pull Jesus aside.

"Hey Jesus," Dan says. "What about all that stuff with my grandmother?"

"Sorry Dan," Jesus replies. "I can't tell you anymore about that. If you want to know more about what's going on with your grandma, you're going to have to read another crappy book."

"Well that doesn't seem fair," Dan says.

"I know," Jesus says, "but what can I say, the guy is kind of a jerk." Then Jesus looks at me and winks.

As I'm leaving, I can hear Dan's voice trailing off. "Wait. What do you mean I have to read another book?" he asks. "There's a book about my grandma? What was the first book?"

Speaking of our hero's grandma, the old lady is still working on her puzzle, and I am going to check on her. This current crisis is temporarily averted. In the grander scheme of things, we are still running out of time. We need that jigsaw puzzle finished.

So there you have it folks. That's our story. I swear to you that every little bit of this nonsense actually happened, or will happen, especially the stuff I did not make up.

Oh, one more last thing, but this is really it, I promise. It has been brought to my attention by a friend - thanks Gus! - that I've never introduced myself to you, not this entire time. I've never explained my role in all of this silliness, or how I came to witness these dire yet hopeful times. My apologies.

    Hello. They call me Bob.

# Epilogue

When Jack22's power comes back, it takes a while for him to gather his thoughts and figure out what's happening. There are some short term memory files that are damaged and can't be retrieved, but eventually he is able to piece things together.

As he recharges, he silently watches the happenings unfold in Alacrán's office, but when he sees that shiny golden cat, he knows he has to have it. He's devising a plan to steal it and escape when the strangest thing happens. Something distracts everyone. Jack22 watches the people make their way over to the windows. They've abandoned the statue. Now is his chance.

Jack22 moves into action as swiftly as his battered robot joints allow him. He sneaks over to the table, grabs the black case with the statue safely inside, and sneaks out to the elevators. On his way out of the building he makes a pit stop in the men's costume area. He quickly changes from Montana Texas to a new persona, César Bolivar, Mexican expatriate and freedom fighter for hire. His ten gallon hat is replaced by a wide sombrero, his leather motorcycle vest by a rug serape. The upper lip that proudly supported a Handle Bar mustache for Montana Texas is now freshly adorned with a thick Pancho Villa.

After donning his new disguise, Jack22 makes one more stop to say goodbye to Computer Tiara.

"What if I came with you?" Computer Tiara asks.

"What if you did?" Jack22 replies.

"Come to engineering," she says.

Jack22 walks out of the front doors of La Ciudad de Oro and onto the sunlit streets of Las Vegas. There is a twinkle in his eye, a black case in his hand, and a microchip with his girlfriend's personality in his pocket. *Wow*, he thinks. *What a beautiful day.*

The end. Again.

Seriously.

COMING SOON

*The Missed Adventures of Jack22, Master of Disguise!*

*In the desert outside Las Vegas. Praise Bob.*

Truant D. Memphis is also the author of Littlethumb Sneezed. You can follow his attempts to save the Multiverse on Twitter as well, @truantmemphis. On the world where his books are being written and published, Truant has a secret identity. His secret identity enjoys the martial arts, playing sloppy guitar and finding new music to freak out about. He encourages you to be kind to animals, feed the homeless, love one another as hard as possible, and for Bob's sake use your turn signal when changing lanes. Peace.

Photo courtesy of the Dread Pirate Dean-Oh!

www.ingramcontent.com/pod-product-compliance
Lightning Source LLC
Chambersburg PA
CBHW070417010526
44118CB00014B/1793